Black Opera

Black Opera

History, Power, Engagement

NAOMI ANDRÉ

UNIVERSITY OF
ILLINOIS PRESS
Urbana, Chicago, and Springfield

Publication of this book is supported by the Manfred
Bukofzer Endowment of the American Musicological
Society, funded in part by the National Endowment for
the Humanities and the Andrew W. Mellon Foundation.

Portions of chapter 6 have been adapted from "Winnie,
Opera, and South African Artistic Nationhood," *African
Studies*, no. 1 (2016), © 2016 by Taylor & Francis.
Reprinted by permission.

Library of Congress Cataloging-in-Publication Data
Names: André, Naomi Adele, author.
Title: Black opera: history, power, engagement / Naomi
    André.
Description: Urbana: University of Illinois Press, 2018. |
    Includes bibliographical references and index.
Identifiers: LCCN 2017056072| ISBN 9780252041921
    (hardcover : alk. paper) | ISBN 9780252083570 (pbk. :
    alk. paper) | ISBN 9780252050619 (ebook)
Subjects: LCSH: Blacks in opera. | Opera.
Classification: LCC ML1700 .A53 2018 | DDC
    782.1089/96—dc23 LC record available at https://lccn.
    loc.gov/2017056072

Contents

Acknowledgments

This project has benefited from generous support from my home institution, the University of Michigan, and the guidance of many people. I was fortunate to receive funding from the UM African Studies Center (the wonderful African Heritage Initiative), the Institute for Research on Women and Gender, a Humanities Faculty Fellowship, and the LSA Associate Professor Support Fund. I was further aided by additional support from Women's Studies, the Department of Afroamerican and African Studies, and the Residential College. A special thanks goes to the Women of Color in the Academy Project for their writing groups and retreats as well as their warm collegiality.

I have been fortunate to have colleagues and friends who have given me very helpful feedback as I have moved through the process of pulling this project together from many diverse experiences and ideas. I am grateful for the extremely valuable comments I have received from people who have read portions of the manuscript at various stages: Evelyn Asultany, David Burkham, Suzanne Camino, Evan Chambers, William Cheng, Mariah Fink, Jennifer Myers, Marti Newland, Josh Rabinowitz, Kira Thurman, and Michael Uy. Many thanks to Mark Clague and his dynamite seminar on *Porgy and Bess* (fall 2017) for reading over and commenting on chapter 4. Special thanks also goes to Abby Stewart, who read through and commented on the full manuscript at a critical point when all the puzzle pieces were coming together, and to Ayanna Okeeva Smith and Marian Killian-Gilbert for inviting me to Indiana University for a short yet stimulating and rejuvenating residency in the fall of 2016. I want to express deep gratitude to my editor, Laurie Matheson, as we have moved through a second project together. I am intensely grateful for Laurie's guidance and shepherding this project through the various stages, including identifying courageous readers who generously gave me critical advice and helped me clarify and strengthen the presentation of my ideas and assembling a wonderful production team (many thanks especially to Jennifer Clark and Julie Gay).

A growing group of scholars who have become friends and supporters over the years in our mutual quest to flesh out sources and shape a historiography of black composers, to practice new formations of intersectional analyses, and to pioneer directions in music scholarship: these dear people include Ellie Hisama, Tammy Kernodle, Karen Bryan, Gwynne Kuhner Brown, Kira Thurman, and Alison Kinney. Thank you for being beacons in the groves of underexplored repertories and populations.

I am fortunate and thankful to belong to a diverse, rich intellectual community in multiple disciplines within the University of Michigan, across the United States, and in South Africa. Most locally in Ann Arbor are Sandra Gunning, Amal Fadlalla, Edie Lewis, Kelly Askew, Cynthia Burton, Terri Conley, Helen Fox, Susan Walton, Beth Genne, Rebecca Schwartz-Bishir, Ruth Tsoffar, Tiana Marquez, Sarah Fenstermaker, Elinor Linn, and Marc Gerstein. More broadly are April James, Nancy Clark, Marnie Schroer, the Callahan family (especially Michael, Susan, and Treana), Donato Somma, and Innocentia Jabulisile Mhlambi. There is a very special group of people who have known me for at least a couple of decades and are particularly marvelous in remembering things about me that help me navigate the sensational as well as the tough times: Caroline Gaither, Rachel Andrews and Kathy Battles, Wendy Giman, and Leone and Ken Litt.

Fueling this project were a few special local hangouts: Zingerman's Coffee Company and the Mighty Good Coffee at Arbor Hills. I also want to express happiness for having Piper, Zeus, and Danny as faithful writing companions.

My deep appreciation goes to Don for his care and support in holding things together on the home front and being a thoughtful listening ear. I also want to mention my love and joy for being Safiya's mom and for having her wonderfully earthshaking presence in my life.

Black Opera

1 Engaged Opera

Throughout this book I present a way of thinking, interpreting, and writing about music in performance that incorporates how race, gender, sexuality, and nation help shape the analysis of opera today. My focus is on how these works, regardless of whether they were written in the distant or recent past, resonate with the issues and experiences of people today: those in the audience and wider contemporary publics. Most musicological analysis, including opera studies, has done its best to reconstruct a viable historical context from what we know of the past to help us understand how we might think about this work in the present. Some of that energy fueled the desire to reconstruct historically informed "performance practice," for example, recreating how Mozart might have first seen and heard his operas (such as the instruments used, the ornamentation improvised, and the materials for the costumes and set designs). This book departs from the solitary goal of understanding how music might have had meaning in the past. While the past is relevant to a general understanding, my larger emphasis is on how these operas have meaning for current audiences. By "audiences" I am referring both to the actual people in the concert hall as well as potential audience members among those who do not attend "classical" (in the general sense) concerts because such venues seem too elitist or outside of their grasp. I am interested in what audiences today see and the connections they can draw to recent and current historical events; this method of inquiry incorporates the shared lived experiences of everyone involved: the performers and the public. Such an approach that brings together opera in a historical context and focuses on how it resonates in the present day points to a type of analysis I call an *engaged musicology*.

Black *Otello*

I start with two true stories about Verdi's 1887 opera *Otello* as it was performed early in the second decade of the twenty-first century. These events provide a context for the impetus of this study. The first happened in the fall of 2012; the second is from the summer–fall 2015.

In the fall of 2012 I took one of my black South African colleagues to a performance of Verdi's *Otello* in the Metropolitan Opera's *Live in HD* series. My colleague was a visiting scholar from the University of the Witwatersrand in Johannesburg, South Africa, and we were part of a small team embarking on a research project that was examining the current opera scene in South Africa. This colleague was in the middle of a six-month stay here at the University of Michigan, and one of my pleasures was going to live opera performances together at the School of Music, Theatre and Dance at the university, and in Detroit at the Michigan Opera Theatre. The Metropolitan Opera's *Live in HD* broadcasts involved a type of hybrid "live" experience as we watched the Saturday matinee performance of the Metropolitan Opera in real time, live streaming to a local movie theater.

While I was excited to share this wonderful opera with my colleague who was fairly new to opera as a genre, I was also a little anxious about this particular performance. It is already a complicated situation with the performance of Verdi's *Otello* and the then-standard use of blackface makeup for the title character. To make things even more awkward, the role of Otello was being sung by Johan Botha, an Afrikaner singer who would be wearing the blackface makeup. I did not know how to think about this—especially given the time period. Here we were, less than twenty years after the dismantling of apartheid in South Africa, where the most brutal regime of white-against-black violence and oppression on the planet during our lifetime had taken place. As an African American woman who was born at the end of the civil rights era, I came of age in the 1980s and 1990s, a time when so many of us thought we were poised for only better and more substantial gains regarding racial inequality and understanding. Yet there we were, sitting in an American movie theater watching one of the most important opera houses in the world utilize the practice of blackface makeup that vividly referenced the painful tradition of minstrelsy, where (primarily) white singers portrayed negative stereotypes of blacks. And I had the opportunity to watch this performance with my black South African friend seeing this minstrel holdover performed by one of her white countrymen in an era that was only a few years past the oppression of apartheid. The timing was also relevant for events developing in the United States. There in the fall of 2012, we were already more than six months past the death of Trayvon Martin and still quite unaware of the upcoming impact his murder and the other public deaths of young black people (primarily young men) would have on the public to kick off a new articulation of racial awareness in the United States.[1]

I sat in the darkened movie theater watching the screen and watching my collaborator watch an Afrikaner in blackface playing the role of Otello. I wanted to apologize, even though that was not the most productive thing to do. I decided that there really was not much I could say to "explain" or even try to justify and try to make sense of what was happening. Instead, I watched the performance and listened to her questions. She wondered about Botha's age, as a way to figure out where he fit into South African history. Though I did not know his age, she estimated that he probably had grown up under apartheid and, as was mandatory, served in the South African military.[2] A confirmation online shows his age to have been forty-seven at the 2012 performance, so he would definitely have qualified to serve in the South African Defense Force when he came of age in the mid-1980s.[3] Botha onstage (through the streaming HD broadcast) and my South African colleague and I in the theater were all in the same age group and yet experienced vastly different lives regarding black-white racial politics during the same period, separated by the Atlantic.

There was very little public comment on the racial politics of the 2012–13 season production of *Otello* at the Metropolitan Opera. The big news was that it was a revival for Renée Fleming (in the role of Desdemona), as it was one of her earliest triumphs with the Met and had been her first Met opening night seventeen years before. In an article he wrote for the *New York Times*, "Returning to a Special Role, Maybe for the Last Time: Renée Fleming in the 'Otello' Revival at the Met" (October 10, 2012), Zachary Woolfe focused on Fleming and said nothing about race or blackface makeup. He praised Fleming, critiqued Botha's stage acting, and then wrote, "To be fair, Mr. Botha may have had other things on his mind. After an uncomfortable first half dotted with stifled high notes, it was announced that he was suffering from allergies. No matter the culprit, his voice settled after the intermission, and its impressive size and bronze color came through." Though "bronze" is mentioned in reference to to Botha, it is only about the sound (vocal color) of his voice—not an uncommon style of commentary—and has no specific reference to race in this context.

The second event took place just three years later, in the summer and fall of 2015. The Metropolitan Opera was going to open its 2015–16 season with a highly anticipated new production by Bartlett Sher of Verdi's *Otello*, this time with Latvian tenor Aleksandrs Antonenko in the title role, with the

Russian soprano Hibla Gerzmava as Desdemona. Displayed prominently in their season book, the Met had put a picture of an Otello with noticeable blackface makeup. Alison Kinney, an opera lover and journalist, was the first to write about the Met's decision not to use blackface after the season brochure "featured a cover image of pale Latvian tenor Aleksandrs Antonenko looking . . . like he'd had a bronzer malfunction."[4]

The question of whether or not to use blackface seems a more straightforward issue than it turns out to be on deeper inspection. Many people outside of the opera world are quite perplexed to realize that—as the past few years of these two examples show—the opera stage is the only stage in the world today where this practice of using blackface makeup for nonblack singers to portray black roles is a regular feature that is practiced, accepted, and—until very recently—never discussed.[5]

These opening stories around *Otello* begin to illuminate what is at stake with the representation of a black character on a stage where the history is to use blackface makeup. This means something in the United States, where the history of minstrelsy, blackface makeup, and negative stereotypes of blacks in the nineteenth century still provide a legacy today. This also means something for audiences who see a white South African singer in blackface makeup and make the connection that he served in the South African military during apartheid, just a few decades before.

In both the United States and South Africa, the opera stage was closed to black singers for decades, and there was a strong mechanism in place in both countries, the enactment of painful and legally enforced practices of white supremacy, that segregated these stages. In an era when science no longer supports a genetic basis for racial differences, we still live in a time when phenotypical differences are legible and the construction of racial difference presents various meanings.[6] In the United States we have seen the first black president, Barack Obama, serve two terms; in South Africa, a steady stream of the first democratically elected presidents, all black, since the end of apartheid: Nelson Mandela, Thabo Mbeki, Kgalema Motlanthe, and Jacob Zuma. Yet both countries still are working out issues about how to write a history that is honest and brings in the diverse experiences of racial difference.

As I write the chapters of this book, I have seen the deterioration of black-white race relations in the United States as long-time hidden practices are getting more national attention: the "new Jim Crow," with incarceration rates and sentencing terms unfairly applied to black people; events where innocent black people are shot by the police and no one is held responsible; and cases where police officers are targeted and murdered.[7] From afar, during my years growing up, the South African protests against apartheid provided a juxtaposition to the racial tensions in the United States. The increasing violence in South Africa with the Sharpeville Massacre (1960), the Soweto Uprising (1976), and the state of emergency under Prime Minister/President Pieter Willem Botha (1985) was dimly reflected in the growing American consciousness of apartheid in the 1980s. In my first year at Barnard College, the Coalition for a Free South Africa at Columbia University assembled a shantytown along College Walk (April 1986) that was also joined by other universities, including Dartmouth and Cornell. The 1990s brought about the triumph in dismantling apartheid and provided the restorative justice model of the Truth and Reconciliation Coalition led by Nobel Prize laureate Archbishop Desmond Tutu. Yet we have, only a few decades later in 2015 and 2016, South African student protests around #FeesMustFall and #Rhodes-MustFall, calling for the decolonization and transformation of South African institutions of higher education. This second decade of the new millennium has brought both hope and discouragement around black-white relations on both sides of the Atlantic.

My goal is not to conflate these two countries around their racial oppressions as being the same. They are separate and have different histories, trajectories, and legacies. Instead, my aim is to bring into focus two complementary operatic arenas, half a world apart, that demonstrate similar and different approaches to situations with much in common—specifically, the new millennium's legacy and articulations of the oppression of black people. This legacy is based on earlier oppression (colonialism and apartheid in South Africa, slavery and Jim Crow segregation in the United States) that had some release at the end of the twentieth century with the dismantling of apartheid in South Africa (and development of their new constitution) and the emergence of a black middle class (despite the growing movement of mass incarceration that targeted blacks) in a United States reaping the benefits of the civil rights movement and desegregation. Yet at the beginning of the second decade of the new millennium, both countries have seen a resurgence of racial tensions in the #FeesMustFall and related movements in South Africa and the #BlackLivesMatter and related movements in the United States.

This book does not essentialize "black experience" into a set of codified events. Rather, it presents alternative narratives informed by theoretical paradigms that draw most heavily on feminist intersectional analysis, Patricia Hill Collins's standpoint theory, bell hooks's model of the margin and the center, and Paulo Freire's pedagogy of the oppressed.[8] As a means of expanding the current narrative of history, by including the legacies of slavery, colonialism, Jim Crow, or apartheid, I show that opera has proved to be a flexible and capacious genre. It can give voice to the different experiences that exist outside the mainstream; with the participation of black composers and librettists behind the scenes, black bodies and embodied stories on the stage, and black audience members interpreting the performance, opera compellingly expresses multiple vantage points than have not been previously engaged.

Calling this book *Black Opera: History, Power, Engagement* is meant to chart a terrain in interdisciplinary opera studies that incorporates a way of thinking about what black opera can be. In this study I go beyond only mentioning black composers and singers, and discuss a historical context and political directive for having black voices telling their own stories and becoming full participants in a genre that had been closed through segregation. Calling something *black opera* might imply that there is a white opera or other identity-related operas; this is not my intention. This book is not the last word on what black opera is, but it is an important starting point for how we can reinvent a term to include new voices, narratives, and experiences. This study does not talk about Latin America, Asia, India, and many other spaces that have been important in black experience. While I cover parts of Europe, the United States, and South Africa, there are still many stories in these places that augment and can shift the telling I present here. Rather than a thorough coverage and listing of all black opera, I seek to initiate a discourse that is capacious and welcomes contrapuntal voices. In this study, I use the terms *black, African American, white, coloured/colored* (a term used during apartheid that I use very limitedly and only in referring to that specific context), and *mixed race* all with caution and care. I realize that these words mean different things across the Atlantic, and my primary goal is to be sensitive and not at all offensive; my apologies if the nuance of my language use causes anyone discomfort.

Behind the Scenes: Crafting this Narrative

As a black opera scholar and fan, I hold myself accountable. To be honest, I had not really noticed the use of blackface makeup until after I had been attending opera regularly for more than a decade. While I was perhaps a little naïve as an audience member, I was also a person of the time who experienced and accepted the cultural conventions around me. The larger picture of opera and social consciousness provide an important helpful context to understand how this could happen.

Let me set the scene. Edward Said's *Orientalism* (which first outlined how the West had constructed a paradigm for seeing the East—a stand-in for basically any non-Western power—as inferior and weaker) was not published until 1978, and his provocative essays on *Aida* that put the opera in the context of colonialism and imperialism were not published until 1987 (and reprinted in 1993).[9] Though there were other people writing about identity and representation, cultural politics, and theoretical frameworks that challenge forms of hegemony (around race, gender, sexuality, and class), this scholarship had been neither fully integrated into the discipline of musicology nor discussed by, or incorporated into, mainstream reviews for audiences of classical music. For me, Said's clear writing in his constructions of power and privilege and his insistence that the arts (literature, music, visual art, theater, and dance) were not innocent of politics, were especially compelling for bringing what was happening onstage into the present day. These writings and my reading across disciplines helped me "see" opera in new ways. Yet even as Said and others were asking questions about orientalism and exoticism in *Aida*, the "on the ground" practical reality of the common practice of blackface makeup was not discussed.[10]

I started going to the Metropolitan Opera in the 1980s while I was in college in New York City. Opera audiences then were a bit different: today, the "realism" onstage needs to be more closely aligned with what we experience in daily life (though I am not claiming that opera is just like real life).[11] The 1980s were still a time when opera was first an aural phenomenon and secondly a visual event. Opera of the time featured elaborate sets and costumes for their sumptuousness, placed less emphasis on a true-to-life representation of action or a compelling imitation of life in the present or the past.[12] Audiences did not expect singers to move around much onstage, and the depiction of "reality" was a very stylized concept. Videos of opera performances were rather rare, and the broadcast of opera on television could never keep up with the demand of a true opera lover; such events were all too infrequent. Many opera fans experienced live opera primarily through real-time Saturday afternoon radio broadcasts sponsored by Texaco; these started in 1931 and continued through 2004, having since been carried forward through sponsorship by the Toll Brothers homebuilding company since 2005.[13]

Of course, the internet (with YouTube and other streaming and downloaded opera performances) was decades away at the time. People learned and got to know operas through audio recordings (records, cassettes, or the then-new media of compact discs). When one was fortunate to be able to attend an opera performance, and admittedly this has always been an expensive art form, it was not uncommon to sit far away from the stage. Singers who were supposed to "look the part" of the role regarding age and weight, and the use of supertitles (or seat titles, that are now used at the Met), were newer conventions in opera that became more standard in the 1990s and early 2000s.[14]

As a student living in the city, I would rather spend my money on more opera tickets for less-expensive far-off seats than only a few opera tickets in the better seats. So I stood for a lot of operas both behind the Orchestra seats on the main floor and way up high in Family Circle, where the sound was exponentially better (yet at the expense of seeing the details of what was happening onstage). The Met is a very large opera house by any standard (it seats almost four thousand; in addition to the orchestra level, there are five horseshoe balcony levels, with Family Circle being the top of the fifth balcony level), and it is easy to grow accustomed to missing specific details onstage.

My purpose in outlining Said's ideas about representation and power, the architecture of the Met, and the emphasis on the aural sound of opera in the 1980s is to clarify how the visual component of blackface makeup in opera was somewhat invisible to so many in the audience. It is not meant to be an "excuse," but rather a way to help explain how so many people did not look at opera closely, even when they were there at a live performance. Of course, the makeup was not invisible, and the audience was well aware of who was singing the leading roles. Additionally, many people were very aware of the race of the singer, and many of the black female singers of that time were among the biggest draws. Roberta Alexander, Martina Arroyo, Kathleen Battles, Harolyn Blackwell, Grace Bumbry, Hilda Harris, and Jessye Norman were not only in my all-time Favorite Singers Club, they were hugely popular with practically everyone.[15]

After the *Blackness in Opera* collection of essays was published in 2012, I wanted to further pursue a direction that had opened up during the research for that project: blackness in opera is something that extends beyond the United States and Europe. In juxtaposition to the operatic tradition in the West, I found compelling cases of opera performance (adaptation and newly composed works) in sub-Saharan Africa. Two case studies came from South Africa (*U-Carmen eKhayelitsha* [2005], and *Winnie: The Opera* [2011]) and one from Senegal (*Karmen Geï* [2001]).[16] As I explored the context around *U-Carmen eKhayelitsha* and saw the final week of rehearsals and first two performances of *Winnie: The Opera* at the State Theatre in Pretoria in the spring of 2011, I found an uncanny and exciting new world for opera in South Africa that promoted and highlighted black people as singers, subjects of operas, and composers working in interracial performance contexts.

This encounter has helped shape how I now think about and approach all opera, especially in terms of how I think about representation in the questions that ground this study: who is being represented, who is telling the story, and who watches and interprets the story. While *Karmen Geï* does not seem to be part of a larger Senegalese operatic tradition that I have found, the two

South African operas opened up a different landscape.[17] The South African operas were not two anomalous examples but instead were indicative of a larger situation and reflect several currents in opera in the United States. As I looked at opera in the United States and South Africa, I saw connections across the articulation of gender, race, sexuality, and nation. For me, opera is no longer a cloistered tradition opened to the chosen few in opera houses dotted across the West. My current world of opera includes these South African voices too and expands the relevance of opera across race, gender, sexuality, and nation. The questions now became, how can a genre that resisted the participation of black people tell us anything about the past or the present in the context of such strong cultures of white supremacy? What can we gain from looking at opera, such an elitist genre, about racial regimes by looking at how race is represented in the past and the present on both sides of the Atlantic?

The history of opera in South Africa is a story that is still being written.[18] In this study, I sketch an outline of specific themes and topics that includes an overview of a few early figures (singers, composers, supporters) who have laid a foundation for the larger Black South African opera scene. My story also incorporates operas written in and about the United States that highlight the vantage points of African Americans. Looming in the background is the European opera tradition that provided a model for bringing music and drama together. Ultimately, I realized that though the worlds of South Africa, the United States, and Europe are distinct with individual characteristics, bringing them all together in my narrative enriched the larger picture rather than limiting it. When I sat these case studies side by side, I realized that similar (though not the same) themes emerged and the bigger story became richer when I kept them next to each other—not fully in conversation, but juxtaposed so that they presented a contrasting whole.

Behind the Scenes: Downstaging Black Voices and a Shadow Culture

The word *downstage* is a blocking term in theater practice and refers to the portion of the stage closest to the audience at the front of the playing area. In studying the downstaging of black voices, I seek to construct a story about race, gender, sexuality, and nation that had been relegated to the margins, to uncover this story and bring it to the forefront of how we have thought about opera at the end of the twentieth century and into the millennium.

I use the term *shadow culture* carefully. I am not implying that black participation in opera is a second-tier endeavor that dimly reflects the glory of the mainstream tradition. Describing something as being in the shadows can inadvertently give an impression that the thing fully illuminated is the true art, and that which is obscured is of lesser importance. This is not at all my intention for discussing blackness in these operas.

The history of black involvement with opera in the United States can be seen as a shadow culture to the all-white and segregated opera scene existent in the United States through the first half of the twentieth century. A similar thing could be said about opera in South Africa up to 1994. Uncovering this shadow culture reveals a different narrative of opera that has a parallel, yet obscured, lineage to the dominant tradition in opera in both countries. This new story of opera achieves much of what the dominant opera culture had accomplished, but it traces different terrain and addresses different questions. In contradistinction to the dominant opera traditions in the United States and South Africa, the shadow cultures I am identifying feature black partici-pation and black subjects in ways that involve a deep engagement and care in representation that is not present in the dominant culture. The dominant culture focuses on stories about black characters in ways that exoticize the subjects; for example, Verdi's 1871 opera *Aida* is a made-up story by Italians and Frenchmen set in the time of the Pharaohs with little knowledge of the historical Egyptians and Ethiopians and makes no reference to living Egyptians or Ethiopians during the late nineteenth century.[19] *Otello* presents a similar situation with a story based on Shakespeare's play *Othello* that has little connection to the real lives of North Africans (Otello/Othello is a Moor) living in European settings and, as the two opening case studies indicate, has a history of being performed by nonblack singers in blackface. The shadow culture of opera brings black perspectives and experiences downstage in our narrative of how the story is told and who is telling and interpreting the story.

For South Africa, a shadow opera culture involves a new post-apartheid situation where, for the first time, blacks are legally allowed to participate and receive training in opera programs. This has had a remarkable effect in less than a full generation; there is currently an incredibly vibrant opera scene with black singers performing at the highest levels in domestic and inter-national opera houses, productions of repertory operas in Western produc-tions, productions of repertory operas in South African settings, and newly composed operas by black South Africans. With operas based on historical figures such as the Zulu Princess Magogo kaDinuzulu, Nelson Mandela, and Winnie Madikizela-Mandela, black South Africans are writing their stories and history into the repertory. In the United States, there is a similar writing of black people's experiences into opera. In this study, I focus on one recently composed work, *From the Diary of Sally Hemings* (2001). I also include adapted works from the past that take nonblack operas and adapt them in black settings: Bizet's 1875 opera *Carmen* presented in two later American settings (as *Carmen Jones* [1954] and *Carmen: A Hip-Hopera* [2001]) and one in a township outside of Cape Town, South Africa (*U-Carmen eKhayelitsha* [2005]). Additionally, I discuss the best-known American opera that focuses on race, Gershwin's 1935 *Porgy and Bess*, and analyze the recent setting from 2011 for the Broadway stage.

The shadow opera culture in the United States is much more extensive than can be included in any one study. There are forgotten or previously lost operas that are resurfacing, and there are recent operas and composers who are writing new stories. A particularly fertile field for this inquiry is in the world of the Harlem Renaissance, with the operas of Scott Joplin, the recently discovered operas of Harry Lawrence Freeman, and the operas of many other composers whose works have been unperformed and hidden from circulation.[20] One of the most important African American opera composers is Anthony Davis, whose operas include topics on black subjects (*X: The Life and Times of Malcolm X* [1986] and *Amistad* [1997]), as well as on themes as varied as science fiction (*Under the Double Moon* [1989]), the abduction of Patty Hearst (*Tania* [1992]), and a contemporary Native American family affected by the past (*Wakonda's Dream* [2007]). Davis's operas tell a story of American life encompassing multiple experiences and vantage points that center-stage race, ethnicity, and gender in a jazz-inspired voice. Davis is also the only black opera composer to have had multiple operas commissioned and performed in major opera houses. Adolphus Hailstork is another black composer who has had multiple operas given professional performances. The Dayton Opera Company commissioned and premiered his *Paul Laurence Dunbar: Common Ground* (1995); Hailstork termed the thirty-five-minute production "an operatic theaterpiece." His second opera, *Joshua's Boots*, called "an opera in one act," was commissioned by the Opera Theatre of St. Louis and first performed in 2000. The opera takes up themes of the Great Migration to the west and focuses on black cowboys and the all-black Buffalo Soldiers.[21] Hailstork wrote his third operatic work, *Robeson*, for the Trilogy Opera Company of Newark, New Jersey, performed in 2014.[22]

Leslie Adams, Regina Harris Baiocchi, George Lewis, Dorothy Rudd Moore, Richard Thompson—these are just a few of the black composers with whom I have spoken who have each composed at least one opera and would write more if there were better opportunities for commissions and performances.[23] Composer Nkeiru Okoye, professor and director of music theory and composition at the State University of New York at New Paltz, is a recent important voice to have emerged on the classical art music scene with symphonic and theatrical works (*The Journey of Phillis Wheatley* [2005]; *Brooklyn Cinderella* [2011]; and *Invitation to a Die-In* [2017], (commissioned in memory of Trayvon Martin), many of which are based on African American diasporic themes. Okoye's largest operatic work (at the time of this writing) is the two-act *Harriet Tubman: When I Crossed That Line to Freedom* (2014).

The emerging group of operas documenting key stories from African American experience continues at the time of this writing. I learned of two new operas in September 2017, the first, a work still in progress, *Little Rock Nine,* being composed by Tania León with a libretto by long-time Anthony Davis collaborator, Thulani Davis. This new work commemorates the integration of Little Rock, Arkansas's Central High School in the fall of 1957.[24] *We Shall Not Be Moved*, the second opera which fortuitously I was able to attend, is a powerful meditation that is part history and set in the present, about the situation that led up to the 1985 bombing of the Move group in Philadelphia, composed by Daniel Bernard Roumain with a libretto by Marc Bamuthi Joseph and directed/choreographed by Bill T. Jones (co-commissioned by Opera Philadelphia, the Apollo Theater, and Hackney Empire in London, premiered in 2017).[25]

There are nonblack composers working with black collaborators and setting stories that focus on black experiences. The collaboration between Richard Danielpour and Toni Morrison on their opera *Margaret Garner* (based on the historical figure behind Morrison's main character in her 1987 Pulitzer Prize–winning novel *Beloved*) is an example of a narrative rewriting history with the black experience of slavery foregrounded into opera. Two other recent examples of the shadow culture include *Charlie Parker's Yardbird* by composer Daniel Schnyder with a libretto by Bridgette A. Wimberly (premiered by Opera Philadelphia [2015]) and Daniel Sonenberg's *The Summer King: An Opera on the Life of Josh Gibson* with a libretto by Sonenberg and Daniel Nester with additional lyrics by Mark Campbell (premiered in Portland, Maine [2014]; revived by the Pittsburgh Opera [2017] and Michigan Opera Theatre [2018]), about one of the best power hitters and catchers in the history of baseball (Gibson [1911–1947] played for the American Negro Leagues and was, in 1972, the second black player in the Negro leagues to be inducted in the National Baseball Hall of Fame).[26] All of these works are part of what I call the shadow culture of opera.

Taking a chance on an opera that is seen as being outside of the traditional canon is not something that happens very frequently, so the performance of any operas in the shadow culture is a momentous event. This is also somewhat true of all contemporary operas on any topic; new opera is considered to be an inherently risky venture. However, operas on controversial topics (such as those focusing on race or homosexuality) tend to be revived less frequently than operas written by white composers on nonblack heteronormative subjects.[27] Known for its opulence and extravagance and requiring a complex combination of talents and skills needed for performance, opera is a genre unlike any other in the musical world. Even in a small-scale venture, fully staged operas include an orchestra, singers, sets, costumes, a production staff (music director/conductor, stage director), and a suitable venue that can accommodate space for an orchestra, lighting, and a stage. For this reason, the ticket prices tend to be more expensive than for performances such as solo recitals, chamber works, choral concerts, and even most orchestral works. The stakes are high for an opera performance, especially after the age of grand opera ended in the early twentieth century.[28] New commissions have been rare and represent a risk for any artistic management. For these reasons, adding to the opera repertory (either by commissioning new ones or reviving lost works) is rare and precarious.

Blackface and Black Bodies Onstage That Matter

There is a complicated issue lurking behind the situation of color/race and casting. When a black person plays a "white" role or one that does not specify race, things are usually seen as being fine. In fact, it even could be said to show "progress," as a playing field seems to have been leveled and black people are able to enter the canonic repertory. Things are not as easy with roles that are specified as being black (or Moorish or African or Caribbean). For a black person to portray such a role, there can be problems. If it is a role with lots of negative stereotypes (for example, Monostatos in *The Magic Flute* or the roles in *Porgy and Bess*), it can feel uncomfortable to have a black person portray such a character: it is as though this performance is somehow reinforcing negative stereotypes. Yet to have a nonblack person put on blackface makeup seems like an insensitive decision (and for *Porgy and Bess* it is not an option for staged performances in the United States due to specifications of the Gershwin estate). An added complication is the way that some roles in opera are for voice types that are quite difficult to find. At any given moment there are not a lot of Wagnerian *Heldentenors* or *spinto* and dramatic sopranos on the planet who can sing those roles at the top opera houses. The same is true for the title role of Verdi's *Otello*—the subject of the two opening case studies here. While many voice types in opera are frequently available, there are a few roles that are notoriously difficult to cast: Otello is one of them. Indeed, this situation would be ameliorated if there were a better pipeline leading to the training and nurturing of young black singers—an endeavor that would surely involve a good deal of effort and resources.

Finding black singers who can portray Otello is a noble, albeit limited, goal. The real issues involve altering the systems of education and access so that anyone in the United States can feel entitled to work hard, recognize if they have an exceptional talent, and expect a fair chance of having a career in the arts. As I write this in 2017, such a goal is not possible for the young children in Flint, Michigan, whose water supply has been contaminated over the past few years with lead and other toxic chemicals through the irresponsible decisions about infrastructure made by a white-dominated state government to save money. Flint, with its poor, predominantly black population, could have been home to a child's voice with the potential to develop into an Otello, yet we will probably never know. Adequate educational opportunities (compared with those available nationally) are not accessible to many children in New Orleans, where they are still recovering from Hurricane Katrina, more than a decade after the storm. The children of New Orleans deserve a music education that could lead them to continue their phenomenal jazz tradition or the even older opera tradition: New Orleans was one of the first American cities to have multiple opera houses in the nineteenth century. The children in Detroit are also suffering. Their schools have operated under a series of emergency managers since 2009, yet they have an incredible recent musical legacy—within the past sixty years—of Motown, jazz, and a thriving music education system that produced world-class classical musicians such as Metropolitan Opera singers George Shirley, Maria Ewing, and Cheryl Studer and leading classical musicians Ruth Laredo (pianist) and opera conductor Thomas Schippers.[29] Recognizing these social realities reveals how the representations of race and blackness in opera are set against a backdrop of lived experience for black and white citizens.

Seeing and Hearing Blackness in Marian Anderson and Leontyne Price

An engaged musicology acknowledges that there is an underlying falsity in the claim behind "colorblind" casting. There is no blindness today regarding black and nonblack casting of roles or roles of any racial/ethnic identity; race and gender are always noticeable: people do not *not* see race and gender. Even if roles are portrayed where these identities are meant to be ambiguous, these are parameters that audience members will always look for and notice. The cultural history of a place will also shape how these features are interpreted. For example, in the United States and South Africa, the history behind black-white racial relationships continues to inform how blackness and whiteness are read and interpreted by audiences. Actors, singers, directors, and audiences are all aware that the personhood of the performer will be read into the characterization of the role and the reception of that actor in that particular role. Audiences may understand that a performer's race is not a featured element of his or her character in the drama; that is not the same as saying that audiences will ignore (or even forget) the racial identity of an actor.

As a counterpoint to the use of blackface makeup in Otello, let's examine two examples—for the United States and the rest of the world—of how race can be an especially powerful tool when a black singer sings a "black role" that is not overwhelmed by negative or minstrel stereotypes: Marian Anderson singing Ulrica at the Met in 1955 and Leontyne Price singing *Aida*—especially in her farewell performance at her retirement from the Met in 1985.

African American singer Marian Anderson became an important figurehead for black participation in opera in the United States and beyond. She was at the center of the highly publicized concert on the steps of the Lincoln Memorial in 1939 when the Daughters of the American Revolution denied her the right to sing in Constitution Hall and First Lady Eleanor Roosevelt stepped in to voice her support of Anderson as an opera singer. Today, many people know that Anderson broke the "color barrier" at the Metropolitan Opera in 1955 when she sang the character of Ulrica from Verdi's *Un Ballo in Maschera*. This was an important symbolic move, for it ushered in a new era of having black singers perform at the Met as well as in other leading opera houses around the world. How might the details of this important debut be interpreted?

Marian Anderson had a career that primarily took place on the concert stage in churches, in celebrated concert halls, and on the steps of the Lincoln Memorial. Generally, she performed classical art song (such as Lieder and songs in French, Italian, and English). Her emphasis was in a non-operatic repertory, except for arias and numbers excerpted from opera. Her legacy is defined as breaking a barrier in opera, yet her actual experience in opera was quite limited; the choice of Verdi's Ulrica for Anderson, therefore, seems to be an uncanny fit for her experience and presence in opera. Ulrica is a major character, but unlike most other major characters in an opera, her presence is quite limited—in fact, she appears in only one scene, in the second half of act 1 (act 1, scene ii). Given the segregation of the opera stage and her resulting limited experience in opera, this opera allowed Anderson to dominate the stage when she appeared, but also to appear only once in the opera. While she was not entirely in the vocal prime of her career when she made this auspicious step in opera (born in 1897, she was fifty-seven years old when she made her Met debut), her performance was momentous and groundbreaking.

The role was also a striking emblem for her debut at the Met. The character of Ulrica is a fortuneteller and, depending on the version of the opera followed, her role is specified as being a "negro fortune teller," in the Boston setting at the end of the seventeenth century (the original setting had been in Sweden around the court of Gustavus III).[30] In this Boston setting, the character of Renato (Captain Anckarstroem in the Swedish setting), the secretary to the governor, also has an ethnic characterization, as he is referred to as a "Creole."[31] In any case, Ulrica is a character who is set apart from others in the opera. In both versions her dwelling is off from the main action of the opera, she is someone who can communicate with the supernatural, and her music is exoticized through the use of tritones, low woodwind timbres, and an invocation to the "Re dell'abisso" ("King of the Abyss [underworld]"). For the first black voice featured on the Met opera stage, Anderson fulfilled and mirrored the role of a foreign character, invited as a featured presence to peer into an alternate plane of reality and predict a new future. Though these stereotypes are not negative in the sense of having a direct minstrel legacy, they do reinforce her character as having an "exotic" heritage and position her "outsider" status both in terms of ethnicity/race as well as geographical location on the outskirts of the town and royal court, where most of the main action takes place. Anderson's "integration" in opera was complete as to her presence on the Metropolitan Opera stage. The role of Ulrica is important to the plot, but it is a small major role (or a major small role), depending on how one sees her position on the margins of the primary landscapes (regarding the principal narrative and geography) of the opera.

In the first generation of black opera singers on the Metropolitan Opera stage that followed Anderson's historic debut, Leontyne Price became a central leading presence with the wide range of roles and exquisite artistry she brought to her performances. Unlike Anderson, whose place in opera was central in a more ideological vein than in practice, Price sang in opera houses all over the world and left a legacy of operatic recordings. She was a celebrated muse for the eminent American composer Samuel Barber, and she sang Cleopatra for the opening of the new Met Opera house at Lincoln Center in 1966 in Barber's *Antony and Cleopatra*. Though the opera was not a huge success, it showed how far things had come in just a little over a decade. Before 1955, black singers were segregated from the Met; in 1966 a black singer premiered the gala opening of the new season in the new opera building in a newly composed opera—certainly this was one of the greatest honors given any opera singer in recent history.

Price was an adventurous singer who excelled in repertory that was both part of the staple diet of her lyric-spinto voice (heroines of Verdi and Puccini) and the ever vocally exposed Mozart roles (Donna Anna, Pamina, and Fiordiligi). She also was a singer of older repertory when such operas were not standard, and she sang Monteverdi's Poppea (*L'incoronazione di Poppea*) and Handel's Cleopatra (*Giulio Cesare*). Price was a singer connected to her time with her early performance of Poulenc's *Dialogues des Carmélites* at San Francisco in 1957 (the same year the opera premiered) early in her opera career when she was only thirty years old (she sang Madame Lidoine).

For me, and I suspect many others, Price's most famous signature role was the title character in Verdi's *Aida*. It was one of her most frequent roles, and it was the one with which she chose to close her career at the Met Opera house in 1985. In the case of Price, the most pristine voice available for the role does not have to don the blackface makeup to sing the mythic captive Ethiopian princess. The whole scene comes together and resonates even more powerfully in the Act 3 Nile scene during her aria "O Patria mia" and the following duet with her father. For many, these moments are when real life and opera life all come together.

We see the conflict Aida endures as she has fallen in love with the leader of the Egyptian army (Radames), her captor. We also know that her father, the Ethiopian king Amonasro, is going to compel her to fight for her country in his attempt to lead a rebellion. In a private moment at night along the banks of the Nile, Aida contemplates suicide as she realizes that her position is completely untenable; there is no way she can both love Radames and be the daughter her father raised her to be. Yet at this point leading into her aria, her destiny still feels unknowable as she is given an impossible situation that has no easy solution. Her aria presents the culmination of her feelings—that she will never see her homeland again; she can never go back, and it will never be recoverable. Her last line is repeated several times: "O Patria mia, non ti vedrò mai più" (Oh my beloved country, I will never see you again). Verdi is known for working with his librettists to ask for "la parola scenica"—theatrically effective language, "the scenic word." Verdi scholars have discussed the importance, especially in his later operas, of his dramaturgy, wherein he would compress a dramatic moment into a powerful, concise statement, or even a single word. The concept of "patria"—homeland, what is familiar, and what is worth dying for—is a featured image in Verdi's operas throughout his career during the Risorgimento (the Italian unification movement that led to the modern formation of Italy through its first Italian parliament in 1861). Though *Aida* is from 1871, in that first generation of Italian unification, the strength of this movement was still a recent memory for its first Italian audiences, and Aida's insistence on "O Patria mia" would have had a strong resonance.

Just when we think things cannot get worse for Aida, her father (Amonasro) arrives unexpectedly and raises the tension to a new level. Though he has only recently been captured, he has figured out the situation between Radames and Aida and has formulated a plan more devastating to her than the suicide she had considered in her preceding aria. In their duet, he systematically breaks down Aida's resolve as he takes her through the destruction of their country to relive that terror. He then presents the solution: through Radames's love for her, she will get him to tell her the path of the Egyptian army while Amonasro hides so that he can lead the rebellion to success. Aida is horrified and immediately refuses. It is then that Amonasro presents his most deadly blow. He outlines the new inevitable bloodshed and suffering for their country that her decision will entail:

> Una larva orribile
> Fra l'ombre a noi s'affaccia . . .
> Trema! Le scarni braccia
> Sul capo tuo levò . . .
> Tua madre ell'è . . . ravvissla . . .
> Ti maledice. . .

> A horrible form
> Comes toward us from the shadows . . .
> Tremble! Its withered arms
> Are raised toward your head . . .
> It is your mother . . . recognize her . . .
> She curses you . . .

At this point, Aida has been reduced to one word, "Pietà!" (Have mercy!) that she repeats, nearing the point of total exhaustion. Amonasro's response is not one of comfort but of even further fury: he repels her and says,

> Va indegna! Non sei mia figlia
> Dei Faraoni tu sei la schiava!

> Go, unworthy one! You are not my daughter
> You are the slave of the Pharaohs!

The climax is achieved; Aida has come to the end of her endurance. The music had been steadily expanding out—the upper strings reaching the top of the range and the lower strings extended down further to a deep lyrical bass line. It is as though Aida has become engulfed in the metaphorical soundscape around her. The moment of judgment has come, and Aida is totally bereft. She finally realizes what she must do—to follow what she was raised to become. Their exchange outlines her decision.

Aida

(trascinandosi a stento ai piedi del padre)	(dragging herself painfully to her father's feet)
Padre! . . . a costoro . . . schiava . . . io non sono . . .	Father! . . . I am not . . . their . . . slave . . .
Non maledirmi, . . . non imprecarmi . . .	Do not curse me . . . do not revile me . . .
Ancor tua figlia portrai chiamarmi . . .	You can still call me your daughter . . .
Della mia patria degna sarò	I shall be worthy of my country

Amonasro

Pensa che un popoplo, vinto, straziato	Think a martyred, defeated people,
Per te soltanto risorger può . . .	Can rise again only through you . . .

Aida

O patria! O patria . . . quanto mi costi!	Oh my country! O my country . . . how much you cost me!

In a masterful use of la parola scenica, "patria" has now transformed from being the thing desired yet unattainable (in her preceding aria, "O Patria mia"), the ideal you choose to follow ("Della mia patria degna sarò"), to the sacrifice you believe in and must make ("O patria . . . quanto mi costi!"). Aida has come of age, and she has made up her mind; she has made a decision in an unbearable situation. Verdi recognized the intensity of this moment dramatically and was adamant to Ghislanzoni, his librettist, that there is no way Aida has the mental or emotional capacity to sing a cabaletta (of la solita forma) that the conventional form dictated.[32] Musically in the orchestration and in the form, the drama showcases this point where expectations are broken and things come to halt.

I find it impossible to watch Leontyne Price sing this scene and not feel its momentousness. I watch and hear Price sing Aida throughout her career and feel how real these words are: "Oh my country, how much you have cost me." It feels like a moment when the drama onstage and the reality offstage crash together, and I feel as if I understand something new—each and every time I experience it. This voice comes out of a body that lived through the end of Jim Crow and segregation, was part of the continuous waves of the Great Migration to the north and west with people searching for safety, a chance to make it, and to thrive. As Price was stepping onto the leading opera stages around the world, people were marching into the burgeoning civil rights movement. Price made her Metropolitan Opera debut in 1961, three years before the Civil Rights Act (1964) was passed and officially outlawed discrimination based on race, color, religion, sex, or national origin.

An engaged musicology helps me to hear Price's body and experiences in her voice. Revealed in this voice is the childhood in Mississippi during the 1930s and 1940s; the proud and puzzled receptions of her operatic singing by her family, community, and audiences around the world; the comments she must have endured. As the regal and long-suffering Aida, Price was the African American singer whose voice fit the character perfectly; in this role she proved so many people wrong for their bigotry and violence. And she made so many things right for those of us who have fallen in love with opera.

Rubrics for Listening and Analyzing across the Chapters

Woven throughout each of the four case-study chapters that focus on specific works (*From the Diary of Sally Hemings*, *Porgy and Bess*, the Mérimée and Bizet nineteenth-century *Carmen* and subsequent black settings of the story in the United States and South Africa, and *Winnie: The Opera*) are three basic lines of inquiry for structuring my analysis of these works. These questions present a loose rubric for setting up the historical context for the work and a more specific analysis of how the text and music create the drama behind the themes of race, gender, socioeconomic status, sexuality, and definitions of nation.[33] Put simply, I ask: Who is in the story? Who speaks? and Who is in the audience? Though each chapter adjusts these questions to directly address the particular situation of each work, the first question refers to who is onstage (or onscreen in the film adaptations) as well as who is not there. This question relates to the representation of the role being portrayed and the identity (racial/ethnic, gendered, any visible marker) of the person playing the character. Is there true-to-color casting where the characters are portrayed by the race/ethnicity of the actor performing the roles, or is there a practice of colorblind casting or makeup used to darken skin tones and alter physical features? Rarely are these issues free of contemplation, for they relate to the accessibility of having people of color perform roles frequently assumed to be white (or nonspecified racially) and opening up opportunities for nonwhite performers to be in mainstream repertoire and productions.

In addition to the importance of who is onstage is the narrative point of who gets to speak—which is more complicated than who we see onstage. I want to further complicate the important statement that the physical presence makes, and the presence of a larger narrative voice; both can be, but are not always, embodied together. For example, while the presence of black bodies onstage for the premiere of Gertrude Stein and Virgil Thompson's *Four Saints in Three Acts* in 1934 was a bold and momentous statement for that production, no one would claim that the intellectual content of this opera was based on black experiences. This is true given the late decision to cast black bodies in the compositional history of the work (it was not conceived as a story told from black voices) and the fact that the semantic content of this work is based less on a linear story and more on experimental abstraction.[34] However, the presence of the black bodies once they are in the opera, performing the text, and inhabiting the roles creates new meanings regarding the aesthetics interlinking blackness and modernism.[35]

At stake with who speaks—who gets to tell the story—are the difficulties associated with determining when, or how, one story can be representative of a specific set of experiences. This is true when a member of one identity group represents a world within or outside his or her own experience. In the case of *Porgy and Bess*, for example, George Gershwin clearly got many things right about a certain black experience in America; but, as I discuss in chapter 4, other aspects of the opera are quite problematic in this respect. The point is that the representation of a specific identity group's world requires special consideration, whoever the authors are. When a world onstage is created by an insider to that community, the concern is not to say there is one monolithic representation more authentic than any other, but that this is one representation from someone who has lived experience in that world. When a world is created by someone outside that specific community, reactions and commentary by members of the represented community warrant careful attention.

The final rubric I bring to each case study has to do with who is in the audience—who interprets the story. How is the narrative perceived, and whose experiences are reflected in the interpretation? Rather than focus solely on the concept of the unspecified or abstract general reader—a device in literary critical theory that harks back to the classic constructions of Roland Barthes's "Death of the Author," which focuses on the reader at the expense of the author ("the birth of the reader must be ransomed by the death of the

author")—I want to find a more flexible type of "reading" that accounts for
the role each of us plays in our analyses. While there is definitely a place for
learning and thinking about these works based on collected historical facts
(reviews of the first performances, sociopolitical contexts for the specific
period, and the like), I propose that envisioning a world at least partially fueled by an imagination of the past allows us to ask questions that go beyond
what we know for sure and complements what we do not know. Though
such an activity could be written off as speculation—a slippery slope that
could feel like anything is possible and everything goes—this imagination
is meant to open up a capacious space for what is not written down or easily
recorded.[36] The power of these works lies in what they offered to their original
audiences as well as what they still can offer us today. Part of that legacy is
how we piece together those stories from the past and write a thicker (in the
Geertzian sense) account of history. To borrow a concept from Ron Radano
and Philip Bohlman, I am inserting my own "racial imagination" into my
reading of these operas. I am taking their formation of a "shifting matrix of
ideological constructions of difference associated with body type and color
that have emerged as part of the discourse network of modernity" to help
shape how I read meaning into these works.[37] My goal is to share what I think
about these works, given the historical facts as well as my own background,
training, and lived experiences.

The context for analyzing a performed work from the standpoint of the
audience has a deeper precedence in theater criticism than in opera studies;
however, there also exists the larger umbrella of literary and cultural theory
as well as performance studies. A grounding text in theater studies is Susan
Bennett's work on theater audiences (*Theatre Audiences: A Theory of Production and Reception* [1990]) and bringing together the cultural context of a
performance along with the spectators' experiences of the event. Stuart Hall
(*Representations*; "Encoding/Decoding") has also theorized about the het-
erogeneity of an audience and how it can lead to a diversity of readings and
interpretations—around encoding and decoding—and how such meanings
are produced, circulated, and reproduced. A particularly helpful study for
my thinking about audiences and publics transnationally, and especially for
her work on the African continent, is Karin Barber's opening up the meaning
and capaciousness of what a text is (especially outside of a written tradition)
and how it can be interpreted by multiple audiences (*Anthropology of Texts,
Persons and Public*) and the ways being in society shape the ways of being
in an audience ("Preliminary Notes on Audiences in Africa"). Jennifer Lyn
Stoever's recent work, *The Sonic Color Line* (2016), provides a new construction of racialized listening along with the "listening ear" that can hear aural

ideas of blackness. Stoever's work reflects many practices I have incorporated myself, and I find her terminology to be helpful in opening up possibilities for new paradigms. Indeed, it is a rich field of scholarship linking performance and interpretation, especially around race and gender, that has informed my hearing and understanding of the case studies in this book.[38]

Looking Ahead

Immediately following this introduction, chapter 2 opens up a dialogue for thinking about opera in the United States and South Africa. It provides an overview of relevant themes relating to the participation of black people in opera in both countries. With a juxtaposition of the situation in both countries, the themes focus on the influence of the minstrel tradition as it crossed the Atlantic from the United States to South Africa, the early performers who broke through color barriers in classical singing, and the institutions that supported these new voices in opera.

In the opening case-study discussion (chapter 3) on the solo-opera *From the Diary of Sally Hemings*, we find the trope of interracial relationships worked out both in the content of the narrative as well as in the creation of the work. The interracial collaboration was between white composer William Bolcom and black playwright/librettist Sandra Seaton, who worked together on recreating a story that has been lost. Thomas Jefferson and Sally Hemings represent both the early stages of American history as well as many of the types of secrets that were hidden around race. In this genre, such possibilities can be drawn musically that bring things to life in the cloak of the imaginary: an effervescence that is held in sound and voice. This story opens up the hidden history of miscegenation between master and slave and threatens that the "purity" of race as categories between black and white are blurred even with the Founding Fathers of the United States.

From the Revolutionary era that began the formation of the United States, the next case study (chapter 4) moves to a moment in history after Emancipation in the early decades of the twentieth century. With the energy of the Harlem Renaissance and the reality of Jim Crow segregation, the matrices of race, gender, and sexuality (in terms of the expression of sexual behavior) are examined in the telling and retelling of the *Porgy and Bess* story. With the development of an "American" operatic voice in the beginning of the twentieth century, Gershwin brings together an "American Folk Opera" that articulates the experiences of African American life from the vantage point of a Jewish man born of Russian immigrant parents and a white Southerner (librettist DuBose Heyward) who grew up among the failed promises of

Reconstruction. Chapter 4 addresses this story as it was told in 1935, awash in minstrel stereotypes, and then adapted in 2011 to rethink how the depth inherent in the original characters could be made more visible. A centered focus on the character of Bess reveals her evolution as a woman whose sexual experience is presented in terms that vacillate between victimhood and choice. The other female characters (Clara, Serena, and Maria) are also examined to flesh out the larger view of black womanhood in the 1930s and the first decades of the twenty-first century. At stake is the way femininity and race are intertwined for black women in the decades following the Civil War and in the present.

The theme of adaptation is expanded in chapter 5, in the case study that follows the character of Carmen from her genesis in the middle of the nineteenth century with Prosper Mérimée's novella (1845–46) through Bizet's opera (1875), the film adaptation of *Carmen Jones* (1954), the MTV hip hopera (2001), and the South African *U-Carmen eKhayelitsha* (2005). As a way to bring these works into conversation with each other to address the way blackness is foregrounded, I rely on the three central rubrics (Who is onstage? Who is in the audience? and Who is reading and interpreting the work?) to focus on the intricacies of representation across the parameters of race, gender, expressions of hypersexuality, class, and nation while they are juxtaposed and held in dialogue with each other. This chapter brings together the same story as it moves across the Atlantic from Europe to the United States to South Africa and becomes a focal point for looking at text and genre. Though each telling is unique, the counterpoint of female characters who push the boundaries of acceptable behavior becomes a transnational lens through which to see how theories shaping womanhood migrate and are translated across international borders. Carmen, as a cipher, becomes a global citizen and measure of modernity for her time.

Chapter 6, on *Winnie: The Opera*, is the only section of this book that had its genesis in another context. When I first traveled to South Africa in August 2010, saw the students at the University of Cape Town, and heard the vibrancy of the new operatic scene emerging, I found out about the upcoming performance of this new opera about Winnie Madikizela-Mandela from my work with Kamal Kahn (head of the Opera School at UCT who had been involved with early stages of the production) and meeting lead librettist Warren Wilensky and composer Bongani Ndodana-Breen at a reception. The opera project sounded interesting, and though I had no idea where it might lead, I knew that I wanted to see this premiere. I was very fortunate to receive generous support and encouragement from several departments at the University of Michigan and was able to go to Pretoria to the State Theatre to attend the final week of dress rehearsals, the premiere, and second performances. I also looked up contacts at the University of the Witwatersrand in Johannesburg. I had the name of one scholar in African languages, linguistics, and popular cultures who was working on the South African opera Mzilikazi Khumalo's *Princess Magogo kaDinuzulu* (2002), at that time the only full-length opera written by a black South African. Additionally, I had the good fortune to meet another Wits professor who is a musicologist, opera scholar, and professional singer (tenor). Innocentia Jabulisile Mhlambi and Donato Somma and I have ended up forming a wonderful collaborative team that has deeply enriched my engagement with this opera and its setting in South African culture. We kept our initial goals modest; perhaps we could write a jointly authored paper that would contextualize and analyze this new expression in black South African opera. Through more funding and support we were able to meet again in the United States and at the Wits Institute for Social and Economic Research (WISER), through a partnership between the University of Michigan and Wits, and our collaboration grew. Parts of chapter 6 were originally published in a cluster of articles in *African Studies* (2016) that focus on this opera and the burgeoning opera scene in South Africa.[39]

The original goal of this article on *Winnie: The Opera* was to introduce the opera so that my South African colleagues could further write about how the opera worked in South African culture. Instead, the piece became a discussion of how this opera in South Africa reflects trends that are going on here in the United States with the presence of a more "official" line of opera dominated by a white culture and a type of "shadow" line of opera that tells the stories of black South Africans and African Americans. It was through this work that I realized that the genre of opera was being used on both sides of the Atlantic to tell an alternative story of racial experience in counterpoint to the dominant narrative.

The more I thought about these opera scenes across the Atlantic, the more it seemed to present an ironic reworking of "using the Master's tools to dismantle the Master's house," to inadequately paraphrase a famous concept articulated by Audre Lorde in her article "The Master's Tools Will Never Dismantle the Master's House."[40] I do not cite this reference lightly, for I believe it to be one of the most compelling statements about the presence of women of color (and can be extended to also include other underrepresented identities) both in the academy and larger hegemonic discourses of power. I refer to this article carefully and respectfully. Lorde's comments were written in response to a feminist conference that excluded the meaningful participation of nonwhite women. You can hear how tired and exasperated Lorde is in her article as she relates how a phone call to her was the token gesture to include and recruit women of color to the event. In the content of the conference papers and the presence of bodies at the conference, Lorde outlines how a method of business as usual is not going to "[re]define and empower" new voices and seats at the table for negotiation and power.

In using Lorde's metaphor of the "Master's tools," I want to resituate the genre of opera from a mouthpiece of the oppressor to a vehicle that can be utilized by anyone. There is nothing inherently "white" or "nonblack" about the music, text, and possibilities within the choices one can make in composing opera. In chapter 6 I discuss Karin Barber's use of the construction of genre and the opportunities for dialogues between African, Western, and other non-Western forms of oral and written culture she outlines that perfectly fit the operatic conversations going on in South Africa.[41] The presence of Winnie Madikizela-Mandela as an operatic subject in this book illustrates how the stylized language of opera can be learned, adapted, and utilized by anyone who has access to the proper training and talent. This is not yet a perfectly "level playing field," and this is a music that shows class and economic status hierarchies; these boundaries need to be forded and dissolved through fiscal subsidies and broader support for the arts. But the ability of opera to articulate the needs, desires, aspirations, and character of anyone across the globe is something we see demonstrated in the shadow, alternative opera scenes in South Africa and the United States.

Through the examination of opera from the vantage points of race, gender, class, sexuality, and other cultural identities, our vision of opera changes. No longer functioning as an exclusively elitist event for the upper crust of society, its use by different populations can transform the way opera works in culture. The case studies outlined in these chapters present readings of canonical as well as lesser-known works that challenge the concept of an art form that is removed from its original time and place. In addition to presenting a set of questions that identify the vantage points of identity in the analysis of opera (for the people onstage, the intended audience, and the ones interpreting the work), the conclusion of this study presents another model for thinking about how opera and classical art music produce meaning today. To conclude this study, I explore the potential of an engaged musicological practice that allows old and new, standard and underrepresented narratives to be voiced in opera. Such a practice would both invite new audiences into the opera house and present traditional opera goers with new realities.

2 Black Opera across the Atlantic

*Writing Black Music History
and Opera's Unusual Place*

This chapter provides a starting point for asking questions about how to structure and shape information about opera in the United States and South Africa that highlights black experience. As these topics become more visible, current scholarship is underway to fill in some of the gaps in these narratives. Because there exists more information about the theorizing, mapping out a list of composers, and forming a history about black music in the United States, I will begin from this vantage point with a few methodological paradigms for writing about black music history in general, and then move on to a historical context for opera in the United States and signature moments we know about for black classical singing, the entrée of black singers into the opera world, and the genesis of breaking down the barriers of segregation. With a quick outline of a few singers from the nineteenth century, I then discuss the interwoven history of minstrelsy with opera, and highlight Marian Anderson's historic contributions.

My discussion of opera in South Africa emphasizes the recent history since the dismantling of apartheid in 1994. I include a short section on the colonial music history in South Africa, focusing on the encounter of American minstrel troupes who traveled there at the end of the nineteenth century. I also rely strongly on the personal narratives of two South Africans involved in the opera scene there. The first is Italian South African Angelo Gobbato, who emigrated to South Africa as a child in the 1950s and has had an active career in opera as a singer, administrator, director, and professor at the University of Cape Town. The second is Soweto-born composer Neo Muyanga, whose musical training took place in Italy and involved extended stays in England, Los Angeles, and Ethiopia. His operas have begun to be performed in South

Africa and, like Gobbato, he sits on several South African artistic administrative boards. The final section of this narrative discusses a few of the early
black South African opera singers who have had international success and
focuses on an opera-theater company, the Isango Ensemble, that draws its
members from the townships around Cape Town and provides an innovative
model for engaging opera in a wide cross-section of South African life.

What emerges from these initial histories of black opera in the United
States and South Africa is both the need for a more fleshed-out texture of
the opera scene in each country and the somewhat surprising revelation
that opera is a space where blacks across the Atlantic are writing themselves
into history. Through the subjects of the operas, the participants onstage, the
composers and librettists behind the scenes, and the publics in the audience,
opera has become a vehicle for representing new identities and narratives.
Despite the segregated, whites-only history and the parallel musical theater
tradition of minstrelsy in both countries, opera has proved to be an unlikely
space for voicing black experiences.

Black Opera in the United States

Many scholars have provided helpful methodologies for pulling together
a narrative, when so much of it has been hidden and dismembered. It is
much easier to report about a history when there is an extant trajectory of
what has happened through an archive of biographies, treatises, articles,
and published musical works. However, this is not always the case for black
music, and so a reconstructed truth is what can emerge. Recent scholars,
including Eileen Southern, Josephine Wright, Samuel Floyd, Portia Maultsby,
Melanie Burnham, Guthrie Ramsey, Rae Linda Brown, Kyra Gaunt, Tammy
Kernodle, Yvonne Kendall, Gayle Murchison, and Eileen Hayes (and this is
not an exhaustive list) have let their academic training and lived experience
work together to formulate questions and pursue a vision of an imagined
past made visible by constructing a history from that which was not always
written down in obvious places.[1] An older generation of elders who lived at
the dawn of the twentieth century also pulled together narratives that named
names and wrote black musical experience into a burgeoning history: William
M. Trotter (*Music and Some Highly Musical People* [1878]), W. E. B. Du Bois
(*The Souls of Black Folk* [1903]), James Weldon Johnson (*Black Manhattan*
[1930]), and Alain Locke (*The Negro and His Music* [1936]). Through those
of us who were there with our own memory combined with the memories
of others, we are forming a history that records a version of the past that
keeps evolving. Though I am not constructing the same type of history, I

have relied on their work and realize that this is a developing story. Later in this chapter I have drawn on these sources to outline a rough history of black opera here in the United States.

Another helpful model for this study has been Ronald Radano's *Lying Up a Nation*. Early on, he outlines threads for exploring what is at stake for the hinge that brings together race and music in the United States. He identifies the importance of a history that places black people at the center of the creative impetus, that allows blackness to be visible and audible as a marker of meaning in music. Though black music may be hard to define explicitly, once we have figured out what black music is, it can act "as the conscience of the American experience, as the sonic truth teller of race and its multitude contradictions."[2] This has been a beacon for the present study in terms of finding a way to encompass a capacious conception of what "black music" is—especially in reference to opera here in the United States and in South Africa. A difficulty in outlining this project has been that it is not specifically about music composed or exclusively performed by black people—indeed, it looks at music that was at times hostile to blacks in terms of representation, the practice of minstrelsy (here in the United States and in South Africa), and participation in the segregated opera houses as whites-only spaces for the first half of the twentieth century in the United States and nearly the full century in South Africa.

Looking to opera as a place for exploring black experience in both countries is not an obvious choice. Yet it is the very unlikeliness of this situation that makes it all the more surprising and rewarding when examined closely. There is a story that has been buried and invisible about black experience in "classical" music that goes beyond breaking the color barriers and having a presence onstage, a story that encompasses what those bodies onstage mean and how they resonate different meanings for diverse audiences. This space of performance has been saying many things simultaneously, and my goal is to open up some of these meanings. In a slight rewording of Radano's statement above, the black music in opera tells many truths about a more inclusive version of American and South African experiences.

*   *   *

Though there had been traveling opera companies presenting opera in English in North America since the mid-eighteenth century, many feel that the history of opera in the United States generally takes off as a more established tradition when Italian opera came to New York with an Italian opera troupe headed by Manuel García in 1825.[3] As the noted tenor for whom Gioachino Rossini wrote the role of the Count Almaviva in his 1816 opera,

Il barbiere di Siviglia (*The Barber of Seville*), García, together with his family, was a distinguished presence in music history throughout the century.[4]
With people like Mozart's librettist Lorenzo da Ponte (1749–1838) teaching
at Columbia University from 1825 (and held a position there from 1827 until
his death), who was also involved with the García opera tour in New York,
opera gained popularity in the United States starting in the late 1820s.[5]

Within two decades, early black singers emerged, more as curiosity acts
where opera was sung. The history of African American singers in the
United States, especially those who sang classical art music (as opposed
to minstrelsy) is still being written; however, already there is scholarship
that outlines several female singers going back to the nineteenth century
(for example, Elizabeth Taylor Greenfield, also known as the "Black Swan,"
and Sissieretta Jones, also known as the "Black Patti") who sang operatic
numbers and gave concerts. Complementing the other black male performers in the nineteenth century who were more frequently known as
instrumentalists (such as Thomas "Blind Tom" Wiggins on the piano and
Francis "Frank" B. Johnson, a bugler and band leader), the vast social constraints embedded in slavery and attitudes against integration and equality
made it virtually impossible for black people to obtain the training or have
formal opportunities for public performance.

Two important arenas provide a context for examining the presence of
African Americans in opera: choral singing and minstrelsy. Both traditions
were active early in the nineteenth century and were then rearticulated after
Emancipation in the 1860s. During the antebellum period, the majority of
African American choral singing has been studied in the context of slavery.
Choral music known as "work songs" accompanied slaves' labor, and they
performed other music after hours in their spare time (such as Ring Shout,
spirituals that provided coded messages to pass information among slaves,
and music for hidden religious services). As in many African communities,
choral music also accompanied rites of passage such as births and deaths and
was present in other social gatherings. Under slavery, music was regulated, as
were many other forms of cultural expression (such as dance). In the freed
black communities, religious choral singing had less scrutiny as a subversive
force, and churches provided a space for black singing.

With the first founding of colleges for black students in the late 1860s after
the Civil War, choral concerts became an early means of formally organized
artistic expression and fundraising. The Fisk Jubilee Singers was the first of
such groups that were hugely successful and made an important name for
black singers who delivered diatonic harmonies and were in tune with the
European arts scene. After Fisk University was founded in 1866 in Nashville,

Tennessee, the school's treasurer and professor of music George L. White organized the first concert tour in October 1871 as a fundraising effort; this first group of ten singers would develop into the Fisk Jubilee Singers. Their primary program consisted of European classical choral works as well as slave songs and religious music by former slaves (many of these songs became spirituals). The spirituals grew in popularity and quickly developed into the main attraction wherever the singers performed. These early choral experiences demonstrate that though the black college singers were capable of singing classical repertoire, audiences were more interested in hearing the spirituals. This marked an important point in the history of harmonizing spirituals and bringing dignity to a form previously sung by black people to black people in less formal settings. It also indicates that having choirs of black people singing European art music was not a sure way to maintain audiences and begins to open up the question of what contexts were needed to support black performers in art music.[6]

As a sharp contrast to the development of concert music sung by black people in dignified settings, minstrel performances by black people before, but primarily after, the Civil War presented a demeaning, albeit entrepreneurial, way for African Americans to make money and perform as artists. Though seen by many as a "low brow" form of entertainment (especially when compared with the repertoire of groups such as the Fisk Jubilee Singers), minstrelsy is the giant specter with which we must contend as we examine black participation in opera. While the two forms are quite distinct—opera and minstrelsy—they provided a complicated, interconnected history for black musicians.

As a genre that started in the first decades of the nineteenth century, one story has Thomas Dartmouth Rice credited as an important early developer of minstrelsy when—according to the story passed down—he decided to imitate a lame black man, presumably a slave, with his ragged clothes, poor English language skills, and awkward physical bearing. "Jumping Jim Crow," came out of this line of the legacy. Though minstrelsy is a genre and formal structure of musical performance that has a long and more complicated history, it is important in black opera history for the precedent it set in representing black characters onstage. The popularity of minstrelsy in the nineteenth century propagated negative stereotypes that reinforced oppressive beliefs about African Americans. This practice became a widespread form of entertainment in vaudeville theater and the popular musical theater stage that allowed white performers to masquerade in blackface and transgress social-class expectations.[7] What was considered to be proper white masculinity was replaced with vulgar stereotypes of black people and gained great acceptance across stages in the United States as well as abroad in Europe and—ironically, yet not inconsequentially—in locations as far-flung as South Africa.[8]

Though minstrelsy had seen black performers in its early decades, before the Civil War minstrelsy was dominated by white men in blackface portraying the black minstrel stereotypes, crossing the lines of race, class, and gender. It was not until the late 1860s, when minstrelsy was already an established popular art form, that it became a common open space for performing blackness in musical theater for white and black performers alike.

One of the most complicated issues in determining the opera legacy for black performers is the context wherein black performers were called minstrels, Ethiopian delineators, and other terms for minstrel performance when they might actually have been singing classical music, including opera arias and scenes. In fact, early minstrel performances were sometimes called Ethiopian Operas. When George L. White took the first students from Fisk University on a singing tour, they did not yet have their signature name. Abolitionist preacher Henry Beecher (brother to noted author Harriet Beecher Stowe) sponsored the singers for a concert, and the newspapers referred to them as "Beecher's Negro Minstrels," thus obscuring the nature of their performance and encouraging their director to come up with an official name for the group. Since the concept of a "year of jubilee" was popular after slavery ended, the "Fisk Jubilee Singers" as a name felt appropriate, became popular, and stuck.[9] Without knowing that the musical singing group Beecher presented was the group from Fisk, it is easy to misunderstand this history noted in the newspapers.[10] Additionally, this case shows that people did not know what to call a group of black singers in the late nineteenth century besides minstrels, even when their music was a glaring contrast to the minstrel tradition and had what would later be called classical art songs by black composers—the spirituals—as their repertoire.

Since black performers were barred from traditional opera performance, the few singers we know of who had operatic training—Elizabeth Taylor Greenfield, Sissieretta Jones, Marie Selika, for instance—are also sometimes described in contexts that could seem like minstrelsy, similar to the situation with the early Fisk Jubilee Singers before they were officially named. Additionally, such operatic singers sometimes formed their own traveling all-black companies or traveled with black minstrel troupes (two noted examples are Elizabeth Taylor Greenfield's "Black Swan Troupe" in the 1850s and 1860s, and Sissieretta Jones's "Black Patti Troubadours" later in the 1890s).[11] As they traveled, black singers performed in various venues: concert halls, opera halls, town halls, churches, and other places. Hence it is not always obvious whether something advertised as a minstrel act really involved classical art songs and opera arias.

Since the pioneering work of Eileen Southern, *The Music of Black Americans: A History* (first published in 1971 with subsequent editions in 1983 and 1997) and Rosalind Story (*And So I Sing: African-American Divas of Opera and Concert* [1990]), the broad strokes outlining the first black people in opera have tended to focus on two singers. The first black opera singer—Elizabeth Taylor Greenfield, also known as "The Black Swan" (ca. 1809–1876)—emerged from slavery and had a career concertizing in the United States as well as abroad. She sang for Queen Victoria in England and was part of the abolitionist movement on both continents. Matilda Joyner Sissieretta Jones, "The Black Patti" (1868–1933), is the next major opera singer for whom we begin to have a complete biography. Born immediately following the Civil War, she benefited from the social movements around Reconstruction and sang concert tours in the United States as well as Canada, Europe, and the Caribbean. Noted musicologist Josephine Wright mentions the Black Patti Troubadours touring internationally and "performing 'kaleidoscopes' of arias and choruses from grand opera."[12] Wright's well-chosen descriptor, "kaleidoscopes," appropriately captures the difficulty in characterizing what these traveling staged performances were really like.

As I write in 2017, the early history of black participation in opera (as performers, composers, and impresarios) in the United States during the nineteenth and early twentieth centuries is still being written and pieced together; however, thankfully, this history is receiving more attention. Just a few examples of the strong recent scholarship that brings together American history, black diaspora studies, and music scholarship is uncovering a new narrative that expands a deeper shaping and engagement of blacks in opera. Musicologist Kristen Turner has written Theodore Drury (1867–ca. 1943) back into history by tracing the Theodore Drury Grand Opera Company, the first long-running black opera troupe in the United States (1900–1907). Turner's research not only puts this company on the map, but it also contextualizes his work as an impresario and singer through the racial-political thinkers and movements of his time.[13] U.S. historian James Cook has written about opera in American nineteenth-century culture through the presence of Jenny Lind, who sang under the sponsorship of P. T. Barnum. Cook's work encompasses a wide range of African American artists (musicians, dancers, and writers) and activists in the United States, Europe, and beyond. Notable for this discussion is his reconstruction of Elizabeth Taylor Greenfield's career with her fourteen-month concert tour of Great Britain (including her singing for Queen Victoria at Buckingham Palace) and her lesser-known abolitionist and benefit activities back in the States during and after the Civil War.[14]

American and German historian Kira Thurman focuses on black classical musicians in Central Europe and has written about early tours of the Fisk

Jubilee Singers in Germany and their reception as black American singers. In addition to writing these events back into history, she asks probing
questions about how hearing music associated with whiteness, particularly
the German Lied as a symbol of German nationalism, coming out of black
bodies challenges assumptions about who sings; referring to reviews of black
performers, she notes that "being black while singing German lieder was an
odd contradiction for many critics."[15] Another important study that opens
up opera in the diaspora includes David M. Powers's remarkable study that
details a narrative for opera during the second half of the eighteenth century
in the French slave colonies of the Antilles with a focus on Guadeloupe,
Martinique, and Saint-Domingue (present-day Haiti).[16] These scholars, along
with others, are leading the way in understanding past contributions to the
somewhat curious, and complicated, situation of black people in opera today.
This includes the welcomed, albeit limited, presence of black women in opera
and the nearly invisible—with infrequent notable exceptions—black male
opera singers. Offstage, a significant gap is the near absence of black opera
conductors, general managers, orchestral musicians, backstage professionals,
and members on boards of directors in domestic and international opera
companies today.

The touchstone moment for black opera history in the United Sates came
in 1939 when Marian Anderson rose to national attention as she sang on the
steps of the Lincoln Memorial in Washington, D.C., to a crowd of seventy-five
thousand people assembled there, many thousands more through the radio
airwaves. This outdoor concert happened after Anderson's manager Sol Hurok
and Howard University failed in their efforts to set up a performance for Anderson at Constitution Hall because the Daughters of the American Revolution
(DAR)—who owned the hall—decided that they could not sponsor a black
person to sing in their building. First Lady Eleanor Roosevelt heard about this
and wrote what would become a famous letter resigning her membership in the
DAR in protest of denying Marian Anderson the right to sing. Excerpted from
Roosevelt's letter is her unambiguous stance: "I am in complete disagreement
with the attitude taken in refusing Constitutional Hall to a great artist. You have
set an example which seems to me unfortunate. And I feel obliged to send in
to you my resignation. You had an opportunity to lead in an enlightened way
and it seems to me that your organization has failed."[17]

Eleanor Roosevelt and the Marian Anderson Committee (which formed in
the wake of the controversy) arranged for Anderson to give her concert on the
steps of the Lincoln Memorial with the National Mall as her auditorium on
Easter Sunday, April 9, 1939. Anderson had risen to prominence before this
event with her success in other parts of the United States and in Europe. She

made her European debut at the Paris Opera House in 1935 and sang for King Christian in Copenhagen and King Gustav in Stockholm; Finnish composer Jean Sibelius was so impressed with her voice that he wrote and dedicated his song "Solitude" to her. At her return to the United States, she made her Carnegie Hall debut later in 1935 and was one of the first African American singers to be invited to sing at the White House, by the Roosevelts, in 1939. In light of all of these accomplishments, perhaps the greatest for opera in the United States is that she was the first African American singer to sing at the Metropolitan Opera in a major role—that of Ulrica in Verdi's *Un Ballo in Maschera*—on January 7, 1955. Though there were a few other black singers performing at opera houses before, the magnitude of the Metropolitan Opera's reputation and the spotlight attending to Anderson after 1939, her entrance at the Met in 1955 opened up a symbolic door for other black singers at that opera house and the other opera houses of the world.

Since Marian Anderson's debut at the Metropolitan Opera, there has been a steady, albeit slow, stream of black singers in major opera houses. As her career showed, it is still not uncommon for African American opera singers to gain acclaim in Europe first before trying to make it in the United States. As a result, there are African American opera singers who have relocated to Europe, a situation not unlike that for jazz musicians. The pipeline for nurturing young black singers in the United States has not grown in proportion to the talent out there. Though there are black singers active in the United States, there are still great barriers, especially in the major opera houses—Metropolitan Opera, Chicago Lyric Opera, Houston Grand Opera, San Francisco Opera, Los Angeles Opera, and opera at the Kennedy Center in Washington, D.C.

There are many small opera companies and impresarios who helped sponsor opera productions of works by black composers or produced operas (in the standard repertory) with black singers in the first half of the twentieth century in the United States. Now complementing the newly rediscovered Theodore Drury Grand Opera Company in the first years of the twentieth century is the better-remembered case of Mary Cardwell Dawson, founder of the National Negro Opera Company, which ran for several years in the 1940s.[18] Recently, the archives of Henry Lawrence Freeman (1869–1954) were donated to Columbia University, and there are nearly twenty operas in this collection. Additionally, Freeman's opera activities in Denver, Colorado, are also coming to light. There are other people who contributed to opera activities by African Americans, but these stories are still mostly buried in archives.

The story of black people in opera is one that starts with the history of the singers and access to singing. For this narrative to continue, we need to recover and further nurture the work of black opera composers (the past and present), black directors, coaches, upper-level administrators in opera companies who are hiring black singers, agents, dedicated teachers (some of whom are opera singers themselves), and opera institutions dedicated to producing works by black composers and hiring black singers in all of their productions. Moreover, this story needs to be expanded through the work of an interdisciplinary team of scholars, librarians, and archivists who are helping the preservation and documentation of the black presence in opera from the past into the present and future.

Opera in South Africa

The story behind the current opera scene in South Africa since 1994 is one that has developed alongside the presence of colonialism and apartheid. In a unique situation compared to other countries on the African continent, South Africa has had a continuous (or nearly continuous) opera culture since the late nineteenth century.[19] Up until the final years of the twentieth century, the South African official opera environment was all white in terms of its primary patrons, audiences, and participants. The members of this opera society were descendants of British and Dutch colonials, Italian exiles from World War II (including former Italian prisoners of war), and a range of expatriates from Europe and the United States.[20] Opera theaters were open to whites only and they were the ones who were a part of the pipeline that funneled singers into the apprenticeships and programs abroad to leading international opera houses and sustainable careers. Yet behind this privileged side of the South African opera world, there was also a unique version of a shadow culture of black opera that had limited access and training, yet with rich connections to the music. Black singers, composers, and audiences were exposed to Western classical and operatic music through choral societies, missionary churches, and educational institutions. Through this contact a strong black connection to singing and opera emerged.

The presence of the Eoan Group, a cultural and community welfare or-ganization for the "coloured" (now more commonly referred to as "mixed race")[21] people in the District Six area of Cape Town opened in 1933 and provides an exception to the all-white South African opera world. The Eoan Group focused on ballet and drama in its first years and then became an important South African opera center from 1943 to 1977, when Joseph Manca brought in a deeper emphasis on the genre.[22] With its target on mixed-race people and elements of a civilizing mission, the Eoan Group was situated in a complicated position regarding whom it excluded and the government funding that supported it during apartheid. In terms of extending the arts (and for a time, a big focus on opera) to some—but not all—nonwhite South Africans, it can be seen as relating to a South African shadow tradition at the end of colonialism and through apartheid. The history of the Eoan Group had been nearly buried until recently, as Hilde Roos had fortuitously come into contact with the group's archival records and has been reconstructing this history back into a larger narrative.[23]

Similar to the realities for black performers in the United States in the nineteenth century, black South African singers were active in choral singing, through schools and especially through the influence of Christian missionaries who believed that singing was part of the colonial civilizing mission. Traveling Jubilee choirs brought the tradition of African American spirituals to South Africa (through white American and black American singers, alike).[24] In addition to choral singing, which was widely practiced in both the United States and South Africa, an unlikely shared musical practice is the American minstrelsy tradition that was brought over to South Africa in the nineteenth century. As early as 1848 there are records of Joe Brown's Band of Brothers in the Cape Colony; the Harvey Christy Minstrels performed in 1862.[25] In 1865 the Christy Minstrels performed for nearly a month in Durban.[26] In 1880 there is reference to "the Kafir Christy Minstrels," a minstrel troupe of black South Africans operating in Durban. Such entertainment continued through the end of the nineteenth century with the well-known Orpheus M. McAdoo and his traveling (alternatively called Minstrel and Jubilee) groups. Orpheus M. McAdoo and the Virginia Jubilee Singers, a group of African American musicians, spent almost five years in South Africa between July 1890 and June 1898.[27] When black singers in the United States performed theatrically, the content of the show was not always easy to determine; such was the case when they performed in South Africa as well. Gwen Ansell writes of the traveling African American groups at the end of the century:

> But with emancipation after the U.S. Civil War, American minstrelsy had evolved into an African-American performance form that was to impress South Africans of colour far more strongly. This new minstrel show retained some of the old stereotypes in its comic segments, but it also revived authentic elements of African-American culture that had survived in slave communities and combined all of this with acting, singing, and playing of a highly polished, concert hall standard, including arias from Verdi operas. For South Africa, it was Hampton graduate Orpheus McAdoo and his American (later Virginia) Jubilee Singers, who first visited Cape Town in 1887 and toured as far as Kimberley and Johannesburg four times during the 1890s, that made the biggest and most long-lasting impact.[28]

I cite this excerpt at length to illustrate not only the similar overlap in South African minstrel shows where the repertoire included "a highly polished, concert hall standard, including arias from Verdi operas," but also to introduce the dynamics of how American minstrelsy influenced white and black South Africans alike. While the history of black participation in the United States needs to deal with the specter of minstrelsy, I argue that minstrelsy also provides an important part of opera history for black and white South Africans.

The transatlantic slave trade has brought much attention to the elements that were passed between African cultures (practices, beliefs, traditions) and the development of African American cultures from the seventeenth century through the nineteenth century in what became the United States. Debates stemming from the theories of E. Franklin Frazier and Melville Herskovits have explored the extent to which elements from Africa were retained, reinterpreted, or reinvented during the devastation of slavery.[29] What has not received as much attention is how components from the artistic cultures of African Americans recirculated to the African continent. This emerging history of how minstrelsy was in the background of American and South African musical and theatrical traditions deserves deeper exploration that this study only begins to address. On both sides of the Atlantic, the practice of minstrelsy presents a haunting feature to the operatic traditions that are now so salient in articulating black artistic expression and possible aesthetics.

During my first visit to the South African College of Music at the University of Cape Town, when I was giving a guest lecture on early Verdi operas in an Italian opera class, I mentioned the chorus that was so popular in the nineteenth century, "Va pensiero" from *Nabucco*, that was an early hit for Verdi and became an anthem for the Italian unification efforts during the *Risorgimento*. Immediately, a few of my students from the townships in the class started humming the tune. I was shocked—most opera fans in the West do not know this opera at all, let alone be able to hum one of its tunes. The students told me they had sung this tune (and, it turns out, many other opera tunes) in their township choirs. I came to realize that though these students might not have attended an opera, they had been singing choruses and adapted numbers from operas in their choirs for generations. This is only one example of the immediacy some of the opera repertory already has with South African black culture and reveals a more than likely connection between these nineteenth-century traveling minstrel and Jubilee groups and the varied repertory they brought with them. While the early histories of South African opera in both white and black cultures are only recently being written, these histories begin to bring into dialogue how blackness in opera has, and continues to be, expressed in diverse settings across the Atlantic.

Two important recent discussions of opera's history in South Africa can be found in recent narratives by Angelo Gobbato and Neo Muyanga. Both are less formal histories than would be in a textbook; nonetheless, they are personal reflections that represent two helpful vantage points for fleshing out the richness of this story.[30] I had the pleasure of meeting Angelo Gobbato, one of the central figures in developing the opera program at the South African College of Music at the University of Cape Town and in supporting opera more generally in South Africa, as he was nearing retirement. I was delighted to sit in on some of the rehearsals for his production of Mozart's *Le Nozze di Figaro* with the current opera program director Kamal Kahn. They were setting the opera in a Stellenbosch vineyard, where the racial-class lines provided by their setting and cast(s) added a thoughtful commentary to the servant-aristocracy themes embedded in the opera.[31] I write "cast(s)" because the opera program (integrated by race, but with a majority of black singers) was so large that they triple cast the roles to accommodate the talent available.

I found Angelo Gobbato's essay featured on the Cape Town Opera House website. The essay opens:

> When I emigrated to South Africa with my family from Milano in 1950, I was seven years old and already determined to pursue a career as an opera singer. The following account of operatic developments in my adopted country over the past fifty years is thus based on personal experience and recollections and should not be read as either an academic document or as exhaustive historical research.[32]

Despite such disclaimers, this unofficial history is a thoughtful and important telling of opera in Cape Town going back to the late nineteenth century, with the most detail on 1950 through 2012. Such statements are important, especially in these early years and stages of understanding opera in South Africa before a more "official" history has been written. From firsthand experience, Gobbato outlines the struggles and triumphs of training singers and presenting operas with black and white singers, when possible. About the 1950s, he writes:

> Although the National Party had already become the ruling party in South Africa and had begun its strict enforcement of Verwoerd's Apartheid Policy, the University of Cape Town had firmly and publically expressed its opposition to this system and, although individual permits had to be obtained with great difficulty, singers of all races were being trained at its Opera School.[33]

A few sentences later Gobbato discusses the other operatic activities, complementing those of University of Cape Town opera program, at that time in Cape Town, including foreign companies that toured as well as further South African opera ventures:

> Under the name of The Eoan Group, these indefatigable workers mounted several seasons of opera in the Cape Town City Hall—a venue which was not only more economical to rent but which was also practically the only theatrical venue in C[ape] T[own] for which permits could be obtained allowing mixed races both on stage and in the auditorium.[34]

Gobbato outlines the greater difficulty in the 1960s and 1970s for finding spaces that allowed for integrated performers and audiences. One example he mentions is the controversy that surrounded the Nico Malan (now known as the Artscape Theatre Centre) performing arts complex when it first opened in 1971 as a "whites only" space. There were boycotts and protests until the government finally changed this policy. However, the oppressive administration was strong; this happened in the period of apartheid crackdowns, such as District Six being declared "whites only" under the Group Areas Act (in the late 1960s), and the beginning of those enforced removals/relocations of people who had formerly lived in its historically multiracial area. The arts reflected this wave of regime change as protest theater flourished and international artistic blacklisting grew. To illustrate how opera became a central symbol of the apartheid control of the arts, Gobbato states about this time in the early 1970s:

> Opera, already considered by many as an elitistic and unnecessarily expensive artistic waste of time, had become synonymous with the Apartheid Government's attempt to establish international credibility for itself and it was predicted that the advent of a new democratic regime would see the well deserved end of all operatic endeavor in the country.[35]

And yet, as Gobbato writes in his history, opera did not die at the end of apartheid. In fact, just the opposite is true: opera has become a hallmark of the artistic scene in South Africa since 1994, yet in a newly born way with an interracial participation of white, mixed-race, and now mainly black singers.

Angelo Gobbato's experiences, participation, and resistance in the evolving artistic landscape under apartheid can be juxtaposed to the experiences of Neo Muyanga, a South African composer born in Soweto during apartheid.[36] Through various opportunities, and as a way to stay safe during the violence of the 1980s, Muyanga was able to study abroad in Italy and later work in the United Kingdom. While in Italy, he received a strong education that included a focus on Western art music, and he was part of a traveling choir that sang madrigals and other classical music. He graduated in 1993 and moved to the United Kingdom to write music for Footprints Theatre company in Nottingham and work in radio for the BBC. During this time, he was also a founding member of the pop band Blk Sonshine, a group that "was about playing acoustic guitars doing a kind of roots, African meets pan-Africanist project" and toured in the United States.[37] En route back to South Africa in 2000, he spent time visiting the Yared College of Music in Ethiopia, which fueled his interest in musics from all over the world. In Ethiopia he became especially interested in Ethiopian liturgical music and their jazz scene.

Coming of age during apartheid and being in exile opened up the possibilities of experiences and influences Muyanga encountered. When he returned to South Africa in 2000, the post-apartheid era and his celebrity for being in Blk Sonshine allowed him to have more mobility and options. He moved to Cape Town, where he did not know a lot of people. Of this time, he said:

> And I'm living inside my own head, reading lots of books about choral music, from outside, reading about American choral music, the Negro Spiritual. I'm hearing Jessye Norman sing, I'm hearing Paul Robeson sing and it occurs to me that there's a conversation among the black intelligentsia in the US that speaks about classical music and speaks about blackness at the same time. . . . So it becomes a very important time for me to try and synthesize some kind of understanding about what the political project is that links South African jazz, American protest song with the church, Martin Luther King, songs like "We Shall Overcome," "N'kosi Sikelele iAfrika" and how that relates to how this community can articulate itself in a slightly different way to the way we had done up until that point.[38]

These are the types of connections that inform Muyanga's compositional voice. He also cites musical influences from the countries where he has traveled, recognizing a strong bond with African American artists. In addition to Jessye Norman and Paul Robeson, he includes Bobby McFerrin, Harry Belafonte; Italians Lucio Dalla and Luciano Pavarotti; and Blk Sonshine and Wu Tang. His interest in international connections are brought in conversation with musical influences from home as he also includes people from South Africa and talks about Sibongile Khumalo: "It's in this investigation of the archive that I'm finding a connection to missionary schooling people like Tiyo Songa and how he becomes this metaphor for the hybridized African."[39]

The bringing together of musical voices from across the Atlantic was bred into Muyanga's formative experience and characterizes an important feature of his music. About Tiyo Songa, he uses the phrase "hybridized African," and this syncretic combination of disparate elements is something he is mindful of. His experiences provide one illustration of the situation wherein South African black composers lived outside of South Africa at points during the struggle and came of age in areas where they had access to better educational experiences around music.[40] The operatic voices such experiences give rise to imply a great deal about powerful directions emerging in opera today for Muyanga, Ndodana-Breen, Khumalo, and others. Though these composers have training in Western classical music, there is also another set of experiences—Western music brought to South Africa during colonization and apartheid, as well as the very diverse South African traditional musics that have been an important part of their culture. The quick rise in the post-apartheid South African vibrant opera scene reveals what I have discussed as the "shadow culture" of opera in South Africa as well as their deeply rooted connection to choral singing and song as a way to interact with oppression (as resistance). Muyanga brings these things together:

> I started engaging with people who were from the choral movement and started working with them on a number of pieces I was writing that I thought could really benefit from a choral treatment. And then it occurred to me that all the conversations I was hearing, and in all the competitions or rehearsals that I was attending, they were singing these arias, these arias from western opera. And they were singing them right before or right after they sang a so-called traditional piece, and there was this great facility with moving from the one paradigm to the other, there was no, it seemed to me, dichotomy with them.[41]

Such a facility to move between different musical styles so smoothly reveals a different thinking about the role and way opera, singing, and Western classical music fits into South African culture in these first decades after apartheid. As the country finds its new voice and articulates a new identity, what it means to be a black South African is evolving. As someone who has worked in many different musical genres and styles, including opera, Muyanga sits on several arts councils and performance boards. He is serious about his roles both as a composer and as someone who helps keep the arts alive in performance.

> I think what my job should be in that space is to help us think through what opera and classical music means for our country today, because it's not the kind of thing that government can get away with saying "oh no this is a western imposition and it's kicked out". . . . [M]y politicking around black opera, and my positioning around black opera is about that. It's a project that seeks to articulate the history of opera in the black communities. And to argue that it's indigenized. It's no longer a western imposition, it's indigenized, it's internalised by many, many people in our communities.[42]

Though it seems to be a radical formation that opera is now an indigenized South African musical form, it is clear to see how Muyanga has brought his experiences together. All of us living in the twenty-first century are removed from the original contexts of opera's flourishing in the eighteenth and nine-teenth centuries, and the likelihood of South Africa's becoming an important opera center might not be obvious to everyone. However, it begins to make sense when tracing the roles that music, storytelling, and singing have had in South African society in the past, over the past several decades, and up through today.

It is useful at this point to focus on a few interconnected themes—singers, places, and spaces. First are the singers. While I am not offering a compre-hensive list, I have chosen a small, representative group of female singers whose careers span the period (1990s to 2016), looking at how their careers got started, where they have come from (where they were born and trained), and where they have been (a trajectory of their career thus far). Next is place, broadly conceived—spaces where opera has been happening: the physical locations of opera houses, schools, and training programs as well as how some directors/producers have factored specific geographies of South Africa *into* their opera productions (for example, the film *U-Carmen eKhayelitsha* sets Bizet's *Carmen* in the township of Khayelitsha). The path of one opera company (the Isango Ensemble) is of particular interest; having emerged on the scene in the first years after apartheid, the group has forged international connections with Western opera houses (primarily in London and the United States) while maintaining an investment in local township communities and South African settings for their productions.

The First Generations of Black South African Opera: Singers

One of the features of the post-apartheid opera scene in South Africa is that there continues to be a steady flow of white singers who are active and entering opera training programs. This history has been noted since the late nineteenth century and has fueled South African opera through the twen-tieth century and the end of apartheid in the 1990s. My focus here is on the entrance of the many black and mixed-race singers who are newly entering opera training programs and auditioning for productions. As we will see, most of these nonwhite singers gain entry into this style of singing through the vast choral networks, primarily through township choral societies that are supplemented by choirs in schools, churches, and community organizations. The black and mixed-race singers include women and men alike, spanning the range of all male and female voice types. This inquiry centers on a few female singers, primarily because such focus provides a strong entry into the discussion of the first wave of these early, newly composed operas with female title characters, which also happen to include the first two full-length operas by black South African composers, *Princess Magogo ka Dinuzulu* (Mzilikazi Khumalo [2002]) and *Winnie: The Opera* (Bongani Ndodana-Breen [2011]). Furthermore, there are a few more women than men who are making faster progress in the upper echelons of the international opera scene (singing in major opera companies and landing recording contracts).

The first singer I highlight has become a beacon for leading classical and jazz vocalists of the generation just ending apartheid and up through the present. Initially nurtured by her father, Khabi Mngoma, a noted music educator himself, Sibongile Khumalo (born in Soweto in Johannesburg, 1957) has enjoyed a career of remarkable breadth and accomplishment.[43] Rightly heralded as "South Africa's first lady of song," Sibongile Khumalo has degrees from the University of Zululand, the University of the Witwatersrand, and an honorary doctorate in music from the University of Rhodes.[44] Her father "was a pioneer of both the reclamation of indigenous music and the creation of new sounds. . . . For men like Mngoma, choral music remained a way of providing authentic forms of expression and development to African students. He saw no contradiction between conducting Handel's *Messiah*, working on original, nationally conscious modern music, and explaining Zulu lyric forms to fellow enthusiast Hugh Tracey."[45] Given this history, it is not surprising that his daughter's musical education is unusually broad and spans classical music with opera and oratorio, indigenous African traditions, and the variety of American and African jazz styles. Given her musical pedigree, it makes sense that Sibongile Khumalo was the creator of the first South African heroine in a full-length opera based on a real-life person who was also a singer, *ughubu* bow player, and composer, as well as important political figure: Zulu princess Constance Magogo Sibilile Mantithi Ngangezinye ka Dinuzulu (1900–1984). In 2002 Sibongile Khumalo sang the title role in the world premiere of Mzilikazi Khumalo's *Princess Magogo ka Dinuzulu* at Opera Africa, based in Durban at the time.[46]

Tsakane Valentine Maswanganyi (born 1979) is part of the subsequent generation of leading South African opera singers; she created the title heroine in the second major South African opera (and the first one fully composed and orchestrated) by a black South African composer. Bongani Ndodana-Breen's *Winnie: The Opera* premiered at the State Theatre in Pretoria in 2011. Like Sibongile Khumalo, Maswanganyi was born in the Township of Soweto in Johannesburg. Maswanganyi's background, unlike the broad musical education of Khumalo's upbringing, is closer to that of the subsequent black opera singers in this early generation working today. When Maswanganyi entered the University of Pretoria, she wanted to study music, but she did not read notation.[47] After a bridge course, she was able to focus on music, and by the time she was in her senior year, she sang in the opera chorus at the State Theatre in Pretoria. She continued her musical training at the Pretoria Technikon and moved on to the Roodepoort City Opera.[48]

In perhaps a more fortuitous than deliberate plan, Maswanganyi became a founding member of Amici Forever, a self-described "opera band" that has produced two albums (*The Opera Band* [2004] and *Defined* [2005]). These albums have topped crossover charts, and the group has toured throughout Australia, New Zealand, and the United Kingdom. Amici Forever has been described as comprising "photogenic, classically trained opera singers who blend contemporary pop with traditional opera" who came together when they were "rehearsing and performing at opera venues around the world."[49] The four members of the group listed on their Wikipedia page come from three countries: two from England, one (Maswanganyi) from South Africa, and another from Brazil. Their repertoire consists of an assortment of classical works, contemporary easy listening music, and popular songs. Most of the arrangements on the two albums have connections to classical, and frequently operatic, works. The first album has tracks based directly on opera excerpts: the famous tenor-baritone duet "Au fond du temple Saint" from Bizet's *Pearl Fishers*, Mozart's act 1 trio from *Così fan Tutte* ("Soave sia il vento"), Rusulka's best-known aria ("Song to the Moon"), and Calaf's aria in *Turandot* ("Nessun Dorma"). Additionally, there are classical works that have been adapted for opera singers, such as "Land and Freedom ("Terra e Liberta")—based on the second movement from Beethoven's Symphony No. 7 on *Defined* and the vocal version of Elgar's "Nimrod" variation from the *Enigma Variations* with the "Lux Aeterna" text added (on *Opera Band*) and the vocal version of Barber's "Adagio for Strings" (on *Defined*).[50] For several tracks there are YouTube videos that include choreographed staged videos (for example, "Prayer in the Night," *Opera Band*) that allow the viewer to feel more connected to the young beautiful singers.

While it might seem easy to think of an "opera band" as catering to a less sophisticated audience or diluting the classics for mass public consumption, such dismissal feels particularly unmerited when taking a broader view of Maswanganyi's path in opera. The tracks on both albums take sumptuously gorgeous moments in music and rearrange them for a small ensemble (four or five voices) with lush (not the original) orchestrations. The voices are classically trained and do not fudge the notes with pop-like slides or sounds of vocal strain. Those accustomed to listening to opera and classical music can be happily surprised with the sonic quality of the music. Given the popularity of their live concerts, the billboard ratings of their albums, and the plethora of superlative YouTube comments, they have a strong appeal to a wide audience—some of whom, presumably, are not familiar with classical music. Maswanganyi's time in Amici Forever seems to have been a larger focus in the earlier part of her career. When I saw her premiere the title role in *Winnie: The Opera* in 2011, her voice was elegant, in strong shape, and there was nothing in her demeanor or sound that seemed at all uncomfortable on the opera stage. Her biography in the opera program mentioned her work in Amici and also listed her many operatic appearances and roles.

I propose that Maswanganyi's time in Amici was not just an opportunity to use her good looks and beautiful voice to earn a little money, though early in any singer's career such gigs are welcomed. Her career exposes the reality of opera in the changing world she was part of. The South African opera culture in the early years after apartheid was readjusting from an all-white environment to something else: one that could include black, mixed-race, and Indian singers. Opera in South Africa was developing a new identity. Maswanganyi belonged to an elite, newly forming group; she was an opera singer in a new world where black South African opera singers were only just beginning to be allowed to exist. The post-apartheid law of the land required state-sponsored organizations to be racially inclusive. Yet in that first generation, opera companies were just beginning to move toward integration. Additionally, audiences were still being (and continue to be) developed and nurtured for bringing opera to a wider swath of people, particularly to include black audiences, who had been banned from opera houses during apartheid. The early part of Maswanganyi's career illustrates the uniquely challenging landscape these first generations of black South African singers encountered. This was not the expected bumpy terrain most Western musicians and artists anticipate when starting a career within the context of grueling competition, inadequate government support, and very few slots allotted to those lucky enough to be successful. While black South African singers had had success in popular music and jazz during colonialism and apartheid, opera was creating a new narrative in the post-apartheid era. This was a case of writing oneself into history.

The careers of Pumeza Matshikiza and Pretty Yende represent another path this first generation of black South African opera singers have been forging, one that appears comparable to the path many black singers in the United States from the past and even into the present have been making. The similarities shared are when someone's talent is discovered, but there are great hurdles to overcome regarding the resources needed to pursue a musical career. These artists confronted many obstacles from multiple sources. Funding and support are needed at an early stage when success is not at all guaranteed. Frequently the rudimentary training that starts ideally at very young ages is something that has been missing, so there needs to be remedial work in the fundamentals. Talent is something that only goes so far; at the highest levels of the opera world, training in languages, acting, and memorization also need to be cultivated. Finally, an important, yet frequently hidden element in career building is the support and connection one has to a nurturing community. While one's family might provide a loving environment, the foreignness of opera and the requisite lifestyle during the training and success of a career might prove to be too great a price. One is hard pressed to "settle down" and form a typical family that involves childrearing with stable and present parenting. For this reason, opera singers (and other top-level performing artists) from all over the world create more individualized plans for achieving professional success and personal happiness. These are not just issues for Matshikiza and Yende; they are things that Khumalo and Maswanganyi have encountered. Yet the difference is that in the first wave of this early opera generation, Khumalo and Maswanganyi were starting careers before the new post-apartheid routes began to emerge. Both of these singers started their major career in innovative ways (notably, singing in multiple repertories and more popular styles) that brought them abroad to international opera houses and back to South Africa.

Matshikiza and Yende both have degrees from the South African College of Music (University of Cape Town), where they worked with Virginia Davids and Angelo Gobbato.[51] Both went on to study in Europe and have found apprentice-like programs that have nurtured their voices and given them time to learn repertoire and the basics of the opera world. Matshikiza studied at the Royal College of Music in London in 2004 and then spent a few years in the Young Artist Programme at the Royal Opera House, where she was mentored by Dame Kiri Te Kanawa. She joined the Stuttgart Opera and has been on their roster since 2011. Her roles include Mozart's Pamina (*Magic Flute*) and Susanna (*Marriage of Figaro*), Puccini's Mimì (*Bohème*), and Bizet's Micaela (*Carmen*). Her first album, *Voice of Hope*, came out in 2014 (Decca Records) and includes opera arias as well as traditional Xhosa songs. Her second album, *Pumeza Matshikiza Arias*, also Decca, came out in 2016 and focuses fully on Western art music with operatic arias and art songs.[52] Yende's path has been similar. After the University of Cape Town, she studied in the apprentice program at La Scala and was mentored by Mirella Freni. In January 2013 she made the news by filling in at the Metropolitan

Opera for the role of Adele in Rossini's *Le Comte Ory*, where her debut made headlines as she stumbled on the scenery during her entrance and fell, but recovered, sang beautifully, and received a strong ovation. By the end of the 2017–18 season, she will have added several other roles to her Met repertory (Pamina, *Magic Flute*; Rosina, *Barber of Seville*; Juliette, Gounod's *Roméo et Juliette*; Elvira, *Puritani*; and the title role in *Lucia di Lammermoor*. Her first album, *A Journey* (released by Sony in September 2016), has famous show-stopping numbers by Rossini ("Una voce poco fa," *Barber of Seville*), Donizetti (Lucia's act 1 aria "Regnava nel silencio," *Lucia di Lammermoor*), Bellini (act 2, "O rendeteme la speme," *I Puritani*), along with other opera arias.[53] Both singers are beautiful, have incredible talent, and are working their way up through European and international opera houses.

The last group of singers I will cover represent another wave of singing talent. They are a few years younger than Matshikiza and Yende and, as I write now, are still in the early stages of their careers. Like Matshikiza and Yende, three of these singers (a woman, Linda Nteleza, and two men, Thesele Kemane and Makudupanyane Senaoana) were students in the South African College of Music (University of Cape Town) and were featured in the recent documentary *Ndiphilela Ukucula: I Live to Sing*, directed by Julie Cohen in 2013.[54] At the time of the documentary, all three were between the ages of twenty and twenty-six, which means that they were on the edges of the "born free" generation of those who grew up after the end of apartheid and are coming of age in a time that bears the legacy of apartheid but is also open to many new opportunities. The film focuses on the lives of the three singers and their preparations for a performance of Offenbach's *Les Contes Hoffmann* at the Artscape Theatre in Cape Town and follows them to the United States, where they were chosen to intern and sing in a production of Kurt Weill's *Lost in the Stars* at New York's Glimmerglass Festival in August 2012. The production of *Lost in the Stars* featured renowned African American bass-baritone Eric Owens along with several other black singers who came together in this work based on Alan Paton's *Cry the Beloved Country*. This South African novel (1948) was written about the situation in South Africa right before the apartheid system was officially put in place, and this production of the opera provided a unique opportunity for black singers from the United States and South Africa to work together on a timely subject about black-white conflict and misunderstanding, still relevant today. Documentary film director Julie Cohen brings a thoughtful and caring approach to this film. Kamal Kahn, the director of the opera program at the South African College of Music since 2009, and Julie Cohen knew each other when they were children growing up, and this connection aids Cohen in her filmmaking; she is able to garner open and warm interviews from not only the three featured singers and their families but also from Kamal Kahn, Angelo Gobbato, Virginia Davids, and several others who are central in shaping the post-apartheid opera culture in South Africa.

All the singers I have discussed represent a path of South African opera that starts with singers (mainly born in townships) who have had little access to formal musical training yet come through the choral society network and then find their way to the South African College of Music at the University of Cape Town or some other university music program for postgraduate work (Khumalo at the University of Zululand and Wits; Maswanganyi at Pretoria Technikon). Sibongile Khumalo is a bit of an outlier, since her father's exceptional musical background helped shape her musical training. Nearly all of these singers then go abroad to help establish themselves, which also acts a bridge to a career in opera through experience, official affiliations with a Western opera house and, they hope, a recording contract with a major label. Though these singers might have early experience singing in South African opera houses (such as the Baxter Theatre and Artscape Theatres in Cape Town, Opera Africa in Durban, and Roodepoort City Opera), they seem to focus their careers abroad. As the newer generations of singers who take advantage of post-apartheid opportunities, it remains to be seen how many singers stay abroad in Europe and the United States and how many return and are able to sustain a top-level career in South Africa.

South African Places and Spaces

There is another model of opera training, singing, and performing that is also based in Cape Town but provides a different, parallel route to the models described above. Before, during, or after a singer has experience with a formal music school program, there is an opera company that nurtures young talent in the townships. On its website, the Isango Ensemble describes itself as "a South African theatre company that draws its artists mainly from the townships surrounding Cape Town. . . . Our company's structure embraces artists at all stages of their creative development allowing senior artists to lead and contribute towards the growth of rising talents." After outlining their international awards and travel, they describe their productions that "re-imagine classics from the Western theatre canon, finding a new context for the stories within a South African or township setting thereby creating inventive work relevant to the heritage of the nation."[55]

The Isango Ensemble started out as Dimpho di Kopane (Sotho for "combined talents") and was founded in 2000 by Mark Dornford-May and Charles

Hazlewood, two artistic directors at London's Broomhill Opera. The early history of this opera company is featured in the documentary *Township Opera*, which outlines their auditioning process and showcases two of their productions (*Yiimimangaliso: The Mysteries* and *U-Carmen*) that were performed at Stellenbosch (as part of Spier festival) and then taken on a very successful tour in London (initially five weeks, extended to nine).[56] In this documentary we learn that Pauline Malefane started out in the chorus but was soon offered the title role in *U-Carmen* when the original leading singer backed out. Malefane was a huge success in the production; moreover, she eventually married Dornford-May and became one of the leading singers in the company as well as part of the company's administrative team.

Dimpho di Kopane went on to make their New York debut October 27– November 28, 2004, with a series of four works in twenty-five performances over a five-week period at Synod Hall in the Cathedral of St. John the Divine in New York City. Rounding out the program of the *Yiimimangaliso: The Mysteries* (based on twelfth-century liturgical dramas translated in Xhosa) and the Xhosa setting of Bizet's *Carmen*, there was *Ibali Ioo Tsoti: The Beggar's Opera* (an adaptation of the 1728 John Gay satirical operetta) and *IKumkani-kazi yeKhephu: The Snow Queen* (a reinterpreted version of Hans Christian Andersen's story set in South Africa and featuring traditional Xhosa music and ceremonies).[57]

Dimpho di Kopane changed names around 2006, when it became the Isango/Portobello opera company, under the management of Mark Dornford-May and Pauline Malefane. Isango has the meaning in Xhosa and Zulu as "gateway" or "port." The company came into an arrangement with the District Six Museum Homecoming Centre and developed a theater in the former old Sacks Futeran building, called The Fugard Theatre, in 2010.[58] Unfortunately, the company had to leave The Fugard due to financial difficulties. Since 2011 the opera company has been known as the Isango Ensemble. On the homepage of their website they trace their history back to 2000 and outline the guiding vision for the productions:

> From the beginning the company has drawn its performers from the previously disadvantaged townships surrounding the city. Isango creates performances with a strong South African flavor by re-imagining Western theatre classics within a South African or township setting and by creating new work reflecting South African heritage.[59]

In the early days of Dimpho di Kopane, the *U-Carmen* live stage production started out in French (the original language of Bizet's opera *Carmen*) and was then translated into Xhosa. The cast at that point had both black and white singers, and the setting of the production had not yet been moved to Khayelitsha. With the great popularity of Bizet's *Carmen* in Xhosa, as well as the Xhosa setting for the medieval Mystery plays (*Yiimimangaliso: The Mysteries*), the evolution of shows that were adapted to the townships clearly illustrates the company's stated mission on their website of "re-imagining Western theatre classics" and "creating new works reflecting South African heritage." *U-Carmen* became the filmed version *U-Carmen eKhayelitsha* in 2005 and was not only incredibly popular in Khayelitsha but also went on to do well at film festivals, winning the Golden Bear for "Best Film" in the Berlin Film Festival and two Golden Thumb awards for direction (Mark Dornford-May) and performance (Pauline Malefane) from Roger Ebert's Film Festival.

One of their most popular productions is a Xhosa version of Mozart's *Magic Flute: Impempe Yomlingo* that scores the Western opera orchestra for marimba, drums, and township percussion, premiering in 2007 at the Baxter Theatre in Cape Town. It then went on to London and Dublin, returned to South Africa in Johannesburg (at the Market Theatre), and then later had a tour to Tokyo that ended in Singapore in 2009. Other Isango Ensemble productions include repertory operas that are given new settings, *La Bohème: Abanxaxhi* (in a live stage version [2012]), which has been made into a filmed version, *Breathe Umphefumlo* (directed by Mark Dornford-May [2015]) that updates the action to the present time with the characters in Khayelitsha ironically fighting tuberculosis (ironically, since TB, "consumption," was the disease for Puccini's Mimì in 1896 and is—sadly—still an issue in parts of the world, including Khayelitsha). Other shows listed in the Isango Ensemble repertoire include musical settings of *Aesop's Fables* (with music, singing, and dance), an adaptation of Charles Dickens's *A Christmas Carol, Ikrismas Kherol*, where Scrooge is a stingy business woman who is visited by three Ancestral Spirits, and a new setting of Robert Tressell's socialist novel that was influenced by his time in South Africa (Cape Town and Johannesburg) during the 1890s, *The Ragged Trousered Philanthropists: Izigwili Ezidlakazelayo*. In 2012 they partnered with the Globe Theatre in London and co-produced a musical version of Shakespeare's epic poem, *Venus and Adonis*; the work opened the Globe to Globe Festival that April. The 2016–17 schedule included a joint production between the Isango Ensemble, the Young Vic in London, and the Royal Opera House at Covent Garden with an opera based on South African author (and Oxford professor) Jonny Steinberg's novel, *A Man of Good Hope* (2015). This show also appeared at the Brooklyn Academy of Music in February 2017.

The Isango Ensemble has been bold and thoughtful about promoting black South African singers in opera after apartheid. They present a new model of how to perform opera in a way that brings together the opulent Western art music legacy with new surroundings. They achieve that almost impossible combination of making something universal by bringing in the utterly specific. The Isango Ensemble is showing us how opera from the past—*Carmen, La Bohème, The Magic Flute*—can become newly relevant. Additionally, their new ventures with Steinberg's recent novel about a Somali refugee who has traveled down the eastern African coast to find a livelihood in South Africa show an engagement with stories that have roots in the present as well as the past. Through their work with the local people in the Cape Town area who love to sing and the connections to international tours and co-productions with Shakespeare's Globe Theatre, the Young Vic, and the Royal Opera House, the Isango Ensemble articulates a salient portion of the new opera scene in South Africa after apartheid.

In a 2010 article Mark Dornford-May wrote before the Isango Ensemble had to leave their space at The Fugard Theatre in the District 6 Museum Homecoming Centre, he outlined a thorny issue around building audiences in the new South Africa. He opened the article with a question:

> "How come the audience is so white?" is perhaps the most frequently asked question by visitors from abroad to our theatre. It is a complex and difficult one to answer and to be honest I know I blush with embarrassment at our continued failure. It is no comfort at all to me but it is not just at The Fugard that this "whiteness" is: I am afraid to say the same is true of every theatre in this city and nearly every restaurant and cinema.[60]

The integrating of audiences is something that the United States has also struggled with. While there are different issues for the nonwhite audiences in Cape Town and in most United States theatrical venues, there are also important similarities. Dornford-May talks about the difficulty of finding transportation that gets back to the townships after 10 P.M. and the short-term goals to get financial sponsorship for shuttles as well as the longer-term goal of "a proper bus/transport plan."[61] Though not an issue in every U.S. city, such logistical issues are still problematic when trying to recruit audiences who live far from theaters and are cut off from certain parts of town after hours due to the lack of public transportation. Another challenge Dornford-May alludes to is the energy needed to attract new audiences to events that have been considered off limits, whether "officially" through apartheid or Jim Crow laws or through internalized cultural biases that the arts (and especially the "elitist" art of opera) are not meant for, or welcoming to, nonwhite audiences. Even when there are black and other nonwhite singers in the show—such attitudes need to be actively overcome.

Through the use of language—translating European languages into Xhosa—in the opera and the placement of stories in South Africa's township settings, the Isango Ensemble is doing a lot to bridge the connection between black South African audiences and the productions. The other South African opera houses, such as the Artscape and Baxter Theatres in Cape Town or the Black Tie Ensemble and Gauteng Opera in Johannesburg, are also reaching out to nurture young singers through apprentice programs and to feature works that combine the standard Western European opera canon with newer works by indigenous composers.

The presence of black composers, singers, and interracial collaborations that feature subjects about black history in American opera is a narrative that has been primarily played out alongside the mainstream opera tradition, albeit frequently obscured in the margins. I have traced this story back to the nineteenth century, and scholars are beginning to find evidence of this tradition in archives, newspapers, opera house records, and recovered materials from private collections. A new chapter emerging in the United States has a connection to the adapted and newer productions seen in South Africa in a related musical-theater arena through the use of spoken word and hip hop.

The most dazzling example is in Lin-Manuel Miranda's *Hamilton* (2015), a story of the establishment of the United States wherein the founding fathers (George Washington, Thomas Jefferson, Alexander Hamilton, and others) are all portrayed by black and Latino performers. "In this telling, rap is the language of revolution; hip hop is the backbeat. In each brilliantly crafted song, we hear the debates that shaped our nation and we hear the debates that are still shaping our nation." These are the words President Barack Obama said to introduce a performance of *Hamilton*—the blockbuster musical that was then playing on Broadway—at the White House for Washington, D.C.– area high school students on March 16, 2016.[62] In these opening comments, the president linked this presentation of the story behind *Hamilton* with the reality of how this work has meaning today.

President Obama is among the many people who understood that the wild success of Lin-Manuel Miranda's *Hamilton* was due to its tapping into something other than being an evening of entertainment that provides a getaway from life's regular events. "The show reminds us that this nation was built by more than just a few great men; it is an inheritance that belongs to all of us, and that's why Michelle and I wanted to bring this performance to the White House. Because *Hamilton* is not just for people who can score a ticket to a pricey Broadway show, it is a story for all of us and about all of us."[63] Audiences have been drawn in because this work says something relevant and pressing about that present time: who matters, who gets to have a voice, and who can make a country great. *Hamilton* has brought us a history of the United States that goes back to the eighteenth century and that, now more than ever, has resonance.

As an area for future inquiry, the success of *Hamilton* seems to build on the currents happening on formal concert stages and opera houses. Both in opera in the United States and South Africa the relevant themes emerging engage how histories are told and who gets to tell them. These works demonstrate that there are audiences who are eager to see their nation, including wider representations of themselves.

3 Haunted Legacies

Interracial Secrets
From the Diary of Sally Hemings

The Sally Hemings and Thomas Jefferson relationship is an "American" story. Through the imperatives of slavery, their relationship was shaped by an alchemy of economic and societal pressures as Jefferson became one of the leaders of a new democracy that depended on capitalistic gain. Concurrently, he needed the financial structure of slavery to build his expansive estate of Monticello; Jefferson was a landowner who governed a large community of men, women, and children in bondage. In the public spotlight, he was the third president of the United States, a leading statesman for a country he helped create, and for which he became a devoted public servant. His private life was shrouded in shadows where his role as master encompassed his relationship with Sally Hemings, a woman he owned as property and the mother of most of his children. Written into the fabric of the early history of the United States is a particular double narrative about how power is unequally experienced according to gender and race.

The Americanness of this story is not just because it involves a "founding father" of the nation, but also because it contains intersecting themes that foreground gender in such a way that men's stories are preserved and told more frequently than women's histories. This is paired with the socioeconomic power Jefferson held over his slaves such that Hemings was bound to the terms he set and experienced the privileges he controlled. As with many stories wherein gender, race, and socioeconomic elements are combined, the dominant story that emerges reinforces the normative conventions around white patriarchal supremacy. It becomes so common that other possible narratives need to be woven together from existing fragments and creativity in order to become audible.

The central primary evidence for the Hemings-Jefferson relationship includes DNA testing from 1998 and the 1873 memoir of Madison Hemings, son of Sally Hemings and Thomas Jefferson.[1] With these materials, plus the larger context of Jefferson's other writings, the history we know of life at Monticello, and research about the lives of slaves and other African Americans, the story of Sally Hemings has been reanimated by the interracial collaborative team of composer William Bolcom and playwright/librettist Sandra Seaton. Through *From the Diary of Sally Hemings*, Hemings has been given a fresh humanity wherein we can hear her imagined voice and view a construction of her interior life. Of course, it is impossible to know what Sally Hemings said: we have no record of her words. Yet she has been envoiced through the text and music that present a new narrative about how her life could have had meaning in its own time—an alternative to the derogatory accounts already out there—and unquestionably creates a new meaning for us today.[2] Florence Quivar, noted African American opera singer, commissioned the project and sang several performances of the work. At the Coolidge Auditorium in the Library of Congress, Seaton recalls that forty-five Hemings descendants were in the audience.[3]

Across the Atlantic: Giving Voice to Sally (Sarah) Hemings and Saartijie (Sarah) Baartman

To put the two sides of the Atlantic in conversation with each other, I bring together two stories about late-eighteenth-century black women, one from South Africa and one from the United States. Both have become emblems for how race, gender, nation, sexuality, and societal position intersect and shape our narratives of the past. They were black women in societies that did not grant them full personhood or allow a space for their voices to be heard. As a result, their stories have been suppressed, revised, and rewritten, depending on who desires to place them in history. They have been resurrected in modern times as curiosities, spectacles, and aberrant deviations to the acceptable social order.

Across the Atlantic Ocean, between the Gamtoos Valley in the Eastern Cape of South Africa; Virginia in the United States; and Paris, France: I open this section in weaving a connective web across two hemispheres by briefly juxtaposing the histories of Sally (Sarah) Hemings with Saartijie (Sara) Baartman, two women with very different fates yet with overlapping stories of how gender (especially in terms of perceived femininity) and race can be articulated.[4] Born in the same era, these two women represent extremes of

how blackness in its varying physical presentations shaped their opportunities and exploitation. Saartijie (Sara) Baartman, a Khoi-San South African
woman, was born before 1790, possibly in the 1770s, the same decade as Sally
Hemings.[5] Baartman was taken to England in 1810 and then to Paris in 1814
to be exhibited and, ostensibly, to provide visual evidence of the inferiority
of darker races based on the physical characteristics of her anatomy. During
her European sojourn she was launched as the "Hottentot Venus" and sub-
jected to a manipulative marketing campaign that dodged abolitionist efforts
to stop the exhibitions and send her back to Africa. Though this consumed
only five years of her life, it was her last five years (she died on December 29,
1815, in Paris), and the created persona shaped by the public circulation of
racist imaginations vastly eclipsed the "real" woman, so much so that when
modern biographers have tried to recover the life of Baartman, the fragments
of history are overwhelmed with the fictive creation of the Hottentot Venus.[6]

Beyond her death, Baartman's body and what she had come to represent
haunted the nineteenth and twentieth centuries. Though there were other
bodies and bones of people from Africa (and other geographical locations)
that were put on display in exhibits, museums, and dioramas, the "Hottentot
Venus" became a cipher for racialized discourse. Several wax moulds and a
body cast were made of her anatomy. Additionally, "her decanted brain, stiff
skeleton and dissected genitalia" were preserved after her death.[7] Her skeleton
and other parts were on display in the Paris Muséum d'Histoire Naturelle
until they were moved to the Musée de l'Homme when it opened in 1937.
In 1976 Baartman's dismembered body was put into storage until parts were
brought out in 1994 to be exhibited at the Musée d'Orsay; within months,
that exhibit was contested and Baartman went back into storage.[8]

In the late 1990s, issues around how we think about both Sally Hemings's
and Saartijie Baartman's legacies resurfaced. In 1998 there was DNA testing
that provided scientific evidence to something that had been hotly debated
on both sides of the issue; the living descendants among the Hemings and
Jefferson families were genetically linked. The tests revealed that the Hemings
heirs were related to men in the Jefferson family. This finding left the possibility that in addition to Thomas, his younger brother Randolph could have
fathered some of Sally Hemings's children; however, that possibility has not
been substantiated, and the DNA testing leads many to acknowledge that
children were born to Sally Hemings and Thomas Jefferson. Although the
issue continues to generate debate at the time of this writing, the larger view
that receives the most adherence is that what had been suspected before 1998
is now generally accepted by many: Thomas Jefferson and Sally Hemings had

a long-term relationship that produced children whose descendants live into the present time.[9]

After the dismantling of apartheid, a campaign in South Africa to repatriate Baartman's remains began in 1995, leading to her eventual return and burial in the town of Hankey, on the Gamtoos River in the Eastern Cape province in August 2002. Her repatriation and funeral brought dignity to her memory. South African President Thabo Mbeki spoke at the ceremony and presented a model for thinking about how to confront and heal from an unjust past.

> A troubled and painful history has presented us with the challenge and possibility to translate into reality the noble vision that South Africa belongs to all who live in it, black and white. When that is done, [then] will it be possible for us to say that Sarah Bartmann has truly come home.[10]

Mbeki closed his remarks with an extended arm across the Atlantic:

> Another African who lived in the Diaspora, this time in the United States of America, for forebears having been transported out of Africa as slaves, sang of rivers. This is the great African-American poet, Langston Hughes.[11]

Mbeki ended his dedicatory remarks by citing the full text of Hughes's poem "The Negro Speaks of Rivers." As Mbeki ended with the poem's final line "My soul has grown deep like the rivers," he then added, "May the soul of Sarah Bartmann grow deep like the rivers."

Sally Hemings and Sarah Bartmann present two accounts of the gendered and racialized injustices that occurred at the turn of the eighteenth into the nineteenth centuries, on two sides of the Atlantic. Hemings's beauty corresponded with a European standard, and she was praised and given better treatment than her peers; Bartmann's dark-skinned body was considered aberrant to European norms, and she was exhibited as a curiosity of nature. While London and Paris exploited Bartmann and led to her early death, Paris provided different prospects for Hemings, as she could have had freedom and possibly passed within white society. From what we can tell, both women had little choice or power to determine their own destinies, and both women suffered, albeit in dramatically different ways.[12] Bartmann's life was cut short from illness she contracted while on a circus-like exhibition route. Hemings quite possibly had a protected life that involved special treatment, and she lived into her early sixties, but she lived in shadows as an unacknowledged companion to Jefferson and mother of his enslaved children. Both women, who they really were as people, are still shrouded in mystery. Their afterlife has generated much interest: the fragmented body of Bartmann continued to be desecrated in museum exhibits until she was finally buried in her home country; Hemings almost disappeared, though she was kept alive through her children and the stories that circulated underground until DNA evidence made the story unavoidable. In 2002 Bartmann was laid to rest with Mbeki's eulogy for her soul to "grow deep like the rivers" back home, as a proper heritage for her people. In 2001 *From the Diary of Sally Hemings* gave birth to an artistic vision of Hemings that began to flesh out a woman with a voice and legacy that tells a new and yet-unheard story of American history.

Who Was Sally Hemings?

In the early years of the United States up through the Civil War, the practice of slavery presented legal consequences for how racial categories were defined. There was no specific legal category that represented the state between freedom and bondage. In South Africa after colonialism, when the apartheid system came into place mid-twentieth century, the categories of white and black were mitigated by the coloured/mixed-race category.[13] Yet even for this in-between group, the variations of privilege stopped abruptly when someone was categorized as black. Passing as white in the United States and South Africa (and undergoing reclassification in South Africa) under apartheid were unofficial acknowledgements that the line determining blackness could be blurry. For both the United States and South Africa, race and nation determined what kind of life one would live.

Yet even in a system with sharp edges, a liminal category arises; the story between Sally Hemings and Thomas Jefferson exposes how these fault lines have meaning. Here we have a complicated yet common-enough scenario with a woman born into slavery and the relationships that arise around her physical attractiveness, her ability to have children, the consequences of oppression and domination, and the proximity of living in close quarters. Sally Hemings, the daughter of a white man (John Wayles) and biracial mother (Elizabeth Hemings) was (by all accounts) beautiful, legally one-quarter black, and the half-sister of Thomas Jefferson's wife, Martha Wayles. When Martha died young, it is not overly surprising that Jefferson might have seen some of Martha in Sally. Sally's mother Elizabeth was also enslaved and the mother of children by her owner (John Wayles, Sally's and Martha's father). Elizabeth was also the daughter of a relationship between Susannah Epps (an enslaved woman) and her owner John Hemings (a Welsh sea captain; see Chart 3.1).[14] We have a situation of sexual relationships over the course of three generations (Susannah Epps, her daughter Elizabeth Hemings, and her daughter Sally) between master and slave that involve continual exploitation, likely coercion, and possible love.

At root is the way a private situation challenges the public laws of the land. How can a relationship that involves love, trust, and safety develop in the context of slavery, cruelty, and brutality? The story of love between Jefferson and Sally puts into question the tenets behind how slavery and domination work.[15] We have to ask ourselves how a slave could accept someone who was keeping her people in bondage, and possibly love that person, and let him into her heart. We also have to question how a master could fall in love with a slave and still treat her people, and his own children, like chattel. The effectiveness of *From the Diary of Sally Hemings* is that it allows such conflicting emotions to exist simultaneously. Through the use of language and music, such complexity can be accomplished and represented.

The provocative title of William Bolcom and Sandra Seaton's dramatic vocal work on Sally Hemings leads the audience to think that there has been a recent discovery—a secret diary kept by Sally Hemings, the slave and companion of Thomas Jefferson. In interviews and in the notes to the recording they are clear that there is no written diary that survives and that the libretto to the work "is ultimately a work of the imagination, albeit an imagination constrained by historical possibility."[16] Seaton has spoken about how she created a voice for the much-discussed and controversial figure of Jefferson's slave with whom we have evidence he had an ongoing relationship. Seaton writes,

> *From the Diary of Sally Hemings* is first of all a work of the imagination, not a piece of historical research. Although I have done my best to insure historical plausibility, the final test of the song cycle in concert is not the factual accuracy of the words but the human truth and emotional power of the music and words, united in the performance of a gifted singer. . . . .[17]
>
> The portrait of Sally Hemings in *From the Diary* is meant to be suggestive rather than complete. The entries record moments rather than tell stories. The ellipses between entries leave spaces for listeners to complete the portrait for themselves; these spaces indicate my own acknowledgement that the whole truth about the relationship between Thomas Jefferson and Sally Hemings will never be told, either by historians or artists. . . . *From the Diary* is an attempt to allow an imagined Sally Hemings to speak for herself.[18]

This story of Thomas Jefferson and Sally Hemings feels remarkably contemporary as different configurations of family and the growing number of multiracial relationships become more visible. Falling in love across class, race, and/or ethnic lines does not have the same taboo resonance it had in the late eighteenth and early nineteenth centuries. The once unimaginable facts—that one of the country's Founding Fathers probably had a long-term (thirty-eight years) monogamous relationship with a woman who was legally his slave feels both shocking as well as remarkably progressive. Such a story brings to light current themes around which one can now construct alternative narratives (for example, how do we ask questions regarding consensual choice and equality in the context of their vast socioeconomic differences?). Moreover, we live in an era wherein the complexity of black-white relationships is given a new visible focus in the racial-ethnic ancestry and upbringing of former president Barack Obama. The stories surrounding the connections between black people and white people are no longer limited to those who might have intimate bloodline relationships or close friendships with people of different racial and ethnic makeups. This present is juxtaposed with the past in the story of Jefferson and Hemings: a president of the United States can now acknowledge a coming together of racial and ethnic backgrounds in ways that were too controversial before. Starting with the present, the national body politic has been led by a person who embodies more of the population than ever before and gave voice to a wider range of our lived experiences.

In this discussion of William Bolcom and Sandra Seaton's *From the Diary of Sally Hemings*, racial formation in the United States is brought to the forefront. The construction of blackness hinges closely on the edges of whiteness (and vice versa—the construction of whiteness hinges closely on the edges of blackness). Different views about racial identity in the first days of the nation are immediately challenged when Jefferson's published ideas about blackness are juxtaposed with his public and private practices. Mixed-race identity is feared rather than explored and denial becomes a part of the nation's history. The music and its story open up a space for thinking about who Jefferson and Hemings could be or might have been. Historical genre, the presence of those involved with the genesis and creation of this work, and the musical language employed enrich the parsing out of details that have no longer survived.

In January 2012, the month of President Barack Obama's second presidential inauguration, the *New York Times* ran an article about two exhibitions on slavery at Thomas Jefferson's Monticello. Music and cultural critic Edward Rothstein refers to Jefferson and writes,

> What does it mean that such a man not only held slaves but also devoted considerable attention to their status, their mode of life and, yes, their profitability? What was the connection between his ideals and the blunt reality? These are not just biographical questions; they are national ones.[19]

In this spirit, I wish to examine how so many things we try to keep separate come together: the public and the private, the political and the personal,

the intimate and the social, the condemned and the condoned. These op-
positional pairs are some of the repercussions of what we have now come
to understand as the long-term, secret, interracial romantic relationship
(possibly a relationship of choice by both parties) between Thomas Jefferson
and his slave Sally Hemings.

Thomas Jefferson hardly needs introduction, at least in a general way.
Schoolchildren around the world are taught that he was a Founding Father
of the United States as it gained its freedom from its colonization by England,
the third president of the United States, and actively involved in forming the
transition from colonies to country. He was the author of the Declaration of
Independence and one of the principal architects of the republic where equality,
freedom, and the pursuit of happiness would become a model for European
nations, as the French Revolution the following decade would prove.

Sally Hemings has become a well-known figure since the 1990s around the
question of whether she was romantically aligned with Thomas Jefferson.[20]
With family charts, the DNA testing, and reconstructing historical data about
where, how, and if Jefferson could have fathered several children with Hemings,
the emphasis has been on proving—scientifically and historically—how and
under what conditions they were "together." There is a lot at stake with pairing
these two people. How can one look back at the Founding Fathers—a term that
hovers on a construction of patriarchy that, on its surface, appears so loving
and comforting as one can take pride in Jefferson's role in nurturing the birth
of the United States—and reconcile that sense with the information that Jefferson, along with many of the other Founding Fathers, owned slaves? What
does one do with the knowledge that Jefferson lived a double life where he
succumbed to, and even needed the economic structure of, owning slaves? Yet
on the other hand, strong evidence points to the fact that he had a committed,
spouse-like relationship with his slave Sally Hemings, who was also the half-
sister of his deceased wife. Hardly anyone could, or even wanted to, believe that
such a glaring dichotomy in this beloved historical figure could exist. But the
relationship could not lie buried in the past; not even the century-old question
that provided the space for this to be a vague possibility was to remain a mystery. Given the developments in science of the 1990s, we now had the (almost)
definitive DNA results that substantiated what had previously been a rumor:
Jefferson and Sally Hemings had conceived several children together.[21] Though
there was still a possibility that a relative of Thomas Jefferson (and not Thomas
himself) had fathered the descendants of the people who claim a relationship
to Sally Hemings and Thomas Jefferson, the DNA evidence was too strong for
most people to simply ignore. At this point, the discourse had to change. Now,
as Rothstein states above, "these are not just biographical questions, they are
national ones."

Yet more biography is in order before we move on to implications for the nation. Though the narratives of these people's lives have been told and retold in history books and biographies, I relate the facts here now in reference to getting a larger picture of how living situations between whites and blacks (owners, slaves, and those relationships that seem to fall in between these two categories) were constructed—especially in Thomas Jefferson's immediate family experience. While a large part of the story of how we see Thomas Jefferson and his relationship with Sally Hemings has been reshaped since the 1990s, the incomplete and selective (yet factually substantiated) biographies below are limited to thinking about the societal master-slave and familial bloodline relationships between these people in order to gain a quick overview of who is connected to whom.[22]

Chart 3.1: Black-White Relationships around Thomas Jefferson and Sally Hemings

John Wayles (1715–1773) was born in England and came to Virginia most likely in the 1730s. He was a planter, slave trader, and lawyer in the Virginia colony. His first wife, Martha Epps, was the mother of Martha Wayles, who became Thomas Jefferson's wife (hence John Wayles was Thomas Jefferson's father-in-law). John Wayles survived three wives and later had a relationship with his slave Elizabeth Hemings. With Elizabeth Hemings he fathered six children, one of whom was Sally Hemings.

Elizabeth Hemings (also known as Betty) (1735–1807) was the daughter of John Hemings, a Welsh sea captain, and an enslaved woman born in Africa (possibly Hausa from Nigeria), called Susannah Epps. Elizabeth and her mother Susannah became the property of Martha Epps (who married John Wayles). After John Wayles's death in 1773, Elizabeth and her ten children (six of whom are said to have been fathered by Wayles, including Sally Hemings) became the inherited property of Martha Wayles and Thomas Jefferson.

Martha Wayles Skelton Jefferson (1748–1782) was a young widow (her deceased first husband was Bathurst Skelton) with no surviving children in 1772 when she married Thomas Jefferson. In her life she had seven children; her only child with Skelton died at the age three. Of her six children fathered by Jefferson, only two daughters—Martha (called Patsy) and Maria (called Polly)—lived into adulthood. Martha was the only wife of Jefferson. She was the half-sister of Sally Hemings (they shared a father in John Wayles).

Sarah "Sally" Hemings (1773–1835) was one of six children of John Wayles and Elizabeth Hemings. Though born to the Wayles household, she and her mother moved to Monticello (sources differ about when this happened—sometime after 1773 but by 1776) when Martha Wayles Jefferson inherited her father's slaves at his death. Sally was a nursemaid and companion to her half-sister's (Martha's) children (Patsy and Polly) after Martha died. Sally accompanied Polly to Paris (1787–1789) when Jefferson was the U.S. Ambassador to France, and she helped attend to Polly as well as Patsy (who came to Paris later) when they debuted in Parisian society. It is thought that during this time in Paris, Sally and Thomas became intimately involved. Evidence supports that they had six children together, four of whom survived into adulthood.[23] These four children were all freed.[24]

As we explore this story, it is evident that the character of the relationship between Sally Hemings and Thomas Jefferson had precedent in early American history. The household Thomas Jefferson married into when he married Martha Wayles Skelton provided a strong model for his later relationship with Sally Hemings. Martha's father John and (later) her husband Thomas, it seems, both turned to long-term relationships with their slaves that each produced several children. Additionally, there is evidence that Elizabeth Hemings (Sally's mother) also had a similar ancestry. Elizabeth's African mother, Susannah Epps, was taken as a type of companion by the sea captain John Hemings from Wales and became the property of Martha Epps, the mother of Martha Wayles Skelton Jefferson (Thomas Jefferson's wife). Martha Epps, brought Susannah and her daughter Elizabeth (Hemings) as part of her dowry when she married John Wayles. So, among multiple generations (John Hemings and Susannah Epps, John Wayles and Elizabeth Hemings, Thomas Jefferson and Sally Hemings) it was not uncommon for a man to father children and have various types of relationships with chosen black female slaves.[25]

Rather than seeing these situations as anomalous or unheard of, *From the Diary of Sally Hemings* asks us to think about such circumstances as fitting into a larger context that makes room for such occurrences to happen.[26] In her notes to the recording, author Sandra Seaton takes a pragmatic stance in her portrayal: "the relationship between Jefferson and Sally Hemings could never be a love between social and political equals."[27] Yet Seaton immediately goes on to present another complementary vantage point when she writes, "Contemporary African American historian and NYU law professor Annette Gordon-Reed, one of the leading authorities on the relationship, cautions contemporary readers against assuming that any relationship between a white man and a woman legally his slave could be more than power and submission."[28] The music and text to *From the Diary of Sally Hemings* present multiple views of this relationship that is hidden in mystery and yet speaks uncannily to the present as interracial relationships continue to be haunted by the specter cast by slavery and furthered by Jim Crow, segregation, and ongoing racial biases and discrimination.

As someone who is thoroughly involved with how the history of the Jeffersons and Hemingses has been revealed, Annette Gordon-Reed's extensive research and writing on this topic has had a marked focus less on the actual outcome of the debate (Were they involved or not?) and more on how this history has been told. She writes,

> The more important feature of the Jefferson-Hemings debate, I believed, was what it said about the views of Americans—and it must be said, some white

Americans—about the proper relationship between blacks and whites. This was not just on the sexual front (not even mainly on the sexual front) but in terms of the proper power relationship between the two groups overall.

The treatment of the story well into modern times is evidence of the continuing grip that the doctrine of white supremacy has on American society.[29]

It is this angle to the story—its telling and retelling of the past up to the present—that makes *From the Diary of Sally Hemings* so important today. One aspect of this significance is the way things are still rather similar—at least in terms of the resistance people in the late eighteenth century up through the early twenty-first century have had to the image of a Founding Father of the United States being involved in an interracial relationship. Gordon-Reed rightly points out that though this was a story about an event in the past—centuries old—it represents relevant feelings a nation continues to have about itself.

Today most mixed-race people face a similar situation as that of Sally Hemings and her offspring. We know from the memoir that Sally Hemings's son Madison Hemings wrote in 1873 that of the four children who survived into adulthood, two lived in white society and two lived in black society; Beverly and Harriet married white spouses and assimilated as white people, while Madison and Eston married "colored" women and lived in black communities.[30] Despite the passage of 150 years since the end of slavery, in the United States a person's identity and how one is treated are still determined by an alchemy of how you look and behave in relation to racist ideology. Though it is a bold statement, for society at large in the United States you are either black or pass as white. Today, while one might claim an interracial/biracial identity, in reality—as it seems to most people—you are classified as "other" or "mixed," with the implication that you are *other* than white or black, or you are *mixed* from black and white. Though relationships between black people and white people are no longer illegal, the social constructions around interracial identity are still in some sense troubled, as there is no comfortable space, wide social acceptance, or shared understanding of mixed racial heritage.[31]

Who Tells This Story: Composer William Bolcom and Writer Sandra Seaton

From the Diary of Sally Hemings is an interracial collaboration between Pulitzer Prize- and Grammy-winning composer and pianist William Bolcom and decorated writer and playwright Sandra Seaton. Bolcom (born in Seattle, Washington- in 1938) was educated both in the United States and Paris. He was part of the mid-twentieth century progressive scene at Mills College and attended the Paris Conservatoire, where he studied with Darius Milhaud and Olivier Messiaen.[32] Hailed as the 2007 Composer of the Year by Music America, Bolcom has a long list of honors and awards for his work in classical art music (including symphonies and operas) and popular musical styles (especially cabaret songs). A distinguishing feature of Bolcom's music is his ability to encompass a style that feels up to date and current in a popular sense as well as to create music that is considered "classical" and at home in the concert hall. It is this feature that has allowed him to write in a wide variety of styles that come together smoothly and sound relevant to his contemporaneous audiences.

Along with a few other composers in the late 1960s, Bolcom was part of a revival of ragtime music that popularized it outside of strictly jazz circles. Bolcom, white himself, was also a strong supporter of the dignity of other types of African American music—notably jazz—before the mainstream concert-going and academic publics deemed such music worthy of a true "art" status. It was through his work on the 1921 black musical *Shuffle Along* that he first met Sandra Seaton. *Shuffle Along* was among the first all-black musical works on Broadway; its music and lyrics were by Noble Sissle and Eubie Blake, and it contained an interconnected plot (about a mayoral race) written by Flournoy Miller and Aubrey Lyles.[33] *Shuffle Along* was both exceedingly popular (it had a run of 504 performances) and helped launch the careers of Josephine Baker, Paul Robeson, and Florence Mills, and included William Grant Still and Hall Johnson in the orchestra. Seaton, a descendent of Flournoy Miller, sought out Bolcom when she learned he had published a book about the musical.[34] Bolcom writes in the notes to the recording of *From the Diary of Sally Hemings*, "The dedication of the cycle, in memory of Flournoy Miller, is in gratitude for his posthumously bringing Sandra's work to my attention."

Sandra Seaton (born in Columbia, Tennessee) is an African American writer and playwright who grew up in Tennessee and then on Chicago's West Side in the 1940s and 1950s, when her family moved north during the Great Migration. She has written more than ten plays and worked in fiction and spoken word. Her degrees are in the liberal arts and creative writing, and she has received research grants and held creative arts residencies at prominent universities and artist colonies.[35] Her works have been performed in cities throughout the United States including New York, Chicago, and Los Angeles.

The collaboration between Bolcom and Seaton began with Florence Quivar (born 1944 in Philadelphia, Pennsylvania), one of the leading opera singers at the time, who was interested in Sally Hemings. Bolcom writes:

In 1999 Florence Quivar, the celebrated mezzosoprano, asked me to compose a song cycle on Sally Hemings. At first I was inclined to say no, because I had seen so many sensationalized portraits of Sally Hemings that I couldn't accept her as anybody real. This is not because I doubted, as quite a number of people still seem to, that Thomas Jefferson both had a long relationship and fathered children with her; I had always been fairly sure the story was true."[36]

Bolcom goes on to express his concern about finding someone who could represent Sally Hemings well in words. He mentions meeting Sandra Seaton in connection with *Reminiscing with Noble Sissle and Eubie Blake* and becoming familiar with her work. "The quiet forcefulness of the character portraits in the two plays of hers that I had seen, *The Bridge Party* and *The Will*, had impressed me mightily. I couldn't imagine anyone who would understand Sally better."[37] Bolcom continues, "Seaton's own plays deal penetratingly with the world of the African American middle class in a refreshingly non-stereotypical way, and I felt that she would understand Sally Hemings better than anyone else I knew."[38]

Bolcom writes about approaching Seaton to get involved with this project:

"If you don't want to do this," I said to Sandra, "I'll say no to the project." Happily, she said yes to my idea of reconstructing a diary of Sally Hemings, and the work which follows—a longer version of the text I set to music—gave me a Sally Hemings I could believe in, one that sings.[39]

The speaker in the text—not surprising, as it was constructed as a diary—is that of Seaton writing in Sally's voice. Much of it is first-person narrative, but there are sections that narrate events and quote other people. Seaton includes quotations from Jefferson's writings at points and indicates this through the use of italics.[40]

Exploring the Verbal Text

My discussion of the text includes two related and very similar versions. There is the text that is in the notes to the recording (which is the same as the text in the published piano vocal score) and there is the slightly longer text that appears in the *Michigan Quarterly Review*, which devoted a cluster of articles to *From the Diary of Sally Hemings* when the work first came out.[41] The journal cluster contains three parts: A "Preface" written by William Bolcom; the text "From the Diary of Sally Hemings," by Sandra Seaton; and "Program Notes," also by Seaton. In the *Michigan Quarterly Review*, the text is slightly longer (only a few lines were omitted in the final version set to music) and is the one Bolcom refers to in the preceding quotation. The longer text is laid out in fifteen sections, as opposed to the four parts with eighteen songs in the musical work. Nothing is contradicted between the two versions of the text in that the general shape of the narrative is the same. The most common difference is a shifting of a few lines of text within a section or between different sections.

The text in the *Michigan Quarterly Review* is slightly different from the text in the piano-vocal score (and recording, which has the same text as the piano-vocal score); this is the longer version of the full text that Seaton gave Bolcom as he was composing.[42] Though not indicated in the score and recording, the text we see in the *Michigan Quarterly Review* includes a few dates and places that position the diary in historical time and location. The opening sections (comparable to the individual songs) contain neither date nor place, but near the end of section II we have "1788 Paris." Just after section III we see "Hôtel de Langeac," which refers to the townhouse that Jefferson moved into in 1785, probably after his elevation to the minister to the Court of Versailles, replacing Benjamin Franklin.[43] The next and final reference to a date is at the beginning of section V, "December 23, 1789," with the text "Back home, at Monticello. . . ."[44]

Perhaps the most telling portion left out of the musical work is the reference to "Calendar" in two lines: "Calendar's warning: 'Marry a woman of your own complexion'" and "Another bawdy line. 'Take to bed your Sally.'"[45] James T. Callender is a historical figure known for a relationship with Thomas Jefferson that was at first friendly (where Jefferson gave him money, primarily as acts of charity) but then grew estranged when Callender demanded that Jefferson make him postmaster in Richmond, Virginia, and Jefferson refused. As a journalist, Callender then worked against Jefferson and "made the first public allegation that Jefferson had been involved in a sexual relationship with Sally Hemings."[46] Though some of what Callender wrote in the *Richmond Recorder* in 1802 was most likely true, the manner in which he reported it was so indecent that it lost most of its effectiveness because of his own reputation and because he undoubtedly offended many of his readers. As historian Joshua Rothman notes, "Callender's reports of the relationship between Thomas Jefferson and Sally Hemings have been casually and categorically dismissed as unreliable—the libelous rants of a scandal-mongering, drunken, and disgruntled office-seeker."[47] The fact that Callender does not appear very much in one version of this text and then is completely cut out of the final version shows that both Bolcom and Seaton were not interested in giving voice to this sensationalist side of the story. The portrayal we get of Jefferson and Hemings is a sympathetic one, yet also complex, one that focuses on an inner world between the two of them, the larger issues and daily problems they could have encountered, and less on how others judged them.

The musical world Bolcom creates for Jefferson and Hemings has sections that are quite tonal as well as dramatic sections that are dissonant and descriptive of the text.[48] In the program notes to the 2010 recording, Bolcom wrote about his musical approach:

> Sally's world was by necessity an indoor, protected, rather quiet one, and the spareness of Sandra's language for Sally, just what I'd hoped for, is answered by a stylistic sobriety in my own music. I opted for a harmonically plain language with a somewhat French atmosphere (evoking Hemings's Paris sojourn), with African American melodic references well to the background.[49]

Bolcom continues, referring to how he saw the character of Hemmings and shaped his presentation of her.

> I did not want to fall into the expected cliché in so much work I'd seen on Sally. She was not a cardboard icon, standing for a group. In every way she was unique, an individual; otherwise, how could she have fascinated someone like Jefferson for thirty-eight years?[50]

Indeed, Bolcom was pleased with Seaton's text and felt that she had given him

> a Sally Hemings I could believe in, one that sings. I feel that Sandra has given us as much of a portrait of the real Sally as we'll ever have. . . . [this Sally was] someone we sense is there, a living presence capable of great dignity and depth—articulate, restrained, and fearless.[51]

In the score to *From the Diary of Sally Hemings*, the description is "Eighteen Songs for Medium Voice and Piano." Originally written for Florence Quivar, a noted mezzosoprano with a rich and warm sound, the compact disc recording is with Alyson Cambridge, a soprano with a higher and lighter voice; the music fit both voices well and indicates that the work may be performed by most mezzos and sopranos alike.

From the Diary of Sally Hemings is a work that spans musical genre. It can be called a song cycle, since it involves a solo singer and a pianist and is not staged. The dramatic elements across the songs form miniature scenes that feel operatic more often than part of a Lieder recital. There are eighteen songs of various lengths divided into four unequal parts. These song titles are the first line of the song, with the exception of the final song (#18), which has the three subsections noted in the table of contents in the piano-vocal score (see Chart 3.2).[52]

Chart 3.2. Organization of *From the Diary of Sally Hemings* in the Musical Score

Part 1
    1. They say I was born old
    2. Martha and Maria
    3. White waves
    4. *Paris, c'est la ville vivante*
    5. The master brings music to his sitting room
    6. I was carrying a tray when he called me
Part 2
    7. They say I was born old
    8. *Come back to America*
    9. Back home at Monticello
    10. *Purple Hyacinth begins to bloom*
    11. My sister ghost
Part 3
    12. Peonies, a perfume box
    13. Mister, our child is frail
    14. A dark winter blue-black evening
    15. Old shoe! Old shoe!
Part 4
    16. A wild man home from the woods
    17. Papers!
    18. Night watch till early morn

Note: Italics are quotations from Jefferson's writings.

The text from the *Michigan Quarterly Review* contains fifteen sections. From here on, I will refer to the eighteen "songs" in the piano score as "sections," since my focus is on how *From the Diary of Sally Hemings* functions as a collection of mini-scenes, part of a larger work that feels more operatic. Later, I discuss the work as a "monodrama," a type of one-character opera or solo opera. This is not to dispute that the work can function as a song cycle; my analysis here focuses on the larger dramatic and generic scheme of the work.

As Chart 3.2 indicates, the eighteen sections are divided into four parts, from the largest number of sections to the fewest, from six in part 1 to three in part 4. However, most of the sections are around two minutes with the exception of #11, "My sister ghost" (4:12 minutes) and the finale to the cycle (#18) "Night watch till early morn," at nearly nine minutes. Part 3 is the shortest, and though the first half (consisting of parts 1 and 2) is longer than the second half (parts 3 and 4), the "weight" of the cycle feels most intense in the second half, especially in the finale (#18), a consequence of its length and the reminiscent text and music from earlier in the work that is quoted in it. In terms of the dramatic effect, the final sections of part 2 (#11, "My sister ghost") and part 4 (#18, "Night watch till early morn") are the longest, and they give the work a feeling of the conclusion of a first half and the finale in a second half—almost like a larger sung drama that divides the pacing into two large groupings, parts 1–2 and parts 3–4. In performance, the work consumes a little under forty-five minutes, with parts 1–2 lasting about twenty-three minutes and parts 3–4 lasting around twenty-one minutes.[53] Despite the layout of the score as a work in four parts, dramatically in performance, the experience is more like a larger work divided into two halves. Given this dramatic pacing, these two parts could also be experienced as two interconnected sections of a one-act opera.

In terms of genre, the piece feels more like a dramatic work, minus the stage direction and acting, than a song cycle. While the intimacy of a song cycle is achieved through the setting for a solo singer and pianist, the dimensions of that genre are expanded as the piano takes on varied roles beyond an accompaniment that provides harmonic support and an atmospheric mood. The piano comments on the action and speaks as an additional voice that quotes previous material in the same and altered forms. The piano provides a sonic environment that is sometimes a simple thematic accompaniment (such as the opening of the work) and sometimes a diegetic voice that responds to the singer's text. When Jefferson asks for "a little music please," the piano plays three measures adapted from Mozart's song "Das Veilchen" K. 476 an octave higher, referencing an eighteenth-century harpsichord sound (#12, measures 21–24).[54] At times the piano looks more like an orchestral reduction with chords that punctuate recitative (for example, portions of #12 and #15), or assumes an adaptive orchestral role as though accompanying a narrative scene, such as in #3, "White Waves," in the story of Sally's grandmother's (Susannah Epps—though not named) abduction into slavery with her life in Africa ("Dahomey child" measures 13–64) and Sally's juxtaposition of her own "voyage of a different sort" (measures 65–78) to Paris, a trip that could have provided her freedom. Vocally, the singer gets to perform in ways that encompass the style of the Lied as well as the wider expanse of the drama of opera. Though she is always "Sally," her voice also takes on the roles of Jefferson, a narrator, her mother Elizabeth Hemings, and once in the opening number the voice of Mistress Jefferson (her half-sister Martha on her deathbed), who all pull the story together. There are numbers in this work that feel like small pieces; arguably, these could be experienced as diegetic moments (songs in the larger picture), and there are sections that are narratives and dramatic scenes. With all of these types of pieces, the whole feels like a larger work that falls in between and challenges traditional generic designations.

Thinking about Genre

From its early reception, *From the Diary of Sally Hemings* has hovered between genres. After hearing a performance by Florence Quivar (the singer who commissioned and premiered the work), music critic and scholar Paul Horsley noted, "Quivar's velvet voice and experienced dramatic touch made this piece seem more like a miniature opera than a song cycle. Pianist J. J. Penna made the intricate accompaniment seem like a well-crafted narrative."[55] *Washington Post* music critic Anne Midgette reviewed a performance of *From the Diary of Sally Hemings* by Alyson Cambridge, in a recital from 2010, where she calls the work "an evocative and gripping text that creates less a song cycle than a monodrama." Later on, Midgette continues,

> Cambridge entered the fray geared far more to the idea of "monodrama" than "simplicity." She clearly meant the whole evening to be Serious and approached it with an operatic sensibility, starting with a big fortissimo in the first section of the work, in a passage describing a memory from Hemings's earliest childhood. She certainly sold the piece, singing it from memory and commitment.[56]

These references to genre, as a monodrama, and the way in which Cambridge performed the work are telling. Cambridge has become close to the work as she collaborated with Bolcom and Seaton during the recording of the piece in 2010 (on the White Pine Music label). As a regular singer at the Metropolitan Opera, Chicago Lyric Opera, and other opera houses, Midgette's review cites how Cambridge performed it from memory with "an operatic sensibility." Calling the work a "monodrama" feels right in terms of genre. Such a designation has a specific music lineage, described in modern times (after its use in the eighteenth century) as being "most often used as a synonym for a one-character opera, as in Schoenberg's *Erwartung* (1909) and Poulenc's *La voix humaine* (1958)."[57] In more casual conversations with Sandra Seaton and Bill Bolcom, I have heard them both refer to *From the Diary of Sally Hemings* as a "solo opera."

The connections between Arnold Schoenberg's monodrama *Erwartung*, Poulenc's *La voix Humaine* and *From the Diary of Sally Hemings* can be seen to go a little deeper. Though the three are quite different, each is performed by a central female protagonist who is caught in midst of memories and thoughts about a relationship we know very little about. We see Poulenc's Elle ("She" in French) in a one-sided phone conversation with her former lover and learn of her depression and attempted suicide the night before. After suspecting him of infidelity, Elle, at the end of the work, is in bed with the phone and its cord wrapped around her neck, murmuring "Je t'aime" ("I love you") into the mouthpiece. It is unclear if this is another attempted suicide or if the protagonist finds some momentary comfort in her uncertain situation. As in *Erwartung* and *From the Diary of Sally Hemings*, *La voix humaine* ends with ambiguity. After witnessing the precarious mental state of Elle for nearly forty minutes, the audience is left with a sense of unknowing about the details of exactly what happened before our view into her experience and what her future will bring.

Schoenberg's speaker was written during the height of his Expressionist period, a time in the beginning of the twentieth century when ideas around dreams, the unconscious, and Freudian psychoanalysis were gaining attention. Marie Pappenheim's text and Schoenberg's music come together to present the psychological state of a woman (the singer) in a hysterical moment of disturbance. Though I do not argue that Sally Hemings fits this characterization, Oliver Neighbor writes about Schoenberg's protagonist in a way that is also prescient of Sally Hemings; in using Neighbor's words about the singer in *Erwartung*, I agree that Hemings also portrays "a means of expressing the multiplicity of contradictory feelings that can arise simultaneously from the unconscious."[58]

Seaton asserts, "*From the Diary* is an attempt to allow an imagined Sally Hemings to speak for herself." In giving a voice to Sally Hemings through the creation of a fictitious diary, Seaton has given us a Sally Hemings with an unconscious. The text of the libretto spans the time from when Sally Hemings was a nine-year-old child before she went to Paris, her time abroad, her time back at Monticello, through the birth of her children, their respective childhoods, and up through Jefferson's death. In her narration we are given glimpses into her character and the creation of an unconscious—one that is shaped by memories of childhood, the experience of being in Paris, and her role as a mother and consort to Jefferson.

Listening to the Music

Musically, the sonic world accompanying Hemings is filled with tunes and musical reminiscences through the repetition of early themes quoted later in the work. This creates an internal world for the central character where she has musical motives and text phrases that were introduced in the beginning of the work and then come back, sometimes the same and sometimes transformed. Through the music and the text, it is as though the listener is brought into a private world of references that had personal meaning for Hemings and Jefferson. In the audience we get to know them and witness these well-crafted, plausible (albeit fictitious) experiences in a collective imagined and emotional recreation.

There are two musical markers that appear several times in strategic places within the larger work across the multiple sections. Both cases of these recurrences unify the work and help the listener make long-range connections. The first case involves three occurrences with a step-wise eighth-note pattern that creates a sense of movement and traversing time. The second case appears twice and contrasts to the first case by providing a slower chordal texture that grounds the listener with a sense of stasis and arrival.

The first aural marker appears in the opening of the work, the first thing we hear. *From the Diary of Sally Hemings* opens in a moderate tempo with an ascending eighth-note pattern and a harmonic centering around D tonic; the sonic world evoked touches on a mixture between major, minor, and a Dorian hexachord modality. The ear hears a rooted connection to a D tonic but cannot settle into one harmonic modality. The opening line of text, appearing in measure 3 and keeping the same ascending eighth-note rhythm in the bass-line of the accompaniment, presents the speaker as one who inhabits the present and past together: "They say I was born old, so so old before my time." This text returns two other times, near the middle of the work as the opening line of #7 (similar melodic shape, different accompaniment) in the beginning of part 2, and at the end of work (#18), this time with the text and almost the same music as the opening. In the final appearance, this opening line provides a feeling of return and nostalgia, as though we were going back to the beginning. Punctuating the work, this opening theme marks the opening and ending as well as near the midpoint to highlight the trope of a journey that ties the past and present together in a dynamic relationship.

The final section of the work (#18) is quite long, acts as a type of microcosm of the whole, and contains the densest references to previous themes. With the return of the opening lines, structurally we are given closure as we are reminded of how this narrative began. The cryptic nature of being "born old" and "so so old before my time" sets up a constancy where something that had started earlier continues after the expected longevity. Appearing in the opening, near the middle, and again at the end aurally marks this theme as having structural importance. Harmonically and textually, we feel a rootedness in something familiar (the tonic pitch D, the familiarity of the text and melodic phrase), but we are not fully grounded in one harmonic or temporal mode; instead, there is a blending of things that are not always brought together (major, minor, modal, and the present and past).

The other striking musical aural marker is a slow chordal texture that appears twice, the first time to the text "Safe in his arms" (#7, start of part 2) and then again at the end of the work (end of #18). In the work as a whole, the piano part overall is a busy and active agent that both acts as a commentator and provides an atmospheric soundscape. Usually, the piano moves steadily in a role that either keeps the action flowing or accompanies in a more jagged way that punctuates the text. At the end of the first number of part 2 (#7) and at the conclusion of the work's finale (part 4, #18), the music suddenly slows down and shifts to broad chords that move homo-rhythmically, almost like a hymn or chorale. The expression marking for both occurrences is the same: "Stately," in a 3/4 meter with a key signature that signals B major, but it is not afraid of chromatic dissonance. There is no other section like it, and its use twice, especially as both times it follows an agitated section of perpetual sixteenth or eighth notes, gives the effect of pulling back on the tempo to make sure you have the chance to breathe and see things differently. Though the text is different for each presentation, in both cases there is a sense of an almost-resolved tension. Through the centering on a B tonic and the slower "stately" tempo of quarter and half notes (with just a few eighth notes added in), the tempo transports us steadily to a calmer state. Each time, however, the text and harmony act at cross-purposes. In #7 the text reassures us with "Safe in his arms" until the very end, with the performance direction "almost whispered" over the sung text: "but still my voice frightens him," as though the singer is sharing a secret that contradicts the outwardly peaceful atmosphere.

In these final moments at the end of the work (part 4, #18), the text lines up with the message of finally being free from the strain of this earth and reunited in heaven: "Mister, we're free to go. Leave our old clothes behind. This time walk with me to the Lord. We'll dress in our new finery, silk robes to meet our Lord." However, in the key signature of B major with the voice ending on the B tonic note with a widely spaced B major chord, the last notes are the lowest octave C-naturals in bass clef, marked pianississimo with a fermata and "lunga" marking. It is as though, almost out of hearing range, the simultaneity of the half-step B-C-natural evokes a ghostly dissonance that haunts the soundscape; one in the foreground in the voice with the B tonic and the other C octaves below in the piano, exceedingly soft, yet resonating in a way that is more felt than heard. This quasi-inaudible last chord of the work is a fitting clash of two chromatic notes, two realities, representing that friction between the evidence of what we know and the gaps for what is missing (along with the friction of living in two worlds, as Hemings and Jefferson did). These two cases of musical reminiscences emphasize bringing together things that do not neatly fit—the past and present, being born already old, safety and danger, harmony and dissonance.

Ghosts: The Legacies of the Past
Haunting the Present

The metaphor of the ghost is one that permeates the full work. In this diary, Sally Hemings writes several times of her "sister ghost," the spectral presence of her half-sister Martha Wayles (the deceased wife of Jefferson). "Mistress Jefferson" (Martha) dies in the opening number in an intimate setting with Sally and her mother (Elizabeth Hemings). The presence of the deceased Martha Wayles is felt in nearly every song, beginning right away in #2, when little Martha and Maria (children of Martha Wayles and Jefferson) and Sally play together right alongside the text Jefferson wrote for his dead wife's grave (italicized).

> Martha and Maria, hands clasped together in the shade of his poplar tree, we skipped and stopped, spied his words on her grave: *If in the house of Hades, men forget their dead, yet will I remember my dear companion.* Most days I sit with Maria and Martha. . . . Inside the big house. Outside, Mother's cabin. . . . [59]

This felt presence is complemented by the first sighting of Martha as ghost in #6, the end of part 1, and is one of the shortest texts.

> I was carrying a tray when he called me. Sally turn this way. Now hold your face to the light. A little over. Master Jefferson looked whiter than a sheet, whiter than I ever was. He cupped my face in his hands and whispered her name.

In this complete text for this number, Seaton has given us a glimpse of Sally and Jefferson's time in Paris when they were falling in love. Seaton shows how it was possible for Jefferson to see Martha Wayles in her half-sister Sally as she grew older and they were away from their familiar surroundings in Virginia. Linking them through the visage of whiteness, we feel the tenderness as "he cupped my face in his hands" and also the complexity when he "whispered her name"—undoubtedly the name of Martha.

The end of part 2, "My sister ghost" (#11) gets to the heart of what had been mounting in the first half of the work: the awkward, painful, and complicated position Sally assumes as the companion to Thomas Jefferson. In her opening line, she invokes the "sister ghost" and then relates two sightings. "One day I called him Tom. He turned, startled: Now hold your face towards the light. He held me close. The earth belongs to the living." Not only is this one of the text reminiscences from an earlier number (#6 "I was carrying a tray when he called me"), the music is also brought back (not exactly, but very similar and definitely audible) and a tempo indication in the score refers directly to the earlier song "Tempo of VI" with the same metronome marking (quarter note = 69). In this section the themes for what is at stake are brought together, and we get a palpable sense of how Sally is both her own person and a probable surrogate link to her dead half-sister.

The second sighting of Sally's "sister ghost" in #11 appears shortly after the first one. The music to this number (#11) is framed in a ³/₂ meter marked "Rich and Warm" (half-note = 46) that surrounds a faster middle section with an eighth-note pulse. With the return of the opening ³/₂ meter (measure 52), the pace slows back down. The text reveals the second sighting,

> Her ghost appears once more, stands nearby. . . . Sister dear, I hold your daughter's trust. Rather me than a mistress who sets her own standard. Rather me than a stranger. Bloodlines! Bloodlines!

As in the opening of this number, the ³/₂ meter contains a sophisticated rhythmic layering. The left hand moves slowly, with the chords changing on the beat once a measure, or even less frequently with notes tied over. The right hand moves slightly more quickly, but with tied-over syncopations, giving the effect of a misalignment between the right hand (treble clef) in the piano compared to the alignment of left hand (bass clef) with the voice. Consistently, the right-hand accompaniment in the piano seems to be rhythmically off by a half note and for ten measures avoids the metric downbeat (measures 52–62). Combined together in the piano and the voice, this musical hemiola (through the rhythmic displacement) is reflected textually through the haunting of Sally's sister ghost (the deceased Martha Wayles). Overall, this polyrhythmic structure gives the effect of things happening simultaneously on different time scales—an apt way for evoking the juxtaposition of different worlds in time and space as we see Sally grappling with the blending of her present with Jefferson and past with half-sister Martha.

The text to the musical score is filled with specific historical details that are all carefully interwoven to fit what we know about the contextual situation—dates Jefferson was in Paris, where he stayed, and people he met; his writings about gardens and the "purple hyacinths," "wild honeysuckle," and "narcissus" that are quoted in the text; and the presence of Sally's mother, her nieces Maria and Martha, and her children Beverly, Harriet, Madison, and Eston.

As Seaton created this world from her research about the Jefferson family, Monticello, and the period during the late eighteenth and early nineteenth centuries in Paris and the early United States, her own experience also played into how she shaped Sally.

My portrait of Sally Hemings is based not only on a study of the growing historical literature on Jefferson and Sally Hemings but also on my own family
history. Growing up as an African-American in the South before the civil rights
era, I heard many family stories about relationships between blacks and whites
outside of the law. Some were love relationships; others were exploitative—some
were probably both.[60]

Seaton's work in the two plays Bolcom mentions above (*The Bridge Party* and
The Will) and her work since *From the Diary of Sally Hemings* has explored
these themes around interracial relationships and African American life in
the past. In her 1994 play *The Will*, she brings to life the details around her
own heritage and how black-white relationships form the unwritten history
of her ancestry. In a carefully detailed story about two families who lived and
worked together side by side in the South during the years immediately following the Civil War, Seaton creates two households—one headed by Cyrus
Webster, a free black man, and the other a poor white neighbor and son
who work on Cyrus's land. Both families have sons who return from having
fought in the Civil War (on opposite sides) but are unable to return to the
coexistence they once had; the white son joins the beginnings of the Ku Klux
Klan, and Cyrus's son Israel wants to be treated with the respect due a soldier
who supported his country. Throughout the play Cyrus Webster attends to
the present situation as his son Israel becomes increasingly hostile toward
the white childhood friend who is filled with racial hatred toward him and
Cyrus's other son, who is engaged to marry Patti, a black opera singer, who is
based on the historical character of Elizabeth Taylor Greenfield.[61] Around the
edges of this main action is the theme of legacy that Cyrus feels both in terms
of honoring his own ancestors and the wisdom he tries to pass on to his sons.

In her "Program Notes" that appear in the *Michigan Quarterly Review*
cluster about Sally Hemings, Seaton writes about a breaking through of this
unwritten history in an act of her great-great-great-grandfather Cyrus Webster.

A gravestone in my hometown in Tennessee describes my ancestor Anna Sanderson as the "consort" of Israel Grant, a white man. The gravestone affirming
this relation to the world was put up by their child, my maternal great-great-
great-grandfather, Cyrus Webster. According to our family oral history, Cyrus,
who lived his entire adult life as a free black, was taken to the basement by his
white relatives and taught to read.[62]

As Seaton had accomplished before *From the Diary of Sally Hemings*, we see
here in *The Will* themes from her own family's past that emerge in her writing,
being worked out through the interactions she imagines in the portrayals

of her characters. As Seaton weaves together knowledge of the period—in this case Southern history and oral family history—we see a reflection of images from our nation's past that have not survived. More significant than a focus on what is historically factual is the connection such stories have to us today as we strive to remember and reconstruct what we desire to know of the past for our living in the present.

In these "Program Notes" Seaton continues to bring the story of Sally Hemings even closer to her family.

> My grandmother often told me stories about my great-grandmother, Emma Hatcher Webster. The child of two teenagers, a local planter's son and the mulatto daughter of the cook, like Sally Hemings, Emma Webster was a quadroon. Emma was raised at the house as a member of the family, but was given the choice of spending the rest of her life there as a single "white" woman, in a kind of limbo, or leaving the family and marrying a black man; she chose the latter. . . . After Thomas Jefferson's death, the census record for the house where Sally Hemings lived with her sons identified the family as white.[63]

By telling this story of Anna Sanderson, Israel Grant, Cyrus Webster, and Emma Hatcher Webster, Seaton writes her own family into a history that had vanished except for a cryptic gravestone, people's names, and fading memories—all fragile threads of an oral history so easily lost or forgotten. Honoring these stories as dramatic plays and narratives brings their existence back to life, even if the details will never be confirmed. In this way we all can experience works such as *The Will* and *From the Diary of Sally Hemings* not just as creative renderings of fiction but as intertextual documents that bring an imagined past to life for those of us today searching for meaning in fragments and incomplete histories.

Seaton's work with Thomas Jefferson and Sally Hemings began with *From the Diary of Sally Hemings* when Bolcom asked her to write a diary. Yet the richness of her research and her connection to the subject came not only from her own family's interracial roots, but also from the times when this national news, the aftermath of the results from the 1998 DNA testing, let the world know the Jefferson-Hemings liaison was something to be taken seriously. In a related vein to the diary that Bolcom set musically, Seaton continued with projects on Sally Hemings. In 2003 Seaton wrote a one-woman drama—*Sally*—set at Monticello in the final days before Thomas Jefferson's death on July 4, 1826. Two years later, in 2005, Seaton wrote a full-length play, *A Bed Made in Heaven*, also set at Monticello, but this time during Jefferson's presidency in 1801 in the wake of the accusations made by James T. Callender about Jefferson and Hemings's relationship. Though the Hemings-Jefferson story definitely had the possibility of tapping into the realm of an eroticized exotic, the scientific DNA evidence helped legitimize the topic so that it began an important conversation the United States was having for the first time with itself—it was the first time black and white people in large numbers were speaking together about the different legacies slavery had from multiple racial, socioeconomic, and gendered vantage points.

Prior to this time most people had not even heard of Sally Hemings; before Annette Gordon-Reed's work, Hemings was not mentioned in standard history books. The few who had heard of Sally Hemings were taught to discredit her possible relationship with Jefferson as slander against his name. Mass media and popular culture in the late 1990s seemed to be unsure about the extent of the racist white supremacist views out there and were not sure whether to celebrate or sensationalize their coverage. A central event that capitalized on both strategies was the *Oprah Winfrey Show* on November 12, 1998, that televised a first-time reunion between the black and white descendants from Jefferson and Hemings. The public demand for more information and exposure to these living relatives that connect back to the past led to numerous interviews and appearances by these newly united family members on radio shows, college campuses, and countless public speaking engagements.

During the same time that Annette Gordon-Reed published her first book (*Thomas Jefferson and Sally Hemings: An American Controversy*) in 1997 and the DNA testing of 1998, Edward Ball—the descendent of a prominent South Carolina plantation-owning family—published *Slaves in the Family* in 1998. Winning the National Book Award for Nonfiction and the Ambassador Book Award for American Studies, this book added a complementary voice to the Hemings-Jefferson conversation at this time as a white man looked back on his plantation roots to see how to make sense of this history. He opens the book with a chapter titled "Plantation Memories," and after a few lines, he writes:

> My father, Theodore Porter Ball, came from the venerable city of Charleston, South Carolina, the son of an old plantation clan. The Ball family's plantations were among the oldest and longest standing in the American South, and there were more than twenty of them along the Cooper River, north of Charleston. Between 1698 and 1865, the 167 years the family was in the slave business, close to four thousand black people were born into slavery to the Balls or bought by them.[64]

Ball then writes about how, as he was growing up, this lore was something that was always hovering in the background. His family's history felt both like it was something that needed to be understood and like a history that existed in fragments that needed a more coherent telling, at least for Edward and his generation in the Ball family. His motives were partially to satisfy his own curiosity, to find out the extent of atrocities or benevolence in his heritage: he found examples of both, as both were part of the economy of the slave trade and plantation business.

In a related connection to the Jefferson-Hemings story, the Ball family provides another case of hidden interracial relationships that also was cloaked in an accepted denial that later, when probed more thoroughly, was found to be true. Despite the family history that the Ball men never slept with their slaves, Edward found that this happened, even more than he initially suspected.

> In fact I found a considerable amount of evidence that in each generation going back two hundred years at least one of the Ball men had a mulatto family. The evidence came from black families who told me about the existence of their light-skinned uncles and aunts whose fathers were named Ball and also from paper evidence on the plantations where you would find, for example, Ball men leaving money to black women and giving them freedom.[65]

As we are now learning, the stories that segregate relationships of men and women by race is a narrative of denial about what happened in the past. The revelation of the "truth" to these relationships is not the most provocative point. What makes these narratives part of a useable past is that these histories are rarely isolated by race, ethnicity, and other identity markers. Instead, the aftermath of slavery, sharecropping, Jim Crow, the civil rights era, and the passage of time have provided us with a distance that requires multiple lenses to understand the "big picture." Edward Ball talks about this in an interview after he finished his book.

> I'm trying to bring together black and white history into a shared history. We know a lot about the white South, perhaps too much. In the past thirty years we've learned a lot about black Americans and their journey, but we still seem to think of American history as a segregated legacy. We either enter the Native American story or the black story or the Irish story or the WASP story, and we don't depict American life as it really was lived, which was side by side, ethnicities elbowing and competing with one another.[66]

The legacy of interracial relationships during the time of slavery and shaped by the restrictions of that era is exceedingly complicated for everyone today, and anyone can be affected by it in a multiple of ways: white people today can be descended from black people, black people have certainly looked at the consequences of rape and unwanted sexual abuse during this time when black bodies were considered property. It is difficult to find these situations and almost impossible to figure out the consent agreements that were or were not in place. Similar to the Jefferson-Hemings reunion on the *Oprah Winfrey Show*, Edward Ball appeared in January 1998 on Oprah's show and met with some of the descendants from the Ball slaves. These were people that he had looked up, gotten to know, and shared the history he was researching about his family. When they were together on the show, Ball apologized to this family. When asked about this in an interview and the possible sensationalistic element of such a public apology, Ball is thoughtful in a way that tries to convey an honesty and move away from something artificial.

> There are, after all, between seventy-five thousand and a hundred thousand descendants of the Ball-family slaves. If I were to begin apologizing to every one of these families it would quickly become a meaningless act.[67]

When he apologized on *Oprah* to the Roper family, he had gotten to know them. He says, "I happened to do it on national television and in that way this symbolic act was heard by maybe eight million people, which might magnify its importance. I'm not against apologizing again, as long as it has meaning."[68]

In a nuanced fashion, *From the Diary of Sally Hemings* is a work of fiction that tells the truth about the past and the present. We do not have Sally Hemings's own words or even know many facts about her. As with many heroic and everyday black people in the United States and South Africa, she was part of a past that was all about erasing anything that made her unique and denying her any individuality. Yet in her narrative is woven the fabric of earliest U.S. history. Her story powerfully illustrates how life in the United States (and this can also apply to South Africa) brings together black people and white people—and the consequences of such relationships are among the most painful parts of these histories. In the United States Hemings's story encompasses the Middle Passage, the history of slavery, segregation, and continued inequality. But by uncovering a hidden past, we see another side. This newly revealed history provides a voice that was known by some but denied by most: black people and white people were part of an interwoven tapestry of the nation's beginning. Though some of these relationships were by force and utterly horrible, there seems to be evidence pointing to the possibility of another side that shows complicated love and longevity in couplings and pairings between black people and white people, in spite of the larger climate of racial hatred and oppression. Even in a time when the dominant narrative presented blacks as "scientifically" inferior (as we see in the contemporaneous life of Sartijie Baartman/Sara Baartman/Sarah Bartmann), there was lived evidence to prove the opposite. Sandra Seaton's own family, the current generations of genetically linked Hemings and Jefferson descendants, and the interracial children born on the Ball family plantations reveal that these previously hidden stories are surfacing in recent generations. These narratives indicate that there were white people and black people who saw beyond the falsely perceived intellectual, physical, and moral differences between the two races. Such history is critical to know if we ever want to move closer to safer and more equitable living between races: that even in the face of a potent, long-lasting evil, there has been evidence mounting to prove the contrary and show that racial harmony one day might not be impossible.

Epilogue

In March 2017 I had an opportunity to be in touch with composer William Bolcom and writer Sandra Seaton to ask if they had any current thoughts or comments about *From the Diary of Sally Hemings*. Seaton keeps up with news around the Hemings and Jefferson history and forwarded me the recent article from the *Washington Post*, "For Decades They Hid Jefferson's Relationship with Her: Now Monticello Is Making Room for Sally Hemings," by Krissah Thompson, about the restoration of the room believed to have been the home to Sally Hemmings.[69] This article outlined how archaeologists have been working at Monticello to restore Sally Hemings's room where "her space will be outfitted with period furniture and artifacts, such as bone toothbrushes and ceramics excavated on the property." In addition to my excitement to hear that Monticello was continuing to better incorporate the stories of the slaves who worked there, I was also dismayed to read in the comments section to this article that there were many people who still denied the possibility of a relationship between Hemings and Jefferson and were hostilely dismissive to evidence revealed in the DNA reports. It seems that this history is still fighting acceptance, despite the credible scientific evidence available.

William Bolcom had attended a performance of *From the Diary of Sally Hemings* by Marti Newland and Artis Wodehouse in New York City in 2013 and "thought they were terrific."[70] He also mentioned a few things he was thinking about as he composed the music,

> Sally grew up in the house with the Jefferson children, read the same books in the library and so forth, and could have been well acquainted with white culture possibly more than with her "own." Not that she would have disdained anything like Juba dancing and syncopation. . . . We know from Gottschalk

that ragtime's roots go way back before it became known as ragtime, just as boogie-woogie existed already in the 1900s (then called "sixteen"), but Sally may not have been anywhere to see or hear this music in an early form very much. Only in the last few notes of *Hemmings* does her black heritage peek out shyly at us; it's there but rather buried throughout the rest of the cycle."[71]

With the CD recording by Alyson Cambridge and this performance by Marti Newland (available on YouTube), it is wonderful to see performances of this work becoming available and, hopefully, more integrated into a regularly performed repertory. As is seen from the liner notes and articles about this work, Bolcom and Seaton did not blithely play with history and fantasy in their collaboration. Instead, they carefully examined the historical and musical contexts at the dawn of the nineteenth century, researched all available information about Jefferson and Hemings, and thoughtfully brought in their own experiences around black-white culture in the United States to flesh out a compelling narrative of this story. Though a musical work might initially seem to be an unlikely place for addressing the larger questions around race, gender, and the founding history of the United States, it is precisely the creative artistic space that allows for multiple interpretations to overlap simultaneously. The incarnation of Sally Hemings as a ghostly presence in U.S. history becomes a way to emancipate her existence into a palpable and plausible embodiment.

4 Contextualizing Race and Gender in Gershwin's *Porgy and Bess*

Since its first performance in 1935, *Porgy and Bess* has had a steep climb into recognition as an opera (instead of something better adapted for the Broadway musical theater stage). Aided by the Houston Grand Opera production in 1976 and the Metropolitan Opera production in 1985, in recent decades the work has finally reached the status as one of the all-time great American operas.

The 1920s and 1930s in the United States encompassed the "folk" of both the Harlem Renaissance and the Great Depression, while currents of immigration, the Great Migration (of black people from the rural South to urban centers in the North and West), and definitions of what "Americanness" meant provided foundational support in the construction of a national cultural and artistic expression. This chapter examines how *Porgy and Bess* is situated in these contexts.

There are three themes of inquiry that shape this study. First is the question "Who tells this story?" since the issues of representation form a centerpiece of this work's reception. Second, with regard to how blackness is staged, is how the context of the U.S. Southern and Jewish immigration for the composer and librettists helped shape the telling of story as well as who is being represented. A unique characteristic of *Porgy and Bess* is that it presents multiple and complex representations of black manhood and black womanhood; this discussion brings in the multiple representations of black people with gendered and racialized identities. And third: though this is a story that focuses on blackness, it reveals things about whiteness and Jewishness. As I explore the contexts around the first performances of *Porgy and Bess*, I am conscious of who has watched and continues to watch this story, how the opera resonated with meaning in the past as well as in productions of the opera and adapted versions for the musical stage today.

I start with two focal points, in extended quotations, that reflect this book's greater emphasis on opera in the United States and South Africa.

First, a quotation from William Bolcom, featured composer of *From the Diary of Sally Hemings* in chapter 3, about American opera in the twentieth century. In a 2006 interview, cultural historian Daniel Herwitz asks Bolcom about historical models in American opera, as Bolcom had become a leading opera composer with *McTeague* (1992), *A View from the Bridge* (1999), and *A Wedding* (2002). Bolcom replied:

> But I have to say, if you ask about models, somebody in the press once asked me what I think are the six most important operas in the American twentieth century. Well, I said *Porgy and Bess*, *Porgy and Bess*, *Porgy and Bess*, *Porgy and Bess*, *Porgy and Bess*, and *Porgy and Bess*. I still feel that way. I don't see anyone even come close.[1]

Second, as *Porgy and Bess* has come to occupy the position of the quintessential "American" opera, it is also one that has been performed in multiple presentations in South Africa after the dismantling of apartheid. Journalist Peter Cox covered a production in South Africa that later toured Europe in 2012.

> When the Cape Town opera company first began performing *Porgy and Bess* in 2006, they produced the opera as it was—an American story. But reviewers and fans began pointing out how the opera was so closely linked to the story of black South Africans.
> With that in mind, the company decided to reset the piece in the Johannesburg township of Soweto. They put the piece in the 1970s, when the country was still under apartheid. The opera's dialogue has been infused with Xhosa and Zulu, and some African musical flourishes have been added to the piece.[2]

Later on, South African singer Otto Maidi (who was performing the role of Porgy) said,

> Even though it was composed by an American, the relationship is that it tells our story as black people. . . . It also informs and also entertains at the same time. Everything which happens in Catfish Row, it's really, really, really, going together with our daily lives in the townships.[3]

With William Bolcom emphasizing the central position of *Porgy and Bess* as a foundation for American opera, the productions in South Africa demonstrate that the black musical idioms and character representations resonate with performers, composers, and audiences across the Atlantic. In this chapter I present a concise history of the composition and performance of the work and explore the context around Gershwin's own words that *Porgy and Bess* was an American folk opera. This designation around American music, the construction of the "folk" for European and black people, and the genre of opera were all multivalent in their specific meanings at that time in the early twentieth century. Regarding race, I delve into meanings of whiteness (specifically around anti-Semitism and immigration) and blackness during the time of the Great Migration and in references to black minstrelsy stereotypes.

Finally, I take advantage of this opera, the only one in the current repertory, to examine these multiple presentations of black womanhood. I read these characters, especially the title character Bess, through the various lenses—through an intersectional analysis that brings together race, gender, and a hypersexuality; in the company of another canonical opera heroine (Donna Anna from Mozart's *Don Giovanni*) in the handling of sexual indiscretion, honor, and revenge; and across time, in the interpretation of Bess's role from her presence in DuBose Heyward's 1925 novel *Porgy* through her role in the 1935 opera and in a millennial adaptation of her role in the production that writer Suzan-Lori Parks and director Diane Paulus reimagined for a modern audience. Finally, I listen to an important early interpreter (Leontyne Price) talk about what Bess meant to her, and I consider this role in the career of a legendary performer who was part of the first generation of black opera singers who sang across the color line in the leading opera houses of the world.

Constructing the Story of *Porgy and Bess*

George Gershwin was born in 1898 in Brooklyn, New York, and died unexpectedly in 1937 at age thirty-eight from an undiagnosed brain tumor. One of his last and most important works was *Porgy and Bess*, which premiered in 1935. His untimely death has led to several questions about *Porgy and Bess*—questions that Gershwin would have most likely addressed when he revisited this work, had he lived to oversee subsequent productions of the opera. *Porgy and Bess* was the first work to engage an almost exclusively black cast in the 1930s and that continues, in varied versions, up to the present day to be a pivotal work that features black performers and a story about black people in the United States. From its premiere in 1935 up through the present, *Porgy and Bess* has mobilized integrated audiences and critically speaks to the ways black people have been—and continue to be—configured in an ever-changing American consciousness.

Turning to the more recent and high-profile production on Broadway in 2012 (with previews in Cambridge, Massachusetts, in 2011–2012) that subsequently went on tour in the United States, *Porgy and Bess* has been presented in a so-called "postracial" society that has seen affirmative action instituted, accepted, and now challenged. The messages of *Porgy and Bess* provide a cautionary tale from the past, a yardstick for poor urban and rural centers today, and a lurking fear for the future. Through various modifications to the story and music, the new version for Broadway (2012) updates the work in ways that resonate differently with contemporary audiences. A picture emerges that highlights the experiences of racially diverse audiences and continues to shape the multiple layers of meaning present in *Porgy and Bess* over time. I seek to ask questions about *Porgy and Bess* that opera scholars have not focused on but are very much a part of the life of *Porgy and Bess* as a work that has been consumed by real people (the audience) who have gendered, racialized, and ethnic identities and who bring diverse vantage points into the theater.

I am especially interested in how *Porgy and Bess* has generated meaning since its premiere in 1935 and up through the 2011–2012 revival on Broadway, *The Gershwins' Porgy and Bess*, directed by Diane Paulus and adapted by Suzan-Lori Parks and Diedre L. Murray, with a widely talented cast led by Audra McDonald (for which she won her fifth Tony Award as Bess), Norm Lewis, and David Alan Grier.[4] This production subsequently went on tour (with different performers). I was fortunate to see this production on Broadway twice in the summer of 2012 and then in March 2014 while the show was on tour at the Michigan Opera Theatre in Detroit.

As a musical or as an opera, *Porgy and Bess* is a work that expresses many issues around gender, class, and what it means to be American. Through articulations of blackness, whiteness, and Jewishness, Gershwin brings together how racial and ethnic discourses of the past still resonate today. I outline this path through a discussion of the folk and the quest in the early part of the twentieth century among white and black critics to find an "American" musical voice that was discrete from European dominance. In narratives around Eastern European immigration to the United States and the Great Migration among African Americans within the United States, *Porgy and Bess* articulates experiences of self-definition. Through the established shadows of minstrelsy, *Porgy and Bess* reinforces these stereotypes as well as breaks past them to allow black performers and audience members from all backgrounds to feel the power and the pain such assumptions reinforce.

Introducing *Porgy and Bess* (1935)

Porgy and Bess the opera premiered at Boston's Colonial Theatre on September 30, 1935, and had a New York opening and run at the Alvin Theatre on

Broadway beginning October 10, 1935. The singers composed an all-black cast (with white singers for the few white roles, all of which speak and do not sing—the Detective, the Coroner, and the Policeman). Todd Duncan (1903–1998), a voice professor at Howard University, was Gershwin's original Porgy. In 1945, Duncan became the first black man to sing a large role at New York City Opera, as Tonio in *I Pagliacci* (ten years before Marian Anderson's historical debut as Ulrica in *Ballo* at the Met in 1955). Anne Brown (1912–2009), a twenty-two-year-old Juilliard graduate, was the first Bess. Many other classically trained singers joined these classically trained leads. In addition, John William Sublett (1902–1986), known professionally as John W. Bubbles (and who was one of the leading tap dancers and vaudeville entertainers of the time), played the leading role of Sportin' Life. Though "Bubbles" did not read music and needed to be taught his role by rote, Gershwin admired his musicianship and defended keeping him on, even when others felt he was slowing down the rehearsals. To help coordinate the large chorus community of Catfish Row, Gershwin enlisted Eva Jessye (1895–1992), one of the leading choral directors of time, who had university degrees in classical music training and pedagogy (Western University in Kansas and Langston University in Oklahoma) and experience working with composer Will Marion Cook and in Broadway shows and motion pictures. In addition to having been the choral director for Virgil Thompson and Gertrude Stein's *Four Saints in Three Acts* that premiered in 1934 (the year before *Porgy and Bess*), Jessye's Original Dixie Jubilee Singers (which later become the Eva Jessye Choir) was an ensemble that performed spirituals, work songs, mountain ballads, ragtime jazz and light opera.

Scholars have noted that Gershwin himself was in between the "popular" music tradition with his Tin Pan Alley past and successful Broadway musicals and was also moving into the "classical-art" music tradition with his *Concerto in F*, *Rhapsody in Blue*, and *An American in Paris*; additionally, he was finding his own compositional voice that included a large dose of jazz traditions. Gwynne Kuhner Brown has written about how Gershwin supported the important collaborative voice that the black performers brought to the first performances.[5] My emphasis here is the wide range in the types of black voices Gershwin brought into this work. As a microcosm of the black musical community, *Porgy and Bess* of 1935 shows that there were black musicians who were involved with so many different styles of music from this time—the vaudeville tap dancing popular tradition, classical opera, jazz, and spirituals and black art choral singing.

Porgy and Bess ran for 124 performances at the Alvin (closing on January 25, 1936) and then toured (Philadelphia, Pittsburgh, Chicago, Washington,

D.C.) until March 1936. Though 124 successive performances of a single opera in New York could hardly be called a disaster at that time, it was considered a box office failure because it lost all of its $70,000 investment and the financial backers did not make money. Gershwin's unexpected death in 1937 prevented him from going back to this production and working out the details for what might have led to one or two final versions of the work: one for Broadway and/or one for the opera house. As it is now, we have the version from 1935–36 that Gershwin oversaw, but it can hardly be considered definitive, since he wrote too much music and parts of the composition were cut during the rehearsal period and after the premiere.[6] We also have several other posthumous versions: a film (1959) that is now withdrawn from distribution, several opera productions following the momentous Houston Grand Opera revival (1976), and the Glyndebourne film that originally aired on television in the early 1990s, directed by Trevor Nunn and conducted by Simon Rattle. There are various stage musical versions that were performed in the 1940s through the 1960s.[7]

The 1959 Samuel Goldwyn movie version, directed by Otto Preminger, with Sidney Poitier, Dorothy Dandridge, Sammy Davis Jr., Diahann Carroll, Pearl Bailey, and others (Maya Angelou appears as a dancer in an uncredited role), presents a constellation of many themes that illustrate how problematic the legacy of this work has been. Using the leading black singers and actors of the time, with a bold and accomplished director, this movie version seems to have been a recipe for success. Yet the complications of staging blackness—visually and aurally—in the joint media of film and opera uncovered challenges around race and representation. One issue was that this movie version uses dubbed voices with classically trained operatic voices behind the Hollywood faces. Robert McFerrin sang for Porgy (played by Sidney Poitier) and Adele Addison was Bess's singing voice (played by Dorothy Dandridge). In a historical moment of racial uplift that led into the civil rights era, the film presented a difficult cognitive dissonance with great acting and musical talent portraying a story based on negative stereotypes, adverse assumptions, and tragic outcomes for the black community. While the 1959 *Porgy and Bess* film has been recalled by the Gershwin family and is very difficult to find, it brings to mind some of the same issues with a black setting of a different opera in the Western European tradition, Bizet's *Carmen*. In 1954, five years before Preminger turned to *Porgy and Bess*, he worked with many of the same performers (Dorothy Dandridge, Diahann Carroll, and Pearl Bailey) in an all-black cast in his exceedingly popular film version of Hammerstein's 1943 musical, *Carmen Jones*.[8]

Unpacking Each Word: American Folk Opera

Gershwin called *Porgy and Bess* an American folk opera. He discussed his ideas and motivations for the work in the article he wrote, "Rhapsody in Catfish Row: Mr. Gershwin Tells the Origin and Scheme for His Music in That New Folk Opera Called *Porgy and Bess*" for the *New York Times* on October 20, 1935, just ten days after the New York City premiere.[9]

Though these might sound like helpful labels, all of these terms "American," "Folk," and "Opera" were not straightforward in the 1930s. Moreover, there are several issues surrounding *Porgy and Bess* that are prevalent in the literature: the question of genre, the intent of race, and the status of the score. The question of genre is relevant because *Porgy and Bess* seems to be a work that can exist in multiple forms. Gershwin's own comments on this topic are both helpful and complicated. What is "American" music at this point in history? To whom does the "folk" refer, and what does that mean in the 1930s? What is opera in the early twentieth century, nine years after Puccini died and as no American composer (or one from another nationality, for that matter) had yet emerged as a leading figure?[10]

American Music: The First Decades of the Twentieth Century

From the end of the nineteenth into the first half of the twentieth century, a few examples stand out to show how the identification of music "native" to the United States became a deep concern for white and black audiences invested in America's musical profile. In 1885, Jeanette Thurber, the prominent New York music patron, founded the National Conservatory of Music and the American Opera Company in New York City. Born in Delhi, New York, she was the daughter of Danish immigrant Henry Meyers (a violinist), who sent her for music training to the Paris Conservatory. While in Paris, she was impressed with the French system of providing conservatory training at the government's expense and decided to emulate this in the United States. Through her music knowledge and funding from her wealthy grocery-merchant husband (Francis Beatty Thurber) Jeanette was able to obtain a charter from the state of New York and open these institutions. Progressive for its time, the National Conservatory admitted women and men, as well as African American and Native American students.

In 1891 Thurber sent piano faculty Adele Margulies (also seen as "Margolis") to Czechoslovakia to invite Antonín Dvořák to become the director of the National Conservatory. Dvořák accepted this invitation and served as director from 1892 to 1895. Thurber sought out Dvořák primarily for his success in finding ways to bring his own Czech (Bohemian) identity into classical European music—symphonies, string quartets, and other orchestral and chamber works. Thurber's goal was for Dvořák to find an "American" voice in the United States that could be woven into a classical art music tradition. As an outsider, he might have a fresh ear to ferret out "folk" materials and create American music. Dvořák's most famous compositions from this period in the United States were his symphony in E minor, known as his 9th Symphony "From the New World," and his "American" String Quartet—written during the summer of 1893, when he was in Spillville, Iowa, a small town in the northeast corner of the state with a sizeable Czech immigrant population. Being in an environment where African American and Native American students were allowed to study, Dvořák probably was exposed, even nominally, to these cultures. At the conservatory in New York, Dvořák met Harry T. Burleigh, an African American composer and singer who would sing spirituals to Dvořák and introduce him to that style of music.[11]

From the time of the premiere of Dvořák's 1893 symphony while he was in the United States, the work was heralded as an "American" work, with the folk music of African Americans and Native Americans considered to be the core of the sound of the nation. Referring to Dvořák, J. W. Henderson, (music critic for the *New York Times*), wrote,

> What he has done is to saturate himself with the spirit of negro music and then to invent his own themes. He has made himself completely the master of the fundamental melodic, rhythmic, and harmonic peculiarities of negro tunes. . . . Having thus learned how negro music is made, Dr. Dvorak built symphonic themes. He made melodies perfectly adapted to the processes of symphonic development. . . . Finally, is it American? The answer to his question depends wholly upon the attitude which the American public decides to take in regard to the sources of Dr. Dvorak's inspiration. That both Indian and negro music share some of their peculiarities with the folk-music of the Old World need not be accounted to the discredit of the composer's attempt. In spite of all assertions to the contrary, the plantation songs of the American negro possess a striking individuality. . . . A national song is one that is of the people, for the people, by the people. The negroes gave us their music and we accepted it.[12]

This assessment that Dvořák found American music to be composed of Native American and African American voices became an important current in early-twentieth-century American culture. Dvořák's prominence in helping find an "American" voice in music was mentioned in black commentaries during the time of *Porgy and Bess*. In 1923 John W. Work II, composer and educator, wrote about the "Negro Folk Song" and mentioned Dvořák's role in helping define this music in the United States:

> After Dvorak had made a thorough study of music in America, he pronounced the Negro folk-song "original and American," adding that if America ever had a national music, it must be based upon the songs found among the Southern Negroes. Confident in the hope that it would be the beginning of the national music, he composed his "New World Symphony," employing thematically and characteristically the Negro folk-music as a basis and inspiration.[13]

By 1930, noted writer, diplomat, and historian James Weldon Johnson outlined the important role that African Americans played in New York City from the prerevolutionary days of the eighteenth century through the Harlem Renaissance with a special emphasis on their musical and theatrical contributions. In his discussion of Harry T. Burleigh, Johnson writes,

> Mr. Burleigh was a student at the National Conservatory of Music in New York while Anton Dvorak was director. . . . He not only studied with Dvorak, but spent a good deal of time with him at his home. It was he who called to the attention of the great Bohemian composer the Negro Spirituals and is therefore in that degree responsible for the part they play in the "New World Symphony."[14]

In this passage about Burleigh, Johnson writes as though it is already an accepted understanding that Dvořák's music gave credence to how American music was being defined; behind the scenes we see the voice of Burleigh and the spirituals. Prominent writer about the Harlem Renaissance and Howard University professor Alain Locke, a leading voice in African American life, also recognized the connection between Dvořák and black music. In Locke's 1936 *The Negro and his Music*, he wrote about Dvořák's "From the New World Symphony":

> In the "Largo" of the symphony, we sense the true atmosphere of a Negro spiritual, and in the Scherzo or fast third movement, Papa Dvorak, without fully sensing it, was nose close to jazz, for he took his rhythms and tone intervals from the shout type of Negro dance. In this important pioneering, the record stands that Dvorak's guide and musical interpreter was the Negro musician and composer, Harry T. Burleigh, then a graduate student at the National Conservatory, Brooklyn, where Dvorak taught during his American visit.[15]

Though Thurber, Henderson at the *New York Times*, and the black critics John Work, James Weldon Johnson, and Alain Locke concurred with the assessment of African American music having important roots for an American voice in art music, not all composers in the United States initially followed Dvořák's lead. For example, one of the pioneering "American" voices during this time was New England composer Charles Ives (1874–1951), who is frequently considered to be the first American composer of note to have studied fully in the United States without traveling to Europe to find his American voice. Ives spent his college years at Yale University, and his music shows marked influence from the music he grew up with, notably church hymns, band music his father conducted, and parlor tunes promoted through sheet music popular in American homes. Being associated with Connecticut his whole life, Ives is considered a quintessential American voice with roots in an ethnicity that speaks of New England's historical connection to its puritanical culture of whiteness. Yet it seems that even Charles Ives became aware of the growing attention African American songs, notably the spirituals, were getting. Shortly after James Weldon Johnson, J. Rosamond Johnson, and Lawrence Brown published their art-song arrangements in *The Book of American Negro Spirituals* (1925), Ives wrote "In the Mornin'" (1929), which has the inscription in the score "Negroe Spiritual." He heard Mary Evelyn Stiles sing it in 1929; she had known the work "from her father, Major Robert Stiles, of Richmond, Va., who heard it when a boy. It is quite probably considerably over 80 years old."[16] In Sinclair's catalog of Ives's work, he notes that Ives has used some of the music from the spiritual "Give Me Jesus" in the accompaniment.[17] Ives scholar Gayle Sherwood Magee notes this as "Ives's ethnographic attempt to record an oral tradition outside of his own white New England repertoire that originated in a parallel past, that of African Americans in Virginia."[18] As we assemble this picture, we see a composer from New England known for finding his own "American" voice and who seems to have had little connection with African American life, near the end of his composing career, harmonizing a Negro spiritual. It seems evident that the spiritual and "black" music at this time had something central to do with American identity. We see leaders in the white and black press as well as the first generation of "American" composers at the turn of the nineteenth century to the twentieth being drawn to various repertoires in black music.

In addition to the rather bold declaration that Dr. Dvořák was using Indian and negro music to create a nationalistic American sound, Henderson also brings up a theme that will resurface in Gershwin's comments about his own use of African American folk music. They both claim to have absorbed the style or an "atmosphere" (to use Locke's word regarding Dvořák) of black music. What is at stake with such comments that allow Europeans, white Americans, and black Americans to emulate the music of African Americans as American music? When a race, or ethnicity, becomes recognizable to a larger public, has it succeeded in representing a nation?

American music, by the time of *Porgy and Bess* in the mid-1930s, was still in the early stages of defining itself and figuring out its own "classical" or "art" music. Though Gershwin started out as a Tin Pan Alley songwriter, his move into more "serious" forms of music has given him a special place in early-twentieth-century American musical identity. His combinations—of popular, "low brow" songs and show tunes along with more "serious high brow" rhapsodies and concertos (*Rhapsody in Blue* [1924], *Concerto in F* [1925])—gets at the heart of what American music was developing into: finding a new, homegrown voice that evolved out of, but was not wholly dependent on, European tradition. Yet this combination, especially when it brought in elements of black music—such as jazz and the blues—was something that conflicted with what many people thought an "American" musical voice should be. In the 1930s, jazz and the blues were still considered rather subversive musical forms associated with lower-class society and negative sides of black identity; many white people and some black people shared these ideas. The artistry and skill in jazz and the blues were not generally appreciated until much later, in the 1960s and 1970s. Langston Hughes's poem "The Weary Blues," published in Alain Locke's 1925 collection *The New Negro*, was an early example, against the norm, of praising and accepting the blues as a genre. Taking all of these things into consideration helps illustrate how Gershwin was pushing the comfort zone of respectable society when he announced that his use of black music was part of an indigenous "American" musical voice.

Who Are the "Folk"?

Gershwin began his October 20, 1935, *New York Times* article, "Rhapsody in Catfish Row: Mr. Gershwin Tells the Origin and Scheme for His Music in That New Folk Opera Called *Porgy and Bess*" with discussion of "folk":

> Since the opening of *Porgy and Bess* I have been asked frequently why it is called a folk opera. The explanation is a simple one. *Porgy and Bess* is a folk tale. Its people naturally would sing folk music. When I first began work on the music I decided against the use of original folk material because I wanted the music to be all of one piece. Therefore I wrote my own spirituals and folksongs. But they are real folk music—and therefore, being in operatic form, *Porgy and Bess* becomes a folk opera.[19]

In this oft-quoted excerpt, Gershwin seems to be saying two things at once: the music is "real folk music," yet he also admits that he wrote all of his own original "folk songs" and "spirituals." I am not the first to notice this; Richard Crawford writes about this claim as an example of "fakelore," a term coined by Richard Dorson in 1950, wherein the "raw data of folklore [is falsified]

by invention, selection, fabrication, and similar refining processes for capitalistic gain."[20]

The use of folk in Gershwin's descriptive phrase about the work is especially
rich with meaning. In the 1930s, the term "folk" had multiple connotations.
Scholars have long engaged in the conversation about folk as coming out
of the European context. And it might be helpful to see this in the context
that George and Ira Gershwin were first-generation Russian Jews living in
America. Crawford carefully outlines the use of "folk" as Broadway folk dramas, the rural-urban divide of how folk music reflects community life, the
development of the American Folklore Society in 1888, and the efforts of the
U.S. government to collect folk music before World War I and increasingly
so during the 1930s Depression, when the Federal Music Project, a New Deal
program, "seeking to shore up national identity during economic hard times,
sponsored folk-related projects."[21]

Ray Allen, professor at Brooklyn College, has also looked into the varied
associations of the "folk" in his article "An American Folk Opera? Triangulating Folkness, Blackness, and Americanness in Gershwin and Heyward's
Porgy and Bess." Here Allen explores more of the meanings of "folk" in black
culture and mentions W. E. B. Du Bois's 1903 *The Souls of Black Folk*, Alain
Locke's formation of the "New Negro," and the discourses around spirituals as
embodying an elevated form of black music in Harlem Renaissance writing.
Allen brings the black and nonblack "folk" together at the end of his article
and argues that *Porgy and Bess* helped elevate Southern blacks to join other
nonblack ethnic groups as folk in the United States during the 1930s. Allan
writes,

> The door had cracked open for the spiritual-singing folk of Catfish Row to take
> a seat at the table where they might dine with Steinbeck's wandering Oakies,
> Lomax's singing cowboys, Henry Ford's fiddling hillbillies, and Grant Wood's
> stoic farmers, who had come to embody a deep and distinctly American mythos
> during the tough times of the Great Depression.[22]

I would like to build on this thinking about the "folk" to explore a larger context. One of the complications in writing about this work is the difficulty in
finding a trenchant way to think about blackness. Too frequently, it seems that
the issues have been framed around the dichotomous inquiry: "Is *Porgy and
Bess* racist or not?" This question usually encompasses the assumed narrative
that the "all-white" team of George and Ira Gershwin, along with DuBose
Heyward (who had written the novel *Porgy* in 1925 and had been involved
with the libretto for the opera), wrote about black Southern life from their
"white" vantage point. I find this binary construction to be rather unhelpful

because it feels like a weak assessment of the situation. From my own vantage point, it seems clear (and somewhat obvious by today's standards) that there are many racist things about this work. How do we put these different perspectives in conversation with each other so we can understand the past and how the past resonates today when this work, in its various versions, is performed?

The representation of black life in the 1920s (the time setting for the opera) reinforces many negative stereotypes around minstrelsy. Additionally, the story presents a black community that gambles, kills each other, and succumbs to dangerous drunken and drug-induced behavior. A few characters show hope, such as the religious Serena, who has high morals; yet she suffers the loss of her husband Robbins in the first scene when Crown kills him over a craps game. The most promising family of Jake, a self-employed fisherman, and Clara, who sings "Summertime" to their little baby (all of whom have such a bright future in the beginning of the opera), is decimated when both parents are killed in a hurricane. Their innocent infant is then abandoned by Bess at the end of the opera when she leaves Catfish Row in disgrace.

The reception of *Porgy and Bess* has undergone a sharp current of criticism. Especially compelling are the critiques of the work in the aftermath of the film directed by Otto Preminger, *Porgy and Bess*, in 1959. The film had a star-studded cast with many of the same actors from the director's *Carmen Jones*, just five years earlier in 1954 (Dorothy Dandridge, Pearl Bailey, Brock Peters, and Diahann Carroll), with the addition of Sidney Poitier and Sammy Davis Jr. Many years ago, the rights of this film reverted back to the Gershwin family and was pulled from circulation by the Gershwin estate; it has been very difficult to see this film for decades.[23] Hall Johnson, Lorraine Hansberry, James Baldwin, and Harold Cruse are among many who denigrated the film for its lack of authenticity and the persistence of negative stereotypes.[24] Cruse was especially damning of the work (as an opera, musical, and the 1959 film) and extrapolated his criticism to a larger situation he saw in the corrupt relationship between Jewish and white people against African Americans. James Baldwin situates the film in the context of the recent death of Billie Holiday (and makes the connection between "happy dust" and Holiday's heroin addiction) and, in his candid and penetrating style, outlines the ways black America during segregation, Jim Crow, and the deadly threat of lynching was all too familiar with the realities in the world of Catfish Row. Era Bell Thompson, an editor at *Ebony* magazine, also agreed that the movie perpetrated outdated, negative stereotypes. She writes, "*Porgy and Bess* ain't necessarily a movie. It's a shame!" She concludes her article referring to the broader adaptations of *Porgy and Bess* and summing up a widely held view: "To a whole lot of Negroes, drama, novel or opera, it is 'plenty of nothing!'"[25] Reading these reactions by African Americans who were thoughtful, reliable commentators of black life in their own time reveals a perspective on mid-twentieth-century experiences that could easily fade into the background with the suppression of the 1959 film version. This history of *Porgy and Bess* is relevant today as we shape the "bigger picture" of how this work has produced meaning since its inception, premiere, and the various productions and settings into a continuously evolving present. The sharp critique of *Porgy and Bess* seems to be a persistent, perhaps indispensable, part of its reception.

On the other hand, even I must acknowledge that there are also many things to love about *Porgy and Bess*. Most of the tunes are already familiar through jazz standards ("Summertime," "I Got Plenty o' Nuttin," "Bess, You Is My Woman Now"), and Gershwin's music has that perfect combination of an undulating Puccini-esque lyricism with catchy syncopations that well capture the rhythms of the English language. Gershwin's music achieves many things at once. It involves full-out operatic singing yet still has moments that feel like spontaneous outpouring of emotion. Serena's "My Man's Gone Now" at the funeral of her husband in act 1 showcases operatic virtuosity and brings on the chills of a new widow's wail. The "Oh Doctor Jesus" chorus during the second act hurricane makes you feel like you have walked into a black church vigil. Gershwin's insistence on a black cast makes going to *Porgy and Bess* a unique experience, and one especially exciting for black audiences, for practically nowhere else in the operatic repertory (before or since) do we have the chance to see so many black people onstage—and in the audience.[26]

What Is Opera in 1935?

With the death of Giacomo Puccini in 1924, the grand opera tradition came to a close. As the composer of *La Bohème* (1896), *Madama Butterfly* (1904), and his last opera *Turandot* (left incomplete at his death), the style and tradition of opera as it originated in Italy ended. Though Richard Strauss was still writing operas in Germany in the 1930s through his death in 1949, the situation with the Third Reich impeded the circulation of his later operas until after his death.

This is not to say that no operas written in the twentieth century have joined the canon. British composer Benjamin Britten (born in 1913) began an important career with his first full-length opera, *Peter Grimes*, in 1945 and wrote many more until his last opera, *Death in Venice* (1973), which premiered a few years before he died in 1976. Italian-American composer

Gian Carlo Menotti (1911–2007) achieved his first major triumph with his chamber opera *The Medium* (from 1947) and continued this success with his full-length opera *The Consul* (1950) and the extremely popular first opera written for American television (*Amal and the Night Visitors*, first televised on Christmas Eve 1951).

This situation left the 1930s opera scene open for new voices. Coupled with the desire to find an American voice in classical art music, Gershwin's *Porgy and Bess* filled a noticeable gap. The highly experimental collaboration between Gertrude Stein and Virgil Thompson, *Four Saints in Three Acts*, which premiered with an all-black cast in 1934 (right before *Porgy and Bess*), did not lead to many future performances or initiate a new direction in opera.[27]

The history of American music, including operatic works, has not fully taken into account the compositions of African American composers. This is largely due to a presumption that black composers were either not interested in writing "art" music in a tradition outside of the spirituals or that there was a lack of opportunities for their training and nurturing. While this second notion is definitely truer than the first, it turns out that more scholars are beginning to pay attention to the presence of and compositions by black composers as such works are being found and rediscovered. We know that Scott Joplin wrote operas besides *Treemonisha* that were lost. We have heard the same about William Dawson. William Grant Still has been considered an "exception" as a composer who wrote operas, symphonies, ballets, and many other works that demonstrated his skill and training in the Western European musical tradition. As pioneering scholars find more works by black composers and then study, reconstruct, and perform this music, we begin to understand that it is possible to develop a richer narrative that more fully integrates black voices into the American musical scene. No longer only participating in the creation and formation of ragtime, the blues, and jazz, we now see that Du Bois's famous construction of the double consciousness of black understanding around white and black behavior can present a new way of thinking about American music. There were many black composers and musicians who were well versed in classical music as well as in popular (ragtime, blues, jazz) traditions. The striking new reality is that black composers brought the vernacular popular styles together into classical music. Hence, William Grant Still's use of the twelve-bar blues form and the style of the spiritual for the first and second themes of the exposition in the opening sonata form movement to his *Afro-American Symphony* is not the only case of such double-consciousness voice in music. Henry Lawrence Freeman's use of the saxophone in his opera *Voodoo* (first performed in 1928) presents another example.[28] These are not "exceptions" to our current view of the music of the

United States; instead, they are part of a larger, unacknowledged tradition that needs to be discovered and incorporated into our story of American music. This is the voice that has been hidden, a shadow culture, of black opera that needs to be excavated from the past.

Over time, people have thought of *Porgy and Bess* as the Great American Opera, as well as a frustrating collection of stereotypes that emphasize a vision of black people who speak in a dialect-ridden English, drink and gamble too much, and have a loose moral code. To some extent, both of these assessments of the work are true. The opera touches on intensely human emotions that lead to both great passion and heart-wrenching devastation. Yet it is the music that touches us and gets under our skin in such a way that it feels like a part of us. And this is what makes Gershwin's opera so easy to love and so difficult to stay mad at.

Immigration and the Great Migration

To say that *Porgy and Bess* was produced by a racially homogenous "white" creative team does not tell the full story. Indeed, there was someone on the collaborative team who personified quintessential American whiteness: DuBose Heyward.[29]

Heyward was from Charleston, South Carolina, and though his family was not as financially prominent as it once had been, he could trace his ancestors back to the signing of the Declaration of Independence. Heyward came from deep roots in a well-heeled Southern white heritage. Conversely, George and Ira Gershwin were born to Russian Jewish parents who immigrated to the United States in the 1890s. In my discussion of immigration and the Great Migration in *Porgy and Bess*, race matters. Though a scientific basis to biological differences rooted in race has been disproved in current scholarship, this was not the case for nineteenth- and early-twentieth-century constructions of race, and this directly affects *Porgy and Bess*. Yet rather than starting with the more expected racial discussion about whether or not *Porgy and Bess* is racially insensitive or how blackness is expressed in the opera, I want to spend time on how different articulations of whiteness can be found in the opera.[30]

Scholars in the field of whiteness studies have examined how European immigrants from the turn of the nineteenth century into the twentieth tried to distinguish themselves from blacks when they arrived in America. Sometimes these strategies included distancing themselves from blacks and trying to climb up a hierarchy where slaves and former slaves were conveniently at the bottom of the socioeconomic and educational structure. But this was not the only tactic, and sometimes immigrants joined in abolitionist and social justice movements that combined forces with African Americans and worked toward common goals of social uplift.[31] Regardless of their individual stance, Jewish people themselves experienced anti-Semitism and were branded with negative stereotypes, some of which were similar to those associated with blacks.[32] At the time of *Porgy and Bess*, this was especially relevant. Karen Brodkin, along with other scholars, cites the 1920s and 1930s as "the peak of anti-Semitism in America."[33] An area that has not received much attention in the *Porgy and Bess* literature is the background to the richness of the interactions between blacks and Jews in the 1910s, 1920s, and 1930s. At this time ragtime and the blues, Yiddish musicals, early jazz and klezmer were circulating alongside each other in popular culture and could provide a more nuanced investigation into Gershwin's experience and use of black musical idioms. My discussion here concentrates less on these provocative musical interactions and more on a context for these types of musical intersections: What happens when we think about constructions of race around whiteness, Jewishness, and blackness in the time *Porgy and Bess* was written, and how might this shape our thinking about this opera when it is performed today?

The themes of motion and relocation are brought to the fore when we think about George Gershwin coming from a family that immigrated to New York City at the end of the nineteenth century. To further enrich this discussion, I want to juxtapose the concept of people moving to America with the counterpoint of people moving within the United States, and specifically with the Great Migration. With this internal reshuffling, we see a moment in American history, post Reconstruction and after World War I, that featured the movement of African Americans from the American South to the North and West. *Porgy and Bess* encompasses both worlds of displacement. For George Gershwin, his parents Moshe (Morris) Gershovitz and Rose Bruskin emigrated from the area around St. Petersburg, Russia, in the 1890s, met, and married in New York in 1895. They lived in (and moved around in) New York's Lower East Side—Ira Gershwin recalls the family moving twenty-eight times during his childhood, before 1916.[34]

Isabel Wilkerson has beautifully and insightfully written about the Great Migration in her Pulitzer Prize–winning national bestseller *The Warmth of Other Suns: The Epic Story of America's Great Migration*.[35] In tracing the journeys and stories of hundreds of people, she fleshes out the themes, places, and rhythms of the lives she documents. As this era recedes into the past, Wilkerson outlines this time from 1915 to 1970, conducting her research at the turn of the turn of the new millennium, when the survivors of this movement are dying. With their stories, this narrative—of extreme poverty, utter lack of opportunities for advancement, and the ever-present threat of lynching in the Jim Crow South—is rewritten into current memory and preserved in history. The caricatures of the vicious white roles in *Porgy and Bess* (the Coroner, the Detective, and the Policeman) feel more "real" when reading page after page of Wilkerson's interviews, as we relive some of the terror and constant fear of stepping out of place. The stereotypes in *Porgy and Bess* are usually leveled at the black characters in minstrel garb, and these are certainly present in the opera with the Jezebel Bess, Sambo Porgy, Crown the Buck, and others.[36] Nonetheless, the equally extreme exaggeration of operatic drama in the white characters serves the story well and brings to life some of the lived emotion Wilkerson captures in her documentary study of the motivations fueling the Great Migration.

Scholars have already noted a connection between some of Gershwin's tunes in *Porgy and Bess* that bear resemblance to the style of Jewish secular (e.g., klezmer and Yiddish theater) and liturgical music. Howard Pollack's 2007 biography of Gershwin picks out "Oh Hev'nly Father" (act 2) as "reminiscent of a 'davenning minyan.'"[37] Geoffrey Block has demonstrated that Sportin' Life's "It Ain't Necessarily So," is similar to the familiar Jewish prayer "*Baruch atah adonai*" in melodic shape and content.[38]

In Sportin' Life's centerpiece number on Kittiwah Island "It Ain't Necessarily So," all of the references to the Bible are from the Old Testament, indeed from the first five books of the Bible, also known as the Five Books of Moses or the Torah (Genesis, Exodus, Leviticus, Numbers, and Deuteronomy). With cleverly crafted lyrics about David and Goliath, Moses found in the Nile by the pharaoh's daughter, Jonah and the whale, and Methuselah (living nine hundred years), these stories work well for the Bible-believing people of Catfish Row. Moreover, these stories would also have resonance for those from the Jewish faith, and would therefore speak directly to diverse religious backgrounds in the first audiences through quotations spanning both Christian and Jewish cultural associations. Regarding the handling of "*Baruch atah adonai*," the adaptation of this well-known Jewish prayer appears strategically as it is featured in the "anti-sermon" ("It Ain't Necessarily So") that Sportin' Life delivers after Sunday church services at the picnic on Kittiwah Island (act 2). Making the connection between these two religious traditions allows us today to have a greater appreciation of this charged moment, laden with religious allusions, staging multiple identities at once.

In the Great Migration from the American South to the North and West, specific urban centers emerged as prime locations for people to settle and relocate. Chief in outlining these paths of migration were the railways that provided transportation to new homes and futures. These connections drew lines between otherwise seemingly unlikely geographic locations: people from rural Mississippi would end up in Chicago; people in Florida would easily travel up to New York City. To facilitate these transitions, locals in the new northern cities would help the migrating southern newcomers settle by providing housing, food, support, and networking.

Not only as a primary means of transportation, the railways also posed career opportunities for blacks to earn a respectable living. For example, a specific subgroup of porters that started soon after the Civil War—the Pullman Porters—were men hired to work on sleeping cars. As workers with gainful employment and wages, they soon formed an influential voice, creating the first all-black union in 1925 and were later important agents in the civil rights movement.[39] Trains offered a primary means of delivery in the Great Migration by physically transporting former slaves and their descendants to the North and metaphorically providing them with a route to a more plentiful and safer Promised Land out of the dangers of the Jim Crow South.

One of the southern areas early-twentieth-century African Americans left were communities like the one presented in *Porgy and Bess*. Catfish Row was based on a real place in Charleston, South Carolina, that their native son DuBose Heyward wrote about; however, Heyward changed the name from Cabbage Row to Catfish Row in his 1925 novel *Porgy*. Cabbage Row is an extended building that contains two structures, each three stories tall, connected by a central arcade. It dates back to the Revolutionary War era, but in the early 1900s this structure was a tenement inhabited by African American families of freed slaves. In DuBose Heyward's time blacks would sell cabbages grown in the building's courtyard from their windowsills and doorsteps, hence the name—Cabbage Row. Today, the place is still called Cabbage Row, as well as "Catfish Row."

Near the end of the opera *Porgy and Bess*, Sportin' Life has a big number that lures Bess to get back on "Happy Dust," leave Porgy (who is temporarily in jail), and join him in a high-struttin' lifestyle in New York City. In fact, this is one of the most memorable numbers in the show: "There's a Boat Dat's Leavin' Soon for New York." I suspect that the catchiness of this tune has obscured a central question: *Why a boat*? Who would take a boat from Catfish Row, South Carolina, to New York City, especially when there were several train routes available and running between Charleston and Manhattan.[40]

From the beginning of the twentieth century, from 1900 to 1967, the Atlantic Coast Line Railroad included the Charleston-NYC route. And even earlier than that, in the middle of the nineteenth century and under a different name, the Wilmington & Manchester Railroad connected to the North

Eastern Railroad, which brought in Charleston in 1857. Today these routes continue, and Amtrak easily makes this journey. While boat travel was not unheard of between Charleston and New York City in the early part of the twentieth century, it was certainly not the most common means of travel for ease or saving time after the mid-nineteenth century. By the 1930s, trains were much faster and made personal travel by boat seem almost anachronistic. Nonetheless, Charleston and Manhattan were important port cities along the Eastern Seaboard for transporting cargo and freight. Going back to the eighteenth century, the prominent Schermerhorn family of New York City set up trade with Charleston for rice and indigo. It would be quite plausible for characters such as Sportin' Life with Bess, or even Porgy later on in pursuit of them, to try to use the least expensive means of travel or try to sneak aboard a ship heading to New York City.

While it is probable that Gershwin's characters would take the train, the main question lurking in the background remains: Why should Gershwin have them take a boat from Charleston to Manhattan? In fact, not even George Gershwin himself took a boat from New York City down to Folly Island (off the coast of Charleston) when he went there to learn more about the Gullah culture in June 1934; we know he took the train.[41] With this unusual second look at these memorable lyrics that flow perfectly, smoothly signifying multiple things at once, we can learn a great deal. "There's a Boat Dat's Leavin' Soon for New York" presents a line of trochaic pentameter that jauntily scans with a swing beat over Gershwin's syncopated setting. With the black dialect presented against the syncopation, we hear the voices of these men from Catfish Row clearly. Yet the black men would probably find more consolation traveling in the company of other black train porters. Who takes a boat to New York City? I argue that it is Moshe Gershovitz and Rose Bruskin, Gershwin's parents, exemplars of the Jewish emigrant experience.

I bring these things to our attention not to nit-pick about transportation routes but rather to expose a broader story of how *Porgy and Bess* can be seen to reflect the experiences of George and Ira Gershwin. They were not only writing about the African American experience (what they knew, what they made up, what they learned while working on the show) but also an immigrant experience that was familiar in their family and to many audience members who would have attended the early productions. These were the first generation of children born to recently immigrated Russian Jewish parents who had made the migration to a "Heav'nly Land" (to quote Porgy's last number of the opera—"Oh Lawd, I'm on my way to a Heav'nly Land"). And like many other Eastern European Jewish people who arrived at the end of the nineteenth century seeking opportunity, they traveled by steamship. Does this bring a little of the Gershwin history into the opera? Were they writing themselves into history, consciously or not? Whatever the reason to use the word "boat" rather than "train," the context around it deserves investigation.

In addition to being a landmark work that represents a created experience of African Americans, *Porgy and Bess* as an "American Folk Opera" fits into the larger history of American music, one that encompasses immigrant white and black folk cultures in the United States, as well as a troubled minstrel past. It might also tell us a little about the experiences of being Jewish—and not quite white—in the 1930s.

The Specter of Minstrelsy

A central issue that links the representation of race and gender in *Porgy and Bess* is the history of minstrelsy in the United States. Begun in the 1820s and popular through the 1950s, minstrelsy is a pernicious way of organizing visual and cultural stereotypes about black people in the United States that can still be felt today. In terms of *Porgy and Bess*, there are two connections I would like to make. The first is the popular origin myth of how minstrelsy began; the second has to do with the specific images that have been borrowed and that lie beneath the surface of several characters.

Though the beginnings of minstrelsy as a practice has been written about and traced back to popular theater in the nineteenth century, one of the most common origin stories of minstrelsy connects back to an Irishman named Thomas Dartmouth Rice (aka T. D. Rice). Several sources identify T. D. Rice, a traveling actor, encountering a crippled black man (a slave, a stableman, the legends vary) who was dressed shabbily and singing about "Jim Crow." T. D. Rice decided to imitate the crippled black man onstage as one of his acts, by dressing in tattered clothes, blacking up his face with burnt cork, and doing a dance that had the famous refrain: "Wheel about and turn about and do it jus so, Ebery time I wheel about I jump Jim Crow." Though T. D. Rice was not the first blackface performer, his Jim Crow performances in the late 1820s became so popular that he has become associated with the early stages of the whole style.

In a provocative coincidence, or perhaps something more significant, in exploring the impetus for DuBose Heyward to write his *Porgy* novel, I came across an oft-cited paragraph from the court proceedings of the *Charleston News and Courier*. In the introduction to the 1928 edition of *Porgy* (the play), Heyward writes about his influences and inspiration for the novel and play:

> *Court proceedings being quoted*: Samuel Smalls, who is a cripple and is familiar to King Street, with his goat and cart, was held for the June term of court of sessions on an aggravated assault charge. It is alleged that on Saturday night he

attempted to shoot Maggie Barnes at number four Romney Street. His shots went wide of the mark. Smalls was up on a similar charge some months ago and was given a suspended sentence.

DuBose Heyward prose: Here was something amazing. I had been familiar with the tragic figure of the beggar making his rounds of the Charleston streets. Thinking in terms of my own environment, I had concluded that such a life could never lift above the dead level of the commonplace. And yet this crushed, serio-comic figure, over on the other side of the colour wall, had known not only one, but two tremendous moments. Into this brief paragraph one could read passion, hate, despair.

Inquiry on my part added only one fact to the brief newspaper note. Smalls had attempted to escape in his wagon, and had been run down and captured by the police patrol.[42]

A side note to this last sentence is that the goat cart (court proceedings) was used in the *Porgy* play from 1927 and the wagon (Heyward's prose) made its way into most productions of the *Porgy and Bess* opera through the 1980s.

Hence the characters behind the so-called beginning of minstrelsy as a genre and the specific inspiration that led to the source for Gershwin's *Porgy and Bess* turn out to be two crippled black men. Crippled black men! Why was it that, around ninety years apart (the 1830s for T. D. Rice and minstrelsy and the 1920s for DuBose Heyward and Porgy), a genre and then source for one of the most contested American operas would come out of such similar roots: crippled black men whose plights were taken up by white men who were fascinated by them. Was it their exotic foreignness? Was it the ridicule? Was it the desperate presentation of humanity?

Returning to Thomas Dartmouth Rice: the character he developed—Jim Crow—also evolved into Sambo and Uncle Tom, the stereotype of docile and not very intelligent black men who were seen as being harmless and who sang, danced, and smiled a lot. Other negative characters that developed out of this tradition were the Buck (a large threatening black man who only wanted to rape women—preferably white women)—and the Trickster (who also could be called "Zip Coon"), a mischievous and dangerous character who brings trouble and cheats people out of their money and honor. In terms of women, the two most common roles are the Mammy and the Jezebel. The Mammy was a large black woman who took care of white families—cooking and cleaning, while her own family fended for itself. She was a domineering presence and was seen as completely asexual. The Jezebel is a highly sexualized black woman who tempts all men (especially white men) and loves to be sexually used. All minstrel stereotypes are limited in the depth of their characterizations and do not allow for fully rounded portrayals. They are shorthand references reinforcing a patriarchal white-supremacist ideology that prevent a role, or narrative, from developing and moving past established racist formulae.

In *Porgy and Bess* these minstrel character types lie just beneath the surface of many characters. Though all of the primary roles in the opera are fleshed out enough to keep our attention and cause us to begin to care about their plight in the plot, the male characters of Sportin' Life as the Trickster (with elements of Zip Coon) and Crown as the overly sexualized and dangerous Buck stay close to their formulaic stereotypes. The women's roles (which I dicuss more fully in the next section) also reference minstrel stereotypes: Maria has elements of the Mammy; Bess is clearly borne of the Jezebel.

The one male character who starts on one track, deviates a bit, and then returns to the minstrel model is Porgy. As a crippled beggar who charms spare change out of strangers, Porgy's seemingly harmless nature easily fits him into the Sambo stereotype when we first meet him. In most productions, his "I Got Plenty o' Nuttin'" reinforces the persona of a poor black man who knows his inferior status and accepts his lot.[43]

In *Blackness in Opera* I wrote about the different constructions of masculinity in early twentieth-century opera and brought Porgy into this comparative picture.[44] As opposed to the heroism of the nineteenth century, the early twentieth century presents a time of crises and antiheroic behaviors in leading operatic men; I demonstrated this in analyses of the male title characters of Berg's *Wozzeck* (1925), Krenek's *Jonny Spielt Auf* (1927), Gershwin's *Porgy and Bess* (1935), and Britten's *Peter Grimes* (1945). Though this is a trend for leading male characters in opera, there also emerged a different moral code for black and nonblack characters; black characters are not punished for their crimes and seem to have lower expectations placed on them. Unlike the tragic endings of their nonblack operatic colleagues, the black leading men do not pay for what they have done wrong; instead, they are forced into the role of the entertainer who sacrifices his humanity for the sake of leaving the audience with a rousing, hand-clapping finale.

In the beginning of the opera, Porgy starts out in line with the Sambo image: he is happy to be back in Catfish Row after the busy day begging in the white city (for the "Buckra" money) and ready to pass the evening gambling with his neighbors. Porgy's character as the Sambo minstrel becomes more complicated and expanded after he falls in love with Bess, especially after the depth of emotion they express in their duet "Bess, You Is My Woman Now" / "Porgy, I's Yo' Woman Now." At this point, the happy-go-lucky Sambo moves into a more three-dimensional characterization wherein he starts to care about someone other than himself. He lives his life with Bess as a family; they take in Clara and Jake's orphaned baby after the hurricane, and he defends Bess's honor by fighting (and killing) Crown when he comes back to Catfish Row to claim Bess. Yet the final vision of Porgy recombines elements of the minstrel character after he learns about Bess running off with Sportin' Life to New York City. While his disappointment is palpable, Porgy reverts to the role of the entertainer as he puts on a happy face at the end of the show and leads the chorus in the rousing final number "Oh Lawd, I'm on My Way to a Heav'nly Land."

Porgy's optimism that he could be reunited with Bess is not what makes his character ring false at the end. What ultimately undercuts his integrity and heroism is that he has not earned them. By the end of the opera, he lives unpunished for the murder of Crown and within the larger context of his reality in Catfish Row: the brutality of Jim Crow and segregation, his crippled body, and extreme poverty. As I wrote in "From Otello to Porgy," "the success of the final curtain is keeping the audience from making the connection between what we *want* to have happen and what lies within the realm of probability; the reality and Porgy's fantasy are two entirely different things."[45] Porgy's rousing final number re-inscribes the artificiality in the heroism of his character. Though he suffers unjust social circumstances, and we want him to triumph above such undeniable odds, his heroism has been ransomed by the minstrel imperative to have us clap and smile at the end rather than have us identify with him as a more true-to-life character who nobly suffers tragic consequences.

Womanhood in *Porgy and Bess*

What is at stake when we think about *Porgy and Bess* as "an American folk opera," an embodiment of minstrel stereotypes, and an intersection of modern-day race, class, and gender dynamics—along with the rubric of a hypersexuality—when the work is performed today? In this section I focus on how racialized and gendered components work in the characterizations for the women in *Porgy and Bess*: Clara, Serena, Maria, and Bess. I extend the section on Bess by analyzing a specific scene (the confrontation with Crown on Kittiwah Island) in two versions, the 1935 opera and the 2012 production on Broadway. I juxtapose characterizations of Bess in the different shaping of this scene. At the end of this section, I bring in another voice—an interview with Leontyne Price—to explore an additional angle: how Bess has resonated with one of her famous early interpreters.

While the opera comes from DuBose Heyward's 1925 novel *Porgy*, and the play *Porgy* that Dorothy Heyward adapted in 1927, the opera was called

Porgy and Bess and increases the voice of Bess—her presence in the drama as a whole—as a more central character. Musically she does not have full-blown solo numbers (as Porgy does), but she has important numbers with the chorus and significant sections of solo singing in duets with Porgy and Crown. Most important, compared with the other women in the opera, Bess is the only character who goes through a significant evolution, changing and developing over time. Even though Serena starts out married and then loses her husband, this happens in the first scene of the opera, and her character is then set for the remainder of the opera. The other women have specific roles they fulfill and primarily remain static in terms of their character and beliefs.

Early in the opera after the overture, Clara opens the first act with the nearly show-stopping, and arguably the most famous, number in the opera, "Summertime." Though this aria has been transformed into every imaginable style, from multiple jazz standards up through Janis Joplin's famous cover with Big Brother and the Holding Company,[46] its original context is as a lullaby that Clara, a new mother and devoted wife, sings to her fussing baby. In the hubbub of the opening scene, which takes place on a Saturday night on Catfish Row, the men are playing a craps game and the women are socializing while the children are running around. Clara's lullaby brings all of the groups onstage together as she walks between the men and women singing to her infant son.

"Summertime" is remarkably high in the soprano range with a slow-moving lyrical line. Musically, Clara's voice provides a counterpoint to the men's and women's choruses, her high, light soprano voice soaring over the more rhythmically active choral interjections. Clara's voice signals her youth and innocence as an attentive and caring mother. In the familiar words to the lullaby ("your daddy's rich and your ma is good looking") she soothes the child to sleep with the message that the living is easy and their family is stable. Clara is married to Jake, a fisherman, who obviously loves his wife and child as he takes the baby and banters with Clara when he playfully sings "A Woman Is a Sometime Thing." This is a young, promising family where we find a well-employed breadwinner, a devoted mother, and family plans for the child go to college. Yet this picture tragically changes through the course of the opera. Clara begs Jake not to take the boat out during the onset of the hurricane season, but Jake is eager to make money for his family. When Jake's boat gets caught and lost in the big storm (at the end of act 2), Clara blindly runs out and perishes as she tries to find him. The young baby with so much to look forward to in the opening scene is orphaned by the end of the second act of the opera.

Far from a minstrel stereotype, Clara is a role that brings an element of integrity to the opera; as a character her behavior feels genuine (she acts like a loving mother and wife) and seems to have the individuality of asserting her own independence. In act 2, when she runs out to look for Jake in the hurricane, she abandons predictability, even at the expense of making an uncharacteristically bad decision. Up to this point, nothing in her role had prepared us to think she would leave her baby and run out into a dangerous storm, risking her life. Such behavior makes her character appear to have its own agency, in that she can make decisions on the spot and not act from a predestined script; her behavior does not follow clear stereotypes but is wrenched between her love and sense of duty as a mother, wife, and young woman. When she and Jake die in the hurricane, a sense of optimism is lost in the plot. The embodiment of the community's hope for the future has been randomly killed off.

From the opening scene of the opera's first act, a trope woven throughout the opera emerges: women bear the consequences of men's shortsighted actions. Serena, the churchgoing, devoted wife of Robbins, is the victim of the first tragedy of the opera when Crown, in a drunken stupor and high on "happy dust" (the opera's name for an early-twentieth-century version of cocaine and/or heroine), kills Robbins over an argument about the craps game. Serena is a soprano with a heavier voice that illustrates her older age and greater maturity than Clara, but she is still a woman in the prime of life. Her lament at Robbins's funeral, "My Man's Gone Now," shows how easily the fate of women on Catfish Row is beyond their control and tied to the fortune of the men in the community. In the second scene of act 1, the funeral of Robbins has Serena pleading with the community of Catfish Row, and then with the funeral director, to help her pay for a proper burial for her husband so that his body is not given to be dissected by medical students. (Serena's concern references the inadequate healthcare and discriminatory medical treatment African Americans have historically received. With evidence based on personal experience and the infamous cases of the "Tuskegee Study of Untreated Syphilis in the Negro Male" (1932–1972) and the use of cells from Henrietta Lacks, Serena's desperation in this scene was real and resonated with original audiences as well as audiences today.[47]) Without burial insurance, the dignified woman who prays and goes to church is brought to grief and vulnerability through the course of bad luck. Nonetheless, she survives and remains both an active character in the plot as well as a strong member of the community.

Like Clara, Serena is not borne of minstrel stereotypes and instead embodies a different type of black woman onstage. With her young innocence, new motherhood, and high, sweet soprano voice that effortlessly soars in lyrical melodic lines, Clara fits the typical ingénue. Serena gives us something different, a black womanhood that is not usually portrayed. She is a woman in love, devoted to her husband, and financially aware (we see that she holds the purse strings when Robbins asked her for gambling money). We also see her character undergo hardship that she regally bears in her move from wife to widow. We hear her huge, controlled, warm, and powerful voice. She sings with the lyrical drama of a *spinto* or dramatic soprano that can also cross over to a well-managed vocal Broadway belt. Serena defies pigeonholing because she takes on whatever she is asked to do. Though she did not have her own children, we know by the end of the opera, after Bess abandoned Clara and Jake's orphan baby and headed up to New York City, that Serena will be one of the leading women in the community who will take over the raising and nurturing of that child (it is Serena who is holding the baby when Porgy returns from jail at the end of the opera). Serena is a single woman who might get married again, or not; however, she knows how to survive without a man (as she aptly lets us know in "My Man's Gone Now"). She is a leader in the community and, to many in the audience who could make the connection, Serena well represents an unsung member of a black middle class who lives a respectable life, even when her financial situation is more precarious and survival depends on bringing the community together for collective empowerment.

Maria is the older matriarch who owns a small restaurant business and is the de facto leader to whom people look when anyone is in trouble. Maria has a mezzo-soprano voice that shows her older age and commanding authority. Maria looks out for Porgy, and the audience knows that Bess has truly been accepted into the community of Catfish Row when Maria befriends her and convinces Bess to go to the picnic on Kittiwah Island. Maria represents the community values and shuns Sportin' Life (in her number "I Hates Yo Struttin' Style"), even when you think he might have worked his way into a partial respectability, with his big number "It Ain't Necessarily So," on Kittiwah Island. Though Maria certainly reflects elements of the Mammy minstrel character type, this is not the full essence of her character, and she upsets the Mammy elements she does express. As the Mammy, Maria is shown out of the workplace and in an all-black world; in the absence of caring for white families, she is as she would be at home. Her character takes her strength of tending the domestic sphere and uses it to hold the community of Catfish Row together.

Maria presents the case of an upended minstrel stereotype who is also given a more fleshed-out persona that becomes nearly three dimensional in her portrayal. Unlike Porgy, whose ending reconfirms the boundaries of a staged black masculinity that constrains his heroism, and Bess, who reverts to her flawed Jezebel ways at the end when she succumbs to Sportin' Life and leaves Catfish Row, Maria acts heroically throughout the opera. As a mezzo-soprano, her vocal and character types come with a deep legacy in opera that pairs deep treble timbres with power, authority, and heroism.

The nineteenth century established a dual connection between the mezzo-soprano voice and a path different from the soprano lead. In the first half of the primo ottocento, the 1810s and 1820s, this voice type frequently portrayed travesti roles wherein mezzos sang as the male heroic lead (for example, the title role of Tancredi, *Tancredi* [1813] and Arsace, *Semiramide* [1823], both by Rossini) before the tenor took over that position. Later in the nineteenth century the low mezzo-soprano less frequently had a leading role, but when she did, she had a different path than the higher sopranos who sang the Romantic heroine. Nonetheless, the mezzo-sopranos retained their connection to strength and access to power. Aspects of ancestry to Gershwin's Maria can be seen in Verdi's Ulrica (*Un Ballo in Maschera* [1859]), a sorceress who can speak with the supernatural, or Wagner's mythic goddess Fricka (who appears in the first two operas of his Ring cycle, *Das Rheingold and Die Walküre*), who safeguards the rules and ultimately maintains order. Though I am not arguing that Gershwin deliberately made any of these connections from nineteenth-century opera, I bring them up to provide examples of how Maria's role has, and can still, resonate with various audiences, particularly those who have experience with opera.

Breaking through the minstrel conventions of the Mammy, Maria, with her deep mezzo-soprano, can also be heard in opera as a voice that has strength that comes from outside of customary sources. She confronts traditional gendered conventions with a strong vocal presence that can be both nurturing and authoritarian as it reinforces the rules and expectations that work outside a presumed white patriarchy. My reading of Maria borrows from, but ultimately inverts, the stereotypes of the minstrel Mammy. Rather than following the master's rules by taking care of his house and children, Maria calls the shots and runs the community.

The leading woman in this opera, Bess, is the abused, drug-addicted girlfriend of Crown, later love interest to Porgy, and ultimately the companion to Sportin' Life when they leave Catfish Row together. She is a soprano that is heavier than the light voice of Clara, not quite as heavy a voice as Serena, and higher in range and timbre than Maria. Like all three of the other women, musically Bess can hold her own as she sings in different situations, and her vocal style adapts to her evolving characterization. Bess's vocal line soars in her love duet with Porgy, and she becomes a bona fide operatic heroine as they declare their love and fidelity to each other. Yet Bess's vocal role also gets heavier and more muscular in the scene with Crown on Kittiwah Island after the picnic. As she fights with him, her music grows more desperate when she tries to resist Crown's strength. Unlike any other female role in the opera, we see three different phases of Bess's character. The opening woman, when she is first introduced and is associated with Crown, is the hussy Jezebel who drinks hard, takes "happy dust," and keeps up with the rough lifestyle required to be Crown's girlfriend. We then see the rehabilitated Bess who seems to get over Crown, loves Porgy, and learns how to be a member of Catfish Row; she becomes an accepted member of the community. After the scene with Crown on Kittiwah Island, Bess is never quite the same, as her spirit has been broken. One of the strengths of her musical line and dramatic path is that as she moves in different directions, her persona can be interpreted in contrasting ways.

Though Bess's role comes out of the Jezebel minstrel stereotype, this is not her static characterization. Throughout the opera, we see how Bess relates to Crown, Porgy, and Sportin' Life as she becomes connected to each one; she retains a sexualized element in her character as she interacts with each man. At various points in the opera, Bess is paired with each one as she enacts different models of desire, consent, abuse, and resignation (as I discuss later in the chapter). We also see how Bess is juxtaposed to the other women in the opera (Clara, Serena, and Maria) and how she incorporates elements from each of their characters into her behavior. Bess has the least direct interaction with Clara and Jake. It is as though their idyllic domestic relationship in the first half of the opera has little relevance to Bess's lifestyle or her aspirations at that time. Yet after the hurricane, Bess becomes the surrogate mother for their abandoned baby and, for a short while, stands in with Porgy as the highlighted mother-father-infant family we see in Catfish Row.

Serena and Maria are two strong figures in the opera and provide important models of black womanhood in Catfish Row. Widowed by the end of the first scene of act 1, Serena then joins Maria as exemplifying the different roles single women take on in the community. This is a lesson that Bess never learns. Bess always remains connected to a man and fails to be steady on her own, whether it is over the short duration of the picnic on Kittiwah Island one Sunday afternoon or for the several days Porgy spends in jail in act 3. Ultimately, Bess has a difficult time living any of the roles of respectable womanhood, and this is where she is undone by the Jezebel roots of her character. She runs out on being a mother and leaves the family she had created with Porgy when Sportin' Life tempts her with drugs ("happy dust") and a life of excitement in New York City. By leaving the South for the North, Bess and Sportin' Life are rejecting the limits of the world of Catfish Row in search of an unattainable future in the North. In the world of *Porgy and Bess*, the promises of the Great Migration outside the South are unreachable and dangerous. However, the world inside Catfish Row is neither a safe haven nor an arena where the inhabitants can thrive. One of the challenges of this opera that keeps it within the limitations of the minstrel world is that the black characters are never far from destruction or devastation; their fates are tied to the bleakest vision of their existence. They are not given a full humanity wherein they can dream possible, plausible, and probable dreams that let them prosper and succeed.

As a way to further explore a deeper characterization of Bess, I turn to two productions of the same scene and discuss the different interpretations the directors and performers present. The two productions come from the opera version (and I will refer to the widely available Glyndebourne production directed by Trevor Nunn) and the recent Broadway musical version (*The Gershwin's Porgy and Bess* [2012]); each presents different sides of Bess and the evolutions of her character.[48] The scene in question appears as act 2, scene 2 of the three-act opera and at the end of act 1 of the two-act Broadway musical—the end of the Kittiwah Island scene when everyone is going back to the boat to the mainland after the Sunday picnic and Bess is detained by her confrontation by Crown. The result is that Crown overcomes Bess and, despite her protests (this is after she had been living with Porgy), Crown drags her offstage for a sexual encounter. In the whole work, this is the most sexually violent scene and the question of interpretation is how the director and performers interpret Bess's nonconsent to Crown's forceful physical sexual advances.

The dramatic situation in both productions takes into account that Bess is in an abusive and destructive relationship with Crown. She asks Crown, "Oh what you want wid Bess?/She getting' ole now....You know how it's always been with me,/These five years I been yo' woman,/You could kick me in the street, And when you want me back,/You could whistle, an' there I was/Back again, lickin' yo' hand." Her text further states that she wants to be with Porgy and that she wants Crown to leave her alone. Her last words in this scene to Crown are "Take yo' hands off me,/I say, yo' hands, yo' hands, yo' hands." With each repetition of "yo' hands" it is possible to hear her music becoming less resolute; a plausible interpretation could see Bess as weakening to the familiarity of always giving in to Crown as he is used to taking whatever he wants.

In the Glyndebourne production of this scene, there is room for uncertainty in how to understand Bess in this scene. Is she a woman worn down by

Crown out of defeat, or is she unsure of how to fight the unhealthy feelings she still might have for him? Though there is no denying that Bess is trying to resist Crown as she struggles to push him away and tells him to let her go, it is possible to watch this scene and feel the ambiguity (about whether or not her resolve against Crown has given way).

Though sexually violent and pushed to an extreme, there is precedent for this type of sexual tension and violence in a canonic opera from the late eighteenth century: the beginning of Mozart's *Don Giovanni*. In a stylized (and usually less explicitly staged) violence, the opening of Mozart's 1787 opera presents a conflict between Don Giovanni and Donna Anna. Immediately following Leporello's opening number about not wanting to be a servant anymore (*"Notte e giorno faticar"*), Donna Anna tries to hold onto Giovanni physically and restrain him from leaving. She sings, *"Non sperar, se non m'uccidi/chi'io ti lasci fuggir mai!"* (There is no hope, unless you kill me, / that I will ever let you go!). We see the two disheveled characters in Donna Anna's bedroom (or, as sometimes staged, at the doorway of her bedroom), where they have recently had a sexual encounter, and it is clear that Don Giovanni is trying to leave while Donna Anna is trying to restrain him from going. Directors have taken liberties with this scene to make it seem that either Donna Anna is wanting to continue the sexual affair that has just happened or Donna Anna has just been sexually violated (no consent given) and is trying to hold on to the masked perpetrator so that he can be punished. Though both interpretations affect the characterizations of Donna Anna—she consented, enjoyed the sexual encounter, and is angry that the masked man is leaving, or she did not consent and is trying to bring justice to her rape—the result in the opera is played out the same way. In the terms of the opera, Donna Anna's virtue has been violated, her father (the Commendatore) is killed while trying to defend her, and she is a woman whose honor must be restored. Regardless of her consent, Donna Anna's integrity is ultimately not compromised because her father was killed protecting her honor. Even if she had briefly consented to the sexual encounter in the moments preceding the opening of the opera, it is all reversed when her father is sacrificed and she devotes the rest of her time (and the mission of her fiancé Don Ottavio) to avenging her father's death. Hence, the issue of "honor" becomes more associated with the Commendatore's death in fighting to defend his daughter and less connected to any actions directly initiated by, or perpetrated against, Donna Anna.

No one dies defending Bess's honor. Instead, one could argue that this is in part why Porgy kills Crown later in the opera. However, those actions also seem to be motivated by the fear that Bess will leave when Crown comes back to claim her; either Bess is weak and will be seduced by Crown, or he will remove her from Porgy by force. When Porgy kills Crown in revenge, any nobility of the action is nullified by its cold-blooded calculation. When Don Giovanni kills the Commendatore, the Don is ultimately punished when the Commendatore returns at the end of the opera and drags Don Giovanni down to hell. Rather than the sacrifice of the Commendatore, Porgy gets away with murder and is never brought to justice. Though his intent might be to defend Bess's honor, Porgy loses something in exchange; he no longer embodies the upright citizen who abides by the law.

In *Porgy and Bess*, the incidents that happened on Kittiwah Island besmirch Bess's reputation, regardless of one's interpretation of those events. In the opera, we know that Crown is violent and dangerous; he killed Robbins in the first act and he now forces himself on Bess. Her honor is compromised because she has a sexual encounter with Crown, after pledging her love to Porgy (earlier in their nearly show-stopping duet "Bess, you is my woman now"/"Porgy, I's yo' woman now"). If Bess is seen as wanting Crown back, she is further flawed for cheating on Porgy. This is not to imply that Bess as a victim of rape should be blamed; she clearly says "no" multiple times to Crown (in the libretto several times she says "Lemme go" and "Take yo' hands off me"). The point here is that Bess is abused by Crown, and her innocence is weighted down by his violence against her, regardless of whether she resisted him forcefully or was weakened in her resolve. When she gets back to Catfish Row from Kittiwah Island she is delirious, sick near death, physically and morally defiled. In addition to physical healing, she seeks moral redemption.

A difficulty in watching this scene today is to reconcile current understandings of sexual violence with those from the past. In both the opera and Broadway version the tension in the drama derives from whether or not we believe that Bess truly loves Porgy and how the director treats the aftermath of her attack. There is no confusion about Crown's violence and coercing Bess to have sex. For most of us today, there is no question that Bess is not giving consent, and this should guarantee Bess's innocence. Today we see Bess as the victim of a sexual crime.

For me, the Broadway musical presents a less ambiguous version of Bess than the Glyndebourne production, one that feels more cognizant of today's understanding of sexual violence and its lingering damaging effects. Though she refuses Crown initially, eventually Bess capitulates, and we see her subjugation as she yields to Crown and returns his violent groping with a desperate submission. Yet this is not a true consent because she is defeated and hates herself for it.[49] During this pivotal scene, we see how she is not just distraught but through this final encounter with Crow, Bess has been damaged in such a way that she never fully gets over it. Even when she goes back to Porgy, he forgives her and she says she wants to be with him—yet there is something broken in her that cannot be fixed. Not all of Porgy's love or the acceptance of Catfish Row can fully save her. The audience senses that perhaps she betrays Porgy at the end of the opera not because Sportin' Life has convinced her to be with him but rather because since Kittiwah Island, she no longer feels worthy of Porgy; her honor and self-worth have been stripped from her. In this scenario, it is possible to see her decision to leave Catfish Row at the end of the opera as though she were operating under a twisted sense of honor: her choice to leave Porgy is her internal logic not to saddle him with her own flawed self.

Unlike Donna Anna, Bess (in both the opera and Broadway musical) has lost her inner sense of integrity. This is all the more poignant, because there is an added scene in the Broadway version, after Bess comes back from Kittiwah Island, where the women of Catfish Row bathe her and help her through her fever and recovery. In the opera she is only seen with Porgy watching over her, but in the musical, one sees Bess more fully integrated into the community where the women have accepted her as one of their own. In what becomes a communal scene in the musical, it is as though the women of Catfish Row baptize and anoint Bess as they wash her and see her through the delirium. It thus feels as if Bess is losing so much more in this musical version, since she has the other women supporting her and even almost overcomes being the lost Jezebel she was at the beginning. In the musical, Bess is forgiven and becomes one of us—one of the community and the audience—who witness her evolution and breaking free of the stale minstrel caricature. Her redemption is within her grasp, she just does not feel she deserves it.

Bess Onstage and in the Audience

Let's explore a complementing interpretation of Bess that starts from a performer's perspective and moves on to illustrate how that view articulates something that has resonated and continues to do so with a lot of women who sit in the audience. In James Standifer's documentary *Porgy and Bess: An American Voice* (1997), Leontyne Prince talks about singing Bess"

> Being Bess was already half of me, I mean most of me anyway . . . it wasn't a matter of sort of accenting this or accenting that. Well, there was little to prepare for. I don't mean saying that [about?] the character itself. I mean being a . . . being wonderfully black . . . wonderfully, a, a, a[n] unhampered [untampered] by, you know having to, I don't know it's just sort of, I'm getting sort of side tracked by, you know a. . . . like here I am, isn't it terrific.[50]

This is not an easy transcription to make, nor is the meaning perfectly obvious; though I think the message gets across more clearly in the live interview. Let me provide a little context.

When she sang the role of Bess, Leontyne Price was early in her career (1953, twenty-five years old). As a student at the Juilliard School she sang Alice Ford (1949, in Verdi's *Falstaff*) and was cast in a revival of *Four Saints in Three Acts* by Virgil Thompson in 1952, right before she was cast as Bess. Later, as her career matured and she became one of the greatest singers in the world, her roles focused more on the standard repertoire of Mozart, Puccini, and especially Verdi. Though she definitely was a progressive singer—as the muse for Samuel Barber and her roles as Handel's Cleopatra (*Giulio Cesare*) and Poulenc's Madame Lidoine (*Dialogues des Carmélites*) show—the mainstay of her repertory was not focused on "black" characters after her early stints as Bess and in *Four Saints*. (The one tremendous exception is the title role in *Aida*.)[51]

My point here is that in the interview for Standifer's documentary, when Price is recalling her time as Bess, she says, "Being Bess was already half of me, I mean most of me anyway . . ." and she refers to Bess as "being wonderfully black." Without trying to simplify Price's characterization of Bess, since she struggled to find the full expression of her thoughts, it is easy to see in the interview that there was an animation to her comments that seem to reflect a sense of ease with understanding where Bess, the character, came from. Perhaps Bess had a backstory that was easier for the young Price, newly arrived in New York City from Laurel, Mississippi, to immediately grasp than the Elizabethan Alice Ford (of Verdi's *Falstaff*) or the other repertory roles she was learning at Juilliard.

Hearing Price talk about her memories of being Bess opens up a suppressed and hidden image of blackness that many black women in the United States have internalized. Bess is the outsider who works hard to fit in, to assimilate, or at least not to be the outsider. Though the neighborhood of Catfish Row is all black, it is not a far leap to see Bess as a metaphor for always being outside the norm. She shows us what it is like never to feel fully accepted. In a palpable way, this makes her connection to Porgy even stronger through Porgy's poignant acceptance of his role as an outsider due to his physical limitations and disability.[52]

Bess's presence proves that there are different expectations for some women (women who fall within expected norms, for instance) than for other women (who fulfill marginalized stereotypes). When it is so rare to see any opera that has at least one compelling, fleshed-out black character, the all-black environment in *Porgy and Bess* highlights multiple types of women, and it is hard for any black woman in the audience not to see herself at least partially represented in the different permutations of black womanhood presented in these roles. Race definitely matters, but as the presumed all-white environment of most operas allows a "universal" connection among the audience, so too does the figure here of Bess as a doomed heroine bid all women to examine her plight. It is not as though her blackness is irrelevant; it is just that everyone is invited to see, understand, and accept or condemn her. Regardless of what these judgments will be, they are—without a doubt—shaped by racial and gendered experience of the observer. Bess provides not only Leontyne Price the opportunity to say "Bess was already half of me," such a powerful role in this opera allows all of us to see things from a vantage point that includes at least some of the marginalized experiences of being an outsider.

Listening to Leontyne Price discuss her interpretation, performance, and internalization of the role of Bess brings together the three central themes of inquiry in this study: who is in the story, who tells the story, and who watches the story. As a Southern black woman born a few years before *Porgy and Bess* was written, her connection to the historical context, her understanding of the minstrel stereotypes, and her experiences of the drastic restrictions during Jim Crow segregation provide a different depth into our understanding.[53] As a performer who brings a role to life and, alternatively, as a member of the audience watching the opera, Price reveals a world of embodied black experience onstage. To the multiple lenses looking into the character of Bess from the analysis of her role in the plot and the direction as she is staged in different productions, the vantage point Leontyne Price explains is one of an audience member who got to jump into the character.[54]

In the nexus of nation, race, and womanhood, the opera and recent musical versions of *Porgy and Bess* speak to us in different yet related ways. The vulnerability and desperation of Bess is both strong drama and a painful story to watch. The artistry of the music and the story are going to affect us in the audience, no matter who we are or how we see the outcome. Leontyne Price's reflections in Standifer's 1997 documentary were made long after she left Mississippi, sang Bess, and retired from one of the greatest opera careers on record. Her enthusiasm and energy in thinking about how Bess was a part of her go beyond her excitement from the memory of singing an early role and penetrate into a deeper reflection of how Bess can still reflect some of the many sides of Price's experiences. The hope and defeat embedded in the character of Bess is something that transcends the space of the opera, and its dramatic impact reaches out to those onstage and in the audience. The opportunity for a connection between the performers and the audience makes this work so powerful. It was a fitting commentary for its time in Jim Crow America, and it maintains relevance still, nearly a century later, as we move through and past the new millennium.

5 *Carmen*

From Nineteenth-Century France to Settings in the United States and South Africa in the Twentieth and Twenty-First Centuries

Arguably the sexiest woman in all of opera, the title character of Georges Bizet's *Carmen* has garnered much attention for well over a century. This is no surprise, for the opera score is filled with seductive melodies and syncopated rhythms, colorful orchestration, and bold lyrics. From her opening manifesto on love in her famous "Habanera" through her final fatal duet with Don José, Carmen audaciously lives life on her own terms. Inspired by the novella of the same title by Prosper Mérimée, Bizet's opera reshapes the narrative and fleshes out a unique individuality for Carmen.

The title character, Carmen, has been referred to as a gypsy since its inception. In this chapter, I use the term "gypsy" sparingly and with caution because increasingly this word has become associated with negative stereotypes. Rather than simply a descriptive term for an understood group of people, this word currently is considered by many to be a racial/ethnic slur. The Romany people have been defined by Central and Western Europe as exotic outsiders who—primarily—came from Eastern Europe, India, and Egypt.[1] The historical origins and accurate migration histories of these people have not been chief factors in their representation. Instead, Western art forms have relied on tropes of thieving, untrustworthy, violent, and licentious people; the "gypsies" of Mérimée and Bizet's *Carmen* stories squarely fit into this category. My aim in this paragraph is to take responsibility for what I am presenting. Many of these stories about Carmen (in the nineteenth century and in later adaptations) pick uncomfortably at wounds around name calling, fears of the foreigner, and internalized racist ideologies. In the analysis and critique of these troubled histories, I wish to acknowledge the pain they can cause and their potency.

My main emphasis in this chapter is to examine how the Carmen story continues to have meaning along the themes of race and ethnicity, gender, socioeconomic levels, sexual desire, and changing definitions of nation. I focus on several versions of the Carmen story, starting with the first two sources in nineteenth-century Paris (the Mérimée novella and the opera by Bizet), through two African American settings in the United States (*Carmen Jones* in 1954 and *Carmen: A Hip Hopera* in 2001), to an all-black setting in South Africa (*U-Carmen eKhayelitsha* in 2005). To accomplish this reading, I begin with themes I find critical to the understanding of the Carmen story in its first nineteenth-century versions—the novella by Propser Mérimée (1845–46) and the opera by Georges Bizet (1875). This reading provides a background to the opera that reinforces ideas in the narrative that are particularly relevant to my discussion of the work (and this section will be a helpful reminder, or introduction, for those who are not as familiar with these various versions of *Carmen*).

Carmen Jones, *Carmen: A Hip Hopera*, and *U-Carmen eKhayelitsha* are available on film and DVD, and are accessible to contemporary audiences. Chronologically, the first work is *Carmen Jones*, which originated as a stage musical written by Oscar Hammerstein II and was first performed in 1943. The version I am going to focus on is the 1954 film adaptation, *Carmen Jones*, directed by Otto Preminger, starring Dorothy Dandridge and Harry Belafonte. The second film, *Carmen: A Hip Hopera* (2001), was produced by MTV, directed by Robert Townsend, and starred Beyoncé Knowles (as she

Table 5.1. *Carmen* Overview: *Carmen* the novella

	Bizet's *Carmen*	*Carmen Jones*	*Carmen: A Hip Hopera*	*U-Carmen*
Date	1984	1954	2001	2005
Film Director	Francesco Rosi	Otto Preminger	Robert Townsend	Mark Dornford-May eKhayelitsha
Setting	Spain, Seville	rural Florida and Chicago	Philadelphia and LA	South African township
Names	Carmen	Carmen Jones	Carmen Brown	Carmen
	Micaëla	Cindy Lou	Caela	Nomakhaya
	Don José	Joe	Derek Hill	Jongikhaya
	Escamillo	Husky Miller	Blaze	Lulamile Nkomo
	[bull fighter]	[boxer]	[rapper]	[opera singer]
Other important characters	Zuniga	Frankie Freschita—expanded [Pearl Bailey]	Lieutenant Miller Zuniga—expanded [Yasiin Bey "Mos Def"]	Captain Gantana
Language	French	English (with dialect)	English (hip hop)	Xhosa

Prosper Mérimée, *Carmen*.
Sections 1–3 appeared in the *Revue des Deux Mondes* on October 1, 1845. Section 4 was published later in 1846.

was still known then before she dropped "Knowles") and Mekhi Phifer. The final film is the 2005 South African *U-Carmen eKhayelitsa*, directed by Mark Dornford-May, adapted by Pauline Malefane (and others), with Malefane in the title role. There are two sub-Saharan African settings of the Carmen story in the early twenty-first century: *U-Carmen eKhayelitsha* from South Africa (2005) and *Karmen Geï* from Senegal (2001); given my focus here on the United States and South Africa, my discussion of *Karen Geï* from Senegal is published elsewhere.[2]

Shaping Carmen: Bizet and Mérimée

An unfortunate irony of Bizet's *Carmen* is that Bizet never lived to see his opera become what it has been for quite a while now: one of the most popular operas of all time. Yet after its premiere, the opera was hardly considered a spectacular success. In retrospect, it is easy to see the primary trouble was that the commissioning theater was not the best fit for the subject matter. *Carmen* was the second opera the co-directors of the Opéra-Comique, Camille du Locle and Adolphe de Leuven, invited Bizet to compose. Though the first opera, *Djamileh* (1872) was not a solid success, they went ahead with a second commission. Since Prosper Mérimée's *Carmen* was not unknown, from the beginning there was concern that the subject matter would be too grisly for the conservative, family-oriented audience of the Opéra-Comique.

Assured by experienced librettists Ludovic Halévy and Henri Meilhac, and the strong support of Célestine Galli-Marié, the first interpreter of Carmen, du Locle and de Leuven went ahead with the plans. But with the underclass cigarette factory workers, the sexuality of the title character, and her brutal death onstage, Bizet's *Carmen* ended up being too shocking for the Opéra-Comique audience. Despite the opening rocky reception, the initial run included forty-eight performances, with the premiere on March 3, 1875. Tragically, exactly three months later on the night of its thirty-third performance (June 3, 1875) Bizet died after complications of a high fever and heart attack. Just a few months later in October 1875, *Carmen* finally gained critical success in a Viennese production where the spoken dialogue (a requirement of the Opéra-Comique) was replaced with sung recitative composed by Bizet's colleague and friend, Ernest Guiraud.

Prosper Mérimée's *Carmen*, published in four installments from 1845 to 1846 in *La Revue des deux mondes* (*Review of the Two Worlds*), carried the subtitle *Journal des voyages;* the periodical had a focus on travel, which Mérimée's novella fit well. Told from the vantage point of a French narrator conducting research in Spain, the story of the bandit Don José and the subversive Carmen seems almost accidentally to become the main focus of the story as the exotic Romany and life of thievery overtake the initial plot. The local color of Spanish "gypsies" and bandits entices the narrator away from his original research and centers his attention on the foreign attractions in Spain. As was common with travel writing in the nineteenth century, the depiction of Spain is less about being historically accurate (though Mérimée had traveled to Spain, he never claimed that his novella was true) and more about the view of Spain by a bourgeoisie Frenchman who knew the tastes of his readers. Mérimée's novella reveals an outsider's fascination with an exotic transgressive "Other."

Challenging the Conventions: Gendered Relationships in *Carmen*

Bizet's opera delineates the different worlds that men and women inhabit. Central to this mission is the addition of the characters of Micaëla and Escamillo (neither is in Mérimée's novella) who help articulate the norms for gender relations. Escamillo is a composite character of the men Carmen has seduced, and he provides a compelling rival to Don José for Carmen by the end of the opera. As a Toreador with a booming bass voice, Escamillo easily captivates the audience with his brash virility in the bullring described in his famous rousing entrance number, "The Toreador Song." He is a logical choice for Carmen; as is seen in their short duet in the final act, their music is well matched as they effortlessly sing of their love for each other.

Micaëla provides an important model of femininity that reflects the expectations of the Opéra-Comique's audience and conventions of late nineteenth-century womanhood. Whereas Carmen is brazen and acts according to her own code of ethics and desires, Micaëla shows us the woman with whom Don José should fall in love. A sincere girl from his village, approved of by his mother, Micaëla is demure and shy. She gets nervous with the attentions from the military officers when she first looks for Don José in the beginning of the opera. Later in the act, when she is finally reunited with her beloved, she is hardly able to voice her true feelings without filtering them through her role as a messenger from his mother. Yet Micaëla is not a weak character, for she ventures into the mountains to find Don José in the third act, after he has left her and the military to follow Carmen and her band of smugglers. Micaëla shows courage as she tells José that his dying mother wishes to see him. More than any other character, Micaëla demonstrates a noble honor in the face of adversity.

Rather than the notorious bandit in Mérimée's novella, in the beginning of the opera Don José is perfectly poised to marry Micaëla and live an honorable life. Bizet's Don José has been softened from being a dangerous outlaw in his own right to being a military corporal trying to abide by the rules and advance. One of the key conflicts in the opera is the progression of Don José from a respectable character to an obsessed, half-crazed stalker who loses control.

In Bizet's opera, we see how the traditional codes of masculinity go askew after Don José encounters Carmen. Hardly even noticing her during her "Habanera," as soon as Carmen sets her sights on Don José, he becomes increasingly unable to resist her demands and charms. Even after he dramatically declares his love to her in his earnest and lyrical second act "Flower Song," Carmen immediately challenges him to prove this love by running off to the mountains with her to live the life of a bandit. Though he initially declines, the circumstances that arise by the end of the act compel him to follow her lead and give up the life he had intended to follow in the military. In the fourth act, after things have gone awry and Carmen has moved on to Escamillo, Don José implores Carmen to remember the good times they had together and begs her not to leave him. As she harshly tells him to leave her alone, the traditional gender dynamics in the relationship are reversed. Though Carmen tries to end the relationship, a nearly hysterical Don José uses every argument he can think of to make her stay: he wants to start a fresh life together with her, he wants to save her and save himself, he still loves her. When she refutes him at each point and says she no longer loves him, his desperation comes through most poignantly when he agrees to remain a bandit and do whatever she wants; he repeatedly pleads with her, "Do not leave me" (Mais ne me quitte pas).

With the crowds in the background cheering on Escamillo, Don José takes action and does the only thing he sees possible. Rather than let Carmen go, he turns her into the victim and brutally stabs her. With the ultimate metaphor of rape and domination, Don José seals his own doom. He has become the worst exaggeration of what he feared most in Carmen in her code to stay true to herself. Unlike Carmen's independence, wherein she allows everyone—and, most important, herself—to make up one's own mind despite pressure to heed convention, Don José has lost control of his actions and his inner sense of justice. Proceeding without a moral compass, he snuffs out the one thing he thinks he loves and effectively kills his own desire to move forward. His final words, which conclude the opera, show his capitulation to the authority he had just disregarded and his consequent admission of guilt: "Vous pouvez m'arreter / c'est moi qui l'ai tuée" (You may arrest me / I was the one who killed her). One interpretation could see Don José as an upright man who Carmen brings down though her seductive power. Another interpretation reveals the character of Don José as being unsure of its destiny and unable to choose what is right in the final round when all of the cards are laid down.

Carmen's Voice: L'amour et la mort (Love and Death)

From her first entrance, Carmen reveals her views about love in the chorus of her famous "Habanera." Delivered over a repeated undulating bass line that intertwines with her curvaceous vocal melody, her message snakes its way through her enticing music.

> Si tu ne m'aimes pas, je t'aime;
> Si je t'aime; prends garde à toi!

> If you don't love me, I love you;
> if I love you, look out for yourself!

Though not the most "healthy" code of behavior for a romantic relationship by any standard, Carmen is honest about her intentions and stays true to them throughout the opera. To look at *Carmen* as a love story promises disappointment, but to think about the opera as a story that explores many aspects of love filtered through gender, ethnicity, socioeconomic conditions, and definitions of nation provides more instruction.

In the first half of the opera Carmen's voice has a distinctive resonance. For noted musicologist Susan McClary, Carmen is the only character whose primary discourse in the beginning of the opera is through diegetic songs (music heard as songs by other characters onstage). In other words, Carmen presents herself in song rather than a regular voice that matches the other characters. Hence, her "voice" is perceived in a special way onstage as well as by those of us in the audience. Her use of song is strategic because she sings things she cannot or chooses not to say. In the "Habanera" she is able to present herself as a so-called "gypsy" performer. In this role, she is expected to exist on the margins of society and be able to spontaneously break into song. In this marginal identity she also is able to reveal herself as a potential lover to the full village in a way that would be too licentious in a spoken context.

A little later in act 1, after mayhem breaks out in the cigarette factory, Carmen does not give Zuniga spoken answers when he questions her about her role in the disorder. Instead, she responds to him in a sing-song "Tra-la-la-la-la" as she refuses to recognize his authority or implicate herself in his interrogation. Later when she is held in jail, she pointedly sings to seduce Don José to get what she desires. She whispers a lilting melody that eventually erupts into the gyrating rhythmic "Seguidilla" that outlines how she yearns to meet him at Lillas Pastia's, drink manzanilla, dance the seguidilla. and show him "le vrais plaisirs sont à deux" (the real pleasures that are for two).

As Carmen's "Seguidilla" was a private number to seduce Don José near the end of act 1, act 2 opens at Lillas Pastia's tavern, where Carmen leads a full-blown *Chanson bohèmien* ("Gypsy Song"), which accelerates into a rollicking dance number. Complete with added dancers and brilliant costumes, Carmen very publicly engages those onstage in the tavern as everyone gets caught up in the repetitive music that accelerates to a frenzied *presto* tempo. Though Carmen has been seducing those onstage since her first entrance, this number is specifically geared toward those of us watching her in the theater. We had witnessed her abilities in act 1, but this is the first time she directs her seductive powers outward to the audience. With the driving rhythm and onstage dancing bodies, we are also caught up in the fervor and are aroused; this number rarely fails to get an impassioned ovation.

In a microcosm of the main themes of the opera, the Fortune Telling Trio in act 3 provides a view into what is at stake and foretells how things will work out. With characteristically bright and sparkly music reminiscent of the playful music of the smuggler's quintet in act 2, Fresquita and Mercedes read their fortune in the cards and see just what they want—romantic love and wealth without obligation. The mood drastically changes when Carmen begins to read her own fortune: death for both her and José. The contrapuntal juxtaposition of Carmen's stark lament and her girlfriends' bubbling refrain illustrates how Carmen has now entered her own sonic and emotional zone. She was never part of respectable society and she now no longer fits within the world of the nineteenth-century image of the gypsies. In an especially effective setting, Bizet contrasts two near homophones in French "l'amour" (love) and "la mort" (death) as Carmen accepts her fate, which becomes so tightly intertwined with both love and death.

Throughout Mérimée's novella, the plot is told by the French male narrator and Don José; rarely does Carmen even speak, though she is described in rich detail by the two men who are fascinated and entranced by her. A critical feature of Bizet's opera is that we finally get to hear Carmen's voice as she speaks for herself and is given a full musical portrayal. For Bizet's earliest audiences, her brazen character was beyond the conventions of the family-oriented Opéra-Comique theater. However, the opera caught on in its revised version within months of its premiere and has remained popular ever since.

There seems to be something almost universal in the timelessness of this opera. Multiple adaptations and new productions of *Carmen* continue to be regularly performed all over the world. Some have estimated the number of adaptations to exceed seventy-five, and there are books devoted to discussing multiple versions and iterations of the Carmen story onstage and in film.[3] Updated versions, in addition to the three black settings I will discuss later in further depth, include Flamenco versions (notably by Carlos Saura [1983]); one in a garage with a mechanic in London (*The Car Man*, choreographed by Matthew Bourne [2001]); another contemporary African setting in Senegal (*Karmen Geï* by Joséph Gaï Ramaka [2001]), and a Bollywood Carmen (presented live and then in a TV film directed by Indra Bhose with music adapted by D. J. Kuljit Bhamra).[4] Clearly, in the new millennium Bizet's heroine has inspired multiple variations that speak eloquently to current times.

Three Rubrics for Approaching Mérimée and Bizet's *Carmens*: Who Is in the Story, Who Speaks, and Who Interprets the Story?

Who Is in the Story?

In the Mérimée and Bizet *Carmens*, there is a clearly delineated presence of the "exotic outsider"—Carmen and her bohemian friends—juxtaposed to the hegemonic "normative" participant. In these nineteenth-century French tellings, the presence of the migrant bohemians is contextualized by a contrasting Western European presence, a type of entry point "tour guide" figure to help the Western audience feel a bit more oriented in the story, rather than the completely foreign experience with nothing familiar. In Prosper Mérimée's novella, this normative presence appears immediately in the opening sentences as an unidentified French narrator. Though the French narrator is in all four parts of the serialized novella, his role is the largest in the opening and final sections. In the opening he sets up the story—he is a French scholar who is traveling to Spain to find the precise location of the ancient battle of Caesar (45 BCE) in Munda, a town on the Mediterranean coast between Gibraltar and Málaga. The beginning paragraph of the novella posits this as a historical problem with scholars disagreeing about the exact location, and provides a purpose for his journey into southern Spain. In fact, Mérimée did write more about the problem of Munda's location in an article he published in the *Revue archéologique* (in June 1844, one year before the *Carmen* serialized novella), and for those reading the *Carmen* novella when it was first published in 1845, the voice of this French narrator could certainly feel as if it overlapped with the voice of its real author—Mérimée—in these first sentences.[5] Some of the first readers of *Carmen* might also have known that Prosper Mérimée had himself travelled to Spain and published a series of "Letters from Spain" in the early 1830s in *La Revue de Paris*, which included dispatches on bullfighting, highway bandits and thievery, and witches—themes and characters all present in the novella.[6]

To both the nineteenth-century readers of Mérimée's *Carmen* novella and to us today, our French narrator comes across as logical and trustworthy; he tells us of his mission in southern Spain to do research on this ancient topic, and his voice of familiarity and ease with these topics is well earned from his past history in his research on classical topics (such as Caesar) and his travel history in Spain. By the end of the first paragraph of *Carmen*, Mérimée, through the voice of his French narrator, provides the perfect segue between his research and the entertainment of a digression:

> Finding myself in Andalusia at the beginning of autumn, 1830, I undertook a rather long excursion to clear up my remaining doubts [regarding the location of Caesar's battle of Munda]. A monograph that I will soon publish will, I hope, leave no doubt in the minds of any well-intentioned archeologists. While waiting for my dissertation to finally resolve the geographical problem that holds all the savants of Europe in suspense, I would like to tell you a little story, it does not take anything away from the interesting issue of the location of Munda.[7]

Thus, the saga of *Carmen* commences through this "little story" as we understand why and how this story has come to be told. Throughout the novella, our French narrator takes us through the action. Don José, the famous Spanish bandit, is introduced through the narrator a couple of paragraphs later in part 1, and the two interact when they share a meal, smoke cigars together, and stay in the same tavern. Though Don José is not fully trustworthy, the narrator has befriended him and shows a code of honor to this friendship when he warns Don José that the authorities are coming to arrest him. In part 2 it is Don José who protects the narrator, repaying him the favor of helping him escape arrest at the end of part 1. Don José saves the narrator from Carmen's deceptive charms after she lures him to her place for a palm reading, and then directs the narrator safely back to his inn. Later in part 2 and for all of part 3, the narrator visits Don José in his jail cell as the latter awaits execution for his crimes. In part 3 Don José takes over the story in his voice, as he tells of Carmen, her history, and their ill-destined time together. Hence, the novella is told in the presence of the French narrator all of the time, even when he is not the first-person narrator. At first he is the one who introduces the story, and we (the reader) are led strategically to the landscape and geography of Spain and the variety of people who live there.

It is presented as a protected space as these new people and places are told by "one of us": the French narrator. By part 3, Don José has become more familiar through the narrator. Though Don José is still a foreigner and part of the shady world of the "Other," the reader feels safe because Don José is locked up in jail and we are given the opportunity to be even closer to the exotic "source" and get his side of the story, without ever being at risk or in any danger. Mérimée's French raconteur can temporarily relinquish narrative control because the threat is contained as Don José tells his story from jail.

Part 4 of the novella was published the following year (1846) and, as in the opening of part 1, is told in the French narrator's now-familiar scholarly voice characterizing the behavior, origin, and languages of the Romany to which Carmen belongs. Such a narrative device frames the novella in an implicit academic fashion; in addition to its entertainment value with the local exotic flavors, the French narrator is careful to position Spain in the larger context of Western European knowledge. The rugged physical landscape, the outlaw and marginalized people, and the dialect Romany languages of Spain have been contained at a safe distance, over the Pyrenees, contrasted with the more civilized world of France.

I am not alone in noting the presence of the narrator and authorial voice of Mérimée in the *Carmen* novella. Paul Robinson and Susan McClary have posited that such a framing device provides Mérimée the narrative control to wrest the story back from Don José and the irresistible Carmen and place it in his own patriarchal voice.[8] My point here complements this stance and emphasizes that the person telling the story is also a formative character in the drama. Though the presence of the French narrator might seem small, his role is critically important as the tour guide figure to help the other French and non-Romany people feel engaged and safe with this unfamiliar and unpredictable material. Even when the French narrator is silent and lets Don José tell the story (for most of part 3), he can be invoked, as though he were sitting by our side, listening to the story along with us.

In Bizet's opera *Carmen* there is no narrator per se, but I would argue that the function of the tour guide/narrator has now shifted to the re-inscribed figure of Don José.[9] Rather than the outlaw bandit that befriends our French narrator, Don José in the opera is a dragoon—an honorable young military officer who is not, at first, distracted by Carmen during her "Habanera" and has been given an upright love interest in Micaëla, who has his mother's approval as a potential wife. Don José in the opera has been rehabilitated as the tenor hero, and the troubled past so prominent in Mérimée's novella has been nearly erased so that the quick reference to it is easy to miss.[10] Micaëla is a character that the librettists Meilhac and Halévy added in order to present a female character who could be a foil to the brazen Carmen and help make the drama more suitable to the family-nature dramas of the Opéra Comique. In Bizet's opera, the final scene in act 4 shows the downfall of the tenor hero as he falls in love with the dangerous Other and is pushed over the edge from being a respectable northern Spanish soldier to the obsessed, love-crazed killer who fell prey to the spell Carmen cast on him in act 1.

In both the Mérimée novella and Bizet opera, Don José is from the north, specifically Navarre, and he is identified as being Basque. In the beginning of part 3 of the novella, as the French narrator turns the story over to him, we hear Don José introduce himself.

> "I was born," he said, "at Elizondo, in the Baztán valley. My name is don José Lizarrabengoa, and you know Spain well enough, sir, that my name tells you immediately that I am Basque and old Christian. If I use *don* it's because I have the right, and if I were at Elizondo, I would show you my genealogy on parchment. They wanted me to enter the church, and had me study, but I hardly took advantage of it. I liked to play handball too much, that led to my downfall. When we play handball, we other Navarrians, we forget everything."[11]

There is no other geographical location that Mérimée could have chosen that would better reflect a dual French-Spanish identity. Located in the northeastern region of Spain, Navarre is part of the Basque country extending between Spain and France across the Pyrenees and approaching the Bay of Biscay in the Atlantic. With a long tradition of having a desire to be its own nation, the Basque identity for Don José from Navarre presents a Spanish man who is as close to France as possible. The Mérimée novella plays up the bandit side of Don José; however, as the quotation above shows, he still has enough of a Western European identity to be able to relate to the French narrator and present a lineage that connects to the church and a class structure that allows him to use the title of *don*. In Bizet, the opposite shading is used for Don José. The Spanish bandit element is gone, and through his access to the malleable Basque affiliation and its transnational Spanish-French regionalism, Don José maintains his Spanish identity yet has been transformed into a relatable figure for the nineteenth-century French audience. While the action of both the novella and opera is placed in Andalusia around Seville in the southern area of Spain closest to the African continent, the nomadic Romany aspect of Carmen's background is contrasted with the northern Basque (almost French) identity of Don José. In both nineteenth-century French versions of *Carmen*, onstage we have the exotic smuggler world of Carmen mitigated through a lens of one of us (whether it be as the non-Bohemian French bourgeoisie or a modern-day audience) interacting with this exotic world, as a proxy—conduit—for access into the drama.

Who Speaks and Who Interprets?

In Mérimée's novella and Bizet's opera, the presence of the French narrator and Don José as a tour-guide figure place an "insider" who is relatable to the nineteenth-century French bourgeoisie audience inside the action of the drama. Though Carmen in the novella rarely speaks for herself, and is most frequently described by the French narrator or Don José, the enactment of Carmen's story onstage in the opera allows her to speak for herself. Her voice is delivered through the author and composer of her words and music, as well as the physical body onstage performing her role. While the representation of the non-European "Other" is a central feature of the Carmen story, a critical factor remains: which perspectives are being represented? I separate out these two points because I want to acknowledge the power of having a stage filled with members from other cultural groups (for example, the wandering Romany populations of Mérimée and Bizet) and especially when other cultural groups are marked through brown bodies, as with the African Americans of *Carmen Jones* and *Carmen: A Hip Hopera*, and the black South Africans of *U-Carmen eKhayelitsha*.

The visible physical differences of ethnically/racially marked bodies present an impact that no one today can ignore. Though I think audiences have noticed these phenotypical differences throughout time, I can speak most confidently of the present: audiences notice obvious markers of identity—especially around race and gender.[12] Moreover, in an environment where there are so few roles for characters outside the Western standard convention (currently still assumed to be white), the visual impact when there are characters onstage who contrast to this presumed norm makes a dramatic statement.[13]

These visible differences among the characters onstage (what comes out in their verbal and musical texts and the embodied portrayal by the performers) present a set of codes for the audience to read. How the audience interprets these codes exposes my last rubric in the analysis. Aside from the differences between audiences in the past and present, I start from the assumption that the audience is always heterogeneous and encompasses multiple experiences and vantage points. In this type of analysis it is possible to make generalizations; however, the main point is that there is not a single dominant "correct" interpretation that wipes out other perspectives. Important to such analyses are the different publics in the past and present who view these Carmen productions. Given the all-black settings in the United States, there are cultural references (such as uncredited roles for African Americans who would be recognizable to contemporaneous audiences, and the political shifting during the civil rights movement that resonated differently with black and white audiences). Similarly, the South African dismantling of apartheid had a profound effect on how new possibilities were articulated, and setting the opera in a post-apartheid township cigarette business signaled a specific moment in history for the political and social economy of the working- and middle-class black South Africans.

Carmen Jones

Everyone who has written about *Carmen Jones*—the 1943 musical and the 1954 movie—has noted and spent time on the fact that this show has an all-black cast. In the context of its time, it followed the first wave of all-black Hollywood films in the 1930s and 1940s (such as *Hallelujah* [1929, MGM], *The Green Pastures* [1936, Warner Brothers], *Cabin in the Sky* ([1943, MGM], and *Stormy Weather* [1943, 20th Century Fox]) as well as musicals and shows on Broadway (such as Noble Sissle and Eubie Blake's *Shuffle Along* [1921] and Hall Johnson's *Run, Little Chillun'* [1933]). Scholars have written about the casting for the musical and Hollywood movie productions.[14] My analysis privileges race within the framework I set out above—who is in the story, who tells the story, and who interprets the story—though not necessarily in that order, and then moves on to other contextual information that situates this work in its original time and today.

The story of *Carmen Jones* is told by Oscar Hammerstein II (1895–1960), a pivotal American theater figure who produced and directed shows, wrote libretti, and was part of many collaborations, the most famous being with Richard Rodgers. Several of their collaborations started as stage musicals and, like *Carmen Jones*, were adapted into films (which included *Oklahoma!* [staged 1943/film 1955]; *South Pacific* [1949/1958]; *The King and I* [1951/1956]; *The Flower Drum Song* [1958/1961]; and *The Sound of Music* [1959/1961]). Hammerstein grew up in the theater business, the son of William Hammerstein (1875–1914) and grandson of Oscar Hammerstein I (1846–1919). Grandfather Hammerstein was a major figure in pioneering opera in the early twentieth century. In addition to his vaudeville theaters, he opened opera houses in Manhattan, Philadelphia, and London. He presented the American premieres of several operas (*Louise, Pélleas et Mélisande, Elektra, Thaïs*, and *Salome* among others), arranged the American debuts of famous opera singers Mary Garden and Luisa Tetrazzini, and included Nellie Melba on his roster. Hammerstein II's father (William) was more involved with managing the vaudeville houses; he ran the Victoria Theatre, located in what was to become Times Square, which he turned into the most successful theater in New York during the first decade of the twentieth century. Though the Victoria Theatre under William Hammerstein was well known for its specialty acts and freak shows, like other vaudeville theaters of the time it also included sketches, parodies, and scenes drawn from "serious high culture" such as opera. "Carmencita," an act with Spanish dancing, was reported to have been especially popular in August 1905.[15]

Through his father and grandfather, Oscar Hammerstein II was presented with an intimate look at how opera could be adapted to, and flourish in, the United States in the early twentieth century. With a combination of opera houses and vaudeville houses in New York City, Hammerstein II grew up in a cultural milieu where opera could be adapted across social standing and economic status. Additionally, his musicals show his fascination with cultures considered outside the American norm—*South Pacific* (1949), set in the Pacific Islands, is about French colonialism and American intervention during World War II; *Flower Drum Song* (1958), set in San Francisco, is about Chinese immigrants and assimilation; and *The King and I* (1951), set in Thailand, is about the relationship between a widowed British governess and the King of Siam in the late nineteenth century. One of his early successes (a collaboration with Jerome Kern), *Show Boat* (1927), featured an interest in the representation of interracial black-white culture set in the South with a move in the plot to Chicago, a possible anticipation of some of the racial world developed in *Carmen Jones*.[16]

Who we see in the film of *Carmen Jones* has generated discussion and debate—and with good reason. It features an all-black cast, and we know that Walter White—head of the National Association for the Advancement of Colored People—decided not to endorse the film because it did not support the integrationist agenda of the organization at that time. But the question of "who is in the film" becomes less clear when we consider that although the visual world of the film is all black, the sound world is more complicated. As has been discussed in the scholarship, the voices of the leading singers were dubbed. Even though the two leading characters were singers in their own right—Harry Belafonte and Dorothy Dandridge—the operatic singing was given to operatically trained voices. By today's standards, the most disturbing case of this dubbing is using a white singer to fill in for a black character. This is what happened for the title character of *Carmen Jones*. The young Marilyn Horne sang Carmen Jones at the very beginning of her career, which would later develop into superstardom as an opera singer (she focused on Handel and Rossini travesti roles, but also included nineteenth-century characters including Bizet's Carmen and Saint-Saens's Delilah). The other two high-profile roles, Harry Belafonte (the Don José character) and Joe Adams (the

Escamillo character) were also dubbed. In an uncharacteristic situation, these roles were dubbed by black men, both of whom had operatic training. Le Vern Hutcherson (1905–1969) sang for Belafonte and had also sung the role of Gershwin's Porgy. Marvin Hayes (1926–1995), had studied singing with Todd Duncan and had worked with Stravinsky (as a student at the University of Southern California) and Poulenc (when Hayes traveled to France).[17]

Though it turns out that most of the dubbing for the all-black cast was done by black operatically trained singers, there is one crucial case of cross-racial voicing—a white singer dubbing a black actor. However, the larger question goes to the perception of voice and race. The Bizet estate expressed concern to Billy Rose, the impresario who oversaw Hammerstein's Broadway production, about the use of black voices for Bizet's opera. Jeff Smith characterizes the concern: "As long as the performers did not sound like African-American singers but adhered to the more 'universal' standards of classical vocal performance."[18] Although the use of the invented black dialect was not considered a problem, the *Carmen Jones* film evidently did not meet the mark for the Bizet estate, and they prevented it from being shown in France until 1981.

The "universal standards of classical vocal performance" present complications regarding racial voicing and casting. The 1954 environment reveals two things simultaneously about racial tolerance and practice. First, there was a strong contingent, represented by the Bizet estate and all who agreed with them, that felt blackness on its own could not yield a "universal standard" of operatic excellence. Second, the box office success of both *Carmen Jones* the musical and the film were undeniable, and audiences were interested in seeing this opera in a black setting.

Jeff Smith has compellingly asked, "Were Dandridge and Belafonte considered 'too black' to sing opera?"[19] Smith links the aesthetics around opera singing and film technology to examine how the dubbing had created "a kind of phantasmic body that registers visually as black but sounds 'white' in terms of the material qualities of its 'voice.' . . . [*Carmen Jones* the movie created] an all-black musical that 'mimes' the voice of white, European culture."[20] While dubbing was not uncommon in Hollywood films from this era, this case of *Carmen Jones* presents a different situation than the common practice at this time. In a metaphorical way, these dubbed voices bring us back to the nineteenth-century French Carmen sources. As we saw in Mérimée's figure of the French narrator and Don José in Bizet's opera, they each provide a familiar "one of us" function in the narrative. The presence of the dubbed voices in *Carmen Jones* serves a similar tour-guide function on a sonic level. It is as if the dubbed voices are also saying to the Bizet estate (which was especially nervous about the singing in the all-black film version) and opera-knowing audiences, "Don't worry, we will take care of the opera." The musical sound coming out of the black bodies was not riddled with the expected swing-jazz or Calypso accent that black actors were thought to "naturally" bring to their singing. Instead, a "passable" musical voice was used: a voice that sounded both black enough, yet also somewhat operatic. The speech employed in the film *Carmen Jones* reveals no attempt by the writers to find black people from the South who were native speakers of the "black English" they were trying to reproduce. Instead, the resulting imagined black dialect was adapted into the screenplay from the musical by Oscar Hammerstein II (who had written the book and the lyrics) and Harry Kleiner, a Russian-born American immigrant who worked as a writer and producer for 20th Century Fox starting in the 1940s.[21] The words that were spoken and sung were a mediated constructed voice similar to the conceit of dubbing—a re-voicing of a meta-language that blended together elements that a white audience thought a black community would sound like.

The audience has been implicated in this vocal drama because of the unusual transparency presented in this case for the practice in dubbing. As Smith outlines,

Unlike other dubbed performances in Hollywood musicals, which were typically uncredited, the voices of Marilyn Horne, Le Vern Hutcherson, and Marvin Hayes were featured in the film's opening credits and were mentioned in nearly all of the film's reviews. . . . The frequent references to the film's use of operatic voices served to reassure audiences that *Carmen Jones* remained closely tied to the Bizet opera.[22]

Twenty seconds into the opening credits we are given a list of the dubbed singers. They are presented strategically and are hard to miss. As the film begins, the first image is the central rose with the red flame behind it and immediately you see "Otto Preminger presents Oscar Hammerstein's Carmen Jones." This text is replaced with a frame that lists the five leading roles ("Starring Harry Belafonte, Dorothy Dandridge, Pearl Bailey, Olga James, Joe Adams"). The next text lists the smaller lead roles ("with Broc Peters, Roy Glenn, Nick Stewart, Diahann Carroll), along with the ghostly presence of the hidden singers ("and the voices of Le Vern Hutcherson, Marilynn [sic] Horne, Marvin Hayes) that lingers on the screen for eight seconds (a long time in this context when people want to get to the film itself).

John McCarten from *The New Yorker* was one of the reviewers who mentioned this dubbing specifically and praised

Dorothy Dandridge, whose configurations are remarkable and whose songs, rendered by Marilyn Horne, have a highly sultry effectiveness. I had no idea

that Miss Dandridge was not singing in *voce sua* until I was given the news
by a press agent.[23]

Marilyn Horne was just twenty years old when she sang the vocal role for
Dorothy Dandridge in *Carmen Jones*, and her "star presence" had not yet
ascended to bring additional luster to the soundtrack when the movie opened.
One of her early leading roles was Hata (also called Agnes), a contralto role
in Smetana's *Bartered Bride*, produced by the Los Angeles Guild Opera (an
organization founded by the city to present opera to schoolchildren) the same
year as *Carmen Jones*; this newly experienced Horne was one of the white
operatically trained singers who helped legitimize the film's connection to
the Bizet opera. She talks about the process of recording the singing voice
of the leading role:

> It wasn't much of a strain—in fact, it was fun. My job entailed working with
> Dorothy Dandridge. I had to listen carefully to her speaking voice and try to
> match the timbre and the accent, so that when it came time for me to record the
> songs, there would be a little bit of Dandridge in my throat. She sang in a register
> comfortable for her, then I mimicked her voice in the proper keys. Later, she
> filmed her scenes with my recorded voice blasting from huge loudspeakers. The
> tendency in dubbing is to overdo your mouth movements. Dandridge didn't and
> was sensational. The sound technicians pieced music and film together and the
> result is a seamless performance by Dorothy Dandridge and Marilyn Horne.[24]

Horne's description continues the conceit of how black and white voices and
bodies come together. With "a little bit of Dandridge in my throat" and the
"seamless performance by Dorothy Dandridge and Marilyn Horne," there
emerges an interracial, cross-cultural element to the sonic world of the film.
I am not alone to notice this, and Smith perceptively writes,

> Although *Carmen Jones* depicts a space of racial segregation on its image track,
> its sound track reflects the prospects of desegregation as an issue associated
> with the civil rights movement of the fifties and sixties. Blacks and whites could
> not intermingle in the diegetic world of *Carmen Jones*, but their voices could
> in nondiegetic and extradiegetic spaces on the sound track.[25]

In her 1983 autobiography, *Marilyn Horne: My Life*, Horne devoted a full
chapter to *Carmen Jones*. In addition to her discussion of auditioning for and
working on *Carmen Jones*, she also provides her views of the experiences
black musicians faced in classical music. She outlines a brief history of how
long it took major opera houses to allow black singers in, and at the time of
her writing in 1983 she says, "We cannot pat ourselves on the backs—there's
still a long way to go."[26] She astutely notes that it was New York City Opera

that had first presented black singers in leading roles in the late 1940s, and it was not until 1955 that the Metropolitan Opera allowed its first black singer, Marian Anderson, to sing.

Horne does not make a direct connection between her own hire as the operatic voice of Carmen Jones in 1954 and the following year having the largest American operatic barrier punctured by Anderson. Yet her views not only provide a lens into what the opportunities were for blacks during the 1950s and 1960s but also examine how she was positioned in this era. In the chapter Horne also outlines the beginning of her relationship with Henry Lewis (1932–1996), a black double bassist and conductor who was part of the pioneering generation of black classical musicians who broke through the types of barriers Horne talked about in her autobiography. Though they had met through the *Bartered Bride* performance in 1954 (Lewis was in the orchestra pit), it was not until this *Carmen Jones* (Lewis again in the orchestra pit) that they began to date. Their relationship was not inconsequential; they later were married from 1960 to 1979 and have one daughter.

Marilyn Horne is configured in the history of *Carmen Jones* as a voice that represented the problematic views of its time. It hardly seems fair to associate her with any of the negative ideology behind the casting; she was a young singer auditioning for a part and not at all included in the decision-making process behind the scenes. Her personal relationship with Henry Lewis is important, for it speaks of her personal code in the midst of a racially politicized time. She met him during the height of the civil rights era and married him seven years *before Loving v. Virginia*, 388 U.S. 1 (1967), the Supreme Court decision that invalidated laws prohibiting interracial marriage in all states. They were together for nearly twenty years and raised an interracial daughter amid the hope, violence, dreams, and disillusion that shaped black-white race relations during the 1960s and 1970s. The chapter on *Carmen Jones* in her autobiography, written just a few years after she and Lewis parted ways, presents her experiences at the beginning of her professional career and personal relationships with a caution that might diminish the politicized nature of her actions, but it also tells the story in a careful manner for her primary readers—opera fans.

Who Speaks and Interprets the Story?

The themes around cross-racial dubbing are taken up by pioneering African American female film director Julie Dash nearly thirty years after *Carmen Jones* in Dash's early film, *Illusions* (1982).[27] Though ten years before what was to become her best-known work, *Daughters of the Dust* (1992), *Illusions* feels connected to *Carmen Jones* by its similar setting during World War II and the uncanny sensation of hearing and watching the voice of a woman of one race come out of the body of another woman of a different race. The film's leading character, Mignon Dupree, is a film executive assistant working in Hollywood in the early 1940s. The opening conflict arises when a dubbing situation is needed (due to the misalignment of the sound and visual tracks) for one of the songs in an upcoming big budget film. The original white actress (who is also the singer) is unavailable to come in and re-record the music because she is overseas working with the troops for the war effort. Dupree finds a black singer (the character of Esther Jeeter) who can fill in. In an almost eerie scene, we see Jeeter singing, perfectly impersonating, the white actress's voice as the film is projected onto a larger screen in the background (hence, we have the reverse situation of Horne singing for Dandridge as Carmen Jones).

But what makes this film such a helpful commentary for Preminger's *Carmen Jones* is that Dupree is actually a black woman "passing" as white in the Hollywood industry. Though members of the audience might, or might not, have picked up on this hidden trope, the secret is first revealed when Jeeter quietly says to Dupree "Oh don't worry. . . . they can't tell like we can," referring to the all-white office and production staff that surround them. At that moment, a good portion of the audience knows what is going on. The more blatant revelation (when the white people on the screen know) comes later in the film when a picture of Dupree's black fiancé is seen. In this commentary Dash is showing that double consciousness that Du Bois writes about, where to survive in white America, blacks need to be fluent in both black and white cultures. The coming together of being able to read across race and social position while being competent in one's job illustrates how Dash is writing her own experience and stories into the history of film.

It is precisely the lack of this kind of agency that makes the situation in the *Carmen Jones* film so uncomfortable. The assumption that the black singers (Dandridge and Belafonte) were attractive and could act but that their singing was not appropriate for opera heightens the exoticization of their presence. We are allowed to see them, but their voices have been replaced by the trained opera singers who are altering and adjusting (almost "dumbing down") their real voices so the audience will hear this as more "realistic." Black bodies could be seen and heard speaking a fictionalized black dialect, but to sound operatic, they were not yet allowed to sing and be heard as themselves.

Black Place and Space in Carmen Jones

The setting of 1954 in the U.S. rural South and Chicago presents several markers that ground this film in historical and cultural meaning. The larger context includes a time when Jim Crow legislation was still strong but was beginning to be dismantled, with the greatest victory being the Supreme Court's *Brown v. Board of Education of Topeka* decision (347 U.S. 483) in May 1954 (four months before the opening of *Carmen Jones*), ruling that the "separate but equal" (from *Plessy v. Ferguson*, 163 U.S. 537 in 1896), in this case with public schools, for black and white students were unconstitutional. In this context, references to education and upward mobility had an especially strong resonance. As the film begins with Joe having been selected for flight school, the energy for this honor is propelled both by the triumph of *Brown v. Board of Education* along with the reputation of the Tuskegee Airmen, the African American military pilots who had been active in World War II, before the military was desegregated in 1948. Joe is not just an average military soldier; he is one of the brightest chosen for leadership and a promising future.

Another strong theme is the Great Migration of blacks from the rural South moving into northern and western urban centers. With the opening scene showing Cindy Lou coming to the military base by bus, she is also deep within a crowd of other black passengers who turn out to be coming to work in the parachute factory next to the military base. This establishing shot that opens the film is strategic not only for setting up the location of the action but also for establishing central themes in the film. Transportation, opportunities in the newly desegregated military, postwar prosperity with both men and women going to work, and crowds of black people dressed well (for work, or especially nicely as in the featured figure of Cindy Lou) are moving peacefully and with purpose—no rioting or protests. All of these activities show us a working- and middle-class black community that is ordered and productive, actively engaged in the postwar American dream.

Watching the opening of the *Carmen Jones* film might have presented a simple morning commuter scene to the majority audience; however, to a black audience, the beginning sequence signaled a chance of new beginnings, and Cindy Lou's journey is imbued with even more purpose and excitement as the audience eagerly waits to see where she is going and whom she is meeting. Obviously, she is ready for something important to happen, and we are drawn into her quest. Later in the film Husky Miller and his entourage are presented as passing through Billy Pastor's in rural Florida as they are on their way to Chicago.[28] Not only is Husky Miller heading to the city, his manager and assistant offer to take Carmen and her friends there with them. The quintet "Whizzin' Away Along de Track" with Carmen, Frankie, Myrt, Dink, and Rum about the clickety-clack of the high-speed train to Chicago is a reference to much more than a casual weekend trip. The movement from Florida to Chicago by train cites a specific journey that is a central part of black history. The hope and energy contained in that number well revitalizes the earlier context it had in Bizet's opera as one of the few "bright" moments of the work when the exotic bohemian world was on display. In Billy Pastor's Café the excitement is brought in for the possibility of new horizons with the promise in the refrain that "it only takes a half a day to be a thousand miles away, Come on away, Chicago! Chicago!" Furman and others are right to note the importance Preminger places on transportation as a signifier of social mobility.[29] Yet the greater meaning of seeing black bodies travel on public transportation must have resonated deeply with the lived experience of those in the audience who had made such a journey themselves or had family members who had traveled these similar routes.

Though there are references throughout the film that speak directly to black experience during the 1950s, the material from act 2 in Bizet's opera—the section in Billy Pastor's Café in the film—presents a particularly dense group of signifiers, some of which other scholars have read in isolation, but not all together. The scene opens focusing on a house-turned-business in the country in the evening. A neon sign marks "Billy Pastor's Café," and as the scene moves into the building we see a well-dressed crowd gathering around a bar, sitting, standing, and talking. In this speakeasy-type place the principal characters gather after hours, relaxing and dancing, outside of work and apart from the more commercial, most likely segregated, all-white establishments downtown. As the opening of act 2 in Bizet's opera, the scene in Lillas Pastia's tavern is an out-of-the-way inn and with Carmen's "Chanson bohèmien" and the most exoticized large group scene in the opera where most productions end up with Carmen dancing frenetically on a tabletop. It is out of this scene that Frankie (Pearl Bailey in the role of Carmen's friend Fresquita) takes up the "Chanson bohèmien," now called "Beat out Dat Rhythm on a Drum." As has been thoroughly discussed elsewhere, this number, originally sung by Carmen in the opera but now given to Pearl Bailey, bears a good deal of the dramatic weight that spells out a jungle-infused vision of primitive blackness.[30] The choreography, added music, and new text all reference a side of black culture that feels far away from the operatic associations evoked in the rest of the film.

Outside of the public gaze in the 1950s white culture of the film, the all-black speakeasy of Billy Pastor's provides a different place—a space more private where the main characters can let loose with less uptight behavior and where there is less chance of a white foreman or passerby showing up unpredictably. Even within the all-black filmic world, this scene presents a different racial dynamic with its contained semipublic-private arena. Billy Pastor's is known within the local black community, but it is public enough to be available to Husky Miller and his crew when they pass through town.

Such places were necessary in the Jim Crow segregated South, and such a space is needed in this postwar climate for an all-black film so invested in showing the plight of sympathetic African Americans. These are not gangsters or ruffians; rather, they are respectable people who can entertain themselves (and us in the audience) with let-loose dancing in a properly specified location (the clean, well-lighted Billy Pastor's Café) on the edge of town.

The moment for the jungle-inspired primitive dancing is strategically choreographed. In a noncredited cameo role, famous jazz drummer Max Roach plays the drums as Bizet's familiar "Chanson bohèmien" sounds in the background when Carmen enters. After Carmen asks the coat-check woman whether or not Corporal Joe has been around, the music gives way to a drum solo that moves us off Bizet's score and into an improvised, uncharted black territory. Though Frankie (Pearl Bailey) remains central to the action, we also have a new troupe of dancers who show up—like Max Roach—also uncredited. Several of these dancers were at the beginning of their careers, but were becoming familiar faces (and bodies) in black films, news, and events of the time. To an aware audience, an up-and-coming group of "who's who," along with more seasoned artists, appear on the screen. Alvin Ailey (1931–1989) and Carmen de Lavallade (born 1931) are the first dancing couple we see—framed in the mirror in the foyer at the coat-check area. Lavallade (with the long ponytail and white dress with the red roses) and Ailey had worked together at the Lester Horton Dance Theater in Los Angeles (a leading modern-dance studio on the West Coast and one of the first to have an interracial company). Four years after *Carmen Jones*, Ailey would go on to found his path-breaking Alvin Ailey American Dance Theater company that is still one of the leading dance ensembles around. Lavallade also became an important dancer and choreographer with the Metropolitan Opera ballet, Alvin Ailey's company, and other theaters on and off Broadway. Two other recognizable dancers at Billy Pastor's are Carmencita Romero (1914–2001) and Archie Savage (1914–2003), both of whom were Katherine Dunham dancers and had also appeared in *Cabin in the Sky* (1943).

In act 2 of Johann Strauss II's operetta *Die Fledermaus*, Count Orlofsky throws a New Year's party where, when available, it is customary for visiting famous opera singers who happen to be in town to drop in, make a surprise visit, and sing a verse or short aria at the party. Such an event provides a fun moment for the cast onstage as well as a treat for the audience to see who is in town and has shown up. In a similar vein, the thrill of seeing Max Roach and these uncredited dancers allowed audiences in 1954 to see some familiar as well as emerging new artists in the party atmosphere of Billy Pastor's. Additionally, for future audiences, even up through the present, it is also exciting to see who was there in *Carmen Jones*, a film that showcased such a dazzling array of black talent at that time.

The song featured at Billy Pastor's tavern, "Chanson bohèmien," is transformed into "Beat out Dat Rhythm on a Drum" and centers this scene on one of the most resonant tropes of the Harlem Renaissance that signaled a black connection to Africa. The presence of the drum—notably the tom-tom—was a frequently used sound image to evoke life before the Middle Passage and slavery. When Pearl Bailey specifically mentions the tom-tom, the image is one that she talks about as absorbing a deep feeling inside. "I feel it beatin' in my bones, it feels like twenty million tom-toms, I know it's twenty million tom-toms, even when I'm deep inside my bones." Not an uncomplicated sign, the focus of this number on the drum and the moment when the drum becomes "twenty million tom-toms" sets up several internal references to how deeply embedded this symbol was inside the imagination of people during this time.

An early and important reference to the tom-tom occurred in Eugene O'Neill's 1920 drama, *The Emperor Jones*, which was made into a movie with Paul Robeson in 1933. In this drama the title character is haunted by the beating of the tom-tom from the first scene through the final moments; the drum is a vehicle for an imagined past as well as an internalized heartbeat. W. E. B. Du Bois, Langston Hughes, and Helene Johnson Hubbell all mention the tom-tom in reference to African music in their writings and poetry.[31] William Grant Still opened his orchestral suite *Africa* with three solo tom-toms (1928), and Shirley Graham (who would later become W. E. B. Du Bois's second wife) wrote an opera in 1932 called *Tom Tom* (based on John Womack Vandercook's 1926 published travel diaries, titled *Tom Tom*, set in the Caribbean). Perhaps the most striking reference in this scene to tom-toms is in the movie *Stormy Weather* (1943, 20th Century Fox), which was one of the first all-black-cast movies released by a major studio and contains an extended "African" scene that included "Diga Diga Do, Diga Do Do," an "African Dance," and a song that opened with "Hear the Beating of the Tom-Tom." In *Carmen Jones*, just moments after the reference to the "twenty million tom-toms," Pearl Bailey moves on to the final verse of the song and brings the music and dancing to a momentary pause when she sings in the second half of the last stanza, "Tomorrow morning let it rain, tomorrow morning let it pour, tonight we're in the groove together, ain't gonna to worry about . . . Stormy Weather . . . gonna kick old trouble out the door!" The tempo slows, there is a momentary pause in the otherwise hyper-energetic dancing, and Pearl Bailey looks right into Max Roach's eyes (whose back is to us, and it almost feels as though she is looking at us in the audience) when she sings those lines. We get the reference and understand the message: eleven years after *Stormy Weather* here is a new musical to show off and feel good about.

Immediately following "Beat out Dat Rhythm on the Drum," we hear the arrival of the last main character to be introduced in the drama: Husky Miller plays the role of Escamillo from the opera, and his entrance showcases another well-known popular number. In Bizet's opera, this is the "Toreador Song," and it tells us who Escamillo is from the description of a bull fight: we watch the struggle with the bull and see the eventual victory for fame and love (presumably a girlfriend is in the crowd). The text for Husky Miller's entrance "Stan' Up an' Fight" works in a similar way to introduce Joe Adams (a noted radio announcer in Los Angeles at the time) as the film's boxing champion, Husky Miller.[32] The choice to change the role of the Escamillo character to a boxer makes sense for the time, given that era of African American boxing history. In the recent past of the film, the legendary Joe Louis (1914–1981) had held the world heavyweight boxing title from 1937 to 1949 and was considered by some to be the best boxer who ever lived. Also during this time in 1954 the famed John Arthur "Jack" Johnson (1878–1946, nicknamed the Galveston Giant), the first African American world heavyweight boxing champion (from 1908 to 1915), was inducted into the Boxing Hall of Fame.

As boxing became more than a sport exclusively for entertainment, the prominence of black boxers became an important achievement in the larger scheme of the civil rights movement. Like Escamillo's "Toreador Song" for bullfighting, "Stan' Up an' Fight" can be read as a description of a boxing match; the opening stanza focuses on Husky Miller's record ("Seventeen decisions in a row an' only five on points; de res' was all K.O." [knockouts]), and the second stanza outlines an outdoor fight in a baseball park. Yet the feeling of the number changes during the second stanza and refrain when certain words are highlighted and the cast joins in for the chorus. The second verse portrays a fight out in the open air where:

> De ring looks small an' white.
> Out in de blackness,
> Out in de blackness,
> you can feel a hun'red thousan' eyes
> fillin' de night.
> . . . .
> People are quiet—
> Den der's a riot!
> Someone t'rows a punch
> An' plants is right smack on de mark . . .
> Somebody's hurt,

You kinda think it's you.
You hang across de ropes—
Da's all you want to do.
Den you look around' an' see your trainer's eyes,
Beggin' you to see it through,
De say, "Remember,
Big boy, Remember—

Chorus
Stan-up an' fight until you hear de bell,
Stan' toe to toe,
Trade blow fer blow,
Keep punchin' till you make yer puches tell
Show dat crowd watcher know!
Until you hear dat bell,
Dat final bell,
Stan, up an' fight like hell!

Setting up the arena with "white" and "blackness" (in the opening lines of this verse), with the people quiet and then there's a riot, feels less like the boxing fight we see near the end of the film and more like a rally for standing up to "fight like hell" for what you believe in. The all-black peaceful gathering outside of Billy Pastor's Café has transformed this familiar popular tune into an impromptu civil rights anthem wherein the semipublic-private segregated space of the film reaches out across the screen into multiracial audiences.

James Baldwin's critique of the film, "Carmen Jones: The Dark Is Light Enough," appeared as "Life Straight in De Eye" in the January 1955 issue of *Commentary* magazine and was reprinted in his essay collection, *Notes of a Native Son* (first published in 1955 and then reissued in 1983 by Beacon Press in Boston). His comments are stinging in a pointed way, for he boldly wrote critically of a film that was undeniably important in terms of the money given to an all-black film at that time, the impressive spectacle it allowed blacks onscreen to achieve regarding showcasing talent, and the large number of black artists it brought together. Baldwin gets to the heart of what the film does not accomplish—it does not show black people as real people with three-dimensional portrayals. Baldwin writes that the "amoral Gypsy" is mapped onto the "amoral Negro woman," the characters "sound ludicrously false and affected, like ante-bellum Negroes imitating their masters," and the sexual chemistry between the two leads "is a sterile and distressing eroticism, however, because it is occurring in a vacuum between two mannequins who clearly are not involved in anything more serious than giving the customers a run for their money."[33] In an era when *Carmen Jones* was successful at the box office, *Life* magazine put Dorothy Dandridge on its cover (the first time a black person had appeared on the cover), and the film was nominated for and won multiple awards, Baldwin's essay could seem to be disgruntled, out of step with the time, and off the mark.[34] Yet his review gives us a penetrating view of how *Carmen Jones* had meaning when it first came out from someone who had his finger on the pulse of the black-white racial climate of the time.

Baldwin comments on the politics of skin color, a theme deep in the black community yet not always perceptible to nonblacks. Baldwin signals this discussion by saying that the film "is one of the first and most explicit—and far way the most self-conscious—weddings of sex and color which Hollywood has yet turned out."[35] He then outlines each of the main characters on the spectrum of a so-called "color wheel,"

> . . . . the color wheel in *Carmen Jones* is very important. Dorothy Dandridge— Carmen—is a sort of taffy-colored girl. . . . One feels—perhaps one is meant to feel—that here is a *very* nice girl making her way in movies by means of a bad-girl part. . . . Harry Belafonte is just a little darker and just as blankly handsome and fares very badly opposite her in a really offensive version of an already unendurable role. Olga James is Micaela, here called Cindy Lou, a much paler girl than Miss Dandridge but also much plainer. . . . Joe Adams is Husky Miller (Escamillo) and he is also rather taffy-colored. . . . Pearly Bailey is quite dark and she plays, in effect, a floozie. The wicked sergeant who causes Joe to desert the army—in one of many wild improbably scenes—and who has evil designs on Carmen is very dark indeed; and so is Husky Miller's trainer, who is, one is given to suppose, Miss Bailey's sugar-daddy.[36]

I have included, at length, these several excerpts to more deeply engage this topic, for they illuminate one of the most penetrating and incisive themes in the film.

References to the "brown paper bag test" and its more modern incarnation in discourses around colorism have been painful and destructive tropes in the black community going back to slavery. Leading black scholars, including Henry Louis Gates Jr, Cornel West, Michael Dyson, Alice Walker, and Toni Morrison (among others), have documented and historicized these terms in thoughtful commentaries.[37] An especially difficult element of this conversation is that the "brown paper bag test" and behaviors around colorism are internalized practices and attitudes that exist within the black community as well as through ideologies that are projected onto the black community by nonblacks. To have Baldwin note the roles by the darkness of the actors' skin color brings to the surface a topic everyone sees and registers but no one in polite society would want to talk about; it encompasses shame and embarrassment. Though the action of *Carmen Jones* is set in an all-black environment, the politics around race are still present. In a different configuration than the one Mérimée and Bizet nineteenth-century French sources provide with the exotic Romany world being told through a white narrator, the internalized opinions concerning the racial dynamics of white supremacy are still operative.

Baldwin spells out the players on each side of the racial divide. The leading characters all have rather light brown skin ("taffy-colored," the right light side of the color line in the world of the brown paper bag test); this includes Carmen, Joe, Cindy Lou, and Husky Miller. The darker characters all have negative associations connected to them. The "wicked sergeant who causes Joe to desert the army," Sergeant Brown (Brock Peters) is the antagonist rival to Joe for Carmen's affections. Rum Daniels, Husky Miller's manager (played by Roy Glenn) is only concerned about keeping his own job and does whatever he can to get Carmen Jones in the entourage, including acting as the sugar daddy to Frankie and Myrt. Pearl Bailey's darker color is filtered through a few complementing lenses. Though Baldwin writes her off as "a floozie" kept by sugar daddy Rum Daniels, she was one of the already-known stars of the time who brought attention to the film. Moreover, as Jeff Smith has noted, Bailey's darkness provides an acceptable arena for the jazzy performance of blackness in the otherwise opera-infused world of the film.

The battle of dark and light is most dramatically played out in the boxing match at the end of the film between Husky Miller and the Brazilian Kid Pancho (an uncredited role played by Rubin Wilson).[38] The fight is an indoor scene in an unnamed Chicago arena with a full all-black audience. Throughout the match the camera focuses on the fight in the ring with jump-cut shots to the general audience, Carmen and her friends (Frankie and Myrt) watching in the front row all dressed up in their finery, and Joe in the background as he sneaks around and finds the storage closet where he will later kill Carmen. The two men in the ring are strikingly differentiated by their skin colors, with Husky Miller looking lighter than he had anywhere previously and Kid Pancho the darkest person we have seen thus far in the film. Their skin color is highlighted by the fact that they are dressed for boxing (wearing nothing except boxing shorts, socks, shoes, and gloves) and we see a lot of their skin through their exposed arms, legs, and torso. Kid Pancho's boxing shorts are a shiny bright white with a purple stripe; the bright white material of his shorts contrasts with the darkness of his skin. Husky Miller's boxing shorts are black with a red stripe; the black of his shorts contrasts with the lightness of his skin. The fight between the two men starts out with some light sparring before Kid Pancho takes the lead in the first round. But in the second round Husky Miller is up to the task and knocks out Kid Pancho. In a scene that stages the boxing match in real time, Husky Miller fights Kid Pancho and wins in the second round after two minutes and twenty seconds. Though we have been rooting for Husky Miller all along—he is the new love interest of Carmen Jones—the defeat of Kid Pancho seems especially harsh. While we had only been introduced to him in the ring (he has no backstory and we know nothing about him except what the announcer says—a South American boxer from Brazil), he seems more like a straw man set up to be defeated by Husky Miller than a real opponent. It is easy to cheer for the light-skinned Husky Miller: he is fully integrated into the story. Kid Pancho is not even a character in the nineteenth-century French sources; his role replaces the bull that Escamillo violently defeats.

The color politics in *Carmen Jones* reinforce the attitudes of its time that are still visible today. In the conclusion of Baldwin's essay on the film he presciently writes that "it is one of the most important all-Negro movies Hollywood has yet produced . . . the questions it leaves in the mind relate less to Negroes than to the interior life of Americans."[39] Such a challenge and indictment help us realize that while this film might feel in some ways dated today, more than sixty years after its premiere, it still resonates boldly with the current hesitations around a black-white integration, where everyone is supposed to start on a level playing field, all voices can be heard just as clearly, and everyone is given a fair chance.

Hip Hopera and Carmen Brown

The term "hip hopera" was used as early as 1994 as the title of the debut album by west coast rapper Volume 10.[40] The seventh track of the album, also titled "Hip-Hopera," was produced by Baka Boyz under the RCA Records label and was released on March 1, 1994. *Oxford Music Online* only lists "Volume 10" and "Beyoncé" for the search on "hip hopera" (and nothing for "rap opera"). In *Wikipedia* the category of "hip hopera" brings up the entry for "rap opera" and lists a few examples, the most compelling being R&B singer R. Kelly's *Trapped in the Closet*, a three-part, thirty-three-chapter saga that outlines scenes in black urban life with connecting musical material throughout.[41] The work was released in various parts from 2005 to 2012. The provocative question of whether hip hop can be extended to the longer form of an operatic scale is not fully addressed in the current examples of hip hopera except for the MTV *Carmen* setting directed by Robert Townsend in 2001.[42]

In 2001 MTV took up the bold decision to cross genre and period by transforming the Carmen story into a new type of musical dramatic performance: the intrepidly titled *Carmen: A Hip Hopera*. With performers who were famous (and several who went on to become more famous), the artists included the film debut of Beyoncé Knowles (while she was still part of Destiny's Child), with the cast filled out by rappers (including Mos Def, Da Brat, Rah Digga, Wyclef Jean, Jermaine Dupri, and Lil' Bow Wow) and actors (including Mekhi Phifer, Reagan Gomez-Preston, Casey Lee, Sam Sarpong, and Joy Bryant). Set in Philadelphia and Los Angeles, the story retains a few, and changes many, elements from the nineteenth-century French sources. As McClary has noted, overall this telling of the Carmen story is strongly reliant on Preminger's *Carmen Jones*.[43]

The use of a narrator, similar to the French narrator in the Mérimée novella, frames the MTV hip hopera. However, rather than the outsider to gypsy culture, here we have a black female rapper (Da Brat) bringing us into the action. In an opposite function to Mérimée, Da Brat as the narrator presents us with an insider to the world of the drama who outlines the main themes for us from her standpoint. The opening prologue introduces us to the norms of the work in terms of the story and the sound world of the hip hopera. The vocal track consists of Da Brat's voice setting up the story; for those who are not familiar with the opera, her opening lines let us know that this is "a classic story retold" and sets up the "tragic tale" and "free spirit" of our leading heroine. With the final line of the opening, "as we fade to the car," we are brought into the main action of the story as the scene changes to police car with Derek Hill (our Don José) and his partner driving around the streets of Philadelphia.

INTRODUCTION [PROLOGUE] BY DA BRAT

Huh, yeah
A classic story retold,
Carmen, a Hip Hopera
watch the drama unfold.
The tragic tale of a girl
Tryin' to capture the gold
With a free spirit, brothers steady tryin' to hold
What would you do for love? (uh huh)
Is the cost too much?
For the object of your desire
you're tryin' to touch
Sometimes beauty is best to be observed from afar
Rise and fall like a star,
as we fade to the car. . . .

Though this introduction, functioning like a prologue, lasts less than two minutes, it sets up visual and aural guides for how this hip hopera works. Aurally, the track of Da Brat's vocal rap is accompanied by the acoustic sound of orchestral instruments (the strings and timpani). The vocals do not start until about forty seconds in. Within the first thirty seconds we are presented with a repetitive violin melody of steady sixteenth notes supported most prominently by an orchestral string section. Deep in the background there are sustained chords with horns and winds filling out the texture that provide a contrapuntal richness to the overall sonic fabric. The string melody is joined by the timpani playing a V-I cadence that supports the orchestral texture both harmonically (grounding the music in a home key) and rhythmically with a steady dotted-figure that helps the listener feel the crisp downbeat.

Visually we have two image tracks that are interspersed as they are juxtaposed. With establishing shots of the iconic statue of William Penn and the Ben Franklin suspension bridge over the Schuylkill River, the action is placed in Philadelphia with an aerial view panning across the full city and gradually focusing on the black neighborhoods, showing aging brownstones, run-down storefront businesses, and areas of urban blight. The camera then focuses on Da Brat with her instrumental ensemble surrounding her on the city street. We see her in the middle gesturing dramatically and waving a makeshift conductor's baton (that turns out to be a single rose—the flower reference to Carmen that cuts across multiple settings of this story), commanding her orchestra of a few violinists, a couple sets of timpani, and music stands standing in for the other players.[44] The screen shifts between a black-white image and filters with different colors (rose, yellow, blue), almost as though it, too, were warming up as it finally moves into regular, full-stereo color by the end of this opening sequence. A crowd begins to form as Da Brat tells her story with a setting in the urban neighborhood, literally in the streets of the people. This introduction guides the audience—the people gathering on the street and those of us in the theaters—and helps orient us to a new musical texture that combines the unsung quality of rapping voices and the reminders of a traditional operatic overture with the full orchestra signaled by the strings and timpani.

At the end of the main action in the hip hopera, the familiar "overture" music with the acoustic strings and timpani once again returns with Da Brat delivering her epilogue; this time there are flashbacks from the movie interspersed that recover the broad strokes of the plot. Unlike the fourth part of Mérimée's novella, this conclusion deals directly, not covertly, with what has just been presented. The supposed impurity of the Romany language Carmen speaks is not turned into an exegesis on the inferiority of Carmen's people, nor do we view the guilt of a man driven too far. Da Brat as the narrator poses questions that help the audience come to its own interpretation: "Who will take responsibility?" Is Hill "the one that she needed or the one that got her killed?" "Or is it Carmen to blame for her own downfall?" Da Brat treats Carmen neither as victim nor predator, but as a possible instigator whose actions should be seen as having consequences. Unlike Mérimée's narrator or Bizet's Don José, we have the voice of the protagonist, a black woman, summing up the action and posing the moral questions at the end. We are not told that we have been contaminated by the Other or have witnessed the downfall of a good soldier. Instead, we are given a eulogy for this new "immortal Beloved."

OUTRO [EPILOGUE] BY DA BRAT

Uh
And that's the story, no life, no more, just the loss.
Caught up in between the negative and positive force
Carmen Brown, sad tale of a life cut short.
Who will take the responsibility when the guns go off?
On one side you have Hill, he got to live with the guilt
Is he the one that she needed or the one that got her killed?
Or is it Carmen to blame for her own downfall?
Did she play with his heart and never loved him at all?
It doesn't matter now because she is resting in peace
And all the playas in the game have to live with the grief
It's only now that she's gone, you will truly discover
The Immortal Beloved Carmen Brown, there will never be another

The connections between Carmen Jones (Dorothy Dandridge) and Carmen Brown (Beyoncé) reflect a deep portrayal of African American women at the middle of the twentieth century and at the turn of the new millennium. As we saw, the reception of Preminger's *Carmen Jones* is situated in the midst of the United States after World War II, at the dawn of the civil rights era. Themes of postwar prosperity, the continuing Great Migration to the north for better opportunities, important symbols of black achievement (seen in the star-studded all-black cast with Dandridge, Belafonte, and Bailey, as well as appearances by Max Roach, Alvin Ailey, Carmen Lavallade, and others) show less of an exoticized dangerous "gypsy" world and more of a "separate but equal" vision of midcentury black culture.

Walter White's concerns about the NAACP publicly endorsing the film dealt with the all-black, non-integrationist setting of the film. Yet ironically, *Carmen Jones* also did a lot to promote an integrationist agenda, albeit covertly. Before the United States was ready to see bodies of different races come together peaceably onscreen, the nation needed to see black bodies at peace onscreen—living lives that were relatable to the white majority audience. *Carmen Jones* laid that groundwork. While there were still stereotypes (for example, poorly spoken English, letting loose in wild dancing), the film showcased glamorous, talented African Americans employed and working to achieve the American dream of career advancement (Joe being chosen for flight school) and access to capital and socioeconomic status (visible in Husky Miller and his entourage). *Carmen Jones* promotes an assimilationist agenda that aims to demystify and de-exoticize America's great Other—black people.

Carmen Brown continues this journey to fit into the American dream at the dawn of the new millennium. Caught up in the bling of the opulent lifestyle Hollywood and hip hop culture seem to offer, our title character now has aspirations to "make it" and achieve the same basic types of success—career recognition and material wealth—that we saw hinted at midcentury in *Carmen Jones*. In Preminger's film Carmen Jones resisted, in part, the buy-in to such an agenda. She showed up late to work, was known as a flirt, and focused on seducing good-looking men. In the added scene (no equivalent in the narrative in the nineteenth-century French sources) when Carmen Jones and Joe are detoured at her grandmother's house en route to the jail at Masonville, we see Carmen dusting off Joe's uniform, cooking him dinner, and talking about his being honest and not like the others (without any irony or condescension, he is a real credit to the race). They banter about his getting married and he says he can imagine her settling down and having children. Though Carmen Jones denies that future for herself, it is clear that she is perfectly familiar with that assimilationist culture and sees its importance for others, like Joe and Cindy Lou. It is not hard to see that Joe suspects that one day Carmen will probably change her mind and become the type of housewife she envisions for him. This is plausible not only because of the ease with which she starts to get dinner ready but also in how she shines his shoes and seems to slip effortlessly into the part of the now-classic 1950s housewife.

Looking back on this scene, many might want to believe that Carmen Jones has a shot at such a future. The assimilationist model of Carmen has her give up the "bad girl" image, but the question is, What would she become? Is there a middle-class midcentury model for a black Hollywood female character? Perhaps a domesticated Hollywood Carmen Jones would suffer from the same pitfalls white women of this postwar period would face; the "problem that has no name" that Betty Friedan would later articulate in her groundbreaking 1963 book, *The Feminine Mystique*. Some in the audience want to assimilate Carmen Jones into that gendered space where women who had had access to employment as "Rosie the Riveter" during the war effort were now displaced as the men came back, and expected to return back to the home (and it would still take a generation for some women to begin to find paths to college). But the realities for black women (and other women of color) were not tied to this same narrative. Though Carmen Jones may move beyond her original exotic bohemian roots, this film also reveals that there is no room for a middle-class black Carmen Jones outside of the factory or domestic sphere for raising children; not only does it not follow the story of Bizet's opera, there is no room for such a character in 1950s Hollywood film. While Carmen Jones is more domesticated from her original roots, the reality of the 1950s Hollywood film allies well with Mérimée and Bizet's story. As the marginalized "Other" Carmen Jones still needs a narrative that is different than the acceptable feminized model allowed for white womanhood.

Carmen Brown, on the other hand, is a more modern woman who lives in a different time. She is a liberated Carmen and has other options available that include a career and access to financial gain. This is a Carmen who has dreams—aspirations—as we see when Hill takes her back to her apartment, ostensibly so she can change into sweatpants before he takes her to jail. While she is re-dressing in the bedroom, we see Hill looking at the books on her coffee table about how to break into acting and several affirmations framed across the mantel: "Never Give Up, You Can Do It!!! Keep your eyes on the stars and you'll be one; Live each day like it's your last." Here is a Carmen who has fully embraced the late twentieth-century dream of capitalism and the pursuit of fame. As audiences look back on *Carmen: A Hip Hopera*, there is an added story of who the voice and body behind Carmen Brown has become: Beyoncé, whose rise to fame as a singer, performer, and media presence truly attained the success of superstardom.

Both Carmen Jones and Carmen Brown are first presented to us in a highly sexualized scene for their entrance number, the Habanera. In *Carmen Jones*, "Dat's Love" is sung by Dorothy Dandridge in a tight red pencil skirt with a plunging neckline on a black peasant blouse; it is an outfit that is inappropriate for her day job in the parachute factory and unlike anything the other women at work are wearing. For its time, the hip-hugging bright red skirt and low neckline sexualize Carmen Jones as she sings about love, freedom, and sexual energy. When Carmen Brown first appears in Lou's Pub in the hip hopera ("If looks could kill, you would be dead") the effect is similar, but turned up several notches. The camera scans over her body several times; first we see her feet, then her feet and thighs, then her feet, thighs and bust and finally her full body. The camera's movements act as though they are caressing her image and this motion forces our eyes to visually paw and grope at her body. We see that Carmen is wearing a body-clinging red sequined dress that looks more like it was drawn on than being removable as clothing. In the neighborhood after-work hangout bar for policemen and their girlfriends, Carmen Brown's presence is almost X-rated.

Yet even in this highly sexualized scene, Carmen Brown challenges the image of only being eye candy. Her entrance starts out as a solo and then move to more of a trio texture in the dialogue with Lieutenant Miller (played brilliantly by Mos Def) and his partner Nathaniel (the late Sam Sarpong). As Miller and Nathaniel are trying to come on to Carmen Brown, she thwarts their efforts,

> But I'm not hearing you, you might as well be mumbling
> See, I have dreams, and with a man, what will become of them?
> There's not a kid out here who can make me believe
> I should postpone my goals, he got tricks up his sleeve?
> Whole bar full of cuffs and you ain't locking me down

Carmen's words echo a late-twentieth-century strand of feminism especially popular with the millennial generation that took for granted many of the political feminist gains of the 1970s and 1980s "second wave" generation while also wanting to embrace a sexier brand of feminism.[45] In a typical lyric that links her voice to the lineage of Motown soul singer Marvin Gaye and also brings together the varied tropes of her curvaceous hips, competitive beauty, and the dangers of stalking, Carmen Brown's Habanera entrance number continues,

> See this is Carmen, voice sweet as Marvin
> I turn out lights, with the switch, when I'm walking
> Girls steady jealous cause they men always hawkin'
> Even got Lou lookin' at me like he stalkin'.
> And I got a mind, too.

Carmen Jones and Carmen Brown personify modes of black womanhood at the middle and end of the twentieth century that are also informed by the actresses who played them. Dorothy Dandridge was undeniably an incredibly talented actress and singer, but her career success was tempered and shaped by the attitudes around race and gender of her time. Though she shared many similarities with Marilyn Monroe, and they reportedly had a strong friend-ship, their fates overlap and differ in striking ways.[46] Both were direct con-temporaries (Dandridge 1922–1965; Monroe 1926–1962), happened to share a middle name (Dorothy Jean, "Marilyn" Norma Jeane), were sex symbols of their time, had multiple marriages, and died of accidental pill overdoses whose stories were initially covered up and still have auras of mystery surrounding the details. While Monroe's unleashed sexuality as the dumb blonde coupled her stage persona and all-American good looks (a busty bombshell), she spent a good deal of time trying to conquer this image and reset the norms by which she had become typecast.[47] For Dandridge, the sexual image had different stakes. Though writing about *Carmen Jones*, Baldwin identifies the more general issue in his comments about the apparent minimizing of the sexual eroticism as a necessity for people to take the film seriously: "Negroes are associated in the public mind with sex . . . darker races always seem to have for lighter races an aura of sexuality."[48] In the complicated racial times when free black bodies were still defining themselves on stage and screen, Dandridge had a different negotiation than Marilyn Monroe with star image, gender, and sex. Attractiveness with less unbridled sexual energy seems to be the choice made for keeping the attention on the seriousness of the film and all it stood for in black achievement.

By the time we get to *Carmen: A Hip Hopera*, young women—of all races in the United States—could flaunt their sexiness in ways that "claim" power rather than exploitation.[49] In addition to being sexy and powerful, this Carmen "has a mind too" and wants to project a multifaceted image that brings all of these things together. Beyoncé's super sexualized first appearance during her version of the Habanera is seen in a different context from that of Dandridge. Rather than the artificial and weakened sexuality Baldwin compellingly theorizes in *Carmen Jones*, Carmen Brown's entrance (as well as her seduction scene with Hill for their "Seguidilla") is smoldering hot with lust and desire wrapped together. Yet throughout the film we see other images of Carmen Brown as she hangs out with her friends and in her first encounter with Blaze (the Escamillo figure, now reconfigured as a rapper). Rather than exclusively the flirtatious vixen, Carmen Brown sometimes appears almost shy, certainly less outgoing than her friends Rasheeda and Nikki (Fresquita and Mercedes in the opera) when they first meet Blaze at the club. Though she might not be loud and "in your face," Carmen Brown exudes a confidence that allows her to think on her feet (when she asks Hill to take her home to change her clothes before going to jail), and to speak self-assuredly and intelligently when she talks about her dreams and desires to be an actress (when she impresses Blaze as she talks about wanting to go to Los Angeles).

The evolution of the Carmen persona shows a broad progression from her original position as a vividly portrayed but mainly silent literary character in Mérimée's novella to Bizet's very vocal and central character in his opera. Seeing and hearing such a bold female character needed a lot of intervention through the depiction of a foreign picturesque setting (complete with exotic bohemian color, bull fights, and seductive so-called Spanish dances), and a helpful "tour guide" type of figure to keep the audience grounded in the norms for nineteenth-century Western (European) behavior. When the story of Carmen on the margins migrates to African American culture in the United States, there is the added dynamic of having Carmen become the representative of black people on the periphery of mainstream white culture. Yet the original relationship between Carmen as an outsider to the others in her novella/operatic world is altered, as there are now all-black settings in *Carmen Jones* and *Carmen: A Hip Hopera*.

These works present an important opportunity to explore what a Carmen figure could do in her own community. Carmen Jones and Carmen Brown are very much articulations of their time with the opportunities and limitations of 1950s and the early millennium in the United States. *Carmen Jones* presents a spectrum of black people at midcentury, the working class of the parachute factory laborers, black soldiers in the newly integrated military, the glitzy world of show business with Husky Miller and his entourage, the mix of classes at Billy Pastor's, and the poor in Carmen's hometown. While the depictions of these socioeconomic levels show a cross-section of black society, they are not fully explored and are presented in rather sanitized ways (on a colorful movie set). Yet even though there is a diversity of class representation, there is little room for Carmen Jones to fit outside the gendered expectations for womanhood of that time. For black women there is the working world and the domestic sphere. In the world of *Carmen Jones*, the high price is death for wanting to look for something different and experience sexual freedom to move from one partner to another.

Unlike Carmen Jones, Carmen Brown is allowed to be motivated by her dream for stardom and fame. This is a world that feels contemporary to its audiences: the urban blight of Philadelphia, the depiction of policemen and "regular" folks at Lou's Pub and at the bar in Philly (after Blaze's first concert when he first meets Carmen Brown and her friends), the figure of famous glitzy rapper Blaze and his crew. From what we see, Carmen Brown is well on her way to realizing her dreams by the end of the film when she is settled in L.A. with Blaze and her friends. Being quite adept at manipulating the gender codes of her time, she uses her good looks and personal drive to move ahead. In the telling of this Carmen story, the price she pays for her ambition is brought on by corruption in the black community, notably through the "bad cop" of Lieutenant Miller and his manipulation of "good cop" Derek Hill. What we have not yet seen in these African American Carmens is a figure who works within her community and has desires that can be achieved.

Additionally, these U.S. Carmens weave in a feature of the Great Migration exodus from her home community (Florida, Philadelphia) to the north (Chicago) or west (Los Angeles) for better opportunities. In the next section I outline a context for opera in post-apartheid South Africa that shows how *U-Carmen eKhayelitsha* adds this new dynamic of a Carmen who is rooted within her own community, albeit equally unlucky in her destiny.

South African Carmen: *U-Carman eKhayelitsha*

Bringing the Carmens Together: Narrators and Audiences

As in the African American Carmens, South African *U-Carmen eKhayelitsha* is adapted to an all-black setting; in this case, the main action takes place in the Cape Town township of Khayelitsha with a few flashbacks that take the story to the rural areas (formerly the Bantustan Homelands, during the apartheid government). All of the characters are black—as in *Carmen Jones* and *Carmen: A Hip-Hopera* and, unlike Mérimée's or Bizet's *Carmen*, there is no presence of a tour-guide narrator to help the audience understand Carmen's so-called mysterious and exotic ways. This is because there has been a radical shift in the vantage points—who is in the story, who is telling the story, and who is in the audience interpreting the narratives.

A process that had its roots in the nineteenth century, present in Carmen Jones and continued through Carmen Brown (in *Carmen: A Hip-Hopera*), is now complete in our title character, U-Carmen. These black Carmens have shown the evolution of the Carmen figure. In 1875 we started with the exotic outsider who titillated and shocked the hegemonic French bourgeoisie audience with her outlandish ways. In the mid-twentieth century, audiences in the United States were also enticed by the sexual allure of Carmen Jones. The lower economic status and sexual nature of this 1950s postwar factory worker continued her enticing presence with the fantasy of racial subservience and the safety of containment within a pre–civil rights segregated environment. Mainstream America had access to a dazzling array of black talent without the threat of having to be too close. On the screen or performing onstage, an unspoken (but strictly enforced through practices such as redlining and Jim Crow laws) respectable distance remained between blacks and whites that prevented the two populations from moving in next door, sitting side by side in school, or—in many states—sharing the same water fountain. By the end of the twentieth century, America once again revisited the black Carmen figure. At this point, the United States was past the civil rights movement of the 1960s and had a strong, albeit bloated, sense of national pride in its socially progressive advances since the 1950s, including a perception of its black-white race relations.

When *Carmen: A Hip-Hopera* was released in May 2001, no one knew that we were on the cusp of a new era of global terrorism after the events a few months later on September 11. No one knew that we would elect our first black president in 2008 and enter such a racially turbulent time that much of the progress of the civil rights gains would be called into question and urgently need readdressing within that decade. Instead, the millennial hip hop Carmen aspiring to the bling lifestyle felt like a clever twist of the "American dream" where anyone with energy and talent could make it big. Carmen Brown, embodied by the young Beyoncé, brought together the smokin' hot body type, a smooth R&B-infused rapping lyrical style, and just enough youthful innocence that, despite the mixed reviews (the movie did not significantly catapult anyone into the spotlight, but neither did it hurt any of the performers' careers), it had rather strong support from black audiences.[50] Even as the century drew to a close, the story was still presented in a segregated setting—an all-black cast where the action was focused in the urban centers of Philadelphia and Los Angeles. With the light honey-brown color of most of the principal characters, the hip hopera reinforced much of the racial narrative seen in *Carmen Jones*. The title character is a party girl who wants to break out of the expectations before her. Carmen Jones resisted the domestic and well-behaved demure girlfriend-fiancé-housewife path represented in Cindy Lou. Carmen Brown resisted the girlfriend-fiancé-housewife path represented in Caela. While Carmen Jones does not present an alternative path, besides working in the factory and possibly marrying into wealth through the boxer Husky Miller, Carmen Brown has aspirations and goals to "make it big" and become a singer and actress. Despite the vast gains black people in America had made, Carmen Jones and Carmen Brown love and pursue segregated dreams, fifty years apart in the United States at midcentury and the dawn of the new millennium.

U-Carmen comes out of these sources but resonates as a different figure. It is as though Carmen has gone home to a space where she is surrounded by her community. We, in the audience, have followed her there and watch her, peering in from the outside we now inhabit.[51] U-Carmen from Khayelitsha not only represents who is in the story, but she is now telling the story; she is the narrator. Those of us in the audience who are not from Khayelitsha are not given an easily accessible, built-in narrator/tour-guide proxy to show us how (or if) we fit in.

As Davis and Dovey have perceptively argued in their discussion of how the opera and the township are brought together through Fernando Ortiz's ethnographic paradigm of transculturation, "Bizet has become a character in Khayelitsha, and Khayelitsha has become inhabited by Bizet."[52] Viljoen and Wenzel have also discussed the way U-Carmen fits into her community in Khayelitsha and articulates different narratives that extend beyond the *femme fatale*; she becomes a more complex and independent South African woman.[53]

In the opening of the film we are introduced to the elements of the township and the setting of the opera through the use of the diegetic sounds of the township, the female factory workers singing other non-operatic songs over Bizet's music, and the fast panning action of the camera (forward and backward) over the landscape of Khayelitsha.[54] In these opening minutes of the film, we are given direction about how to watch and listen to this telling of Carmen. As the camera introduces us to the township visually, we are also alerted early on to the contrapuntal sonic soundscape that will bring together Bizet's music, the diegetic sounds of Khayelitsha's honking car horns and crowing roosters, and the multiple instances throughout the film when diegetic singing of non-operatic Xhosa songs and ululation are layered on top. The use of the French narrator in Mérimée's novella and the "he is one of us" aspect to Bizet's Don José in the opera are now presented through the filmic devices of the genre where the sound and visual techniques replace the use of a specific character in the story who guides the audience through the narrative. As Khayelitsha is written into operatic history, multiple opera audiences are brought into these new narratives. Those not familiar with opera but part of Khayelitsha see themselves in Bizet's tale. Those familiar with opera but outside of Khayelitsha see Bizet in the township. And those familiar with neither Khayelitsha nor Bizet experience a story that opens up the possibilities of how opera can have meaning in new spaces for unexpected populations.

U-Carmen

The entrance into the exoticism of the Carmen story is reconfigured in *U-Carmen eKhayelitsha*. The film presents a new incarnation of the narrator figure. Unlike the framing device of the same narrative voice in the Mérimée novella (of the French bourgeoisie academic) or Da Brat outlining the story from the gendered and racialized position of our protagonist (in her prologue and epilogue), here we have two disembodied "voices" surrounding the film. These bookends open with the voice of Mérimée, spoken in the opening minutes of the film while the camera pulls out from a close-up of

U-Carmen's face. The final bookend is the vacant voice of the landscape that the camera center stages once U-Carmen has been silenced.

In the opening we have Mérimée's words from his novella, translated into Xhosa (appearing as English subtitles across the bottom of the screen) spoken by a baritone voice, describing the figure of Carmen.

> In Spain for a woman to be thought beautiful she should have thirty positive qualities. Or to put it another way, it must be possible to apply to her three adjectives, each of which describes ten parts of her person.[55]

This quotation of Mérimée's authorial voice is paired with the visual "voice" the camera provides that immediately links Mérimée as narrator with what we see. During Mérimée's words (presented both in Xhosa and English) we see the image of Pauline Malefane's face come into focus as the embodiment of our Carmen. After the close-up, the camera pulls back and reveals the location, a small photo shop in Khayelitsha. The camera dynamically pans around the township, and the narrative voice reciting Mérimée's words gives way to the soundtrack of daily life starting morning routines. A Western orchestra begins tuning up, then moves into the downbeat of Bizet's sparkling rousing overture. The establishing shot in this opening sequence does several things simultaneously when it brings together Mérimée's words introducing the image of Pauline Malefane as our U-Carmen and the importance of "looking" through the close-up camera angle in the photo shop. As if the conceit of translation were not salient enough, we have the aural marker of the Xhosa language (an Nguni click language that immediately sounds the foreignness with the pops of the clicks on *x*, *q*, and *c*) and English interpretation in subtitles.

In Mérimée's novella and in the role of Da Brat in the hip hopera the narrating figure frames the story as the first and final scenes. Unlike the energetic and hectic opening scenes of *U-Carmen eKhayelitsha*, the end of the film, with its final sonic and visual landscapes, is contained in one long, slow shot of the camera pulling back from the stabbed, dead Carmen. Unlike the animated beginning with the bright orchestral timbres and the colorful visual texture of Khayelitsha, the conclusion of the film is nearly silent and the visual rhythm has slowed down to an extreme long shot pulling away from the scene. In the last moments of the film, we hear the dull roar of the wind and see the passing cars in a maze of highways that give the scene an impersonalized ghostly feel.

The stark, postapocalyptic nature of the end of the film seems vaguely appropriate. For even though this film represented an early example of South

Africa's new and exciting entrance into an international arena for film and opera, it also carried some of the weight of its brutal history with apartheid. One of the things that makes *U-Carmen* so effective is that the story is completely in the present moment with the recent history of apartheid woven in through its indomitable legacy and a few strategic flashbacks in the characters' memories. The past is embedded as it haunts the present but does not take over the future. There are a few overt references to the apartheid past, but the focus of the film is on the sumptuous sound of the voices and the still-new situation of hearing opera sung in Xhosa and seeing it set in a township. The stark reality of the poverty in Khayelitsha is noticeable and unlike traditional opera performances in Western opera houses; but once the audience settles into the film, these initial matters tend to revert to the world of the film and point to the *verismo*, gritty realistic element of the original late-nineteenth-century context of Bizet's opera.[56]

U-Carmen eKhayelitsha takes the construction of realism/*verismo* and extends it to a new level with its hyperrealistic setting and the use of a cast that is at home in the township (with the performers either from there or nearby locales). Most *Carmen* productions present Carmen as an exceptional character who is different from her peers—she is sexier, more exotic, more liberated, more peculiar, more outlandish . . . more *something*. U-Carmen embodies any member of the Khayelitsha community whose experiences stand in for a modern South African heroine. In this Carmen we see a different side; she lives by modest means, works in a cigarette factory, and raises her child within the community as a single mother. Malefane reveals her thinking about the role of U-Carmen: "Carmen is just an ordinary person, any normal woman who wants to live life to the fullest." She continues, "A lot of people see Carmen as strong all the time . . . sometimes she does those things because she wants to protect herself from the public. She's a fighter, she's fragile." Regarding this last juxtaposition between the strength and potential weakness, Malefane notes, "Carmen is quite fragile inside. On the inside she is quite vulnerable."[57]

We see U-Carmen fleshed out with strength and these vulnerabilities. Unlike other Carmens, U-Carmen gets beaten up by the police in the second-act tavern scene (Bizet's Lillias Pastias; now at Bra Nkomo's shebeen) and suffers humiliation. She is a struggling Carmen and emerges as an even more sympathetic character when we learn that her Don José (Jongikhaya) has a violent past and is beating her.[58] When she tries to move on, she seems more like a woman trying to escape an abusive relationship than the usual, somewhat fickle Carmen figure who tires of Don José and rejects him just because—it seems—she needs a change of pace.

In the final scenes when Jongikaya stalks U-Carmen at the concert arena and kills her outside by the side of the highway, she easily fits the profile of a domestic-abuse victim, killed by her abuser. Presented like a crumpled red blotch along the side of the road next to the refuse and garbage blown against the fence, U-Carmen becomes a stand-in for other women who suffer the consequences of violence that is passed down from the state through the oppression of institutionalized racism that gets recirculated and dispatched onto loved ones and hapless bystanders who get in the way. While U-Carmen is a strong character who shows a degree of agency in her decisions, she is also presented as a victim of a larger societal violence reflective of the white supremacy and patriarchy of her environment. Jongikhaya is also a victim of this same environment. His aggression toward her is borne of systemic and internalized codes of violence, self-hatred, racism, shame, and misogyny.[59] Though these larger elements of institutionalized racism and patriarchy are elements in the other black versions of the story (*Carmen Jones* and *Carmen: A Hip Hopera*), it is different in the South African context where the immediate history of apartheid lingers so closely in the background and is in the psychological and physical memories of the cast, production crew, and early audiences from 2005. Both U-Carmen and Jongikhaya suffer from the legacy of apartheid, which combines the mix of violence and patriarchal oppression in domestic relationships as well as in the institution of the nation. U-Carmen's situation moves from representing the very personal to embodying the experiences of any woman in Khayelitsha.

Carmens and Death

All three—Carmen Jones, Carmen Brown, and U-Carmen—wear red when we see them in their first appearance. This is true for almost all Carmens on the opera stage as well as in the vast number of other adaptations. Regularly, the color red continues to be connected with Carmen's character and it is not unusual to see her associated with this color throughout the production. However, in an unusual move, Carmen Jones and Carmen Brown both wear white when they are killed. Such a color scheme speaks to a deeper trope in each film. As has already been discussed, their Habanera scenes, like all Habanera scenes, are meant to show them off in sexual roles. Yet both African American Carmens undergo a transformation that adds a different layer of interpretation to their murder. In the earlier nineteenth-century French sources, the exoticism of the bohemian Carmen was always kept in the forefront, visible in her contrast to the role of French narrator in the novella and the tour guide stand-in—Don José—in the opera. The nineteenth-century

Carmens needed mediation as well as punishment by the end with her death so that an expected social order could be restored; Carmen's disruption of that social order needed to be stopped.

With the all-black versions of the story, the difference between Carmen and the other people in the narrative has dissipated and the distance between the insiders and the outsiders to the story is gone. The murders of the black Carmens resonate differently than in the earlier versions. Carmen Jones, Carmen Brown, and U-Carmen are not a contagion to the communities onscreen or in the audience; instead, they have been brought into the mainstream of the world of their respective films and cultural times. Since they are now members of their larger community, there is a new element of sacrifice to their deaths. Carmen Jones and Carmen Brown are still outliers to the norms of their societies; as mentioned above, they do not fit squarely into the conventional models of womanhood for their respective times. But now there is room for them. Neither had been as deeply connected to the original criminal element of the earlier sources. Both women are flirtatious, but we also see different sides of them with the domestication potential of Carmen Jones (when she cooks dinner in the side trip at her grandmother's house as Joe is taking her to Masonville) and the girlfriend/woman-with-career-dreams/aspiring actress/singer in Carmen Brown. While Carmen Jones is still dealing with the limited gender and segregationist racial politics of her time, Carmen Brown has been liberated and emancipated, to certain degrees, regarding the reality of her aspirations. It is possible to imagine Carmen Brown making it big as a famous superstar; in fact, Beyoncé already has.

Both African American Carmens have assimilated into their cultural surroundings enough so that American white and black audiences of their time could imagine meeting and knowing such characters. Hence, both characters were less foreign to their audiences. But it is the way that each African American Carmen is killed that changes the nature of the larger meaning of her death. Carmen Jones wears white and is strangled by Joe. Right before he kills her he sings: "String me high up on a tree/so that soon I will be/with my darling/ my baby, my Carmen." With the overt reference to hanging in his lyric ("String my high up on a tree") and his choice of strangling her, rather than the original stabbing in the opera, Carmen Jones becomes a cipher for lynching, a horror very real in 1950s America. Her wearing white speaks to a larger sacrifice of unwarranted and unjust killings of black people at its time. Wearing white exonerates Carmen Jones from the guilt of crime (despite Joe's comments that he is killing her for revenge and not letting her two-time anyone else again) and places her as a different type of victim.[60] Carmen Jones is not the sexually deviant underclass so-called gypsy Carmen from the nineteenth century. I am not arguing that her death is meant to represent a private lynching; a character like Joe would not lynch Carmen. Rather, I assert that the direct references to lynching would resonate with many in the audiences of the time. With Carmen Jones dressed in white her death points more to a symbolic sacrifice rather than punishment. In 1954 she is stopped for trying to have too much, live too grandly, and move beyond (what might have been considered for the politics of the time) her "proper" station.

Carmen Brown also lives life to the fullest, and she wears white when she dies. However, she is killed for other reasons. One of the complicated changes in the hip hopera adaptation is the increased size of the role of Lieutenant Miller, portrayed brilliantly by rapper Mos' Def. Miller takes the position of Bizet's Zuniga—the police superior to the Don José character—Derek Hill. In the opera Zuniga's main function is to provide a rival to Don José at the end of act 2 during the tavern scene at Lillias Pastias. Zuniga shows up right after Carmen and Don José have a fight. As Don José was going back to his dragoon barracks, he sees Zuniga come to court Carmen. The two men get into a fight and, having disrespected his superior officer, Don José definitively chooses the outlaw life of Carmen and her smuggler band over his life as a dragoon. As a character, Zuniga appears at the beginning of act 1 and he has a role at the end of act 2 to show Don José caught in a power struggle with his commanding officer and to provide a romantic rival to Carmen.

In the hip hopera, Lieutenant Miller's is a major role that serves more as an example of a dirty, bad-cop foil to the clean, good-cop image of Derek Hill (as Don José). After Da Brat's opening prologue, the scene moves between two cop cars (one with Miller and his partner, the other with Hill and his partner). We first see Miller collecting hush money from a local drug dealer that immediately shows he is on the take and working with the gangster crowd. As both Miller and Hill respond to a stolen-car call from headquarters, we see Miller plant drugs on one of the perpetrators, deny it, and then threaten Hill when he tries to speak up. Miller emerges as the bad cop yet the smooth and confident rapper; his character becomes much more interesting than the hardly noticeable Zuniga from the opera and almost steals the show.

The "good cop" family-values man Hill represents (with his engagement to Caela) versus the "bad cop" with close gangster dealings that Miller embodies reflects a larger trope of black urban life. The double lens in which society views black people during the time of the hip hopera tends to shift between praising those working within the system of middle-class values and, conversely, being hyper-suspicious that all black people have a tendency toward thug-like behavior, cavorting with drug dealers and corrupting the halls of law enforcement. Miller and Hill bring both sides of this conflict to life; Carmen Brown becomes a player against this background.

By the end of the hip hopera, Carmen Brown has moved closer to her goal of fame and is with Blaze in Los Angeles. Derek Hill who initially went to L.A. to follow Carmen Brown is hiding out from the law and has gone to warn Carmen that the corrupt Miller is in town. Backstage during one of Blaze's concerts Hill tries to warn Carmen of the danger, but Miller (hiding in the rafters) sees them both, and he shoots and kills Carmen. As Hill pursues Miller, he shoots Miller in self-defense and kills him. The last scene before Da Brat's epilogue/outro is a montage that intersperses the flashbacks Hill has of meeting Carmen, the rise and fall of their relationship with the future news and media coverage of the reported violence at Blaze's concert where Hill is blamed for killing Carmen Brown and Miller in a fit of jealousy and rage.

An element that makes the hip hopera feel relevant and truer to life is the ending where the news media gets things completely wrong in their coverage of this "black on black" crime. Audiences (up through today) watch the film and understand that so often the officially reported story does not have the full truth when it comes to crime among black people (as well as many other communities of color). With the complementing story of crime in black neighborhoods and police corruption, Carmen Brown becomes a pawn in a larger narrative. While she is still a character who stands for young black millennial female-gendered power, she also becomes a symbol of the innocent caught in the crossfire. Hill presents no motive for killing Carmen; his stated reason for being there is to protect and save her from whatever Miller has planned. Hill believes that Miller would hurt Carmen in order to get to Hill, and the audience has no reason to doubt him. Miller has proved to be an immoral character who would have no problem killing to cover up his own corruption. Hence, when Hill's prediction comes true, Carmen Brown's death has little to do with her own behavior and more to do with how she is caught in the crosshairs of patriarchy gone wrong. Wearing white highlights the virtue in Beyoncé's brand (just beginning as she was becoming a solo artist). She is a Carmen whose sexiness has lost its threat and has become desirable by men, women, and transgendered people as a feature to possess or to emulate. So many of us now want to be this millennial Carmen.

U-Carmen in South Africa's township of eKhayelitsha dies wearing Red. But even though she was created after the other Carmens, and in post-apartheid South Africa, there is something less sacrificially heroic in her death than the other black American Carmens (Carmen Jones and Carmen Brown), whose deaths seemed to be connected to shining a light on larger causes, legible just below the surface, of injustice. U-Carmen's death feels brutally realistic and violent outside against a chain-link fence, next to a major highway. After her death, the camera pulls back and for a few long minutes the music has stopped, the diegetic noise of the cars on the freeway takes over the sonic soundscape, and the red crumpled heap of her body against the side of the road seems more like a red blotch of refuse than a once-living person. This is an everywoman Carmen who has no magical exotic powers and no belief that her dreams, optimism, and aspirations can save her. Now she has become easily disposable.

This is a Carmen whose story has ended even before the cameras stop shooting. It is as though everyone else has gone away; there are no mourners, the police have left, and the medical examiner will pick up the body of U-Carmen—labeled and ready to go—when it fits into an already-busy schedule. In the bureaucracy of post-apartheid life, she will wait her turn in death for entrance into the morgue. This Carmen is unlike other versions of the Carmen story where the curtain comes down and the film ends with her friends crying around her and Don José dejectedly taking responsibility. Those Carmens have a heroism ascribed to their death. Those Carmens died center stage and we are still mourning their deaths as the films end. In Khayelitsha, it is as though her specific death has already become old news before we can leave. The cameras continue to roll, capturing a vast emptiness of violence past and the aftermath of death is still felt: the death of U-Carmen, those who came before, and those who will come after. This is a telling of Carmen in the midst of the apocalypse. The specter of apartheid hovers in this film as a ghostly character. We witness something that has unfolded and is still unfolding before us. This is a story that begins as it ends, or whose ending signals a beginning.

In the black settings of the Carmen story, the Carmen figure becomes an increasingly more integrated member of both her onscreen community and the audiences sitting in the theater. Within the South African Carmen the juxtaposition between the familiar and the foreign seems to be practically erased so that the film has a fairly homogenous group of characters, a story set with members from the township of Khayelitsha. The cultural world presented is recognizable and understandable to its home audience. South Africans can see their own land and people so that the separation between the Self and the Other so prominent in Mérimée and Bizet virtually collapses.

Yet the element of exotic fascination continues, even if it is configured differently in the nineteenth-century French versions, wherein the French were presenting Spain to the French—the implied audiences for Mérimée and Bizet (even though in reality this was not a homogenous public, they catered to expected conventions).[61] In the new millennium, audiences are anticipated to be more diverse, especially with the distribution of film being a global phenomenon.

U-Carmen eKhayelitsha has gone beyond the local opera audiences and has become a global text. The multiple publics who are exposed to the film far exceed its original audience or modern opera-going audiences in any one location. As mentioned above, this South African version presents a glimpse into an experience that is not seen in traditional Western opera productions. In standard productions of *Carmen*, opera audiences today are used to having the character of Don José act as our heroic figure; the Spanish soldier who is engaged to the girl next door (Micaela). When he falls in love with the racial and ethnic Outsider (Carmen), we are a little nervous but expect him to civilize her to our patriarchal code and make the best of the situation. The tragedy is his when he is unable to tame her and is driven to kill her when her wild ways cause him to snap in an obsessive pathological break. Yet in the last moments of the opera he redeems himself when he does not flee the scene but instead "returns to his senses" and turns himself in. Though we know he will be punished, he ends the opera as a good citizen to the moral code as he admits his wrongdoing and accepts his punishment.[62]

What we are not used to is a production where Carmen is part of an African community around her. The African American context of *Carmen Jones* and *Carmen: A Hip Hopera* is accessible to most audiences through iconic visions of black America in the rural South (as in the first part of *Carmen Jones*) or in the African American urban experience in Chicago, Philadelphia, and Los Angeles. Traditional opera audiences are not used to having this exotic tale told from a different angle.

The invention of U-Carmen in South Africa gives birth to a new viewer who destabilizes the function of the earlier nineteenth-century transgressive presence of Carmen. Non-African viewers familiar with the French Carmen stories understandably feel disoriented when first seeing this South African Carmen; the Western normative vantage point has been shifted and the heroine formulates new terms of womanhood. Inversely, it is now the specifically non-African publics that have been decentered. Those of us in the audience who are not South African are now exoticized, as we are outsiders to the localized knowledge of South African culture. In a new gesture for a telling of Carmen, the experiences of South African audiences are mirrored back in the films. In terms of who is representing whom, the stakes have also changed and it is no longer the exotic Other who is being defined by a Western narrator. Instead, we have a new articulation of sub-Saharan Africa that takes into account the experiences of postcolonial, post-apartheid cultures and repositions who is on the outside looking in.

6 *Winnie*, Opera, and South African Artistic Nationhood

Winnie: The Opera, composed and orchestrated by Xhosa composer Bongani Ndodana Breen, is the first full-length, fully orchestrated opera by a black South African composer. Working alongside Breen on the libretto was the interracial team of Warren Wilensky and, in the last stages, Mfundi Vundla. I write about *Winnie: The Opera* for its historical importance as a leader in black South African opera, as well as because I had the opportunity to see the last week of rehearsals, the premiere, and the second performance.[1] Hence, along with the other nonfilm case studies in this project (*From the Diary of Sally Hemings*, Gershwin's 1935 version of *Porgy and Bess*, and Bizet's *Carmen*), I have experienced this work as a member of the audience. Like the 2011 Broadway production of *The Gershwins' Porgy and Bess*, *Winnie: The Opera* is also unavailable as a commercial DVD recording (at the time of this writing) and I experienced the operatic presentations of both as live performances.[2]

Winnie: The Opera fits into as well as challenges conventions around what is considered "South African" music. The opera breaks the model of thinking that "traditional" South African music has no deep connection to music on other continents. Scholarship has documented the syncretic components of South African jazz (such as Marabi and Jaiva), hip hop (and Kwaito), and other popular musics that show how traveling minstrel troupes in the late nineteenth century interacted with mission hymns to help create isicathamiya and the intercontinental dialogue of jazz musicians who produced global variations of musical genres.[3] Given the colonial and apartheid history to South Africa, and the long-term encounters with the West, the musical tapestry of post-apartheid South Africa interweaves musical diasporas together.

Author's POV

We see less scholarship on how interracial collaborations between black and white South African musicians and performers have been influenced by Western musical forms that are considered "art music" or music for the concert stage. This discussion of *Winnie: The Opera* helps fill that gap and positions the work at the center of a conversation about musical genre, identity, and nation building in Europe, the United States, and South Africa.

In the other case-study chapters, I have written as an audience member who is proficient and knowledgeable in the cultural codes for the specific works. As an opera scholar, I am well versed in the conventions of the Western European operatic tradition. As an African American who grew up in the United States, I have experienced black-white racial dynamics from a black perspective. (This is not to imply that there is only one monolithic understanding of these issues but rather to value direct insider experience.) Finally, as someone who has grown up in the United States, I am able to speak about American nationhood as a citizen. My subject position in each of these arenas does not mean that I have an exclusive copyright on the "black American experience." Instead, I refer to these things to highlight that my experience relates directly to the areas of identity and representation I analyze.

My personal experience does not encompass what it means to be South African, someone who has lived through the horrors and eventual dismantling of apartheid, or a citizen of the new post-apartheid South Africa. My vantage point changes in this chapter and my point of entry has shifted so that I now write about an artistic culture that, in many aspects, I approach from the outside. For this reason, I have changed the type of analytical inquiry and structure of my discussion. My three-pronged investigation (who is in the story, who wrote the story, and who interprets the story) is still relevant, but my experience draws from a different reservoir. While it is possible for me to identify the subjects and creators for the first two questions, the depth of interpretation is limited by my non–South African experience. For that reason, I leave that level of textured analysis to my South African colleagues.[4]

The strengths I bring to this chapter are the questions that place *Winnie: The Opera* in a larger comparative framework that includes the Western opera tradition, opera in the United States, and the representation of blackness in opera more generally. I locate my discussion of *Winnie* within these three separate currents in relationship to each other. Though they might seem unrelated at first, my initial purpose was to juxtapose the United States and South Africa in relationship to how the two countries are using opera to express new narratives around representation. However, rather than narrow my focus exclusively on these two traditions, it turns out that early models of European opera are relevant to the larger story around nation that I want to tell. In order to situate and contextualize how I have brought together canonic European opera, recent operatic activity in the United States, and the current opera scene in South Africa since 1994, I needed to construct a framework for discussing these three elements in relationship to each other. For this I invoke strategies that postcolonial and feminist writers have used to expand what is considered the normative—hegemonic and canonic—and have applied that to the landscape of how music in general, and opera specifically, are discussed.

I have found helpful Homi Bhabha's placing of "the location of culture" as an in-between space that allows previously ignored or oppressed voices to be heard alongside (and sometimes commenting on) the dominant narrative.[5] His articulation of the "unhomely" where culture and the dynamics of power intersect is relevant for thinking about how black musical voices in South Africa are speaking to and about dominant and oppressed discourses. In my adaptation of Bhabha's constructions, these voices include the presence of the physical bodies producing the sounds on stage, the stories being told, the sounds of the linguistic languages being heard, and the musical styles employed. The use of opera as a relatively new musical genre for black South Africans illustrates Bhabha's in-between space where "unhomely" works combine discourses from dominant and oppressed groups into a new dialogue.

In *Feminist Theory: From Margin to Center* African American theorist bell hooks identified a common practice in previously silenced groups when they are initially beginning to find their voices in a public forum. Frequently a subgroup articulates one way of telling the full group's story and leaves out other equally valid versions that should be part of the larger narrative. Originally writing in the early 1980s, hooks names the complications of developing a feminism that reflects the lives of white, middle-class women to the exclusion of other experiences around race and class, specifically the experiences of women of color and working-class and poor women. She imagines an expansive construction of feminism that includes a wider range of voices that can handle multiple narratives simultaneously. I cite hooks as a key voice, yet she belongs to a larger conversation that has included Audre Lourde, Patricia Collins, Alice Walker, and Gloria Anzaldúa, among others.

The model of the center and a margin that reflects a counternarrative existing outside the recognized norm is especially helpful for my explorations of how opera in the United States has developed over the past forty years. Most opera narratives have focused on the traditions in Western Europe. As the voice of American opera came to tell its story, experiences of the composers from the hegemonic racial/ethnic groups dominated the narrative. As a counterpoint to the energy *Winnie: The Opera* reflects in South African culture toward opera, I identify two leading voices who have become associated with successful directions in American opera: Philip Glass and John Adams. I then supplement this dominant discourse with a different narrative, one that is more inclusive of a broader portrayal of American experiences, represented in recent operas about African Americans who have been relegated to the margins into a shadow opera culture.

Since the 1970s, opera studies have looked at representations of the "Other" in terms of an exoticized or orientalized figure. Based heavily on Edward Said's *Orientalism*, this discourse has been framed around the power dynamics surrounding the West's hegemony in defining the East as weak and subordinate. Though this paradigm was helpful in asking questions around who has the power to define whom, Said's orientalism focused on the East-West dichotomy (invoking an exotic Eastern foreignness) and positioned the primary vantage point as the West looking at the East. Music scholars have extended this examination to explore how the "exotic" works in opera, and the focus has primarily been on representations of the "Other" by Westerners working within the European tradition.[6] Recent operas in South Africa give us the opportunity to ask different types of questions. This growing South African scene goes beyond being an issue of how the West represents the non-West. Here is a situation where the non-West is fluent in the musical languages of the West but is also employing additional "languages" in terms of musical allusion and sound, historical context, and cultural references.

Through a different lens than orientalism, one way South African opera might be better articulated is through a newer paradigm, the Global South, which draws upon global studies and transnationalism.[7] An examination of opera that opens up the Global South allows for a more comprehensive view of the North, specifically Western norms in opera, queried from a different perspective: the vantage point of South Africa. In this way, the Global South speaks for itself and in dialogue with the West as South Africa becomes an important producer of operas. Moreover, the vantage point has shifted; it is now South Africa that gets to redefine opera on its own terms through its adaptations of Western operas in South African settings and the creation of new South African operas.

Cultural anthropologist Karin Barber discusses how genre can open up such dialogues between African, Western, and other non-Western forms of oral and written culture. While her inquiry usually focuses on poetry and theater, her compass of a "text" is capacious and brings together multiple forms of cultural and artistic practices that effortlessly include opera. Barber's constructions of genre and text invite ways to think about South African opera as it relates to Western opera. With both articulations belonging to the same genre of opera, I seek to dismantle a hierarchical relationship between an original and a copy, parody, or imitation. Instead, I engage a theoretical framework that operates cross-culturally. In a helpful formation of these ideas, Barber writes that "genre is the principle by which texts converse with each other."[8] Later on, she further extrapolates, "genre is thus the key to the relationship between an individual work and a larger tradition."[9] Hence, we see how genre—in this case, opera—can generate the power to reach across culture and geography to create complementing narratives of black bodies, experiences, and voices on both sides of the Atlantic.

With a specificity toward South Africa after apartheid, literary and cultural historian Sarah Nuttall uses the concept of "entanglement" as a "means by which to draw into our analyses those sites in which what was once thought of as separate—identities, spaces, histories—come together or find points of intersection in unexpected ways."[10] Nuttall's rubric for expressing the entwining and twisting together of disparate elements provides a fitting metaphor for the complications behind the genre of opera in South Africa. First being popular with whites throughout the twentieth century and up through apartheid, since 1994 opera has a new resonance with the black world as it writes itself into history through this same genre. In this use of entanglement, I posit that opera in the black world fits into Nuttall's entanglement framework as it signals a counterracist move and works toward desegregation.[11]

I have outlined a theoretical context to analyze the post-1994 opera situation in South Africa as it replaces a previously all-white practice with the newer scene in which black and mixed race South African stories and participation are being added to the artistic tradition.[12] The question of opera as a chosen genre might seem jarring to some, since it could represent the height of white Western European elitism. However, rather than being eliminated and rejected out of hand, opera is being transformed to do different things. No longer a borrowed replication of a foreign tradition, South Africa—specifically black, mixed race, and white South Africans—is creating a new vision and function for opera. South African opera brings together a new interracial collaboration between white, mixed race, and black South Africans that present Western and traditional South African inspired narratives performed by the bodies and voices of all of its citizens.

After this examination of how opera functions as a genre, my discussion of *Winnie: The Opera* looks to its immediate context in South Africa. Continuing the line of inquiry into how opera tells stories about mainstream and marginalized culture, I provide a brief outline of how opera has long had ties with political meanings since its inception in the sixteenth century (and especially in the nineteenth century, when opera was used to assert a country's national identity in music and narrative). I then juxtapose the way the United States and South Africa have supported dual strands of opera making where the voices and stories of black citizens present contrasting narratives to the established mainstream and use the genre to write themselves into history. This discussion picks up on the construction of a shadow opera culture introduced in chapter 1 by exploring different shadow threads in U.S. and South African operas. The rest of this chapter will then focus on the case study of *Winnie: The Opera* to present the overall structure of the opera and how the work taps into different interpretations and roles for Winnie Madikizela-Mandela as a complicated and conflicted heroine and leader in the nation.

Recent Black Opera in South Africa

Though opera had been associated with white European culture in South Africa, black South Africa is now putting its mark on the form and structural organization of opera. The musical and textual meanings are now imbued with a new set of layered codes. Those familiar with the Western opera tradition can see the roots and relationships of the canonic repertoire in both the recent South African productions of the standard operatic repertoire as well as in the newly composed South African operas that began to emerge in the years immediately following the dismantling of apartheid. Mzilikazi Khumalo's *Princess Magogo kaDinuzulu* (2002) and Bongani Ndodana-Breen's *Winnie: The Opera* (2011) represent the two largest and most established full-length operas written by black South African composers within the first two decades after apartheid.[13]

These two recent operas represent a South African operatic voice that is both modern and new—particularly since South African opera by black composers had not existed earlier. Moreover, these new works point in multiple directions simultaneously. They represent original stories—of two notable South African women—whose lives had been lived in the spotlight for the deeds of the men associated with them as well as actions in their own right. In the larger international context, modern women's lives present a welcomed complement to the trend of male protagonists featured in recent operas by (who have become) the more mainstream American composers Philip Glass and John Adams.[14]

Musically, the South African operas have forged their own voice. Both Western and South African operas employ operatic singers supported by a full Western orchestra. Frequently in the South African operas, the European orchestra instruments are complemented by traditional African instruments that have moments when they are featured on their own as well as times when they blend in with the full orchestra. The musical organization fits into a typical through-composed musical texture (used by many contemporary Western operas) that can be interspersed with strophic songs for diegetic moments when the characters onstage are singing a song. In fact, the presence of "song" is used several times in *Princess Magogo kaDinuzulu*, who herself was a singer, and in *Winnie: The Opera*, most notably during the end of the first half, when Winnie goes to Pondoland and the village women sing her praises. Though Khumalo and Ndodana-Breen both have their own musical sound, the general style is similar to a post-Romantic harmonic language that is present in most modern opera written since the second half of the twentieth century (for example, Benjamin Britten, Gian Carlo Menotti, John Corigliano, William Bolcom). By "post-Romantic" I am referring to a musical style that has points of tonality interspersed with less tonally focused sections and a frequent reliance on melody or a lyrical quality in the vocal line as well as the orchestra. While the South African operas utilize classically trained orchestral musicians, there is also the use of traditional African musicians who play South African instruments.

African languages (isiZulu in *Princess Magogo kaDinuzulu* and isiXhosa in *Winnie: The Opera*) are incorporated and give the operas a unique diction wherein the vowel-driven African languages, to a Western listener not familiar with African languages, can almost pass for Italian (the language opera was conceived in, and whose vowel-based nature makes it easy for the words to flow together). Yet intermittently the isiZulu and isiXhosa vowels (and consonants) are interrupted by the sonic marker of the "click" sounds that both *Nguni* languages share. To an ear used to hearing Italian opera, the "click" sounds shift the almost-familiar aural world into a stark new soundscape that highlights the foreign nature of this linguistic terrain. While *Princess Magogo* is entirely in isiZulu and *Winnie* uses isiXhosa but relies heavily on English, the sonic signifiers of the "click" sounds in the African languages, embedded within a vowel-saturated context, provide the audience with a syncretic linguistic experience, somewhere between Western opera and South African singing. These two South African operas provide a foundation for building upon Western opera in a way that opens up a space for African stories and histories to be told in their own African languages.

How Opera Tells History: Narratives of Opera Past and Present

The topic of Winnie Madikizela-Mandela and the genre of opera might seem unlikely ways of articulating a new nationhood. Yet within the context of opera—both past and present—there is a relevant history about how the genre has provided a space for underrepresented perspectives. In narratives of Western European opera, this space has elevated such voices into the discourse of high culture while also providing a flexible medium for keeping up with evolving musical styles, musically setting different languages, and developing new narrative strategies. From the earliest days of opera history in Italy at the end of the sixteenth century up through the past forty years in American opera, there are similarities in how opera has gone about the cultural business of expressing national identity. This new operatic movement in South Africa finds resonance with the past and present in how larger national concerns can be echoed musically.

European Opera and National Identity

With a long history that spans several centuries, opera is a dynamic, ever-changing genre that has its roots in a group of Florentine intellectuals at the end of the sixteenth century who were looking for a way to emulate their idea of the power of ancient Greek music. They had read about the affective power of music from Plato and Aristotle and, despite not having full musical exemplars of what they were trying to reinvent, they came up with a type of music mixed with drama that developed into opera in the early seventeenth century. As opera grew in popularity, the genre came to move between court entertainment and presenting a space for displaying the embodiment of royal power and spectacle. For example, Louis XIV was not just the major patron of opera but also appeared on stage himself in opera ballets. Seventeenth- and eighteenth-century European courts came to rely on opulence as a key feature in opera as was seen in the importation of Italian opera across the continent in opera houses in London, Lisbon, Hamburg, Leipzig, St. Petersburg, and many other cities.

In contrast to its early history in the royal courts of Europe, opera in the nineteenth century began a mass movement into a broader public audience that included a wider range of social and economic classes.[15] With the availability of printed sheet music and pianos in many middle-class homes throughout Europe and the United States, operatic numbers (tunes from popular arias, choruses, and ensembles) were performed and known by regular people too, not just royals and aristocrats.

A special case existed in Italy during the middle of the nineteenth century: opera took on a leading role in the Italian Risorgimento (the Italian unification movement to oust foreign governance, primarily the Austrians and the French, and install an indigenous Italian ruler). The leading Italian composer of the time, Giuseppe Verdi (1813–1901), and his operas became symbols of the people's connection to the political struggle. More than exclusively the upper strata of society, indeed a larger, broad cross-section of Italy's population was now engaged with opera and its new meaning for an Italian national identity. Verdi's choruses (most notably "Va pensiero" from *Nabucco* [1841]) became anthems for the Risorgimento unification movement, and these works were sung in homes and played in the streets. The respect for Verdi's works gave way to his name becoming an encrypted slogan (Viva Verdi!) that had the additional meaning of supporting "Vittorio Emamuele Re Di Italia" for the first leader of the unified Italy. In fact, Verdi was even elected into the first Italian parliament, where he served from 1861 to 1865.[16]

Though Italy, the birthplace of opera, presents the strongest case in the second half of the nineteenth century, other nationalism movements during this time also saw their goals reflected in opera. The areas around Moravia and Bohemia supported a Czech operatic tradition (with singing in Czech) through Bedřich Smetana, Antonín Dvořák, and Leoš Janáček, precisely while a Czech nationhood and identity were moving into modern formation. Richard Wagner solidified a German operatic tradition with operas based on German and Nordic folklore and developing a musical style that perfectly fit the consonant clusters and linguistic characteristics of the German language. Russia was also finding its voice in the operas of Pyotr Illyich Tchaikovsky, Modest Mussorgsky, and Alexander Borodin, among others, that featured Russian politics, history, and literature, large choruses representing the Russian people, and singing in the Russian language. In these countries Italian opera (frequently with imported Italian music and singers) had been popular since the eighteenth century. It was not until the second half of the nineteenth century when the national identities of many European countries were shifting—to local ethnic rule in the Czech areas, to a unified Germany from the Prussian states, to a weakening of the tsarist regime that would lead to revolution in the early decades of the twentieth century—that opera in these countries adapted more indigenous elements (native language, composers, and subject matter).

Such examples provide a history of opera that is not usually emphasized or told. Instead of focusing on the major composers whose works have survived or the operas that are still in the repertory, this narrative suggests that opera embodies an expression of national identity for new voices. This is especially true when opera is written about a specific country's history—with its own national heroes and geographical locations—and composed in the vernacular language of that country (such as American operas in English, Czech operas in Czech, Russian operas in Russian, or South African operas in isiZulu and isiXhosa).

Narratives of American Identity in Opera

The ascendance of American opera composers toward the end of the twentieth century brought a new voice to the international opera scene. In addition to a musical sound that felt more accessible, the subject content regularly included recent history that was immediately relatable to the audience. With several operas based on the lives of Americans, the United States was writing itself into the venerable tradition of opera. The drama in these political operas stemmed from controversial topics and figures in history. The use of the atomic bomb in World War II is problematized in operas by both Philip Glass and John Adams, revealing the weighty legacy this lethal weapon has had on the memory of its citizens (particularly those who grew up during this time) whose country first deployed it. Both Glass's *Einstein on the Beach* and Adams's *Dr. Atomic* question the ethics around the decision to use the atomic bomb. In an opera that presents a more concrete narrative arc than *Einstein*, Adams's *Dr. Atomic* focuses on the moral issues about deploying the bomb. In this telling, American born J. Robert Oppenheimer is placed at the center of the drama. Additionally, *Dr. Atomic* creates an imminent anticipation of doom throughout the opera in the nervousness and agitated propulsion in the music that transfers the mental anxiety of the characters onto the audience through an unsettling sense of disquiet and impending disaster as we all wait for the test launching of the first atomic bomb to happen (the opera ends right as the bomb is deployed).

Still alive in 1987 when Adams's first opera, *Nixon in China*, premiered, former President Richard Nixon was considered by the American public as a figure who was moving into the role of the wise, experienced senior statesman with his groundbreaking trip to China emerging as the highlight of his presidency. Yet Nixon was still remembered as the president who resigned on the verge of being impeached amid the horrendous state of affairs in Vietnam and a wiretapping situation that exposed unprecedented lies and paranoia. Though these quick examples only skim the surface of the richness of this topic, the larger point is to highlight how a new national voice in opera (in this case mainstream America) has taken some of its central historical moments to retell in operatic form. The complexity of how drama, music, and text can enrich a narrative and say many things simultaneously makes opera a powerful medium. With an emphasis on presenting different sides of a controversy and avoiding final judgment, the genre of opera has proved to be an excellent arena for juxtaposing conflict and passionate feelings. Through a monumentalizing of the spectacle and drama in a nation's identity, opera provides a way for multiple sides to get compelling exposure.

While the post-apartheid vibrant opera scene in South Africa presents a different voice—an interracial collaborative voice between black and white South Africans—from the previous mainstream of opera in South Africa before 1994, a contrasting picture of mainstream American opera may be seen in a group of works based on black experience that premiered between 1986 and 2005. Compared to the dominant white culture of South African opera during apartheid and the mainstream American opera found in the work of Glass and Adams, these emerging black opera traditions in South Africa and the United States present evidence of a shadow opera situation. Though written and performed separately, and never presented as an official operatic cycle, the black shadow culture of American operas outlines signature points in black history. For a sample representative of an alternative American history focused on black experiences, I briefly construct a narrative out of five operas from this shadow culture as an example of the richness of the operas hovering on the margins. Presented chronologically by the periods they outline, I bring together operas that focus on the Middle Passage, *Amistad* (Anthony Davis and Thulani Davis, 1997); slavery, *Margaret Garner* (Richard Danielpour and Toni Morrison, 2005) and *From the Diary of Sally Hemings* (William Bolcom and Sandra Seaton, 2001); and the civil rights era, *X, The Life and Times of Malcolm X* (Anthony Davis and Thulani Davis, 1986).[17] Added to these four recent works is the highly publicized revival of the most controversial opera about blackness in the repertory, *Porgy and Bess* (1935). This opera shows black life in the early twentieth century as it rubs against the ideals of the Harlem Renaissance, the Great Depression, and the poverty of the Jim Crow South. In 2011–2012, the work was transformed from Gershwin's enigmatic characterization of an American folk opera on the opera stage into a new adaptation for the musical theater stage. Consequently, and unlike the vexed operatic version, the work received much attention and praise on Broadway (as well as a small amount of critique) as *The Gershwins' Porgy and Bess*; Audra McDonald won her fifth Tony for her portrayal of Bess.[18]

Not surprisingly, since different composers wrote the four recent works separately over the span of a couple of decades, the historical chronology of these operas does not present a linear narrative. Anthony Davis, the only black composer (ever) to have had multiple operas commissioned and performed by major opera companies, outlines the chronological bookends of the timeline presented in these five works. His two operas, *Amistad* (about the 1839 slave revolt aboard the Spanish slave ship that eventually docked on the coast of New York and became a case heard before the U.S. Supreme Court) and *X, The Life and Times of Malcolm X* open up the black experience in a telling of slavery's origins through the question of freedom. *Amistad* sketches the fate of the Mende West Africans as they arrive in 1839 in the United States, where the international slave trade was outlawed, the abolitionist movement was in its early stages, and the country was still deeply invested in bondage. *X* brings us to the world of civil rights leader Malcolm X, who questioned the relative freedom of blacks a century after Emancipation. Through his use of jazz and the trickster figure, Davis writes operatically while pulling in black-based musical and literary idioms. Both of these operas also interact with popular film versions (Steven Spielberg's *Amistad* [1997] and Spike Lee's *Malcolm X* [1992]) and the different telling of each story by these two iconic directors as they reflect different visions of the same material. In the late twentieth century, film has arguably occupied a similar position of social commentary that opera had in the past; through such a lens, new opera-studies criticism explores relationships between opera and film.[19]

Margaret Garner, based on the historical figure about whom Toni Morrison built her award-winning novel *Beloved* (1987), premiered in Detroit (co-commissioned with the Michigan Opera Theater, the Cincinnati Opera, and the Opera Company of Philadelphia). Italian American composer Richard Danielpour paired with Morrison as librettist and produced an opera filled with black spirituals, call-and-response singing, and a grisly narrative that hauntingly reproduces rape, infanticide, and lynching onstage. Paired with *From the Diary of Sally Hemings*, these two works feature reincarnated voices for the title heroines when virtually nothing survives in their original voices.[20] The theme of recreation is central to all five operas, as the stories are reconstructed from history yet told from new vantage points. As new works are created and the controversial *Porgy and Bess* was successfully re-adapted for the Broadway stage, these seemingly familiar stories are recast in ways that speak directly to contemporary audiences; they articulate innovative things about how race and gender are configured in African American operatic heroism set in the United States today.

When seen all together, these five productions present a new narrative of blackness, one that retells central moments of African American history and incorporates distinctive portrayals of heroism in opera that bring together race, gender, and underrepresented sociohistorical perspectives. Now, at the turn of the twentieth and twenty-first centuries in the United States, during a time when many see affirmative action as a policy of the past and new formations of a so-called postracialized identity are being constructed, opera emerges as a genre that is capable of retelling the history of black enslavement, segregation, and integration. Black identity has become open to different interpretations. As Barack Obama completed his second term as the first black president of the United States, protests and riots in response to police brutality and the widely held perceived failure of the justice system to work for African Americans caused many to call this time a new stage of the civil rights era.[21] In this environment opera has become a new space for articulating how quintessential experiences and achievements of African Americans can be represented. Making this story even more unusual, and linking it to black opera in South Africa, is that it has taken place in an art form that had largely been closed to black composers and musicians.

None of these American operas about black experiences have had the circulation or attention given to the above-mentioned operas of Philip Glass and John Adams. In fact, until Marian Anderson sang at the Metropolitan Opera in New York in 1955 and opened a symbolic door for many other black singers who were classically trained, with few exceptions opera in the United States had been segregated; the major opera houses and careers in opera were closed to black singers. Yet since the beginning of the twentieth century black singers and composers in America had been involved in operatic activities, albeit most commonly in all-black ventures and in nearly isolated obscurity. In the first half of the twentieth century many singers in the black church and community aspired to sing opera, despite the lack of performance venues open to black classical singers. When George Gershwin cast his landmark 1935 opera, his leading singers already had classical operatic training: Todd Duncan (Porgy) was on the Voice Department faculty of Howard University, and Anne Brown (Bess) was a graduate student studying voice at The Julliard School. With opportunities closed in the first half of the twentieth century for a strong participation in opera by blacks in the United States, it is all the more surprising that by the last decades of the century opera became an arena for exploring how race and gender reflect the changing portrayals of black-white relations in the United States.

A similar thing could be said about opera in South Africa. During apartheid opera was an exclusively white domain, with the black populations maintaining a strong culture of solo and choral singing in churches and civic choirs.[22] Yet since 1994, opera rather quickly became a space that black singers and composers moved into. Like both streams in American opera, South Africa is producing newly composed works on cultural and political figures, writing their own South African history into the genre of opera: Princess Constance Magogo KaDinuzulu (Khumalo, *Princess Magogo kaDinuzulu* [2002]) and Winnie Madikizela-Mandela (Ndodana-Breen, Wilensky and Vundla, *Winnie: The Opera* [2011]). *The Mandela Trilogy* presents the situation where a white South African compositional team was commissioned to write three scenes from Nelson Mandela's life (composers Péter Louis van Dijk, Mike Campbell, and the librettist Michael Williams). Moving chronologically through Mandela's life, the first act (by van Dijk) captures the style of traditional rural music, the second act (by Campbell) has elements of a jazz musical, and the third act (by van Dijk) is more operatic in style.[23] To a greater extent than in the United States, South African national artistic ministries and private industries are supporting opera; in addition to new works, black opera companies are staging adaptations of Western canonic operas (such as Mozart's *Marriage of Figaro*, Puccini's *La Bohème*, and Bizet's *Carmen*).[24] European opera has also seen many adaptations, and this tradition has continued into the United States. As discussed in chapter 5 on settings of Bizet's *Carmen*, there are a few notable cases of all-black settings (*Carmen Jones* and *Carmen: A Hip Hopera* are two). What makes the South African situation unusual is the larger number of adaptations into all-black settings. In the United States a significant contrast can be seen in the adaptation of Puccini's *La Bohème* by Jonathan Larson in *Rent* (1994). While there were several characters who were black, there were also white, Jewish, and Latinx characters who were central to the racial/ethnic make-up of the ensemble. In the United States it is almost unheard of to see an all-black opera cast outside of *Porgy and Bess*; in South Africa, this is becoming a norm with the Isango Ensemble and in productions for other opera companies.[25]

The example of South Africa provides a compelling foil to both American opera scenes: the recognized masterworks of Glass and Adams alongside the newly emerging narrative of African American opera. In a genre that frequently signals elitism, foreign languages, and overwrought staging of old-fashioned topics, the past few decades have shown opera to be a medium open to experimentation and new directions. Unlike the situation in post-1994 South Africa, opera houses in the United States have recently been quite slow in moving toward racial integration. Though American houses have been a bit stalled in getting greater numbers onstage, like South African opera, the orchestra, and the various production and technical crews are still primarily white. Nonetheless, opera is providing a space that reconfigures race and gender and reveals a new narrative in the United States and South Africa about how black audiences and performers have had a long-time engagement with singing (primarily in churches and community organizations) in styles that have allowed a few singers who are vocally ready to move into opera. With these recent operatic productions, across the globe in the United States and South Africa, blackness is being newly staged.

Winnie: The Opera Onstage

The world premiere of *Winnie: The Opera* at the State Theatre in Pretoria on April 28, 2011, was an important and triumphant event. The theater was packed and even the "real" Winnie Madikizela-Mandela was in attendance. At the end of the opera, after the final curtain call and with the entire cast and production team onstage, she took her place with them and spoke from prepared remarks as well as extemporaneously. Raising her fist to the sky, she shouted "*Amandla!*" (Power!). The audience rose to their feet and shouted "*Ngawethu!*" (The power is ours!) right back in response. After an exhilarating performance, Madikizela-Mandela's presence added further excitement. She said that she liked the opera and felt this was the biggest honor and the best praise she had ever received from South Africa, her home country. She also admitted to not having ever been in the State Theatre before that night; however, she revealed that she had considered bombing it before, during the years of apartheid.

Winnie Madikizela-Mandela, known as "Mother of the Nation," is a controversial figure who is beloved and fierce, heroic and infamous. Yet *Winnie: The Opera* is not entirely alone in presenting such a formidable leading female character on the international opera stage; a few recent works also defy this stereotype, and Winnie fits right in with these strong willed women: *Madame Mao* (Bright Sheng [2003]) and *Powder Her Face* (Thomas Ades [1998]), based on the life of the Duchess of Argyll.

Winnie: The Opera also belongs to a handful of canonic operatic heroines who challenge the traditional suffering damsel in distress and present an alternative to the innocent who is unjustly punished in the end. There are a few repertoire operas that defy conventions and showcase a different type of heroine. *Winnie* evokes the drama behind the contested positions of both sixteenth-century Tudor heirs to the throne (Queen Elizabeth I and Mary Stuart) in Donizetti's 1834 *Maria Stuarda*, the forcefulness and violence of Puccini's *Tosca* (1900), and the steadfast vengeance of Strauss's *Elektra* (1909).

Winnie the woman has become a legend in her own time. Thrust into the public eye for decades while her husband Nelson Mandela was a political prisoner for twenty-seven years on Robben Island (1963 to 1990). As a new bride and in her twenties, Winnie Mandela raised their two girls when Nelson was away; she faced intense public scrutiny, several arrests and imprisonments (including eighteen months of torture in a death cell). Yet while much of her life has been lived publically, there is also an enigmatic side that causes us to wonder how she can hold such contradictions. Neither her heroism nor the controversy surrounding her can be denied, and it is these qualities, the intertwined victim-perpetrator-heroine, that ask who Winnie Madikizela-Mandela really is. *Winnie* does not answer these inquiries unequivocally but allows the intensity of these questions to fuel the drama embedded in the story of the opera.

As mentioned above, *Winnie* is not a stand-alone opera in South Africa after 1994; it belongs instead to a larger movement in South Africa that involves how the new nation sees itself as well as how it aspires to be seen.

Several major opera companies have either begun or gained new momentum in South Africa since 1994: Opera Africa in Durban, the Isango Ensemble opera company (in Cape Town), Black Tie Ensemble (based in Pretoria), the Gauteng Opera (based in Johannesburg), the Cape Town Opera (the professional opera company), and the very active opera program at the University of Cape Town that produces its own season and sometimes collaborates with the Cape Town Opera.[26] All of these opera companies, including more that are starting up, receive state and private funding and are supplemented by multiple young-artist programs that train young students and help finance their musical education in country and abroad.

Winnie: The Opera came out of an independent production company (Vundowil) that was founded as the opera was being completed. The project started out as *The Passion of Winnie*, a digital opera (projections of photos, chamber orchestra of sixteen, two soloists—Winnie and Columbus, her father—and chorus of eight who also double on smaller solo parts) and premiered in Toronto on June 8, 2007.[27] At that point the work was one act and Mfundi Vundla had not yet joined the creative team. Madikizela-Mandela was invited to the premiere but was publically denied a visa due to her political troubles and was unable to attend.

Winnie as an opera is a deliberate undertaking that received generous national and private funding, premiering in one of the leading venues, the State Theatre, in the country's capital city of Pretoria. As an especially attractive feature in the post-apartheid world of South Africa, the work brought together a large interracial group collaborating on the same project behind the scenes (in the creative team of the composer and librettists), the production team, and onstage with the singers, dancers, and actors. While the singers were black (except for the few white characters), the orchestra and production crew (lighting, sound, costumes, and make-up) were for the most part white. Shirley Jo Finney, an African American visitor new to South Africa, was the director. Bongani Ndodana-Breen is Xhosa and mentions in his program note that he is the first black South African to write and orchestrate a full-length opera. Warren Wilensky, a South African Canadian film director, wrote the first version of the libretto for *The Passion of Winnie* and was joined by South African media mogul Mfundi Vundla in the revision for the full-length opera.[28]

Winnie: The Opera is not an opera that simply shows a good-faith effort. Nor does it attempt to "try" to be an opera. *Winnie* is an opera that both belongs in the canonic opera repertory and shows new directions for the future of the genre. I write these words realizing that at this point the opera has only been performed four times during its initial run (with the premiere on April 28, 2011) and I am making a rather bold statement. I stand behind this assessment and I hope this opera gains the wider recognition it so richly deserves with continued performances. It has captured the movement for bringing together an event and characters that are timely, topical, and political. The opera is relevant—not only for South Africa but also for the United States, Europe, and any other operatic tradition in the twenty-first century. It has brought a compelling humanity and depth of drama to several of its characters—especially its leading lady—that makes it feel like an opera, as opposed to a musical or operetta.[29] We get to know their motivations and we *care* about them, even if we do not agree with them or are particularly sure if we can like them for their controversial actions. It is a work that brings together a full Western orchestra and tonal/post-tonal tunefulness combined with a postmodernity that uses TV media clips and projected animation screened in the background.[30] It also presents an insider's view of African traditions, from the *ilobolo* bride price negotiations and rituals at the end of act 1, to the adaptation of a Xhosa song sung by the Madikizela women in Pondoland in the beginning of that scene (act 1, scene 3). Musically and linguistically (with text sung in English and Xhosa) the opera presents an intertextuality that shows a syncretic coming together of traditional South African and Western European elements into something that references each population and is relevant to a new mixed audience that reflects the global reach of these issues.

Although this is a story that has an international reach, it is still rooted in South Africa. Perhaps most important, it is told by South Africans about South Africa. I had the privilege of witnessing this story being told for the first time by South Africans—a fully South African cast (a situation that would probably change when the opera is performed in different countries). At a time when Apartheid was less than fifteen years in the past and the people being depicted were still living, I was able to watch this opera debut in Pretoria—the capital city of a country where most of the cast and audience members vividly recall what this system of oppression felt like firsthand.

The Truth and Reconciliation Commission

The Truth and Reconciliation Commission (TRC) hearings had multiple meanings for South Africans and elicited many emotions and strongly held ideas about how South Africa was pursuing justice in its new form of government. For the new nation, and especially relevant to this opera, the TRC was an important moment for understanding who Winnie Madikizela-Mandela had become. Chaired by Archbishop Desmond Tutu and based in Cape Town (though they convened at several locations throughout South Africa), the hearings ran from April 1996 through the end of July 1998. Madikizela-Mandela was subpoenaed by the TRC and testified in September and October 1997.

After having been banished to Brandfort in the Orange Free State in 1977, Madikizela-Mandela moved back to Soweto in 1986. That same year, she helped resolve an internal conflict within the Orlando West branch of the Soweto Youth Congress [SOYCO] that led to the development of the Mandela United Football Club (MUFC),[31] an organization that played soccer matches as well as provided a personal security detail for Madikizela-Mandela. It was through the MUFC that her alleged activities took a more violent turn, primarily the disappearance and presumed accountability for the deaths of many people. The most notorious and tarnishing charge was the abduction and murder of alleged police informer, fourteen-year-old Stompie Seipei (also known as Stompie Moeketsi and James Seipei). In its report on the matter, the TRC admitted to the difficulty of parsing out the details of what really happened; they received three versions of the killing from multiple witnesses (Jerry Richardson, Katiza Cebekhulu, John Morgan, Johannes "Themba" Mabotha, and Paul Erasmus). Even though "each version was explored in the Investigation Unit's report to the Commission," the commission said that it had "not been able to establish conclusively the veracity of any of these versions."[32] The TRC found Ms. Madikizela-Mandela responsible for Stompie Seipei's abduction and that she "was negligent in that she failed to act responsibly in taking the necessary action required to avert his death."[33]

Winnie: The Opera mentions Stompie Seipei and includes a role for his grieving mother. For the first South African audiences who saw the premiere, the opera relives some of a process that was pivotal in the creation of the new South Africa at the end of apartheid. For future South African audiences and non-South African audiences, the depiction of the TRC hearings for Madikizela-Mandela document a specific historical moment that articulated a way of coming to deal with a horrendous past that also wraps gender, politics, and nation together. Given the prominent position of the TRC in *Winnie: The Opera*, after the opening prologue it is the first and last scenes that bookended the opera with real SABC (South African Broadcasting Corporation) television footage discussing the TRC and juxtaposes so many of the public and private, personal and political personae of Winnie Madikizela-Mandela.

More than any other part of the opera, these scenes at the TRC with Madikizela-Mandela have a direct immediacy. Unlike the rest of the opera, which moves back in time to explain what shaped Winnie's experiences in the past, the opening of act 1 and the opera's conclusion represent the present time of the opera (1998) and are supplemented by media coverage both in the paparazzi chorus of the opera as well as in the SABC real television footage of the event. For many people at the opera's first performances and into the present, Madikizela-Mandela's reputation has been altered and shaped to include this horrific information. The prominence of the Truth and Reconciliation process in the opera brings an unsettling issue to light. Despite the best energies and intentions of those involved with the TRC, sometimes the "truth" is not recoverable. And despite the spectacle and pageantry of opera—a genre we all know is staged and not "real" life—it sometimes provides the most compelling presentation of multiple truths when a single truth does not feel fully viable.

As an African American who had not yet spent a lot of time in South Africa, my experience of the TRC hearings as they are presented in *Winnie: The Opera* felt very close to the way I had heard about them in the United States. I was quite impressed with a country that had just gone through the brutalities of apartheid and was willing to acknowledge head-on the atrocities of racism and undergo the process of restorative justice. This system allows the victims and perpetrators to move toward some understanding of reconciliation rather than an abstract system of punishment. The critique of not prosecuting the guilty seemed to be outweighed by the benefit of having an open conversation about the crimes, to provide evidence against a false retelling of events, and to begin a process of healing through forgiveness.

Anthony Holiday, a South African political activist against apartheid and philosopher, scholar, and journalist, presents a trenchant analysis of how the TRC juggled the difficult combination of amnesty, remorse, and catharsis among the victims and the victimizers. In his essay "Forgiving and Forgetting: The Truth and Reconciliation Commission," he outlines two primary functions of what he saw the hearings could do. First, they became a repository for facts, collecting a political legal history about who, what, where, and when. Second, they provided a space for dealing with the "psychological facts, pertaining to how people now felt about what had been done to them."[34] On the first point, the TRC could work well, and there have been pages of testimony recording the experiences and the commission's findings about what was reported (most of this is publically available online). The second point, argues Holiday, was more difficult to achieve given the complicated nature of how displays of remorse and forgiveness most naturally exist in private settings and appear less successful when conducted in such impersonal, state-sponsored venues. Yet despite this challenge, Holiday observed that

> it rapidly became clear that these public displays of emotion were an essential part of what Tutu and his commissioners meant by "reconciliation." They meant a kind of psychotherapeutic "healing," the efficacy of which largely depended on

its taking place, not within the cloistered privacy of a confidential confessional, but in a public arena and under the scrutiny of the mass media.[35]

A central critique of Madikizela-Mandela after her final TRC hearing is that she did not show enough remorse or compassion for her alleged victims, even though she eventually admitted that things had not gone as planned. Near the end of their special report on the Mandela United Football Club (where most of Winnie's hearing is addressed), the commission characterized her behavior throughout the process:

> She refused to take responsibility for any wrongdoing. It was only at the end of her testimony, under great pressure from Archbishop Desmond Tutu, presiding over the proceedings, that she reluctantly conceded that "things had gone horribly wrong."[36]

It is perhaps this feature of the outcome of Madikizela-Mandela's public experience at the TRC that the opera Winnie can best address. At the very end of the opera Archbishop Desmond Tutu eloquently implores her to show the type of remorse and compassion Holiday wrote about in his analysis of the TRC. In his dramatic scene when he addresses her, Tutu sings:

> I speak to you as someone who loves you very deeply
> Who loves your family very deeply
> . . . .
> Stand up and say there are things that went wrong
> . . . .
> You are a great person
> You don't know how your greatness would be enhanced
> If you were to say sorry, things went wrong, forgive me.
> I beg you

Cast as a baritone, the same voice type her father Columbus is given, Tutu's words have a soothing effect on Madikizela-Mandela, and she begins her response: "Thank you very much for your wonderful wise words/That is the father I have always known in you." She continues with an apology to Stompie Seipei's mother and then utters her famous words, "Things went horribly wrong."

In the elevated genre of opera, the public gets to relive this moment in history and contrast it to Madikizela-Mandela's enigmatic demeanor that was found lacking in real life. Onstage, the opera directors and women who portray Winnie can add their own understanding to how they interpret her words and behavior. In the heightened spectacle of each opera production, Winnie is reinvented and the audience gets to rethink how she was shaped by her ordeals during apartheid. The reconciliatory capacity attached to the public catharsis produced by the TRC once again appears within grasp during each performance as the country is given further opportunities for national healing.

Organization and Structure of the Opera

There are two ways the final draft of the libretto and the program for the premiere of the opera divide the number of acts and scenes in the work. This final draft of the libretto for *Winnie* presents the opera's structure in four acts with various scenes (Table 6.1). The program for the premiere condenses the structure into two acts with three scenes each (Table 6.2). In comparing the two versions, all of act 1 and scenes 1 through 3 in act 2 in the final libretto are called act 1 in the program for the premiere. Both versions then have an intermission. Act 2, scenes 5 through the end of the opera are called act 2 in the program from the premiere. Below are diagrams of each version of the organization. In Table 6.2 I have written short synopses of each scene.[37]

Table 6.1. Structure of the opera in the final draft of the libretto

Overture
Prologue: *Mothers of the Missing*

Act 1
    Scene 1: A gymnasium, Mayfair Johannesburg
    Scene 2: Prison

Act 2
    Scene 1: Pondoland (1956), Dawn
    Scene 2: Pondoland, Dawn
    Scene 3: Columbus's Vision

Intermission

[*Act 2 in program for the premiere*]
    Scene 5: Train to Brandfort—1950–1980
    Scene 6: Brandfort—1981
    Scene 7: Brandfort
    Scene 8: Brandfort—Dusk

Act 3
    Scene 1: TRC Projection
    Scene 2: Orlando West, Soweto
    Intersticial [grand pause]

Act 4   Scene 1: TRC Hearing Conclusion

Table 6.2. Structure of the opera in the premiere program

[Overture—not noted in the premiere program, but an orchestral introduction was played before the Prologue]
Prologue: *Mothers of the Missing*
Act 1 *Scene 1: Gymnasium Hall—Johannesburg, 1998.* The ninth and final day of the "Winnie Hearings" in the Truth and Reconciliation Commission [TRC]. *Scene 2: Prison—Pretoria, 1969.* Winnie is tortured during her eighteen months of solitary confinement. *Scene 3: Hills of Pondoland, 1956.* A twenty-one-year old Winnie tells the women of the Madikizela clan that she has met Nelson Mandela, a Thembu prince, and hopes to marry him. Members of Mandela's family arrive for the *ilobolo* (bride price negotiations). While their success is celebrated, Columbus (Winnie's father) expresses his concern for the marriage.
Intermission
Act 2 *Scene 1: Brandfort, late 1970s.* Winnie is banned to Brandfort in the Orange Free State and put under house arrest. Even at this remote location, she is pursued by the foreign press. *Scene 2: Orlando West Soweto, 1980s.* A scene in Soweto with the Mandela United Football Club (MUFC) that is led by Jerry Richardson and overseen by Winnie. The MUFC performs a Toyi Toyi (a militant dance-like piece associated with the protest movement). Winnie addresses the crowd at a mass funeral, the police open gunfire, and chaos ensues. *Scene 3: Gymnasium Hall—Johannesburg, 1998.* Back to the final day of the "Winnie Hearings," where the TRC chairman, Archbishop Desmond Tutu, implores Winnie to apologize for her actions.

The version performed at the premiere was the one outlined in the program. Despite the fact that the second half of act 2 and all of acts 3 and 4 were condensed into act 2, the first half of the evening before the intermission (prologue and act 1) felt a little longer than the second half. The overall effect worked well dramatically and kept the pacing moving smoothly, with the second half feeling like it moved expeditiously to the conclusion.

The souvenir program booklet, available for purchase at the performances, provides the outline of the opera (yet with more description of each scene in the printed "Opera Synopsis" than I have given in Table 6.2). In the lovely full-color booklet, there are the expected lists and pictures of the cast, the KwaZulu-Natal Philharmonic Orchestra, the Gauteng Choristers, the production and design teams, and stills of the performance (taken during rehearsals). Additionally, there appear a few opening statements that are not usually contained in an opera stagebill. There is the "Foreword by the Ministry" (by Paul Mashatile, Minister of Arts and Culture, and Dr. Joe Phaahla, Deputy Minister of Arts and Culture), "A Message from Mrs. Winnie Madikizela-Mandela on *Winnie, the Opera*," and "Music notes from the Composer" (Bongani Ndodana-Breen). This frontmatter provides official statements from both the government and "Winnie" herself that support the opera as well as provide a helpful guide from the composer for the audience to gain a better sense of the how the music is organized and what to listen for.

After a short orchestral overture (or prelude), the opera begins with a prologue that focuses on eight women surrounded in darkness and bathed in a glowing light. They are dressed head to toe in white, with white wraps on their heads and translucent veils across their faces.[38]

> The Mothers of the Missing scour the earth, endlessly searching for any sign of their loved ones. These women exist in a twilight world of grief and longing. They gather fireside, and smear ash on their bodies as token of their mourning.[39]

Their costume takes its cue directly from Xhosa traditional dress, specifically *Amagqirha* (medicine men and women), a connection some South African audiences probably make instinctively.[40] In any case, they appear almost ethereal and not fully of this world, making stronger their relationship to those living and those missing. Mothers of the Missing sing a multipart choral hymn that becomes a central musical theme used throughout the opera to highlight pivotal events. The gorgeous, lush sound of the counterpoint between these eight women's voices transports the listener to a nostalgic musical place that feels at once new and familiar. Ndodana-Breen writes that the "Mothers' theme is original music but borrows very heavily from the music heard at black funerals during the 1980s, where standard church hymns were sung very slowly with improvised added layers of harmonies."[41] As this mournful hymn is transformed throughout the opera, this first presentation with the richness of the female ensemble stays with the listener and becomes almost like a haunting memory when it recurs.

As a segue into the first act, the first scene opens with two janitor sweepers preparing the courtroom for the ninth and final day of the "Winnie Hearings" in the Truth and Reconciliation Commission. As the hall opens to the public, there is an explosion of movement and sound; the beginning of act 1 juxtaposes several layers of activity with the vibrant energy of the dance troupe depicting the paparazzi of the international media and the singing chorus, representing the general audience of South Africans who have come to witness the TRC hearings. While the anticipation grows for Winnie's entrance, she finally appears off to the side, almost anticlimatically, at first hardly noticed by anyone else onstage. In mid-conversation with her daughter Zindzi, Winnie searches her purse for her glasses. This first image of the title character is telling, for it removes the hype that everyone has been set up to expect with a grand entrance. Moreover, the glasses function as a metaphor that comes back at the end of the opera in the final scene as Winnie, again looking for her glasses, seems to ignore TRC Chairman Archbishop Desmond Tutu when he is asking her to apologize. In the actual TRC proceedings, Winnie was reported to have been fumbling with her glasses; this was variously reported on as her defiance and distraction.[42] I would like to suggest that this real event from the TRC is taken up in the opera and extended. In the opera, the glasses provide a metaphor that illustrates the clarity of Winnie's physical eyesight and visionary gaze; these are the lenses through which she views the world. Her searching for her glasses signals an intention, on Winnie's part, to try to see things distinctly not on her own, but as they are seen by everyone else. As a recurring image for sight (and insight), wide-open eyes—most likely Winnie's—projected against a black curtain are presented between various scenes as a visual trope that takes the theme of watching, witnessing, and judging from Winnie's experiences onstage to our experience as spectators in the audience.

The spectacle of the opening of act 1, scene 1 is followed by an intimate scene of torture, set several decades earlier in a prison in Pretoria, between Winnie and the prison guard Major Theunis Swanepoel, a recurring figure who follows Winnie throughout her life in the opera and who is determined, unsuccessfully, to extract her confession. In his moving aria, Swanepoel is not apologetic for his torture of her, nor does he try to explain his political philosophy. Instead, the critical element that focuses his character is the emphasis brought to his hands. The text of his aria explains how he sees his hands not primarily as instruments of torture but rather as the part of him that is meant to build, nurture, and help things grow. When he goes home, his hands are busy raising children, planting gardens, and fostering a safe community. The strength of his role is that he is not a caricature that can be quickly written off as a simplistic villain. This aria shows us another side of him that becomes more human. In essence, this makes him even more menacing because we in the audience want him to change—and he seems capable of change—despite his unmovable quest to bring Winnie Mandela down. Though he could easily be the villain in the opera, embodying the persecution by the white apartheid government, the opera is more complicated in its portrayal of good and evil. Swanepoel is the white government agent who physically and emotionally tears Winnie down year after year. Yet the real placement of evil is in the effect of that torture and how it transforms both of them. For Winnie we see the evolution of her youthful idealism on the eve of her engagement to Nelson Mandela in scene 3 of act 1, when she is first attracted to Mandela and his revolutionary causes, through the height of the apartheid struggles in the late 1980s presented in the penultimate scene of opera in act 2. For Swanepoel, his first-act aria from

1969 is juxtaposed to his later appearances in the second half of the opera in the late 1970s and 1980s, wherein he continues to harass Winnie; he becomes a parody of the moral compass he tried to emulate early on in his life and is reduced to an ineffectual specter that periodically haunts Winnie.

In addition to Swanepoel's textual accent on hands in his aria, the opera visually highlights the trope of hands more generally. One of the animated short film clips projected onstage later on in the opera is the active image of moving hands that are building, shaping, and molding things. In a conversation with William Wilensky (co-librettist) I had mentioned the power of these animated hands during the animated short and how they seem to refer to several characters in the opera who shape and move the narrative along (particularly Swanepoel, Winnie, and Columbus—her father). Wilensky said that this short film was originally intended to be shown during Swanepoel's aria, but the production team found it to be too distracting from the aria. So it was placed later in the opera during an instrumental interlude with no other action onstage. The decision to use the animated short later becomes very effective as it links Winnie not just to Swanepoel but to the two men who are shown to have the greatest influence on "shaping" her—her torturer and her father—in this telling of her story. (Though many might expect her ex-husband Nelson Mandela to play an important role, in this opera he is not a developed character and is a presence only referred to by others.)

The first half of the opera (act 1 in the program) ends with a scene set in 1956 that provides the earliest look at Winnie—twenty-one years old as she goes back to her home in Pondoland and announces her interest in "a Thembu prince"—Nelson Mandela, whose Thembu clansmen later approach Winnie's Madikizela people to discuss the *ilobolo* (bride's price) and celebrate the traditional slaughtering of a cow to seal the couple's engagement. This scene provides a fitting finale to the first act with the framing of the opening portion with the all-women's chorus and Winnie singing traditional songs in Xhosa and the closing traditional *ilobolo* ceremony with the full chorus onstage. The act ends with Columbus having the last word and singing his concern about his daughter marrying a revolutionary. His caution adds to the intensity of the drama, for at this moment in the opera we are most removed from the present. This is the earliest point in the narrative, just prior to Winnie's becoming officially engaged—and we get to see Winnie right before she marries Nelson Mandela, when her role in the whole saga will be set into motion. Here the opera allows us to see Winnie, unequivocally full of potential and innocence, before she is who she eventually becomes.

One of the most powerful elements of *Winnie: The Opera* is that it takes us back to a Winnie the audience has either forgotten or never knew, a Winnie who certainly does not exist anymore. While opera Winnie comes to embody South Africa—as the ever-complicated "Mother of the Nation"—the opera brings us back to a point before any controversy. There is joy in the Madikizela women's Xhosa hymn to Winnie in Pondoland; the language belongs to her clan, the music fits the fabric of traditional Xhosa song, and we are steeped in the tradition of the homeland. We are far from every other location in the opera—the TRC hearings in Johannesburg, the prison of Pretoria, her banished exile to Brandfort, and the township of Soweto. Here is Winnie, and South Africa, in the prime of their existence. The new role opera Winnie will take up as "Mother of the Nation" when she lives her life as Winnie Mandela in the second half of the opera is far from the unsullied memory this moment has recreated. Opera Winnie in her youth, just before her marriage as the soon-to-be "Mother of the Nation," is juxtaposed with the "Mothers of the Missing" who haunt the opera's prologue with their mourning and wailing of grief. A new identity for South Africa has emerged in this opera and we, as the audience, see the post-apartheid nation through the lens of *Winnie: The Opera.*

As South Africa defines itself as a nation built on post-apartheid values, the opera stage—as it has been in Europe and the United States—has become an arena for working out nuanced cultural issues around gender, power, heroism, and modernity. With the first full-length operas by a black South African based on the life of such a strong female political figure—Winnie Madikizela-Mandela—this new South African voice in opera resonates with the Western European tradition where women's voices are specially marked and get to carry power and authority. As a political woman whose public life was also shaped by her private roles of mother and wife, her negotiation between the professional and domestic spheres are given operatic treatment that help shape new memories of a modern nation. Winnie Mandela's courage, as the waiting wife for so many years when Nelson Mandela was imprisoned and in her own experience with torture, is juxtaposed with her admitted guilt at the Truth and Reconciliation Commission hearings. This opera, which boldly opens up an opportunity for a millennial operatic heroine—a divorced, convicted woman living today in a South Africa she helped to build—is not only modern in Pretoria but also for the rest of the world. In post-apartheid South Africa, opera has become a critical space that fuses past histories with current aspirations for the future while also engaging intersections of gender with race and nation.

Conclusion

Engaged Musicology, Political Action, and Social Justice

There are many hurdles to overcome in making opera more accessible to a broader audience. It is an old and revered genre that is frequently considered to be either elitist or overly intimidating. Since there is no mandatory music education that includes opera studies in the United States (and this is true in many other parts of the world), the genre can appear to be remote and exclusionary. While there are exceptions, most opera requires an orchestra in the pit, singers onstage, sets, and costumes; it is an incredibly expensive endeavor to pull off. Moreover, there are not opera houses on every corner, let alone in every city; it is often not easy or convenient to attend. If you happen to have an opera house within easy traveling distance (by car, bus, or train), the ticket prices tend to be prohibitively expensive for many people. This list of hurdles to opera's accessibility continues. One of my goals is to show in print what I have experienced in real life many times: opera can be relevant, provocative, and empowering. Opera is an art form that has potential for being a site for critical inquiry, political activism, and social change.

Unlike the audiences for the very first opera performances in seventeenth-century northern Italy (in court theaters and a limited number of public theaters) that represented a rather small percentage of the general public, the audiences I envision in this book are vast. They encompass a diversity of publics and include the people I sit next to in opera houses across the world; my friends who are opera lovers; my friends who do not know much about opera but are willing to learn more; and the many students I teach in my classes in addition to music majors (I frequently have undergraduate engineers, business school and liberal arts students, and student athletes). These audiences also include people who attend pre-concert lectures, academic conference sessions, and other adult-learning venues; they go to university alumni camps and enrichment opportunities, they listen to National Public Radio interviews, and some have been incarcerated at the local women's prison where I volunteered and team-taught women's studies and opera classes for four years.

My approach to this book has been greatly shaped by feminist theory and pedagogies that originated outside the academy; these influences are reflected between the lines in the opening paragraphs above. I have long admired the capaciousness of many of bell hooks's ideas. From the title of her books, such as *Feminism Is for Everybody: Passionate Politics*, to her definition that "simply put, feminism is a movement to end sexism, sexist exploitation, and oppression," to her stance encouraging scholars to write in a style that is easily accessible and readable, I have tried to use these concepts in the presentation of my ideas about opera and how I write.[1] I do not claim that "opera has to be for everyone"; I know it is a stylized genre that might not appeal to all people. However, I ask questions and frame my inquiry in ways that open up spaces for anyone who might want to learn more. I treat issues that opera scholarship has not deeply engaged regarding how race, gender, sexuality, and nation are contrapuntal voices working in ways that reinforce their coming together and at times in ways that seem to be in opposition. I argue that the identities of the opera's creators (the composer and librettist), the interpreters (the performers onstage), and the people in the audience matter greatly and produce multiple simultaneous meanings of an operatic production.

A good deal has been written about the importance of understanding the background of a composer and the immediate context around the genesis of a work. On the other hand, the contrasting position has argued that the arts need to be freed from the weight that there is only one "true" interpretation locked inside the world of the artist. It would be an oversimplification to say that such debates have been resolved. There are valid reasons to want to understand an original performing context for a work and the composer's intentions—as far as we can decipher and interpret—for thinking about a work. The contemporaneous aesthetics surrounding art are also central for gaining a deeper knowledge about how a work could have been seen and heard by its original audiences.[2] Many of my colleagues have written textbooks about and will teach using such a pedagogy for understanding an artwork in its own time. I also have written about this approach in my first book, *Voicing Gender*, with the construction of the "Period Ear," which explores the conventions in the early-nineteenth-century Italian opera tradition for understanding how a woman's voice could be heard to sound as multiple types of roles across gender and character. A blameless female heroine, a woman who can do terrible things and still survive the end of the opera, and the male heroic lead could all be performed by the same singer throughout her career during the first half of the nineteenth century in Italy. Hence, understanding contemporaneous primo ottocento aesthetics for opera helps us see how voice types and character types for women changed over the nineteenth century; women were not only allowed to successfully challenge male domination in the beginning of the nineteenth century, but during this time women also frequently performed as male characters and embodied this patriarchal authority.[3]

Yet there are also compelling reasons to look at works from the past in terms of how they resonate today. In his seminal essay about the supposed interdependent roles of the author and the reader, Roland Barthes places a new importance on the reader: "The reader is the space on which all the quotations that make up a writing are inscribed without any of them being lost; a text's unity lies not in its origin but in its destination." A few sentences later he ends the essay with the bold statement that "the birth of the reader must be at the cost of the death of the Author."[4] I find this a compelling challenge to attend to the voices of the composer and the listener alike. In the case of opera, the "readers" are the people doing the interpreting: audience members.

However, what makes music performance different from reading written texts, as Edward Cone and others have written, is the added role of the performer.[5] As I explore in this book, the performing body is not a neutral zone or a blank slate. This body has multiple overlapping identities in terms of the expression of gender, race and ethnicity, and national origin—to name the particular markers I have analyzed in the greatest depth (but certainly not the only important areas of representation). Moreover, the bodies in the audience are also ciphers of meaning that can read, and be read, in multiple ways. I have extended the line of inquiry around artistic interpretation to include these different people: the artists (who, in most cases here, are the composer and librettist), the performers onstage, and the people in the audience.

I am writing from the vantage point of the audience. As a black woman, my voice interweaves my experiences of gender and race. Such racialized and gendered experiences inform Patricia Hill Collins's "black woman's standpoint" theory, a model that shows how people who share a social situation may express shared and similar experiences that empower collective consciousness and political action.[6] I also am aware that marginalized communities interact with the dominant culture in ways that can be damaging as well as liberating. In his study *Education for Critical Consciousness* Paulo Freire provides the paradigms of "integration," the behavior of a flexible democratic system that employs critical thought, and "adaptation," the assimilation to an authoritarian oppressive regime, as ways to respond to the dominant culture.[7] In my study, I read the voices of opera creators, performers, and audiences in an integrative mode inspired by Freire. I do not categorize all of opera as outdated exemplars of an irrelevant genre that speaks only to white, European Western audiences. To do so would both oversimplify and deny the artistic treasures of Western civilization to nonwhite people due only to a perceived scientific difference based on skin color, a misleading visual marker that has no scientific basis.[8] Artistic and intellectual achievement based on scientific genetic differences between people of different racial and ethnic categories has been disproved. Vast differences in achievement due to social and economic injustice and systemic prejudice based on racial and ethnic difference are another matter, and those have been assumed in this study. As a genre, opera is not inherently flawed with racist sexist negative stereotypes. Instead, it works as a mouthpiece, a conduit, through which a reflection of a society's cultural ideology—which may include those stereotypes—can be heard and seen.

Returning to Freire, I find his analysis of overcoming oppression to be helpful in my goals for engaging opera in this book. He outlines a process in which both the oppressed and the oppressor struggle to see each other as more fully human and, thus, they both regain their humanity. As an art that speaks through text, music, and staging, opera employs many of our senses and allows us to see life situations reenacted on the stage in ways that encompass the grandiose as well as the subtle and nuanced. It is a genre that elicits a wide range of our emotions (love, anger, joy, fear, and so on); it makes us think and feel. I find opera to be in an important, albeit unlikely, position to make changes regarding how we can think and feel about ourselves, as well as new situations and, possibly, new groups of people. Freire states that "the pedagogy of the oppressed . . . is the pedagogy of people engaged in the fight for their own liberation." Through its role in shaping how we see ourselves and others, opera, as I see it, has a role in this liberation.[9]

In my work I show how blacks in the United States and South Africa have recently used the genre of opera not just as performers (especially as singers) but also as composers and librettists.[10] Not only are operas from the Western European tradition being performed in traditional productions across the world with black performers, but they are also present in avant-garde stagings where the action is placed in all-black settings and given new meanings. Additionally, black artists are working with nonblack artists in interracial collaborations and composing new stories with narratives around black experiences. Opera has become a space where black people are writing themselves into history. In a genre where blackness had been routinely seen in negative stereotypical ways, a new generation across the Atlantic in the United States and South Africa is rewriting the terms for representing blackness in opera.[11] I read such a move as empowering and liberating and one that can harness political action.

To help distinguish between current directions in musicology and the engaged musicological analysis I am talking about, the next sections include a discussion of "public musicology," a recent construction of the American Musicological Society. I then bring in two real-life situations where my training as a musicologist and my experience in charged musical situations presented opportunities to examine what is at stake with an engaged musicological ideology. The first experience is about a cutting-edge recent production of Bizet's *Carmen*; the second is about a concert-version performance of Mozart's *Die Entführung aus dem Serail*.

Public Musicology and an Engaged Musicology

In the August 2013 issue of the American Musicological Society's *AMS Newsletter* the president of the AMS, Christopher Reynolds, wrote about three new initiatives: a new member directory, a new blog, and a newly endowed plenary lecture at the annual meeting. The new AMS blog had its genesis in postings to the AMS list (a moderated musicology discussion listserv) in 2011 and discussions at the AMS's board of directors' retreat in March 2012 about the discipline's "relevance and viability to the world at large."[12] Reynolds related that, prodded by an email "lamenting our relative invisibility, many—including [Reynolds himself]—identified the variety of ways in which individual members have successfully made an impact outside of academia and professional journals."[13] Later on Reynolds wrote:

> The [AMS] Board wanted to find a way to communicate what it is we do in language that would be accessible to constituencies we want to reach, including performers and concert-goers. After considering various possibilities we agreed at our March 2013 meeting to launch an official AMS blog, which we dubbed *Musicology Now*.[14]

In this introduction to the new AMS blog, the emphasis seems to be on the lack of recognition that musicologists receive and the frustration that important information about music is not reaching a wider audience. The target audience as stated are "performers and concert-goers." The description of the new blog followed.

> *Musicology Now* is a blog from the American Musicological Society, written by its members for the general public. It seeks to promote the results of recent

research and discovery in the field of music history, foster colloquy, and generate enthusiasm for the subject matter. Using links, images, and sound, it references conversations within and around the academy and in the principal institutions of music making around the world.[15]

Here the targeted audience is mentioned as the general public, and through the use of technology (links, images, and sound) the focus "references conversations within and around the academy" as well as the leading international performance institutions. From my further investigation of public musicology in practice, the primary concerns seem to be a desire to make research from the academy known to the classical music community and to discover a way to celebrate the work of people doing musicology outside traditional academic positions.[16]

There is nothing in my construction of an "engaged musicology" that is at odds with the AMS "public musicology"; however, they seem to occupy different spaces. An engaged musicology is more of an ideology that incorporates the vantage points of the current diverse publics interpreting a work. In addition to the traditional tools of musicological analysis, engaged musicology emphasizes how a specific musical work has meaning today. In public musicology the emphasis seems to be more on an educational desire to share the accepted knowledge of specialists with a less-informed audience. It is a dissemination issue rather than how the interpretation engages the experiences of the audience. Public musicology presents a "musicologically correct" discussion of the music. An engaged musicology finds a way to incorporate some of the experiences of the public into an historically informed interpretation.

In a recent alumni publication from a musicology department at an Ivy League institution I saw an article about their graduate students involved in a new "public service initiative." I was eager to see what they were doing—connections to the immediate community, outreach to public schools, addressing the inequities of education where exposure to classical and art music repertories are left to the wealthier families of the community who can afford lessons for their children—the opportunities could be endless. As I anticipated reading about this, I also wished that there had been a public-service music forum for students when I was in graduate school. Instead of seeing graduate students out in the community "field," the newsletter showed a picture of graduate students sitting around a seminar table in a classroom working on their laptops participating in a "Wikipedia Edit-a-thon." My initial response was twofold: I was both disappointed that this was the chosen activity (and not something more grassroots, such as what I mentioned above) and, upon further consideration, also pleased that these students were creating and updating entries and jumping into a realm that would, indeed, have a broad impact on the public who sought accurate and dependable information about music. Subscriptions to the *Oxford Music Online* dictionaries (the online gateway to the *New Grove Music Dictionaries*) that are the standard scholarly reference for the most critically correct musicological information are prohibitively expensive for the average person who does not have access through a university or other institutional affiliation. Wikipedia is free (provided you have basic internet access) and serves as the go-to reference for most people who need information on anything, and though the classical/art music entries can be riddled with inaccuracies, it is nevertheless a source people frequently use and trust. Despite my initial reservations, I decided that it was good that these top musicology graduate students were helping to make a public resource on music knowledge stronger and better.

I have characterized public musicology in a way that is not exuberantly flattering because I think it has yet to reach its potential. I honor what I sense to be the energy behind wanting to find a way to bring the knowledge and exciting ideas that musicologists (people who are scholars and lovers of music and, frequently, performing musicians) want to share with others who are not researchers. These "Others" range from professional musicians to elementary music teachers, lawyers with subscriptions to the symphony, and people who never go to concerts and might be intimidated by the gatekeeping around classical music culture (for example, walking into most opera houses is a daunting event when it is your first time). I am encouraged by the recent voices in musicology (including some on the *Musicology Now* blog) who are questioning and exposing areas for growth and deeper inclusion within the discipline. William Cheng's recent monograph, *Just Vibrations: The Purpose of Sounding Good*, moves boldly with a critique of the vicious culture so present in many humanities disciplines (including musicology) and a call to move toward a more compassionate aesthetics for acknowledging what is valued.[17] This includes not only a social justice element to our endeavors but also a moral component. As I understand this articulation of justice, what is needed more than a "do no harm" attitude is a reparative mission that helps heal and strengthen along the way. It is this re-envisioning of the experts, audiences, and publics that an engaged musicological practice brings together in the type of music analysis I am presenting in this book.

Trans Carmen in Prison

Another example of a critically engaged musicological practice involves concerts and opera productions that speak directly to the experiences and cultures of current audiences. Let me outline a recent production of Bizet's

Carmen that takes the issues of gender, sexuality, class, and setting in new directions. Whereas *U-Carmen eKhayelitsha* brought the opera into the townships of South Africa, Opera MODO (a fairly new independent opera company in Detroit, Michigan) sets the opera in an all-female minimum-security prison with a countertenor, alternating with the more traditional mezzo-soprano, in the title role.[18] Both singers portrayed a transgendered female Carmen. The publicity materials announcing the opera and soliciting funding for support make the association between this opera setting and the hit HBO series *Orange Is the New Black* with the connection between a women's prison and the prominence of a transgender woman character "'Carmen' as operatic 'Orange Is the New Black' featuring transgender Carmen." In further statements, the website outlines that this production

> will bring a new dynamic to a story familiar to seasoned opera lovers while also appealing to new audiences through a modern and more relatable setting. Finally—and most importantly—we will feature a character from the underrepresented and often misunderstood transgender population. The role of Carmen, in particular, is significant because she is the ultimate seductress who garners power from her feminine beauty and sexuality. A transgender Carmen showcases a role model for the transgender community who is not seen as atypical in regards to her gender, but rather, one who is praised as an ideal of beauty and desire.[19]

The connection between the prison setting and a transgender woman is provocative, but the element of casting a countertenor to sing Carmen adds another dimension. The sound of a countertenor voice is not a well-known timbre to many people outside the classical music world, and it is not even familiar to all opera fans. A countertenor's voice is a treble timbre that comes from a man singing in his head voice. This type of falsetto is also described with terms around the vocal mode (second-mode phonation) and pharyngeal production.[20] The art of such singing has gained new ground since the important strides by Alfred Deller (1912–1979) in the first half of the twentieth century and has become a newer specialty since the early 1990s. There is a generation of singers who have bought this singing style into prominence (Derek Lee Ragin, David Daniels, Brian Asawa, Darryl Taylor, Philippe Jaroussky, and John Holiday to name just a small group).[21]

There is an uncanny experience of hearing a countertenor, especially in a live performance. With the level of expertise today, many countertenors can sound like women singing—the vibrato, the richness, and the vocal timbre can make experienced opera listeners wonder about the gender-sex identification of the singer. Most countertenors sing roles in opera that were originally written for the castrato singers of the seventeenth and eighteenth centuries in roles by composers from Nicola Porpora in the seventeenth century through Handel and Mozart in the eighteenth century, and even Rossini in the early nineteenth century. Such an association with music written for castrati only heightens the countertenor's connection to a gendered ambiguity. While modern countertenors are genetically male singers who have perfected a way of singing that can make them sound like a female singer, the castrato tradition involved the orchiectomy surgery to a young boy before he reached puberty and altered the circulation of growth androgens; hence, the "sex" (genetic identification) of a castrato person once adulthood was reached has been debated and is mitigated through cultural contexts.[22]

Casting Carmen, one of the greatest sex symbols of unbridled feminine desire and power in opera, as a transgender woman indeed showcased a new role model for the transgendered community. The sonic world of the opera was cut down in size (a small chorus, a reduced orchestra) and the performance venues were not traditional stages but large rooms and open spaces where the orchestra was interspersed within the audience and the audience sat just a few feet away from the singers. I was fortunate to attend two (of the four) performances of this production of *Carmen*. In one performance Carmen was sung by the countertenor and Don Jose was a soprano (sung by a woman). In the other performance, Carmen was sung by a woman performing the role as a man singing as a trans woman and Don Jose was the same soprano who sang opposite the countertenor Carmen.[23] The male characters sung by men were Le Remendado, Moralès, and Escamillo, who also doubled as guards for the women's prison and male chorus.

Though a description of these performances might almost sound kitschy and campy, that was not at all the effect in person. With major funding from the Knight Foundation, the company also partnered with the Ruth Ellis Center, a place for at-risk LGBTQ youth.[24] In the program, Danielle Wright, executive director and founder of Opera MODO, wrote an extended welcome and program notes for her vision of the production and its dramaturgy. She also included information about the local trans community in Detroit:

> We hope that this production begins a dialogue in metro Detroit about LGBTQ reception and inclusion in society. In order to further facilitate this, we've partnered with the Ruth Ellis Center and incorporated a sensitivity training into our rehearsal process in order to be sure we are doing all we can to represent the LGBTQ community appropriately. I never realized how many parallels the story of Carmen has with recent events in the Detroit trans community until we started digging deep. There have been at least five murders of trans women in the past two years—murdered by their partners. Partners who could not

understand that they loved someone who finally had the freedom to become themselves. My hope is that in attending these productions, our community will be inspired to grow in its awareness to provide help, jobs, support for the trans community.[25]

At the beginning of both performances I attended, Danielle Wright came out to the audience, welcomed us, and said a version of these program notes to us in person. She also asked us to honor the five murdered trans women in a short silent memorial to them.

To the first performance, I was able to bring two colleagues/friends who have extensive experience working and volunteering in the Michigan Department of Corrections. One friend is a playwright and scholar who writes about the arts in prisons around the world and coordinates a large student network of volunteers who run drama programs in the Michigan prisons. The other friend had been incarcerated for a couple of decades (her life sentence was commuted in the early 2000s) and has become a leading figure in Michigan reentry initiatives and prison creative-arts programs. In comparison, my experience with prisons was rather limited; however, I had volunteered as a women's studies teacher in one of the Michigan women's correctional facilities for four years in the early 2000s.[26] All of us were impressed with the sensitivity and care the production brought to depicting life on the inside. My friend who had been incarcerated said they really captured the feeling of the waiting and monotony of the evenings—especially Sunday evenings—and trying to fill the time with cards, such as the staging of the Card Trio (between Carmen, Fresquita, and Mercedes) in act 3. She also thought that the depiction of the pent-up physical energy and tension felt compelling and rang especially true (Escamillo, a retired boxer, is the prison warden and his entrance in act 2 is staged as a choreographed boxing match between two prisoners).

The group of people directly involved—Danielle Wright, the singers, the musicians in the orchestra, the stage crew—were wonderfully dynamic, highly trained, and much younger than the usual crowd associated with opera (all seemed to be under thirty-five years old). From their biographies in the program, most of them had graduate degrees in vocal performance and all had sung in opera productions before. Many of them had performed in multiple professional opera companies and highly regarded training programs. It was clear that though these young people were at an early stage of their careers, this was not a beginning step for them. All them were accomplished musicians and had professional experience.

The members of the audience were a diverse group that included friends and family of the singers and people like me who had heard of this performance but had no connection to the performers. Many of the audience members (though not all of us) were under forty years old, a rather rare occurrence and strong deviation from the usual opera crowd. In all my years of opera-going since the mid-1980s, I had never experienced anything like this in terms of a young, highly professional group doing an activist version of a canonic opera, tucked away in unusual venues. The performances during the first weekend took place in downtown Detroit at the Carr Center (on East Grand River Avenue), an arts center with performance space and art galleries that features programming for Detroit youth. The second weekend, the performances were located at the Jam Handy, also in downtown (on East Grand Boulevard). Unlike the Carr Center, with established arts program-ming, the Jam Handy building feels like a large warehouse that helped "create a raw atmosphere for the prison setting." Danielle Wright continues in her program notes, "The Jam Handy provides a uniquely 'Detroit' backdrop for the production. The space is deconstructed and bare, but is also known to Detroiters for housing creativity in the city through programs like Detroit Soup" (Detroit Soup is a micro-granting dinner that celebrates and funds creative projects in Detroit).[27] The Jam Handy sits among the areas of Detroit that have suffered from urban blight and are still undergoing reinvigoration. Unlike opera houses that frequently have their own, or shared, parking lot, attending the evening *Carmen* performance at the Jam Handy gave me (and a friend) the opportunity to see and momentarily walk in the neighbor-hood, one far different than those surrounding the Michigan Opera Theatre or Orchestra Hall (where the Detroit Symphony Orchestra performs). The cutting-edge experience of this performance began even outside the theater.

Opera MODO's February 2016 production of *Carmen* has a new relevance for many reasons. The connections to the present moved into the theater and performance. The diversity of the audience felt celebrated; in a production that featured issues around the LGBTQ community, it seemed as though the many members of the gay community in the audience were more vis-ible and welcomed than at other opera performances I have attended. The audience was not only united by our familiarity with the series *Orange Is the New Black* but also because we all had heard Danielle Wright tell us of the Ruth Ellis Center down the street, the five recent murders of trans people in Detroit, and we had just spent a few moments together in silent tribute honoring their memories and the people they left behind. This experience far exceeded my initial thoughts about an engaged musicology that could examine opera in terms of how it fit into its time and place. Writing about this production makes me feel like opera is approaching a new frontier.

Challenges in Performing Mozart's *Entführung* in Post 9/11 Michigan

Another opportunity for an engaged musicological practice involves themes in repertory works that are affected by current political situations and now resonate in complicated ways with contemporary audiences. I had the opportunity to be involved in such a situation with a concert performance of Mozart's late eighteenth-century opera, *Die Entführung aus dem Serail* (*The Abduction from the Turkish Seraglio*) (1782). I sat on the board of an orchestra in Michigan, in a region that has one of the largest Middle Eastern populations in the world outside the Middle East.[28] In a subcommittee meeting I learned of this programming and that the concert was to be the following month (January 2016). While the music is wonderful, this opera contains many unflattering stereotypes of Turkish (and Muslim) people. The opera is an odd genre of being a *Singspiel*—a hybrid of an *opera seria* (with highborn "serious" heroic) characters and situations and *opera buffa*, with more comedic characters and situations. The opera was written before Mozart's most famous operas (the three Da Ponte collaborations, *Marriage of Figaro* [1786], *Don Giovanni* [1787], and *Così fan tutte* [1791]; and *The Magic Flute* [1790]), and this opera provides a slightly earlier look at some of the characteristics we have come to associate with the later operas. Hence, it is a great choice for presenting an opera Mozart composed before he fully settled into his later style.

The comedic element from the *Singspiel* genre and the presentation of the Turkish and Muslims made me feel a bit uncomfortable in the post September 11 environment, especially for a performance in Michigan. I offered to write something from which a statement (a few paragraphs, perhaps) could be taken and inserted into the program. This would need to be an insert since the official program (cast, notes, advertisements, and the like) for the season was printed months before. I wrote my piece to provide an educational context for the board (which includes the executive director and conductor, both *ex officio*), thinking that it could be excerpted and revised according to what people decided. I started with a quotation from Ralph Locke's book on exoticism, the most recent and comprehensive study on this topic.

> "Turkish" operas present a particular problem nowadays. Mozart's Osmin
> (in *Die Entführung aus dem Serail*), for example, is unquestionably nasty, and
> his nastiness is understood as tied up with his adherence to real or supposed
> Turkish customs of the day (such as a man's forcing himself upon a woman
> or threatening to impale his Christian adversaries). We need to be brought to

laugh at certain of his excesses and character flaws—such as his secretly enjoying wine, despite the strictures of the Qur'an—or else the opera does not work. Yet to laugh at Osmin for his graceless womanizing or his religious hypocrisy smacks today of ridiculing the large culture region and the major world religion that he so insists on representing. (*Musical Exoticism*, 322)

After Locke's strong and helpful comments I then continued with an essay containing a detailed discussion so that the board could draw from this material in coming up with a statement for the program insert. My comments ended up being a little longer than I anticipated, but I wanted to present the topic as usefully as possible.

> In our January concerts, we like to commemorate one of the most important and celebrated composers in the Western European musical tradition: Wolfgang Amadeus Mozart, born on January 27, 1756. Rather than censor the elements in his music that reflect outdated beliefs of his time, we choose to perform his important works and provide educational and historical context to help us understand how these works fit into their past and how they continue to have meaning in our time today.
>
> Mozart was in the early generation of Western European composers who incorporated so-called "Turkish" elements in his music. His opera *Die Entführung aus dem Serail* K.384 (1782) frequently tops the list of classical works written that include "Turkish" or "Exotic" elements in Western European music. Mozart also used these elements in some of his other works (most famously, K.331 the "Rondo alla turca" Piano Sonata and K.219, his "Turkish" Violin Concerto) and he was joined by the leading contemporary composers who also followed this practice (e.g., Haydn, Symphony #100; Beethoven's "Turkish March" in the finale to his 9th Symphony). Later in the nineteenth century such "Turkish" elements become less common, though they still continued. However, the theme of exoticism—evoking a place, people or social milieu that feel foreign to the intended audience—continued strongly through musical portrayals of China, Japan, India, the Romani (Roma), Northern Africa, Sub-Saharan Africa . . . the list continues.
>
> Some of the historical context behind Mozart's reference to Turkish elements can be seen in the close geographical proximity between Vienna and the Ottoman Empire, the location of modern day Turkey. The last siege of Vienna by the Turkish was in the 1680s and by Mozart's time in the end of the eighteenth century, the threat was far enough in the past that it was something artists and composers felt more comfortable referring to in their work.
>
> One of the primary references to a "Turkish" sound was to the Janissary music, an elite troop of the Ottoman empire that had their own bands of musicians (called *mehter*). These Janissary bands played at functions such as announcing the arrival of special dignitaries and accompanying the military to

inspire soldiers on the battlefield. Much of the Western European reference to the Turkish Janissary band was in the West's perceptions of their music. Large instruments (bass drums, timpani), triangles and cymbals were used for their ability to penetrate through large spaces that could be heard across outdoor open fields. Other musical elements that became associated with a "Turkish" style include: the use of a simple harmonic vocabulary, sudden shifting from one tonal area to another, repeated notes, repeated rhythmic patterns, quick melodic decorations (e.g., short trills, frequent turns), and sudden contrasts in dynamics with an emphasis on loud playing, among others.

Beyond Mozart's exotic score, we want to acknowledge several competing elements: (1) the libretto reflects the attitudes of a specific time, the end of the eighteenth century; (2) the European perceptions of that time regarding Turkish and Arabic culture were not fully accurate then, and certainly do not represent our views today; and (3) music is not "innocent" of political content—these works carry cultural meaning.

In the context of life after the events of September 11, 2001, and the more recent acts of aggression in the past few months (e.g., the San Bernardino, California, attack on December 2 and the Paris massacre on November 13 are only the two largest), we realize that though we are living in a time of religious extremism that has been leading to violent and painful consequences, these actions do not represent the views of most Arabs, people who are Muslim, or people from the Middle East. With our orchestra based in Michigan we live in a region that is home to one of the largest populations of the very diverse communities of people who are Arab, Muslim, and have roots in the Middle East. Our goal is to welcome everyone to our concerts.

Scholars have long recognized that parts of the world with hegemonic power tend to define other parts of the world in a weaker or less than equal status. In 1978 Palestinian literary theorist and cultural historian Edward Said forged a groundbreaking path by looking at these issues in his book *Orientalism* and set out helpful constructions for thinking about how the West has defined the East that extends beyond geographical locations and includes ways of engaging other people, culture, and beliefs. In the past decade, ideologies surrounding the "Global North" and the "Global South" have been added to how economies of privilege have shaped our perceptions and interactions with different parts of the world. Symphonies, opera companies and classical music institutions today need to be more assertive in addressing the political content embedded in art. As we strive to share the beauty and energy these works continue to hold, we also recognize the need to engage the ways these works resonate in multiple meanings for contemporary audiences.[29]

I sent these comments to the executive director and the one other person on the subcommittee of the board who had also expressed concern about the programming and was supportive of including some statement in the program insert about the context of the work. The board member wrote back right away and said, "Beautifully done." A few days later, I received a very nervous, yet well-intentioned, phone call from the executive director. I appreciated her desire and energy to talk about this and find a way to handle the situation. From my vantage point, and that is the only vantage point from which I can tell this story, it seemed that she felt I had made a compelling argument but I had moved into very risky territory that would bring a lot of negative attention to something that no one in the audience or board would really notice. Though my statement was not circulated to the board, I think the executive director showed the statement to a few others and came up with a different statement to put in the program insert:

> As with a number of Mozart operas, the plots give offense to some. If you are one of them, we ask your forbearance. Our aim is emphatically not to offend but to share the fruits of one of the great geniuses of classical western music.

When asked my opinion, I said that I felt this was too general a statement; rather than evade the real issues, it was important to mention something about the real problems pertaining to Islamophobia—people who are Turkish, Muslims, and the stereotypes that are associated with them today. The following sentence was then added in front of the ones above:

> The plot of *Die Entführung aus dem Serail* is tied up with conflicts between the Viennese and Ottoman Empires at the end of the 18th century—and associated with perceptions of Turkish and Arabic culture at that time—which certainly do not represent our views today.

I share these comments in an effort to illustrate a few of the challenging aspects of pursuing a nascent model of an engaged musicological practice today. This was a difficult experience on several levels. I did not enjoy picking apart an opera whose music I have enjoyed yet was also making me increasingly uncomfortable in the present political climate. I felt uncomfortable for having enjoyed this opera in the past without thinking of how hurtful its messages were, and I was uncomfortable for the current realization that this portrayal of the broadly conceived "Turkish" was inaccurate and needed some sort of intervention. Additionally, it was not fun trying to bring these ideas to a group of good people, whom I worked with and had admired, and who are dedicated to bringing classical music to audiences today. I felt as though I was an irritating nudge who was implying (not so subtly) that something needed to be done that they had not noticed. It was very awkward to play the role of a social conscience that no one saw the need for. I believe that I did the right thing, and I am grateful to the executive director for her patience and willingness to listen to me, even though I am not sure she fully agreed with my standpoint. It is one thing to do "activist" work when people are being poisoned by toxic water or when an emergency manager has been appointed to take over a school system (two cases I mentioned in the introduction regarding Flint and Detroit, Michigan, respectively). It is quite another thing to take a stand on an issue that is not about life and death wherein the stakes seem to be so different. The emotional weight of this work is tough when you bring such things to people's attention and you run the risk of alienating the very people who had been your allies.

My goal in this book has been to demonstrate a way of asking questions and engaging a range of topics that more closely matched my experience of sitting in the opera house, movie theater, at home, or any other venue for seeing and/or hearing opera performed. I found that the questions I had were not only mine but were also shared by many when I began to talk about them. After I spent time analyzing and writing about the case studies and their cultural contexts in this book, I realized that the type of engagement I had forged with opera could apply to other musical genres, practices, and inquiries. In this conclusion I present this model, with opera as the jumping-off point, for thinking about an *engaged musicology*. While my analysis has focused on the ways race, gender, sexuality, and nation shape the tools we bring with us to a work, there are other intersectional themes that can be highlighted to reflect how a work has meaning among different audiences. Though we might not have noticed, or want to admit it, the types of questions we bring to our work are directly tied to our perspectives and experiences. Even if we receive a classic education that employs canonical methodologies, relies on recognized readings, and practices approved pedagogies, we are all unique vessels as we acquire this training and embody our differences. A challenge for those of us who study music is the realization that art frequently resonates outside of a single exclusive period, geographical space, or ideology. In performance, the same work is presented to everyone at the same time. However, art touches us in a variety of ways and has very different consequences and interpretations, depending on who we are. We hear, see, feel, and interpret things differently. This book, written by a member trained inside the academic musicological tribe from a vantage point outside many of their shared experiences, honors those differences.

Notes

Chapter 1. Engaged Opera

1. Trayvon Martin was fatally shot by George Zimmerman, a neighborhood-watch volunteer, in Sanford, Florida, on February 26, 2012. Martin was seventeen years old and was walking home from a convenience store after having purchased candy and a soda; he was unarmed.

2. Under the apartheid system, white men had two years of compulsory military service, followed by camps at intervals. This was abolished in 1994. The End Conscription Campaign, begun in 1983, was an anti-apartheid organization connected to the United Democratic Front and opposed the conscription into military service in the South African Defense Force. See Conway, *Masculinities*.

3. Johan Botha (1965–2016). His homepage states, "After his studies and his debut in 1990 he came to Europe. His international career developed quickly after initial engagement in Germany." http://www.johan-botha.com/biography.php?lang=en. Wikipedia lists his birthplace as Rustenburg, South Africa, in 1965. https://en.wikipedia .org/wiki/Johan_Botha_(tenor).

4. Kinney, "As the Met Abandons Blackface" (quotation on p. 4 of 14).

5. The publicity around the Met's decision not to use blackface makeup for Otello might have a larger effect on the opera industry and could be the beginning of a new practice. Time will tell. But up until 2015, putting racialized makeup on singers for the title roles of *Otello*, *Aida*, or *Madama Butterfly* and *Turandot* ("yellowface" makeup) was an assumed practice generally not commented upon. An early article that commented on "yellowface" is Guilford, "It's Time to Stop Using 'Exoticism.'"

6. Roberts, *Fatal Invention*.

7. Michelle Alexander, in *New Jim Crow*, has raised a national awareness of how the "war on drugs" of the 1980s and 1990s led to racial targeting for incarceration and sentencing practices. This is one of the factors in the background to the Black Lives Matter movement.

8. A further discussion of the theoretical paradigms by Patricia Hill Collins, bell hooks, and Paulo Freire is taken up in the conclusion of this study.

9. Said, "Imperial Spectacle"; Said, "Empire at Work." "Imperial Spectacle" was first published in 1987 and then became more widely available when it was republished as "Empire at Work" in his collection *Culture and Imperialism* in 1993.

10. della Seta and Groos, "O cieli azzurri"; Bergeron, "Verdi's Egyptian Spectacle"; Robinson, "Is *Aida* an Orientalist Opera?"

11. From the origins of opera through the present, the issue of "realism" and "real life" have been discussed with regard to reception and analysis. From the discourse of verisimilitude through *verismo* through the concern since the early 1990s for opera singers' bodies to be thin, lithe, attractive, and sexy to contemporary audiences, opera is concerned with a construction of reality that connects to, and reflects, its time.

12. Several sets by Franco Zeffirelli later in his career typify this trend with his productions of *La Bohème* (1981), *Tosca* (1985), and *Turandot* (1987) at the Metropolitan Opera in New York that had ornate, busy, and extremely complicated sets. This visual spectacle in the set almost made it less important to focus on what the singers looked like (in fact, in some scenes in *Turandot* it was almost difficult to find the singers in the ornate sets); hence, the singers were there primarily to provide aural pleasure rather than a "realistic" visual portrayal of the operatic character. As I witnessed many times, it was not unusual for the audience to clap for each new set as the curtain opened at the beginning of the act.

13. The Texaco broadcasts were originally co-sponsored in 1931 and then moved to full Texaco sponsorship in 1940. See Pogrebin, "ChevronTexaco."

14. The Metropolitan Opera unveiled its use of supertitles in the Met Titles, a system that displays the text on screens behind seatbacks (because the proscenium is too large for the more conventional supertitles) on October 2, 1995. Tommasini "Reinventing Supertitles."

15. I mention black female singers (and not even all the singers of that era) and no black male singers because there were very few black men singing at the Met. This is a deeply pressing topic and has been discussed thoughtfully by Wallace Cheatham (*Dialogues on Opera*) and Alison Kinney ("Conversations with Black Otellos").

16. The adaptation of Bizet's *Carmen* opera on the African continent in South Africa and Senegal led to an article for a journal issue on Opera and Citizenship (see André, "*Carmen* in Africa").

17. Joseph Ramaka's *Karmen Geï* (2001) is most efficiently seen in a context of Senegalese film. I have not found a burgeoning opera scene in Senegal; however, there might be a fruitful exploration in the wider region of opera in the Sahel (for example, *Bintou Were, A Sahel Opera* [2007], composed by a collaborative team) and the Sahel Opera organization.

18. At the time of this writing I know of a few South African scholars working on extended projects (monographs, articles) on opera in and around South Africa: Innocentia Jabulisile Mhlambi, Donato Somma, Grant Olwage, Thomas Pooley, and Hilde Roos. The complicated layers of operatic activity during colonialism, apartheid and post-apartheid, provides a rich environment for South African opera studies.

19. For a further discussion of the historical context for Verdi's *Aida* see Said, "Empire at Work," Gauthier and McFarlane-Harris, "Nationalism."

20. *American Music Review* 45, no. 1 (Fall 2015) is devoted to Harry Lawrence Freeman's *Voodoo*, the archive of his works given to Columbia, and the conference "Restaging the Harlem Renaissance: New Views on Performing Arts in Black Manhattan" (June 26–27, 2015).

21. Information about Adolphus Hailstork's operas appears at his music publisher's website (Theodore Presser Company, http://www.presser.com/composer/hailstork-adolphus/); see also Banfield, "Hailstork, Adolphus Cunningham," and Hailstork's entry on the AfriClassical.com website (African Heritage in Classical Music), http://chevalierdesaintgeorges.homestead.com/hailstork.html#21. At the time of this writing, the Theodore Presser Company website mentions that Hailstork is currently composing *Robeson*, an operatic theater work written for Trilogy: An Opera Company in Newark, New Jersey. On the *Trilogy: An Opera Company* homepage they state that their focus is "on the works of black composers as well as works reflective of the Black Experience." Their mission statement includes their commitment to "maintaining diversity within its hiring practices." http://trilogyaoc.homestead.com/page04.html.

22. Ronni Reich, "Robeson Opera Opens at NJPAC," *Star-Ledger*, November 25, 2014. http://www.nj.com/entertainment/index.ssf/2014/11/robeson_opera_opens_at_njpac.html. See also Kozinn, "Living Colour and Robeson Opera."

23. Leslie Adams (*Blake* [1986]), based on the nineteenth-century novel by Martin Delany about a slave who traveled throughout the southern United States and Cuba to plan a large-scale insurrection, Regina Harris Baiocchi (*Gbeldahoven: No One's Child* [1997], about Zora Neale Hurston, Langston Hughes, and their patron Charlotte Osgood Mason), George Lewis (*Afterword* [2015], about the Association for the Advancement of Creative Musicians in Chicago), Dorothy Rudd Moore (*Frederick Douglas* [1985]), Richard Thompson (*The Mask in the Mirror* [2009], about relationship between Paul Laurence Dunbar and Alice Ruth Moore).

24. Smittle, "Glimpse of the 'Little Rock Nine'"; Cooper, "Little Rock Nine Inspire an Opera."

25. I saw the New York City Apollo Theater premiere (October 6, 2017). For more information see Kimberly C. Roberts, "'We Shall Not Be Moved': A Candid Commentary on Our Society," Philadelphia Tribune, September 19, 2017, and Salamishah Tillet "A Police Bombing, Homes on Fire and an Opera the Grapples with It All," *New York Times*, September 15, 2017.

26. Hyde, "The Summer King."

27. While the sexualized nature of gender is a main subject in opera, I am referring to operas such as *Harvey Milk* (composed by Stewart Wallace with a libretto by Michael Korie) from 1995, based on the gay activist politician; *Patience and Sarah* (composed by Paula M. Kimper with a libretto by Wende Persons) from 1998, heralded as an early mainstream gay-themed opera; and *Brokeback Mountain* from 2014 (composed by Charles Wuorinen with the libretto by Annie Proulx), based on her 1997 short story. Two well-known cases of earlier operas that highlight gay desire are Berg's 1935 *Lulu*, with the lesbian character the Countess Geschwitz, and stagings that play up same-sex

desire through cross-dressed conventions (for example, the opening of *Der Rosenka-valier* or operas with travesti roles by Handel, Mozart, or Rossini).

28. As an opera scholar, I am well aware of how controversial it is to imply that a grand opera tradition ended in the early twentieth century with the death of Puccini (1924). There are definitely wonderful now-established operas written afterward (such as those by Menotti, Britten, Prokofiev, Shostakovich, to name just a few) as well as many of the composers in this study. However, I am referring to the general "grand tradition" of the long nineteenth century.

29. Thomas Schippers (1930–1977) is the only one in this group who grew up outside the Detroit area, in Portage, Michigan, an area near Kalamazoo.

30. The issue of Verdi working with (and despite) the censors of his time is a rich area of Verdi scholarship. Writing his opera *Un Ballo in Maschera* is the greatest difficulty he encountered in his career; the opera was originally intended for the Teatro San Carlo in Naples but ended up being moved to the Teatro Apollo in Rome due to troubles with the Neapolitan censors. One of the difficulties was the setting of the opera in Sweden and the situation of regicide onstage when King Gustavus III is assassinated. This was changed to a setting with a fictitious Riccardo, Count of Warwick and the governor of Boston. In the Swedish setting, Ulrica's racial identity is not indicated, and she is called "Mam'zelle Arvidson." Parker, "Ballo in maschera, Un."

31. Though there are different meanings for the term "creole," a basic use for the word is in the colonial setting for children born in the colonies—children of mixed parentage from the colonies and the New World or children born of colonial parents in the New World. Renato's being a Creole is not necessarily an indication of his racial difference.

32. Bergeron, "Verdi's Egyptian Spectacle."

33. I use the term "sexuality" in this study primarily as a way to explore how gendered conventions express sexual behavior (for example, the hypersexualized association of behavior, as with the minstrel Jezebel caricature, or acts around sexual violence and domination). Less prominent in these case studies are the issues surrounding lesbian, homosexual, or bisexual identities. Chapter 5 includes a discussion around trans queer themes in a 2016 production of *Carmen* by Opera Modo.

34. As John Rockwell, author for the *New Grove Dictionary of Opera* entry titled "*Four Saints in Three Acts*," writes that the synopsis he produces for his entry is "drawn from Grosser's scenario; it could not be deduced from Stein's words alone."

35. For a discussion about the multiple layers of meaning blackness and modernism project in *Four Saints in Three Acts*, see Barg "Black Voices/White Sounds."

36. This thinking of time and the act of interpretation relates to themes by Johannes Fabian in his exploration of how our position with various Others (the West and the "rest," the present and the past, the anthropologist and the subject) shapes our discussion and analysis. See Fabian, *Time and the Other*.

37. Radano and Bohlman, "Introduction," 5.

38. Stoever's "Listening Ear" has a lot in common with my construction of the "Period Ear," which I used more generally to understand the historical and cultural context

around "listening" to gender and race/ethnicity in early-nineteenth-century Italian opera (see *Voicing Gender*). Other important studies that have influenced my thinking about black performance include DeFrantz and Gonzales, *Black Performance Theory* (especially "Introduction: From "Negro Expression" to "Black Performance") and, about listening, opera, gender, and race, Eidsheim, *Sensing Sound*, and Hutcheon, *Theory of Adaptation*.

39. The five-article cluster appears in *African Studies* 75, no. 1 (2016): "Introduction, *Winnie: The Opera* and Embodying South African Opera;" André, "*Winnie*, Opera, and South African Artistic Nationhood"; Somma, "'Just Say the Words': An Operatic Rendering of Winnie"; Mhlambi, "Embodied Discordance: Vernacular Idioms in *Winnie: The Opera*"; and "'The Musical Thread': Neo Muyanga on Opera and South Africa; A Conversation between Neo Muyanga and Donato Somma," an interview with another up-and-coming opera composer.

40. Lorde, "Master's Tools."

41. Barber, *Anthropology of Texts*, 42–44.

Chapter 2. Black Opera across the Atlantic

1. For additional pioneering work, see Catherine Parsons Smith (esp. on William Grant Still), Carol J. Oja (on William Grant Still, the black presence on Broadway, and black virtuosos during the civil rights era). Newer projects are emerging as well: David Gutkin's "American Opera, Jazz and Historical Consciousness, 1924–1994" (unpublished dissertation) has a section on the operas of Harry Lawrence Freeman; Gutkin and Marti Newland co-edited a special issue of the *American Music Review* (vol. 45, no. 1 [Fall 2015]) with an emphasis on Freeman and opera during the Harlem Renaissance. These represent a few new directions in a field that needs much more work.

2. Radano, *Lying Up a Nation*, xv.

3. For a deeper background into the beginnings of opera in North America and the United States, see: John Dizikes, *Opera in America; Elise Kirk, American Opera; and Katherine Preston, Opera on the Road.*

4. In addition to Rossini's *Barber* with Manuel Garcia I, Manuel García II (the son) was a baritone and leading vocal pedagogue; he wrote one of the most influential singing treatises of the bel canto singing technique. The two daughters, Maria Malibran and Pauline Viardot, became important singers and musical figures in their own right.

5. Information on Lorenzo Da Ponte is from Tim Carter and Dorothea Link's entry, "Da Ponte, Lorenzo," *Oxford Music Online.*

6. Graziano points out that with the right management, such as Major Pond managing the "Black Patti" in the 1880s, "white audiences would attend popular events with high-art programs in which the races were mixed" ("Early Life," 580). Kristen Turner's work discusses the Theodore Drury Grand Opera Company, an all-black opera company that had strong black patronage from 1900 to 1907 ("Class, Race, and Uplift").

7. Several authors have discussed the transgressive elements of minstrelsy. See Cockrell, *Demons of Disorder*, for an especially strong discussion of the subversive

nature of whites blacking up in this tradition; regarding whiteness, social class, and sexual perversion, Lott, *Love and Theft*.

8. For sources on minstrelsy in South Africa during the nineteenth century see Ansell, *Soweto Blues*, 13–17; Cockrell, "Of Gospel Hymns"; and Erlmann, "Feeling of Prejudice."

9. Southern, *Music of Black Americans*, 228. Graham in *Spirituals and the Birth of a Black Entertainment Industry* also mentions the naming of the Fisk Jubilee Singers as having connections to Leviticus 25: 39–55 and the biblical emancipation of the Hebrew slaves.

10. The use of such terms, "minstrels" and "minstrel shows," caused confusion in its own time up through today. Luckily, there are scholars (James Cook, Sandra Graham, Kira Thurman, among others) who are looking up historical performances and programs to help clarify what repertoire was being sung by black solo artists and chorale groups.

11. Chybowski, "'Black Swan' in England" and "Becoming the 'Black Swan'"; Graziano, "Early Life," 545, 561.

12. Wright. "Jones, Sissieretta." The Black Patti Troubadours used the term "Operatic Kaleidoscope" in the nineteenth century in their programs. Marta J. Effinger-Crichlow mentions the term as well in "Jones, Madame Sissieretta Joyner."

13. Turner, "Class, Race, and Uplift."

14. Cook, *Arts of Deception*. His current project on the first African American artists, writers, and activists to market their careers globally is under contract with Norton.

15. Thurman, "German Lied," 569n83.

16. Powers, *From Plantation to Paradise*.

17. National Archives and Records Administration. "File copy of the letter from Eleanor Roosevelt to the president general of the DAR." http://www.archives.gov/exhibits/american_originals/eleanor.html.

18. See Bryan, "Radiating a Hope." Bryan is working on a book-length study of Dawson, titled *A Place on the Stage: The Legacy of Mary Cardwell Dawson and the National Negro Opera Company*, forthcoming from the University of Illinois Press.

19. For the early history of opera in South Africa see Malan, "Opera Houses in South Africa."

20. For information about Italian prisoners of war from World War II, see Donato Somma, "Mythologising Music: Identity and Culture in the Italian Prisoner of War Camps of South Africa," unpublished thesis for the University of the Witwatersrand, May 2009. http://wiredspace.wits.ac.za/handle/10539/7005. See also Somma, "Madonnas and Prima Donnas."

21. To non–South Africans, the nuances around what being coloured/colored means today are complex. In some conversations I have had with South Africans, the term "mixed race" refers to people who are black South African (for example, a clan affiliation such as Xhosa Zulu, Ndebele, and the like) and something else (for example, white, Malay, Indian); these people feel that after apartheid, "coloured"

can now be synonymous with "mixed race." Being biracial or mixed race can mean having parents who are not biracial or mixed race or colored. Other people feel that coloured/colored in South Africa today is something more specific that retains closer ties to the past. This position posits that being coloured/colored is different; as Eusebius McKaiser points out, "the criterion for being classified is clear: both of your parents must be colored." (See McKaiser "Not White Enough, Not Black Enough"). This means that in order to be coloured/colored today, both parents must fit the apartheid-era classification of being coloured/colored.

22. A quick history of these points with the Eoan Group can be found in Roos, "*Eoan—Our Story,*" esp. 190–91.

23. See Roos, "Remembering to Forget the Eoan Group," and Muller and Roos, *Eoan: Our Story.*

24. See Cockrell, "Of Gospel Hymns." Cockrell writes, "Spirituals were first sung in Durban in 1889, not by a black choir but by a forty-voice white ensemble conducted by a Mr. MacColl" (423).

25. Ansell, *Soweto Blues,* 14–16. Veit Erlmann mentions the troupe as the Christy Minstrels in Cape Town in August 1862 ("Feeling of Prejudice," 334).

26. Cockrell, "Of Gospel Hymns," esp. 419. Cockrell outlines several cases of minstrelsy in South Africa by American and British troupes as well as internal South African troupes. The American and South African troupes involved white and black performers in blackface.

27. Erlmann, "Feeling of Prejudice," esp. 331.

28. Ansell, *Soweto Blues,* 15.

29. E. Franklin Frazier (*The Negro Family in the United States* [1939]) was a sociologist who argued that "slavery was so devastating in America that it destroyed all African elements among black Americans." Melville Herskovits (*The Myth of the Negro Past* [1941]) was an anthropologist who argued that "African traditions had survived in black cultures in the Americas." A helpful source on this topic and this debate is Holloway's *Africanisms in American Culture,* esp. pages 3–4.

30. I found Angelo Gobbato's essay of the opera scene in South Africa on the Cape Town Opera website, http://www.capetownopera.co.za/index.php/company/history in the fall of 2015 and last saw it posted there in June 2016. The information about composer Neo Muyanga is primarily from his website, http://www.neosong.net/index .html, and the published interview, Somma and Muyanga, "The Musical Thread."

31. I was fortunate to sit in on a few rehearsals (sadly, I was not able to be there for the final performance) during my first trip to Cape Town (July 2010). To triple cast Mozart's *Figaro* is quite an accomplishment since the opera already has a large cast. Most educational opera programs double cast the roles to allow young voices a rest (not to sing two performances in a row) and give more students opportunities.

32. Angelo Gobbato's history of the opera scene in South Africa (hereafter cited as Gobbato's History) is no longer on the Cape Town Opera website (http://www .capetownopera.co.za/index.php/company/history) and it has not been replaced with another history of the company. I last downloaded this history in early June

2016. The history is not dated, but clues in the essay (the memories from "over the past fifty years" when Gobbato mentions having emigrated to South Africa in 1950 in the beginning and the "production of *Porgy and Bess* that is currently playing in Berlin" at the end) seem to refer to the present time of the essay as September 2012 when the CTO went on tour and sang the choir for *Porgy and Bess* (with Sir Williard White and Latonia Moore with Sir Simon Rattle conducting at the Berliner Festspiele on September 14, 15, and 17, 2012). See http://www.berlinerfestspiele.de/en/aktuell/festivals/musikfest_berlin/archiv_mfb/archiv_mfb12/mfb12_programm/mfb12_veranstaltungsdetail_41218.php.

33. Gobbato's History.

34. Ibid.

35. Ibid.

36. Information about Neo Muyanga can be found on his website: http://www.neosong.net/index.html, and in Somma and Muyanga, "Musical Thread."

37. Somma and Muyanga, "Musical Thread," 87.

38. Ibid., 90–91.

39. Ibid., 90–93, quote on 93. Tiyo Soga (1829–1871) was a South African journalist, minister, and translator, and also a musical composer of hymns.

40. South African Bongani Ndodana-Breen is another composer who has spent some formative years in Canada and the United States. He is the composer of *Winnie: The Opera* (2011).

41. Somma and Muyanga, "Musical Thread," 75.

42. Ibid., 95.

43. Khabi Mngoma (1922–1999) was the head of music at the University of Zululand and "had worked in the cultural sphere as artist, teacher, publisher, organizer (of cultural activities), choir conductor and singing coach, historian, and administrator." See Khumalo, "Graduation Addresses."

44. See Khumalo's website (http://www.sibongilekhumalo.co.za/biography.html) and her Wikipedia entry (https://en.wikipedia.org/wiki/Sibongile_Khumalo). Also see Paul Maylam, "Citation for Sibongile Khumalo: Honorary Graduand, Rhodes University, 18 April 2009," http://www.ru.ac.za/media/rhodesuniversity/content/ruhome/documents/citations09/CITATION%20%20FOR%20%20SIBONGILE%20%20KHUMALO.pdf.

45. Ansell, *Soweto Blues*, 115

46. Despite having the same surname, Mzilikazi Khumalo and Sibongile Khumalo are not related. *Princess Magogo ka Dinuzulu* (2002) was the first full-length opera by a black South African composer. Trained in the tonic-sol-fa tradition, composer Khumalo was aided in the orchestration of this work. Bongani Ndonana Breen's *Winnie: The Opera* (2010) was the first full-length opera by a black South African composer that was also fully orchestrated by the composer.

47. The inability to read music was not an uncommon situation after the Bantu Education Act was passed in 1953 and took the education of blacks away from the state-aided mission schools and enforced a new inferior pedagogy that worked as an education for servitude.

48. The Pretoria Technikon merged with two other institutions to form the Tshwane University of Technology in 2004. Information about Maswanganyi's career is gleaned from her page in Wikipedia, https://en.wikipedia.org/wiki/Tsakane_Valentine _Maswanganyi. The Roodepoort City Opera is located in Johannesburg. Through different configurations (and managements) this municipal theater was where white South African Tenor Johan Botha got an early start in his career in 1989.

49. The first quotation in this sentence is from James Christopher Monger's "Artist Biography: Amici Forever" on the AllMusic.com website: http://www.allmusic.com/ artist/amici-forever-mn0000197340/biography; the second is from the "Amici Forever" Wikipedia page: https://en.wikipedia.org/wiki/Amici_Forever.

50. The AllMusic.com website provides track listings for both albums (*The Opera Band* and *Defined*) and lists the source for the number.

51. Virginia Davids was also a singer in the Eoan Company opera activities in the Cape Town area.

52. For information on Pumeza Matshikiza, see Isokariari, "Cape Town Soprano"; Picard, "Pumeza Matshikiza"; Tonkin, "Pumeza Matshikiza"; see also https://en.wikipedia .org/wiki/Pumeza_Matshikiza, and http://www.deccaclassics.com/us/artist/matshikiza/ biography.

53. For information on Pretty Yende, see Fonseca-Wollheim, "Little Time to Prepare"; Renee Montagne, "Pretty Yende: An Opera Star Whose Rise Began with a Fall," Deceptive Cadence, NPR, *Morning Edition*, March 20, 2015; Zemsky/Green Artists Management homepage for Pretty Yende, http://www.zemskygreenartists.com/artists/ pretty-yende; http://www.roh.org.uk/news/opera-and-music-201617 states that Yende made her Covent Garden debut as Adina in Donizetti's *L'elisir d'amore* on May 28, 2017. As this book goes to press, Yende's second solo album, *Dreams*, produced by Sony, was released in November 2017 and with mid-nineteenth-century Italian and French repertoire.

54. At the time of this writing, the documentary film *Ukucula: I Live to Sing* is available through the PBS website, http://www.thirteen.org/programs/i-live-to-sing.

55. Both quotations come from the Isango Ensemble website, http://site.isango ensemble.org.za.

56. *Township Opera*. Produced and Directed by Anthony Fabian, BBC and Elysian Films, 2002. 59 mins. Another beautifully photographed history of this opera company is in Driver, *Short History of Dimpho di Kopane*.

57. Allen, "South African Troupe."

58. District Six is a part of Cape Town that has great historical value. It had been a racially integrated area with Cape Malays, Xhosa, mixed race, and smaller numbers of whites, Afrikaners, and Indians. During apartheid it was reclassified as a whites-only area and forcibly relocated many in the late 1960s through the early 1980s. Since 1994, the government is still working to recognize older claims of former residents. The Fugard Theatre was named for Athol Fugard (b. 1932), an Afrikaner playwright whose work strongly opposed the apartheid system.

59. http://site.isangoensemble.org.za.

60. Dornford-May "Working."

61. Ibid.

62. "President Obama Welcomes the Broadway Cast of *Hamilton*," https://www
.youtube.com/watch?v=V3bNmhbvU2o. President Obama delivered remarks before
a performance of "*Hamilton* at the White House" on March 14, 2016.

63. Ibid.

Chapter 3. Haunted Legacies

1. These sources will be discussed in further depth later. DNA testing from 1998
revealed that the descendants of Sally Hemings are from someone in the Jefferson
family, almost without a doubt Thomas, but possibly another relative in the Jefferson
family. The other evidence of the relationship is in the memoir that Madison Hemings,
the son of Sally Hemings and Thomas Jefferson, wrote and published in 1873. There is
a body of secondary literature about this relationship and current historical debates
about it. Two leading analyses on the Jefferson and Hemmings story are by Annette
Gordon-Reed (*Thomas Jefferson and Sally Hemings* [1998] and *The Hemingses of
Monticello* [2008]) and Randall Kennedy ("Sally Hemmings and Thomas Jefferson).

2. *Envoice* and *envoicing* are terms that have been used in music studies to give agency
to hidden and less audible meanings in musical works. Frequently used to empower
a marginalized message, in recent usage the terms have been used by James Deaville
("Envoicing of Protest") and Carolyn Abbate ("Opera; or, The Envoicing of Women").

3. Personal email correspondence with Sandra Seaton, June 12, 2017.

4. In this section I will use different names for the person whose Koi-San birth name
has been lost. She has been called: Saartijie and Sara Baartman. In his eulogy for her
funeral with the repatriation of her body back to South Africa, President Thabo Mbeki
called her Sarah Bartmann, and I use this spelling in the balance of my discussion.

5. Crais and Scully, *Sara Baartman*. Page 1 of the book's introduction places Baartman's birth in the 1770s.

6. Ibid.

7. Quereshi, "Displaying Sara Baartman," 245.

8. Ibid., 246–47.

9. An excellent starting place for a discussion of the DNA testing and a bibliography of the relationship between Sally Hemings and Thomas Jefferson can be found
on the Monticello website: https://www.monticello.org/site/plantation-and-slavery/
thomas-jefferson-and-sally-hemings-brief-account. Additionally, the possible kin-
ship relationships between Hemings and the Jefferson family have been scrupulously
documented by Annette Gordon-Reed in *Thomas Jefferson and Sally Hemings*. Also
see Whooley, "Objectivity and Its Discontents," and Bay, "In Search of Sally Hemings."

10. Thabo Mvuyelwa Mbeki, "Speech at the Funeral of Sarah Bartmann, 9 August
2002," http://www.sahistory.org.za/archive/speech-funeral-sarah-bartmann-9-august
-2002.

11. Ibid.

12. Though it could seem that Sally Hemings was given a choice to stay in Paris
and become a free person, there was no guarantee or infrastructure to ensure that

she would be able to survive and take care of herself. Additionally, she had no way of enforcing a promise that Jefferson would give her a comfortable and privileged life if she returned with him to the United States. Discussion of the arrangement Jefferson promised Sally Hemings if she were to return from Paris with him can be found in Meacham, *Thomas Jefferson*, 217–19.

13. In South Africa, the Population Registration Act (1950) organized people into three main racial categories: Black, White, Coloured (those of mixed race). Indians (from India), Chinese, Malay (Indonesians), and other racial/ethnicities brought over through colonialism were put in different categories.

14. Various sources list "Epps" and "Eppes" for Elizabeth Hemmings's mother, Susannah. For consistency, I will use Epps.

15. For a discussion of the dynamics of domination (and possible love) between master and slave in physical relationships see Brown, "Black Rapture."

16. Seaton, "Program Notes" (recording notes); quotation appears on the second (unnumbered) page.

17. Ibid.; quotation appears on the fourth (unnumbered) page.

18. Seaton, "Program Notes" (*Michigan Quarterly Review*), 627. These "Program Notes" include some of the same information, but are a little different than the "Program Notes" that accompanied the recording of *From the Diary of Sally Hemings* (White Pine Music) in 2010.

19. Edward Rothstein "Life, Liberty." The two exhibits were "Slavery at Jefferson's Monticello: Paradox of Liberty," National Museum of American History in Washington, D.C. (January 26–October 14, 2012), and "Landscape of Slavery: Mulberry Row at Monticello," held at Monticello.

20. Though many in the general public only became aware of Sally Hemings in the 1990s after the DNA testing and ensuing controversy, there have been many others who believed and passed down an oral history of the Hemings family and the Jefferson-Hemings legacies from Monticello since the nineteenth century. As an historical and archeological site, Monticello has also become a leading place for understanding slavery in Jefferson's time and place. Among others, Lucia Cinder Stanton, Monticello's Shannon Senior Historian, has published about and aided in studying Jefferson's life and slavery at Monticello. "Getting Word: African American Families of Monticello" is an oral history project that also follows and archives interviews to preserve a formerly hidden history: https://www.monticello.org/getting-word. Thanks to Sandra Seaton for letting me know about the "Getting Word" oral history project.

21. There has been much discussion and debate over the scientific validity of whether or not Jefferson and Hemings had a sexual relationship and if they had children together. Additionally, the nature of the relationship, if it existed and bore children, is impossible to know given the complicated dynamics of consensual romantic love and the larger context of the master-slave economic reality during this time. Important sources include the two books by Annette Gordon-Reed (*Thomas Jefferson and Sally Hemings, Hemingses of Monticello*) and the narrative and bibliography on the "Thomas Jefferson: Monticello" website: http://www.monticello

.org/site/plantation-and-slavery/thomas-jefferson-and-sally-hemings-brief-account. Additional sources include Lanier and Feldman, *Jefferson's Children*, and Bey, "In Search of Sally Hemings."

22. The information about these people is gleaned primarily from the Monticello. org website and the presidential biography section on whitehouse.gov website. See also Gordon-Reed, *Thomas Jefferson and Sally Hemings* and *Hemingses of Monticello*.

23. Many people believe that Sally Hemings and Thomas Jefferson had six children together, two who did not survive childhood (Harriet I, 1795–1797, and a daughter born in 1799 who did not survive infancy) and the four who lived into adulthood (Beverley 1798–1873, Harriet II 1801-after 1863, Madison 1805–1877, and Eston 1808–1856). See https://www.monticello.org/site/plantation-and-slavery/thomas-jefferson -and-sally-hemings-brief-account.

24. Thomas Jefferson's will provided for the freeing of five of his slaves, all of whom had close connections to Sally Hemings: Burwell Colbert, a relative of Sally's; John Hemings, Sally's younger brother; Joe Fossett, another relative of Sally's; Madison Hemings (Sally's son); and Eston Hemings (Sally's son). See Gordon-Reed, *Thomas Jefferson and Sally Hemings*, 38–39. Beverly and Harriet (children of Sally Hemings) were allowed to leave Monticello, a euphemism for being granted their freedom (Gordon-Reed, *Thomas Jefferson and Sally Hemings*, 25, 26, 201; Meacham, *Thomas Jefferson*, 495–96. The only slaves Jefferson freed (as specified in his will, or those he allowed to unofficially leave) were all directly connected to Sally Hemings.

25. The information in this paragraph is also laid out in Chart 3.1.

26. Scholarship that puts the Hemings-Jefferson relationship into an interracial context during its time includes Morgan, "Interracial Sex," 52–84, and Rothman, "James Callender," 87–113.

27. "Program Notes," *From the Diary of Sally Hemings* liner notes, unnumbered pages.

28. Ibid.

29. Gordon-Reed, *Thomas Jefferson and Sally Hemings*, viii. This "Author's Note" was added in 1998 after the results of the 1998 DNA testing showed that Sally Hemings and Thomas Jefferson most likely bore children together.

30. "The Memoirs of Madison Hemings," reprinted as appendix C in Gordon-Reed, *Thomas Jefferson and Sally Hemings*, 245–48. These memoirs were originally published as "Life among the Lowly, No 1," *Pike County (Ohio) Republican*, March 13, 1873.

31. This paragraph is not meant to imply that such interracial/"mixed"/biracial categories are not gaining acceptance and understanding in the United States. I mean only to imply that at the time of this writing, such categories are a long way off from being as fully understood as the categories of "white" and "black." This will probably continue to change into having "in between" categories become more widely accepted. This paragraph focuses on black-white relationships; other interracial relationships (such as white-Asian, Native American-Latino, and any other combinations) have overlapping yet different histories and meanings.

32. Bolcom was at Mills College from 1958 to 1961 when he first studied with Milhaud and received his master's degree. Bolcom again worked with Milhaud when he attended the Paris Conservatoire later in the 1960s.

33. *Shuffle Along* was revived on Broadway in 2016. It opened on April 28 but closed early on July 24, when the management decided not to replace the lead, Audra McDonald, who took maternity leave. This revival was staged at the Music Box Theatre and was directed by George C. Wolfe, choreographed by Savion Glover.

34. Kimball and Bolcom, *Reminiscing.*

35. Sandra Seaton has degrees from the University of Illinois (Urbana-Champaign) and Michigan State University. She has been a professor at Central Michigan University and has had residencies at Yaddo, Hedgebrook and Radgale artists' colonies. She received the Society for the Study of Midwestern Literature's Mark Twain Award, which included having a full issue of the publication *Midwestern Miscellany* devoted to her work (Fall 2013, guest editor Arvid F. Sponberg).

36. Bolcom, "Preface," 611.

37. Ibid.

38. Bolcom, "Program Notes" (recording notes).

39. Bolcom, "Preface," 611–12.

40. This is a practice in the *Michigan Quarterly Review* text (discussed herewith) as well as in the recording text and musical score.

41. Seaton, "*From the Diary of Sally Hemings.*"

42. Bolcom, in his "Preface" (610–12), identifies this as the complete text Seaton gave him.

43. See the Monticello website, https://www.monticello.org/site/research-and -collections/hôtel-de-langeac.

44. December 23, 1789, is the date Thomas Jefferson, his daughters, and retinue (including Sally Hemings) supposedly returned to Monticello. http://www.monticello.org/ site/plantation-and-slavery/appendix-h-sally-hemings-and-her-children

45. Seaton, "*From the Diary of Sally Hemings,*" 619.

46. Gordon-Reed, *Thomas Jefferson and Sally Hemings*, 59.

47. Rothman discusses excerpts from Callender's reports in "James Callender and Social Knowledge," which are included in Appendix B, "James Callender's Reports," Lewis and Onuf, *Sally Hemings and Thomas Jefferson* (259–61).

48. For a review essay of the score *From the Diary of Sally Hemings*, see Carman, "Music Reviews." For a review of the recording see Rosenblum, "Bolcom," and Sullivan, "Bolcom."

49. Bolcom, "Program Notes," *From the Diary of Sally Hemings*, Alyson Cambridge soprano, Lydia Brown piano. White Pine Music, CD recording, 2010.

50. Bolcom, "Program Notes."

51. Bolcom, "Preface," 612.

52. This listing of the divisions and song titles is from the table of contents of the piano vocal score, *From the Diary of Sally Hemings*, Edward B. Marks Music Company and Hall Leonard Corporation, 2001.

53. The times in this paragraph refer to the recording of *From the Diary of Sally Hemings*, sung by Alyson Cambridge, with Lydia Brown on the piano. White Pines Music, recording label of Central Michigan University, 2010.

54. Wolfgang Amadeus Mozart's Lied "Das Veilchen," K. 476, was composed in Vienna and dated June 8, 1785. It is one of the only texts by Johann Wolfgang von Goethe that Mozart set. Perhaps fittingly, in its reference to Jefferson and Hemings in Paris at the beginning of their relationship, Goethe's text ("The Violet") is about a young maiden who tramples over a violet (metaphor for a lover's heart) without noticing the pain she has caused. Many thanks to William Bolcom, who pointed me toward this Mozart reference.

55. Horsley, "Song Cycle."

56. Midgette, "Alyson Cambridge Offers Ambitious but Flawed Recital." The "flawed" in the title refers to Midgette's less positive review of the two other works on the program, Jeffrey Mumford's setting of poems by Sonia Sanchez (*Three Windows*) and *Tres Mujeres* with music by Adam Schoenberg setting the poetry of his wife Janine Salinas Schoenberg.

57. McLucas, "Monodrama."

58. Neighbour, "Erwartung."

59. Seaton discusses using quotations from Jefferson's writings in the note to the piano-vocal score and indicates where they are through the use of italics (p. 68).

60. Seaton, "Program Notes." *Michigan Quarterly Review*, 625.

61. Elizabeth Taylor Greenfield (ca 1809–1876), also known as the "Black Swan," is one of a handful of black operatic singers known to us from this time. She sang for Queen Victoria and was known for her concertizing where she sang Handel, Bellini, and Donizetti, among others (she sang concerts and recitals because there were no venues that allowed black operas singers to sing onstage). By calling the opera singer in *The Will* "Patti," Seaton is also referencing the exceedingly popular Adelina Patti (1843–1919), a European opera singer whose fame extended into the United States when she made her debut in 1859 at New York at the Academy of Music in *Lucia di Lammermoor* and later sang at the White House for President Lincoln in 1862. "La Patti" (as she was known) sang a similar repertoire as Elizabeth Taylor Greenfield, and Seaton presents a rich musical reference in naming the opera-singing fiancé of Cyrus Webster's other son "Patti." The subtle references continue as Mathilda Sissieretta Joyner Jones (1868–1933) was also an early black singer who was known in her time as the "Black Patti," referencing Adelina Patti.

62. Seaton, "Program Notes," *Michigan Quarterly Review*, 624.

63. Ibid., 624–25.

64. Ball, *Slaves in the Family*, 1.

65. Bacon, "Inheriting Slavery."

66. Ibid.

67. Ibid.

68. Ibid.

69. Thompson, "For Decades."

70. This performance, sponsored by MELODEON, was performed on November 3, 2013, at Christ and St. Stephen's Episcopal Church, New York City. https://www.you tube.com/watch?v=ifOF8LTYa_4.

71. Personal email correspondence with the author, March 22, 2017.

Chapter 4. Contextualizing Race and Gender in Gershwin's Porgy and Bess

1. Herwitz, "Writing American Opera," 525.

2. Quotations from Voice of America, freelance journalist Peter Cox writing http://www.voanews.com/a/south-africans-remake-porgy-and-bess-musical/1403616.html "South Africans remake *Porgy and Bess* Musical" by Peter Cox, July 12, 2012.

3. Cox, "South Africans."

4. The critical edition of the musical score of *Porgy and Bess* is scheduled for release in 2018; at the time of this writing, access to this score is not available. It will be published by the Gershwin Initiative based at the University of Michigan, general editor Mark Clague. *Porgy and Bess* will appear in Series Four: Operas, edited by Wayne D. Shirley. Connected to the lack of a definitive performing edition, there have been different versions performed of *Porgy and Bess* (whether Porgy's "Buzzard Song" is included is variable, whether the opera opens with Jasbo Brown's Blues scene or another scene, and so forth) reflect these differences. Sometimes a version has been called "*The Gershwins' Porgy and Bess*"—a title used for adaptations by Trevor Nunn (1993 and 2006), Diana Paulus, Suzan-Lori Parks and Diedre Murray (2011) (to be discussed later), and a London production directed by Timothy Sheader (2014) based on the version by Parks and Murray. Trevor Nunn first directed the opera in 1986 for the Glyndebourne Festival. This version was expanded and adapted in 1993 for Television and aired on the BBC in Britain and PBS in the United States.

5. Brown, "Performers in Catfish Row."

6. In fact, until 2018 there has not been an "official" standard version of *Porgy and Bess*, since productions up to that point needed to decide which music to include and which to cut (due to time constraints). Before 2018 I had seen the opera several times, each one slightly different from the other (sometimes Porgy's "Buzzard Song" is included, sometimes the introduction with Jasbo Brown's blues piano is included; Maria's cursing Sportin' Life in "I Hates Yo' Struttin' Style" and several others were added or left out depending upon the directorial vision).

7. A good source for exploring these multiple versions of *Porgy and Bess* is Noonan, *Strange Career of Porgy and Bess*, esp. chap. 5.

8. Preminger's 1954 film *Carmen Jones* was well received and nominated for several Oscars (including Best Actress for Dorothy Dandridge in the title role). See Smith, "Black Faces, White Voices." A discussion of *Carmen Jones* appears in chapter 5 herewith.

9. The Boston premiere of the work was at the Colonial Theatre on September 30, 1935. The New York premiere was at the Alvin Theatre on October 10, 1935.

10. Richard Strauss (1864–1949) was still writing operas, but by 1935 his most popular operas were behind him (*Salome* [1803], *Elektra* [1809], *Der Rosenkavalier* [1911]), and his later operas tended to be more obtuse in meaning (for example, *Die Frau ohne Schatten* [1919]; *Die Ägyptische Helena* [1927]; *Daphne* [1937]). An exception may be seen in *Arabella* from 1932, first performed in Dresden in 1933. Though it was performed the next year at London's Royal Opera House, it did not come to the Metropolitan Opera until 1955.

11. The relationship between Burleigh and Dvořák is discussed in Snyder. *Harry T. Burleigh* (see esp. chap. 5).

12. Henderson, "Dr. Dvorak's Latest Work."

13. Work, "Negro Folk Song."

14. Johnson, *Black Manhattan*, 116.

15. Locke, *Negro and His Music*, 106–7.

16. Magee, *Charles Ives Reconsidered*, 161–62, endnotes on 211.

17. Sinclair, *Descriptive Catalogue*, 717.

18. Magee, *Charles Ives Reconsidered*, 161.

19. Wyatt and Johnson, *Gershwin Reader*, 217.

20. Crawford, "It Ain't Necessarily Soul," 27.

21. Crawford, "Where Did *Porgy and Bess* Come From?" 708.

22. Allen, "Triangulating Folkness," 256.

23. One discussion of the difficulty in finding a print of the *Porgy and Bess* (1959) film appears in Masters, "David Geffen." On a few occasions, I have heard that there have been special viewings of Otto Preminger's *Porgy and Bess* (1959) film since it was withdrawn in the early 1970s. I write about this film from having seen photographic stills but not the film itself. Hence, my comments about the film are based on the essays I cite by Hall Johnson, James Baldwin, and Harold Cruse. I rely also on Lorraine Hansberry's interview with Otto Preminger on Irv Kupeinet's *At Random* TV show mentioned both by Cruse (*Crisis of the Negro Intellectual*) and Era Bell Thompson in "Why Negroes Don't Like *Porgy and Bess*."

24. Johnson, "*Porgy and Bess*"; Baldwin, "On Catfish Row"; see also an interview with Preminger in *Variety*, May 27, 1959, 16. Cruse adds his own assessment and discusses those of Hansberry and Johnson (*Crisis of the Negro Intellectual*, 100–111).

25. Thompson, "Why Negroes Don't Like *Porgy and Bess*," 54.

26. At all performances of the work I have seen (in American urban centers that happen to encompass large black populations) black folks come out to the opera when *Porgy and Bess* is showing.

27. *Four Saints in Three Acts* and *Porgy and Bess* are not frequently seen to have much in common besides their use of nearly all-black casts; they were premiered a year apart (1934 and 1935). Other similarities between the two works are that Eva Jessye was the choral director for both productions and Leontyne Price was asked by Thompson to sing in *Four Saints* (in 1952) right before she was cast as Bess in *Porgy and Bess* in 1953. For a more thorough discussion of *Four Saints in Three Acts* see Barg, "Black Voices/White Sounds."

28. I was fortunate to see a performance of Freeman's opera *Voodoo* in a concert performance during June 2015 at the Kathryn Bache Miller Theatre at Columbia University during a conference that celebrated the donation of Freeman's archive to Columbia. Not as a "jazz" sound, this opera showcases the use of the saxophone for a dramatic dark timbre during the conjure scene. Along with *Voodoo*, Freeman wrote what is estimated to be twenty operas. Cooper, "*Voodoo*."

29. A version of this section appeared as "Immigration and the Great Migration: *Porgy and Bess* in the Harlem Renaissance," in the *American Music Review*, vol. 40, no. 1 (Fall 2015): 17–21.

30. A sampling of the excellent literature that mentions *Porgy and Bess* and blackness includes Crawford, "It Ain't Necessarily Soul"; Allen, "An American Folk Opera?"; and Brown, "Performers in Catfish Row."

31. The literature on how immigrants to the United States navigated racial identities between black and white include Ignatiev, *How the Irish Became White*; Guglielmo and Salerno, *Are Italians White?*; and—especially helpful for this study—Goldstein, *Price of Whiteness*.

32. See Goldstein, *Price of Whiteness*. A picture is reproduced from 1902 (with the caption "Is the Jew White?"), which is described as "a Jew with protruding lips and dark, kinky hair, physical traits that were often attributed to blacks in popular culture" (45).

33. Brodkin, *How Jews Became White Folks*, 25–26. Brodkin also cites Gerber, *Anti-Semitism in American History*, and Dinnerstein, *Uneasy at Home*.

34. Crawford and Schneider, "Gershwin, George."

35. Wilkerson, *Warmth of Other Suns*.

36. A discussion of the minstrel stereotypes in *Porgy and Bess* appears later in this chapter.

37. Pollack, *George Gershwin*, 46. Pollack, in this connection between "Oh Hev'nly Father" and the davenning minyan, cites Maurice Peress as making this observation about the similarity in the counterpoint.

38. Block, *Enchanted Evenings*, 77–78, ex. 4.2 (b). Several internet sites also mentioned a connection between Gershwin and this Torah blessing. Thanks to saxophonist Jeff Siegfried for helping me understand that this is a very well-known Jewish prayer; it is the beginning of many blessings and frequently used over food. By referencing this prayer, Gershwin was using something that would be familiar to his Jewish audience.

39. Tye, *Rising from the Rails*; Allen, *Brotherhood*.

40. The Atlantic Coast Line Railroad (1900–1967) included Charleston–NYC; under a different name (the Wilmington & Manchester Railroad connected with the North Eastern Railroad—which brought in Charleston in 1857). https://en.wikipedia.org/wiki/Atlantic_Coast_Line_Railroad.

41. "On June 16, 1934, George Gershwin boarded a train in Manhattan bound for Charleston, South Carolina. From there he traveled by car and ferry to Folly Island, where he would spend most of his summer in a small frame cottage." David Zak,

Smithsonian.com, August 8, 2010. http://www.smithsonianmag.com/arts-culture/summertime-for-george-gershwin-2170485/?no-ist. This is also mentioned in Wyatt and Johnson, *George Gershwin Reader*, 184.

42. DuBose Heyward, in Heyward and Heyward, *Porgy: A Play in Four Acts*, xi.

43. An effective revision of Porgy's character in the 2012 Broadway version by Paulus and Parks presents Porgy with aspirations; his love for Bess has transformed him and he now desires to be more of an able-bodied man, which he equates with getting a leg brace to walk with more ease. His rendition of "I Got Plenty o' Nuttin'" comes right after he and Bess first consummate their relationship and contains a clever sly subtext, where "nuttin'" is a stand-in for sexual experience.

44. André, "From Otello to Porgy."

45. Ibid., 24–25.

46. Joplin's cover of "Summertime" was recorded with Big Brother and the Holding Company on the last album they made together where Joplin was the lead singer, *Cheap Thrills* (Columbia, 1968).

47. For more information on the "Tuskegee Study of Untreated Syphilis in the Negro Male" see the Center for Disease Control website, "U.S. Public Health Service Syphilis Study at Tuskegee" https://www.cdc.gov/tuskegee/timeline.htm. Combined with the recent book (*The Immortal Life of Henrietta Lacks*, by Rebecca Skloot, 2010) and movie of the same title (directed by George C. Wolfe with Oprah Winfrey and Elise Renée Goldsberry in 2017), the issues of African Americans not being treated ethically, not being fully informed, and not given the opportunity to consent for how organs and medical tissues are used are still relevant and pressing as these stories continue to emerge from the past.

48. For an overview of the Broadway production see Als, "A Man and a Woman."

49. Though not articulated in such terms in the 1930s when the opera was written, today we can understand an interpretation of Bess as a victim of domestic violence and battered person syndrome (also known as battered women's syndrome).

50. Standifer, *Porgy and Bess*.

51. Leontyne Price was the inspiration behind Samuel Baber's *Anthony and Cleopatra* as well as his *Hermit Songs*. I discuss Price as Aida in the introduction to this book.

52. Shortly after Porgy's entrance in act 1, as we are just getting to know him, he says "When Gawd make cripple, he mean him to be lonely. Night time, day time, he got to trabble dat lonesome road."

53. Leontyne Price, born in 1927, was raised in Laurel, Mississippi.

54. Other excellent sources for thinking about Bess in *Porgy and Bess* from the performer's perspective (especially from interviews of singers who portrayed Bess) can be found in Standifer, *Porgy and Bess*, and Brown, "Performers in Catfish Row."

Chapter 5. Carmen

1. *Romani* as an adjective can also be *Romany* and *Rom*. These people call themselves *Romani* as well as *Roma*.

2. I discuss the Senegalese *Karmen Geï* and South African *U-Carmen eKhayelitsha* in a separate article: see André, "*Carmen* in Africa."

3. A few of the best sources that provide an overview of the Carmen adaptations are: Powrie, Babington, Davies, and Perriam, Carmen *on Film*; Zanger, *Film Remakes*; Davies and Powrie, Carmen *on Screen*.

4. The adaptations of Carmens vary from stage productions (such as Matthew Bourne's *The Car Man* [loose adaptation], in 2000 at Theater Royal in Plymouth, England, and later at Old Vic in London) to films for the cinema and TV. See Hickling, "Bollywood Carmen," and Davies and Powrie, Carmen *on Screen*.

5. Dibbern, "Literary Sources" (see esp. n2 and n3, p. 264, re: the opening of the novella).

6. These "Letters from Spain" were published between January 1831 and December 1833 in *La Revue de Paris*. Dibbern, "Literary Sources," 238.

7. Ibid., 264.

8. Robinson, "Mérimée's Carmen"; and McClary, "Genesis of Bizet's *Carmen*."

9. I also discuss the position of Don José (in Bizet's opera) as a proxy for the Mérimée novella French narrator in my article "*Carmen* in Africa.".

10. *Carmen*, act 1, Jose-Micaëla duet. Jose: "Et bien, tu lui diras/que son fils l'aime et la vénère/et qu'il se repent aujourd'hui;/il veut que là-bas sa mère/soit contente de lui!" (Well then, you'll tell her—/that her son loves and reveres her/and that today he is repentant;/he wants his mother back there/to be pleased with him!). Such a line implies that Don José is making up for a negative past deed. The implications of this are fleshed out with a backstory added in *U-Carmen eKhayelitsha*.

11. Dibbern, "Literary Sources," 277. Opening of part 3.

12. I speak as someone living in a specific historical moment, aware of the brutal racial history of the far and recent past as well as the continuing legacy of such violence today.

13. My point here is that such difference is noticed. I discuss further the ways this difference is noted in the introduction to this book about recent productions of Verdi's opera *Otello*.

14. A good starting point for such conversations about casting in the musical and film *Carmen Jones* are Fauser "Dixie *Carmen*" and Smith, "Black Faces, White Voices."

15. Review from the *New York Dramatic Mirror* (August 12, 1905), Dodge and Rogers, *Indian Territory Journals*.

16. *Show Boat* as a musical in 1927 was also made into film versions (1929, 1931, and the influential MGM 1951 version). For more information on the various versions see Decker, *Show Boat*. For a discussion connecting the representation of a sexual persona with Dandridge in *Carmen Jones* and casting the role of Julie in the 1951 MGM film version of Show Boat see Gilbert, "American Iconoclast," esp. 235–37.

17. Murphy, "Alumni Spotlight." Hayes went on to have a successful performing, recording, and teaching career at Cal Arts and Pomona College.

18. Smith, "Black Faces, White Voices," 32.

19. Ibid., 31.

20. Ibid., 37.

21. Obituary, Harry Kleiner (1915–2007), *Classic TV History* (blog), https://classictvhistory.wordpress.com/2008/02/11/obituary-harry-kleiner-1915-2007.

22. Smith, "Black Faces, White Voices," 33.

23. Horne, *Marilyn Horne*, 76.

24. Ibid., 75.

25. Smith, "Black Faces, White Voices," 40.

26. Horne, *Marilyn Horne*, 71.

27. Two helpful sources for thinking about Dash's film *Illusions* and gender and race are "The Politics of Being Seen," by S. V. Hartman and Farah Jasmine Griffin, and "Reading the Intersection of Race and Gender in Narratives of Passing," by Valerie Smith.

28. The setting for *Carmen Jones* the musical has always been in the American South; a 1942 version preparing for the musical was set entirely in North Carolina, and a 1943 version placed the action of the second half in Chicago. The film moves the action to southern Florida in the beginning and then Chicago for the second half. See Fauser, "Dixie Carmen" (130) for a discussion of the versions of the Hammerstein musical.

29. Furman, "Screen Politics," 127; "Apropos Dis an' Dat (Preminger, 1954)" in Powrie, Babington, Davies, and Perriam, *Carmen on Film*, 103.

30. Smith, "Black Faces, White Voices," 33–37.

31. Du Bois, "What is Civilization?," 208–9. Langston Hughes, "The Negro Artist and the Racial Mountain" (first appeared in *The Nation* on June 23, 1926). Helene Johnson Hubbell, "Poem: Little Brown Boy," appeared with a few other of her poems in a collection edited by Countée Cullen, *Caroling Dusk: An Anthology of Verse by Negro Poets* (New York: Harper, 1927). See also *The Portable Harlem Renaissance Reader*, edited by David Levering Lewis (New York: Penguin, 1994), 277–78. Based on a one-act play with incidental music she had written earlier, Shirley Graham Du Bois's opera *Tom-Tom* premiered July 7 and 9, 1932, in Cleveland, Ohio. The opera was commissioned by the Stadium Opera Company (precursor to the Cleveland Metropolitan Opera) and was not performed again. Graham and W. E. B Du Bois started their relationship in the late 1930s and did not marry until 1950. Material about the tom-tom is from an unpublished paper, "Tom Toms and the New Negro: What is *Africa* to William Grant Still?" presented to at the 35th Annual Conference of the Society for American Music, Denver, 2009, by the author.

32. Joe Adams (born 1924) was one of the first black radio announcers (getting his start on Art Grogan's Santa Monica station KOWL) in the 1940s and went on to have a top-rated daily show. Adams went on to have other roles in film and TV and later became Ray Charles's manager and a major philanthropist. See http://www.visionaryproject.org/adamsjoe/ and http://lasentinel.net/joe-adams-a-true-living-legend-from-watts-to-the-world.html; http://www.lawattstimes.com/index.php?option=com_content&view=article&id=1633:joe-adams-legendary-manager-musical-genius-ray-charles-goes-1-on-1-with-lawt-lawt-exclusive-jordan-high-school-graduate-is-shepherd-of-the-legacy-of-musical-genius-ray-charles-and-was-the-first-black-on-radio-proving-that-hard-work-pays-off&catid=27&Itemid=117.

33. Baldwin, "*Carmen Jones*," 46, 49, 52.

34. The 1954 *Carmen Jones* film was nominated for and won the following awards: Dorothy Dandridge was nominated for an Oscar for Best Actress in a Leading Role;

this was the first time a black actress had ever been nominated for this award; Herschel Burke Gilbert was nominated for an Oscar for the Best Music/Scoring of a Musical Picture; the film won a Golden Globe for the Best Motion Picture (Musical/Comedy); Joe Adams won a Gold Globe for the Most Promising Male Newcomer; Otto Preminger was nominated for the Palme d'Or Best Film at Cannes; and Otto Preminger won the Bronze Berlin Bear at the Berlin International Film Festival.

35. Baldwin, "*Carmen Jones*," 50.

36. Ibid., 50–51.

37. For discussions of the "brown paper bag test," its early origins and its practice in New Orleans up through the beginning of the twenty-first century, see Gates and West, *Future of the Race*, and Dyson, *Come Hell or High Water*. For an early use of the term "colorism" regarding the black community see Walker, "If the Present Looks Like the Past." Toni Morrison's recent novel, *God Help the Child* (New York: Knopf, 2015) is also about this topic within a mother-daughter relationship. Recent theorizations of "colorism" have extended to any nonwhite community, including people from Japan, China, Korea, India, Pakistan, Iran, areas in the Middle East, and others.

38. Rubin Wilson, better known as Reuben Wilson, is a soul jazz organist. Born in Oklahoma in 1935, when he was five years old his family moved to Pasadena, where he got into music and boxing (which landed him his role in *Carmen Jones*). http://www.last.fm/music/Reuben+Wilson/+wiki. Listed as Rubin Wilson in an uncredited role on the IMDb: http://www.imdb.com/title/tt0046828/fullcredits.

39. Baldwin, "*Carmen Jones*," 53.

40. "Volume 10." *Encyclopedia of Popular Music, Oxford Music Online*.

41. The *Wikipedia* entry for "rap opera" (https://en.wikipedia.org/wiki/Rap_opera) contains a link to the page "*A Night at the Hip Hopera*," the title of the third album by the Kleptones, released in 2004. Rather than hip hop, this album falls more under the description of "bastard pop" for fusing together samples and soundbites from the rock group Queen as well as movies, television, and other songs. Other works mentioned seem to be more in the line of concept albums that aim to include (or are awaiting funding to expand to) a video component. These albums include hip hop artist Prince Paul's *A Prince among Thieves* (1999, Tommy Boy/Warner Bros.); alternative hip hop *Deltron 3030*, the 2000 debut album by the group of the same name (produced by Dan the Automator for 75 Ark); and nerdcore hip hop Ytcracker's *Introducing Neals* (2014).

42. Since the beginning of this project and at the time of this writing, there are more artistic events calling themselves hip hopera. Two striking examples include the term that some people have used to discuss Lin Manuel Miranda's show *Hamilton* (2015) and Opera Philadelphia's educational program, Hip H'opera, in collaboration with Art Sanctuary and local schools. This program was connected to the creation of *We Shall Not Be Moved* (by composer Daniel Bernard Roumain and librettist Marc Bamuthi Joseph), an opera incorporating hip hop elements (co-commissioned and co-produced by Opera Philadelphia, the Apollo Theater, and the Hackney Empire in London) and premiered in Philadelphia September 16, 2017.

43. McClary, "*Carmen* as Perennial Fusion."

44. The flower is an important symbol in Bizet's opera. Carmen gives Don José a flower after she first sees him—a symbol of her enchanting him. In act 2 we find that he has kept the flower and sings his "Flower Song" to her when he declares his love for her. The rose is important in *Carmen Jones* as the central visual image in the opening credits with a red flame behind it. It is also the flower Carmen Jones gives Joe after she sings her Habanera ("Dat's Love"). After Da Brat uses the rose as a baton in the introduction, the last image is of her throwing the rose up into the air. At the end of the hip hopera, Da Brat ceremoniously places the rose on the road as she symbolically lays Carmen Brown to rest.

45. Another contemporaneous example of a millennial generation feminism is the movie *Legally Blonde* (MGM, directed by Robert Luketic and starring Reese Witherspoon), released two months after *Carmen: A Hip Hopera* in 2001. In the film, after being dumped by her boyfriend, sorority bombshell Reese Witherspoon decides to use her brains and her looks to get into and thrive at Harvard Law School. The movie was a big success and led to the 2003 sequel, *Legally Blonde 2: Red, White and Blonde*, the 2009 direct-to-DVD spin-off *Legally Blondes*, and the 2007 *Legally Blonde: The Musical* (that played in San Francisco, New York City on Broadway, and in London's West End. https://en.wikipedia.org/wiki/Legally_Blonde.

46. The friendship between Dorothy Dandridge and Marilyn Monroe has not received a lot of attention, perhaps because interracial relationships during the time (even a nonromanticized friendship between women) were not popular. Some internet discussion can be found at http://thegentlemensfoundation.blogspot.com/2013/08/the-friendship-of-marilyn-monroe-and.html.

47. Though Monroe's last completed film, *The Misfits* (United Artists [1961], written by Arthur Miller, directed by John Huston, starring Clark Gable and Montgomery Clift) was not a commercial success, it was seen as a possible new direction for Monroe into more serious and dramatic roles.

48. Baldwin, "*Carmen Jones*," 53.

49. We see women of color such as Jennifer Lopez (JLo), rappers Lil' Kim, Rihanna, Missy Elliott, and Queen Latifah, actress Kerry Washington, and later Bey (Beyoncé) herself, who have projected a sexualized brand, while also being strong and savvy businesswomen.

50. Steven Oxman, "Review: 'Carmen: A Hip Hopera' *Variety*, May 2, 2001. http://variety.com/2001/tv/reviews/carmen-a-hip-hopera-1200468590. Jill Kipnis, "DVD Sales Boom in Urban Market," *Billboard*, September 14, 2002, 96. Kipnis writes: "Peter Busch, VP of video for Minnetonka, Minn.-based Musicland, says the chain has experienced strong DVD sales with a variety of urban titles, including *All About the Benjamins, Carmen—A Hip Hopera*. . . . He adds that 'urban DVDs are a winning formula for the studies. They don't have to spend a lot on them, the titles gain national notoriety, and they do very well on home video.'" Though informal evidence, I have found, in teaching this hip hopera in its first fifteen years, my black students overwhelmingly enjoy this film and have heard about it before we cover it in class.

51. I have written about the relocation of Carmen in two sub-Saharan settings with Carmen in Senegal and South Africa and how the vantage points have changed for those in the audience. See "*Carmen* in Africa."

52. Davies and Dovey. "Bizet in Khayelitsha," 50.

53. Viljoen and Wenzel, "Same, yet Different."

54. Davies and Dovey, "Bizet in Khayelitsha," 42–46. I have also discussed this opening sequence in "*Carmen* in Africa."

55. The quotation in the film is longer; this is just an excerpt from the first few sentences.

56. I am referring in this situation both to the *verismo* element of Bizet's original *Carmen* (1875) as being an early part of this late nineteenth century Italian and French artistic movement (primarily in literature and music) as well as the realistic component for today of having the setting of this film be a real community: the township of Khayelitsha.

57. "Interview with Pauline Malefane" under the Extras and Interviews for the DVD *Township Opera* (directed by Anthony Fabian, Elysian Films [2002]).

58. In a flashback during the first duet between Jongikhaya (Don José) and Nomakhaya (Micaela), we see an accidental tussle between Jongikhaya and his brother turn more violent. This provides a context for the plot point later on (act 3), when we see U-Carmen talking with her friends and they say that she got together with Jongikaya too quickly and that he has been beating her.

59. For a connection to Achille Mbembe's discussion of violence in the postcolony of South Africa and the internalized PTSD issue of violence in post-apartheid South Africa see André, "*Carmen* in Africa," 64–65. Viljoen and Wenzel ("Same, yet Different," 62) also discuss violence, specifically domestic abuse in South Africa.

60. The text for Joe: "You tramp. You're no good. You never were. Two-timin' me like it don't count for nothin'. Well it does. You ain't never gonna do that to no man again."

61. I am referring to the idea of an imagined community, particularly in the nineteenth century with the spread of print media and the perspectives of national identities. See Anderson, *Imagined Communities*.

62. In this reading of Don José as the hero, his behavior can be seen as similar to Radames's actions at the end of act 3 of *Aida*, when he turns himself in for treason after he reveals the battle secrets to Aida (and Amonasro in hiding). Katherine Bergeron writes about this as an example of one of the facets of the colonial Egyptian *siyasa*. Gauthier and McFarlane also write about this moment in *Aida* as an example of a colonial domination through the model of the panopticon.

Chapter 6. Winnie, Opera, and South African Artistic Nationhood

1. Much of the material in this chapter appears in or is adapted from my article "*Winnie*, Opera, and South African Artistic Nationhood," *African Studies*, 75, no. 1 (March 2016): 10–31.

2. Excerpts from the Broadway production of *The Gershwins' Porgy and Bess* and *Winnie: The Opera* are intermittently available on YouTube, promotional, and other

websites. There is a commercial audio recording of the Broadway *Porgy and Bess* with the original cast (Audra McDonald, Norm Lewis, David Allen Grier), P. S. Classics, 2012.

3. See Erlmann "Migration and Performance"; Ansell, *Soweto Blues*; Taylor, *Global Pop*; Meintjes "Paul Simon's *Graceland*."

4. Two excellent analyses of *Winnie: The Opera* by South Africans are Mhlambi, "Embodied Discordance," and Somma, "Just Say the Words."

5. Bhabha, *Location of Culture*.

6. For important directions in newer studies of exoticism in opera see Locke, *Musical Exoticism*; Sheppard, "Revealing Masks" and "Exoticism"; Taylor, *Beyond Exoticism*; and Ingraham et. al. *Opera in a Multicultural World*.

7. Dirlik's "Global South" and López's "Introduction: The (Post)global South" are two helpful articles that give an outline of the concepts and ideas around the origin and uses of the term Global South.

8. Barber, *Anthropology of Texts*, 43.

9. Ibid., 43.

10. Nuttall, *Entanglement*, 11.

11. Ibid., 12.

12. I refer to black and mixed race, which is an imperfect way of including the racial category formally known as "coloured" under the apartheid system.

13. Operas performed in South Africa include canonic repertoire operas (frequently in updated productions, including two film productions: Bizet's *U-Carmen eKhayelitsha* [2005] and Puccini's *La Bohème* [*Breathe Umphefumlo*] [March 2015]) and new operas such as the Cape Town *Five: 20—Operas Made in South Africa* (five newly composed operas on South African themes, twenty minutes each) in November 2010; *Mandela Trilogy*, Stephenson and Williams, 2011; *Flower of Shembe*, Muyanga, 2011; *Ziyankomo and the Forbidden Fruit*, Mnomiya, 2012). An additional discussion of recent South African opera is outlined in André, Somma, and Mhlambi, "Introduction."

14. I will elaborate on these two composers' works later in this chapter. Philip Glass began his operatic career with a trilogy of Great Men (*Einstein on the Beach* [1976], based on Albert Einstein; *Satyagraha* [1979], based on Mohandas K. Gandhi; and *Akhnaten* [1983], based on the Pharaoh Akhenaten/Amenhotep IV of Egypt). John Adams's operas include *Nixon in China* (1985), based on the life of President Richard Nixon; *Death of Klinghoffer* (1991), based on the life of Achille Lauro victim Leon Klinghoffer; and *Dr. Atomic* (2005), based on the life of American physicist J. Robert Oppenheimer.

15. I have simplified this early history to express the predominant trend of opera originally being part of an aristocratic European culture. There were exceptions, such as the opera scene in Venice, which had the San Cassiano public theater (opened in 1637) that included a still rather exclusive yet broader public than what we know of opera in other theaters and cities.

16. For more information on Verdi and the Risorgimento, see Gossett, "Giuseppe Verdi and the Italian Risorgimento."

17. In this list of operas, I have named first the composer and then the librettist (for example, the operas *Amistad* and *X, The Life and Times of Malcolm X* were composed by Anthony Davis with the libretto for each written by Thulani Davis—cousin to Anthony).

18. I discuss the original 1935 version and the 2011 Broadway adaptation of Gershwin's *Porgy and Bess* in chapter 4 of this book. Audra McDonald has won her sixth Tony, another one since *The Gershwins' Porgy and Bess* (2012), for her performance as Billie Holiday in *Lady Day at Emerson's Bar and Grill* (2014). In 2015–16 she starred in the production of *Shuffle Along*, the remake of Noble Sissle and Eubie Blake's landmark all-black musical from 1921.

19. See Citron, *Opera on Screen*; Davis and Dovey, "Bizet in Khayelitsha"; Joe and Gilman *Wagner and Cinema*; Levin, *Richard Wagner*.

20. Precedents for other studies that "re-create" voices/experiences when nothing survives (Miles, *Ties that Bind*; Sharpe, *Ghosts of Slavery*; and Fabi, *Clotel*). *From the Diary of Sally Hemings* has been referred to as a "solo opera" (so-called by composer Bolcom and librettist Seaton) and as fitting into the tradition of a monodrama (see chap. 3).

21. The civil unrest 2013–14 was fueled by three highly publicized civil rights cases wherein unarmed African American men were killed and the known perpetrators were not held responsible (two of whom were white police officers). In February 2012, unarmed seventeen-year-old African American Treyvon Martin was fatally shot by George Zimmerman, a rogue member of his community neighborhood watch in Florida who was found not guilty at trial. Over the summer and fall of 2014 the police shooting of unarmed eighteen-year old African American Michael Brown in Ferguson, Missouri, led to his death; the grand jury did not indict the white police officer. In Staten Island, New York City, unarmed African American Eric Garner was accidently killed when a white police officer had him in a stranglehold for allegedly selling loose cigarettes. In December 2014 a grand jury decided not to indict the officer. Throughout the time of my writing, editing, and preparing this book for publication, very sadly, many more black men and women have been victims of police brutality. This is a situation that is not new but has recently come to light more prominently.

22. Much has been written about South African black and colored choral traditions (see Olwage, "Discipline and Choralism" and "Scriptions of the Choral;" Jorritsma, *Sonic Spaces*; and Muller, *Rituals of Fertility*) with a special emphasis on migrant workers and the isicathamiya and mbube singing styles (Erlmann, "Migration and Performance"; Coplan, *In Township Tonight!*). The Eoan Group, a coloured arts and civic organization based in Cape Town since 1933, had an active opera company in the 1950s–1970s and provides an exception to the all-white opera scene before 1994.

23. The Cape Town Opera presented the world premiere of *African Songbook: A Tribute to the Life of Nelson Mandela* at the Artscape Opera House in 2010; after the premiere the title was changed to *Mandela Trilogy*. The work was commissioned to capture three periods in Mandela's life by two nonblack South African composers, Péter Louis van Dijk and Mike Campbell. The work has been revived in Johannesburg and Durban (2010); Cardiff, Wales (2012); Munich, Germany (2014); Ravenna, Italy (June

2016); and in the United Kingdom (Wales, Ireland, and England, August–September 2016). http://mandelatrilogy.com/index.php/performance-listings.

The Cape Town Opera website describes the work as "an encounter with traditional rural music, a jazz musical, and an opera—representing the diversity of expression in contemporary South Africa." http://www.capetownopera.co.za/touring/mandela-trilogy.

24. Mozart's *Marriage of Figaro*, set in the Stellenbosch wine region outside Cape Town, performed by the University of Cape Town opera program, September 2010. Puccini's *La Bohème* translated into Xhosa as *Abanxaxhi* and adapted into the present time in South Africa by the Isango Ensemble, March 2012. This adaptation has been produced on film as *Breathe Umphefumlo* (directed by Mark Dornford-May, Fortissimo Films [2015]). With a different name (Dimpho di Kopane) the Isango Ensemble also translated Bizet's *Carmen* from the French into Xhosa, adapted it into modern-day Khayelitsha as *U-Carmen eKhayelitsha* in 2005.

25. In the United States there are a few all-black opera companies, such as the Harlem Opera Theater and Opera Ebony, who are doing excellent work with productions, vocal competitions, and support for getting more black people interested in and performing opera. A comparison between the United States and South Africa is also influenced by the different racial/ethnic populations in both countries. For the United States, the white majority is contrasted to a variety of underrepresented people who are black, Latinx, Native Americans, and from multiple Asian countries.

26. Portobello Opera became Dimpho di Kopane, which is now the Isango Ensemble opera company.

27. For information about *The Passion of Winnie*, see Meersman, "Singing Winnie in Toronto."

28. Mfundi Vundla (b. 1946) is the creator of the first English soap opera in South Africa after apartheid, *Generations*. He got involved with the Winnie opera project after hearing about *The Passion of Winnie* (when Winnie Madikizela-Mandela was denied a visa by the Canadian government to attend the premiere) and helped turn the work into *Winnie: The Opera* through his experience with film, television, and media. He helped revise the libretto and procure funding for the State Theatre premiere.

29. The distinctions between musical theater genres—such as opera, operetta, and musical—are complicated and deserve rich discussion. My point here is to use the composer's designation for the work as an opera and, in my subjective opinion as an opera scholar, support this categorization for the emotional and musical weight and pathos in *Winnie: The Opera*.

30. As a side note, projected animated scenes in the background is beginning to feel like a South African characteristic, given the work of William Kentridge with his several opera productions; this was quite an integral feature of his acclaimed 2010 production of Shostakovich's satirical opera *The Nose*, Kentridge's first production to premiere at the Metropolitan Opera in New York. He followed this with a 2015 production of Alban Berg's *Lulu* at the Met that also used animated scenes projected in the background.

31. Tutu, "Special Investigation," 555, paragraph 2.

32. Ibid., 569–70, paragraphs 59–60.

33. Ibid., 570, text after paragraph 60.

34. Holiday, "Forgiving and Forgetting," 54.

35. Ibid.

36. Tutu, "Special Investigation," 578, paragraph 99.

37. In the program for the premiere, there were longer descriptions for each scene in the "Opera Synopsis."

38. The Mothers of the Missing bring to mind several international women's organizations that have worked nonviolently for human rights and justice. The Mothers of the Plaza de Mayo in Argentina have a close resonance with the mothers whose children disappeared during the "Dirty War" in the military dictatorship from 1976 to 1983. Other related groups include the vast international network of the Women in Black and—possibly—the Black Sash organization in South Africa that began in 1955 and still continues today.

39. Program booklet, "Opera Synopsis."

40. Thanks to my colleague Donato Somma for bringing my attention to the *Amagqirha* of the Xhosa tradition and their visual connection to the Mothers of the Missing.

41. Program booklet, "Music notes from the Composer."

42. Thanks to my colleague Donato Somma for bringing to my attention this fact about the TRC hearings and how they were reported on in the news.

Conclusion

1. hooks, *Feminism Is for Everybody*, 1.

2. The discourse around performance practice in musicology is an example of the ways musicology as a discipline reconstructed (through treatises, contemporaneous accounts, and other historical documents) ways to perform music from Gregorian chant through the Renaissance and beyond that incorporated traditions not written down. The discipline has also been self-reflective in how much we can ever fully know about the complete authenticity and historical accuracy of such performances; it is impossible to recreate such performances exactly, partially because we are different people living in a different world with the experience of hearing music that has come after the period we are recreating.

3. André, *Voicing Gender*.

4. Barthes, "Death of the Author."

5. A select list of writings on this rich topic include Cone, *Composer's Voice*; Abbate, *Unsung Voices* and "Music—Drastic or Gnostic?"; Cavarero, *For More than One Voice*; Levin, *Unsettling Opera*; Eidsheim, *Sensing Sound* and "Sensing Voice."

6. Collins, *Black Feminist Thought*, 21–32.

7. Freire, *Education for Critical Consciousness*, 21.

8. A helpful overview of the arguments around the construction of race and its failed scientific basis can be found in Roberts, *Fatal Invention*.

9. Freire, *Pedagogy of the Oppressed*, 53.

10. With one exception (*Carmen Jones*, written for Broadway in 1943 and made into a film in 1954), the operas this study come from productions since 2000. Several of the operas were composed after 2000: *Carmen: A Hip Hopera* (2001), *From the Diary of Sally Hemings* (2000), *Winnie: The Opera* (2010); some of them from before: Bizet's *Carmen* (1875) and *Porgy and Bess* (1935). I focus, however, on more recent adaptations of the older works (*U-Carmen eKhayelitsha* [2005] and the Lori Parks production of *Porgy and Bess* [2011]).

11. For an overview to this topic, see André, Bryan, and Saylor, *Blackness in Opera*.

12. In the "President's Message: Covering the AMS" in the previous year's *AMS Newsletter* (vol. 42, no.1 [February 2012]: 2), Anne Walters Robinson also mentions public musicology as something to focus on: "How can we do 'public musicology' better?"

13. Christopher Reynolds, "President's Message: Three New AMS Initiatives (Public and Private)," *AMS Newsletter* 43, no. 2 (August 2013): 2.

14. Ibid.

15. Ibid. This description of the AMS blog was given by its inaugural curator, D. Kern Holoman, someone chosen by the board.

16. This assessment is based on an investigation of the *Musicology Now* blog and two conferences billed as being Public Musicology. The first conference, "The Past, Present and Future of Public Musicology," Westminster Choir College of Rider University, January 30–February 1, 2015, http://musicinnewjersey.com/conference. The second conference, "'It's Still Rock and Roll to Me': The Music and Lyrics of Billy Joel, a Public Musicology Conference Hosted by Colorado College, October 7–8, 2016" (on *Musicology Now*, this conference is also mentioned as being co-sponsored by the AMS: http://musicologynow.ams-net.org/2016/03/a-billy-joel-conference-this-fall.html). An article that moves in other directions and begins to expand the focus is Bonnie Gordon's "The Perils of Public Musicology," *Musicology Now*, February 22, 2016, which brings up challenges around race in terms of the University of Virginia's Arts Mentors program (which she founded and coordinates) and musicology debates.

17. Cheng, *Just Vibrations*.

18. I am getting the sense that in the 2010s a new movement of small opera companies with predominantly younger singers performing edgy productions of canonic repertory opera has begun. Alex Ross has written about it recently in *The New Yorker*, "Operatic Startups: Small Companies in New York Take on the Met," April 4, 2016, and I have heard of other companies doing similar things. What seems to be a new, and I feel very welcomed, direction with Opera MODO is their care and sensitivity around representation and social justice as they meaningfully incorporated current issues around violence to the LGBTQ, and especially trans, communities.

19. https://www.patronicity.com/project/transgender_carmen_as_operatic_orange _is_the_new_black#.

20. Negus et al., "Falsetto."

21. A provocative situation exists in the context of black male singers who have risen to prominence as countertenors in opera careers. There are several black coun-

tertenors who are professionally employed in top opera companies (Derek Lee Ragin, Darryl Taylor, John Holiday, G. Thomas Allen) and others I have heard coming up in smaller venues.

22. For more information about premodern and modern discussions around "sex" and "gender" see Laqueur, *Making Sex*. For more information about theorizing gender in the castrato and opera see André, *Voicing Gender*, and Feldman, *The Castrato*.

23. Opera MODO performed *Carmen* in Detroit on February 19 and 20, 2016, at the Carr Center (311 East Grand River Avenue) and on February 26 and 28, 2016, at the Jam Handy (2900 East Grand Boulevard).

24. The mission of the Ruth Ellis Center is "to provide short-term and long-term residential safe space and support services for runaway, homeless, and at-risk lesbian, gay, bi-attractional, transgender, and questioning (LGBTQ) youth." http://www.ruthelliscenter.org/about-ruth-eliss-center.

25. Danielle Wright, program notes to the Opera MODO production of Bizet's *Carmen*, February 19, 20, 26, and 28, 2016, in Detroit, Michigan.

26. I wrote about this experience in "Teaching Opera in Prison."

27. The quotations are from Danielle's welcome in the program notes to the performance of Bizet's *Carmen*, February 19, 20, 26, and 28, 2016, at the Carr Center and the Jam Handy. Detroit Soup has become associated with the Jam Handy since 2010 given their use of the space for their dinners. For more information, see http://detroitsoup.com/faq.

28. "Demographics," Arab American Institute Foundation (2014). Michigan is ranked second in the United States (after California) for having the largest population of Arabs. https://d3n8a8pro7vhmx.cloudfront.net/aai/pages/9843/attachments/original/1460668240/National_Demographic_Profile_2014.pdf?1460668240.

29. My comments also included a select bibliography: Dirlik, "Global South"; Locke, *Musical Exoticism*; Pirker, "Janissary Music"; Rushton, "Entführung aus dem Serail, Die"; Said, *Orientalism*.

Bibliography

Abbate, Carolyn. "Music—Drastic or Gnostic?" *Critical Inquiry* 30, no. 3 (2004): 505–36.
———. "Opera; or, The Envoicing of Women." In *Musicology and Difference*, edited by Ruth Solie, 225–58. Berkeley: University of California Press, 1993.
———. *Unsung Voices: Opera and Musical Narrative in the Nineteenth Century*. Princeton, N.J.: Princeton University Press, 1993.
Agawu, V. Kofi. *Representing African Music: Postcolonial Notes, Queries, Positions*. New York: Routledge, 2003.
Alexander, Michelle. *The New Jim Crow: Mass Incarceration in the Age of Colorblindness*. New York: New Press, 2010.
Allen, Morgan. "South African Troupe Dimpho di Kopane Reinvents *Carmen, The Beggar's Opera* and Hans Christian Andersen in NYC." *Playbill*, October 7, 2004. http://www.playbill.com/article/south-african-troupe-dimpho-di-kopane-reinvents-carmen-the-beggars-opera-and-hans-christian-andersen-in-nyc-com-122338.
Allen, Ray. "An American Folk Opera? Triangulating Folkness, Blackness, and Americaness in Gershwin and Heyward's *Porgy and Bess*." *Journal of American Folklore* 117, no. 465 (Summer 2004): 243–61.
Allen, Robert L. *The Brotherhood of Sleeping Car Porters: C. L. Dellums and the Fight for Fair Treatment and Civil Rights*. Boulder, Colo.: Paradigm, 2014.
Ally, Nurina, and Shireen Ally. "Critical Intellectualism: The Role of Black Consciousness in Reconfiguring the Race-Class Problematic in South Africa." In *Biko Lives! Contesting the Legacies of Steve Biko*, edited by Andile Mngxitama, Amanda Alexander, and Nigel C. Gibson, 171–88. New York: Palgrave Macmillan, 2008.
Alpert, Hollis. *The Life and Times of* Porgy and Bess: *The Story of an American Classic*. New York: Knopf, 1990.
Als, Hilton. "A Man and a Woman: *Porgy and Bess* Reimagined." *New Yorker*, September 26, 2011.

Anderson, Benedict. *Imagined Communities: Reflections on the Origin and Spread of Nationalism*. London: Verso, 1983.

Anderson, Paul Allen. *Deep River: Music and Memory in Harlem Renaissance Thought*. Durham, N.C.: Duke University Press, 2001.

André, Naomi. "*Carmen* in Africa: French Legacies and Global Citizenship." *Opera Quarterly* 32, no. 1 (Winter 2016): 54–76.

———. "From Otello to Porgy: Blackness, Masculinity, and Morality in Opera." In André, Bryan, and Saylor, *Blackness in Opera*, 11–31.

———. "Teaching Opera in Prison." In *The Intersectional Approach: Transforming the Academy through Race, Class, and Gender*, edited by Michele Tracy Berger and Kathleen Guidroz, 258–66. Chapel Hill: University of North Carolina Press, 2009.

———. *Voicing Gender: Castrati, Travesti, and the Second Women in Early-Nineteenth-Century Italian Opera*. Bloomington: Indiana University Press, 2006.

———. "*Winnie*, Opera, and South African Artistic Nationhood." *African Studies* 75, no. 1 (March 2016): 10–31.

André, Naomi, Karen M. Bryan, and Eric Saylor. *Blackness in Opera*. Urbana: University of Illinois Press, 2012.

André, Naomi, Donato Somma, and Innocentia Jabulisile Mhlambi. "Introduction, *Winnie: The Opera* and Embodying South African Opera." *African Studies* 75, no. 1 (March 2016): 1–9.

Ansell, Gwen. *Soweto Blues: Jazz, Popular Music and Politics in South Africa*. New York: Continuum, 2004.

Bacon, Katie. "Inheriting Slavery." Interview with Edward Ball. *The Atlantic Online*, February 26, 1998. https://www.theatlantic.com/past/docs/unbound/bookauth/eballint.htm.

Baldwin, James. "*Carmen Jones*: The Dark Is Light Enough." First published as "Life Straight in De Eye" in *Commentary*, January 1955. Reprinted in *James Baldwin: Collected Essays*, edited by Toni Morrison, 35–41. New York: Penguin / Random House, 1998.

———. "On Catfish Row: *Porgy and Bess* in the Movies." First published in *Commentary*, September 1959. Reprinted in *James Baldwin: Collected Essays*, edited by Toni Morrison, 616–21. New York: Penguin Random House, 1998.

Ball, Edward. *Slaves in the Family*. New York: Farrar, Straus, and Giroux, 1998.

Banfield, William C. "Hailstork, Adolphus Cunningham." In *International Dictionary of Black Composers*, vol. 1, edited by Samuel A. Floyd Jr., 518–23. Chicago: Fitzroy Dearborn, 1999.

Barber, Karin. *The Anthropology of Texts, Persons and Public: Oral and Written Culture in Africa and Beyond*. Cambridge: Cambridge University Press, 2007.

———. "Preliminary Notes on Audiences in Africa." *Africa: Journal of the International African Institute* 67, no. 3 (1997): 347–62.

Barg, Lisa. "Black Voices/White Sounds: Race and Representation in Virgil Thomson's *Four Saints in Three Acts*." *American Music* 18, no. 2 (Summer 2000): 121–61.

Barnard, Rita, ed. *The Cambridge Companion to Nelson Mandela*. Cambridge: Cambridge University Press, 2014.

Barthes, Roland. "The Death of the Author." 1968. In *Image, Music, Text*, translated and edited by Stephen Heath, 142–48. New York: Hill and Wang, 1977.

Batiste, Stephanie Leigh. *Darkening Mirrors: Imperial Representation in Depression-Era African American Performance*. Durham, N.C.: Duke University Press, 2011.

Bay, Mia. "In Search of Sally Hemings in the Post-DNA Era." *Reviews in American History* 34, no. 4 (December 2006): 407–26.

Bennett, Susan. *Theatre Audiences: A Theory of Production and Reception*. New York: Routledge, 1990.

Bergeron, Katherine. "Verdi's Egyptian Spectacle: On the Colonial Subject of *Aida*." *Cambridge Opera Journal* 14, no. 1/2 (March 2002): 149–59.

Bhabha, Homi K. *The Location of Culture*. New York: Routledge, 1994.

Block, Geoffrey. *Enchanted Evenings: The Broadway Musical from Show Boat to Sondheim and Lloyd Webber*. 2nd ed. New York: Oxford University Press, 2009.

Bolcom, William. *From the Diary of Sally Hemings*. Piano-vocal score. E. B. Marks / Hal Leonard, 2001.

———. "A Preface to *From the Diary of Sally Hemings*." *Michigan Quarterly Review* 40, no. 4 (Fall 2001): 611–12.

Born, Georgina, and David Hesmondhalgh. *Western Music and Its Others: Difference, Representation, and Appropriation in Music*. Berkeley: University of California Press, 2001.

Brodkin, Karen. *How Jews Became White Folks and What That Says about Race in America*. New Brunswick, N.J.: Rutgers University Press, 1998.

Brown, Gwynne Kuhner. "Performers in Catfish Row: *Porgy and Bess* as Collaboration." In André, Bryan, and Saylor, *Blackness in Opera*, 164–86.

Brown, Kimberly Juanita. "Black Rapture: Sally Hemings, Chica da Silva, and the Slave Body of Sexual Supremacy." *Women's Studies Quarterly* 25, nos. 1–2 (2007): 45–66.

Bryan, Karen M. "Radiating a Hope: Mary Cardwell Dawson as Educator and Activist." *Journal of Historical Research in Music Education* 25, no. 1 (October 2003): 20–35.

Caplan, Lucy. "A Small Step toward Correcting the Overwhelming Whiteness of Opera," *New Yorker*, May 18, 2017. http://www.newyorker.com/culture/culture-desk/a-small-step-toward-correcting-the-overwhelming-whiteness-of-opera.

Capote, Truman. *The Muses Are Heard*. New York: Random House, 1956.

Carby, Hazel V. *Race Men*. Cambridge, Mass.: Harvard University Press, 1998.

Carman, Judith. "Music Reviews: *From the Diary of Sally Heming*; Eighteen Songs for Medium Voice and Piano by William Bolcom and Sandra Seaton." *Journal of Singing—The Official Journal of the National Association of Teachers of Singing* 68, no. 5 (May 2012): 599–602.

Carter, Tim, and Dorothea Link. "Da Ponte, Lorenzo." *Oxford Music Online*. New York: Oxford University Press.

Cavarero, Adriana. *For More than One Voice: Toward a Philosophy of Vocal Expression*. Stanford, Calif.: Stanford University Press, 2005.

Cheatham, Wallace McClain. *Dialogues on Opera and the African-American Experience*. Lanham, Md.: Scarecrow, 1997.

Cheng, William. *Just Vibrations: The Purpose of Sounding Good*. Ann Arbor: University of Michigan Press, 2016.

Chybowski, Julia J. "Becoming the 'Black Swan' in Mid-Nineteenth-Century America: Elizabeth Taylor Greenfield's Early Life and Debut Concert Tour," *Journal of the American Musicological Society* 67, no.1 (Spring 2014): 125–65.

———. "The 'Black Swan' in England: Abolition and the Reception of Elizabeth Taylor Greenfield." *American Music Research Journal* 14 (2004): 7–25.

Citron, Marcia. *Opera on Screen*. New Haven, Conn.: Yale University Press, 2000.

Clark, Nancy L., and William H. Worger. *South Africa: The Rise and Fall of Apartheid*. 2nd edition. London: Longman Pearson, 2011.

Clark, Robert L. A. "Local Color: The Representation of Race in *Carmen* and *Carmen Jones*." In *Operatic Migrations: Transforming Works and Crossing Boundaries*, edited by Roberta Montemorra Marvin and Downing A. Thomas, 217–40. Aldershot, Eng.; Burlington, Vt.: Ashgate, 2006.

Coates, Ta-Nehisi. *We Were Eight Years in Power: An American Tragedy*. New York: One World Publishing. 2017.

Cockrell, Dale. *Demons of Disorder: Early Blackface Minstrels and Their World*. Cambridge: Cambridge University Press, 1997.

———. "Of Gospel Hymns, Minstrel Shows, and Jubilee Singers: Toward Some Black South African Musics." *American Music* 5, no. 4 (Winter 1987): 417–32.

Collins, Patricia Hill. *Black Feminist Thought: Knowledge, Consciousness, and the Politics of Empowerment*. New York: Routledge, 1990.

Cone, Edward T. *The Composer's Voice*. Berkeley: University of California Press, 1974.

Conway, Daniel. *Masculinities, Militarisation and the End Conscription Campaign: War Resistance in Apartheid South Africa*. Manchester, Eng.: Manchester University Press, 2012.

Cook, James W. *The Arts of Deception: Playing with Fraud in the Age of Barnum*. Cambridge, Mass.: Harvard University Press (2001).

Cooper, Michael. "At a Moment of Racial Tumult, the Little Rock Nine Inspire an Opera." *New York Times*, October 1, 2017.

———. "*Voodoo*, Opera by the African-American Composer H. Lawrence Freeman, Is Revived." *New York Times*, June 21, 2015.

Coplan, David B. *In the Township Tonight! South Africa's Black City Music and Theatre*. 2nd edition. Chicago: University of Chicago Press (2008).

Cox, Peter. "South Africans Remake *Porgy and Bess* Musical." Voice of America, July 12, 2012. http://www.voanews.com/a/south-africans-remake-porgy-and-bess-musical/1403616.html.

Crais, Clifton, and Pamela Scully. *Sara Baartman and the Hottentot Venus*. Princeton, N.J.: Princeton University Press, 2008.

Crawford, Richard. "It Ain't Necessarily Soul: Gershwin's 'Porgy and Bess' as a Symbol." *Anuario Interamericano De Investigacion Musical* 8 (1972): 17–38.

———. "Where Did *Porgy and Bess* Come From?" *Journal of Interdisciplinary History* 36, no. 4 (Spring 2006—Opera and Society: Part 2): 697–734.

Crawford, Richard, and Wayne J. Schneider. "Gershwin, George." *Oxford Music On-line*. New York: Oxford University Press.

Cruse, Harold. *The Crisis of the Negro Intellectual: A Historical Analysis of the Failure of Black Leadership*. 1967. New York: New York Review of Books, 2005.

Davies, Ann, and Phil Powrie. Carmen *on Screen: An Annotated Filmography and Bibliography*. Woodbridge, U.K.: Tamesis, 2006.

Davies, James, and Lindiwe Dovey. "Bizet in Khayelitsha: *U-Carmen eKhayelitsha* as Audio-Visual Transculturation." *Journal of African Media Studies* 2, no. 1 (2010): 39–53.

Deaville, James. "The Envoicing of Protest: Occupying Television News through Sound and Music." *Journal of Sonic Studies* 3, no. 1 (October 2012). http://journal.sonicstudies.org/vol03/nr01/a05.

Decker, Todd. *Show Boat: Performing Race in an American Musical*. Oxford: Oxford University Press, 2015.

DeFrantz, Thomas F., and Anita Gonzales, eds. *Black Performance Theory*. Durham, N.C.: Duke University Press, 2014.

De Lerma, Dominique-René. *Bibliography of Black Music*. Westport, Conn.: Greenwood, 1981.

———. "A Musical and Sociological Review of Scott Joplin's *Treemonisha*." *Black Music Research Journal* 10, no. 1 (Spring 1990): 153–59.

———. "Opera." In *Encyclopedia of African-American Culture and History*, vol. 4., edited by Colin A. Palmer, 1682–86. 2nd edition. Detroit: Macmillan Reference, 2006.

della Seta, Fabrizio, and Arthur Groos, "'O cieli azzurri': Exoticism and Dramatic Discourse in *Aida*." *Cambridge Opera Journal* 3, no. 1 (March 1991): 49–62.

Dibbern, Mary. "Literary Sources." In *Carmen: A Performance Guide*, 237–310. Hillsdale, N.Y.: Pendragon, 2000.

Dinnerstein, Leonard. *Uneasy at Home: Anti-Semitism and the American Jewish Experience*. New York: Columbia University Press, 1987.

Dirlik, Arif. "Global South: Predicament and Promise." *Global South* 1, nos. 1–2 (2007): 12–23.

Dizikes, John. *Opera in America: A Cultural History*. New Haven, Conn.: Yale University Press 1993.

Dodge, Richard Irving, and Will Rogers. *The Indian Territory Journals of Colonel Richard Irving Dodge*. University of Oklahoma Press, 2000.

Dornford-May, Mark. "Working on the White Face of Theatre." *Cape Times*, November 18, 2010. http://www.artlink.co.za/news_article.htm?contentID=25972.

Dovey, Lindiwe. *African Film and Literature: Adapting Violence to the Screen*. New York: Columbia University Press, 2009.

Driver, Camilla, ed. *A Short History of Dimpho di Kopane: A South African Lyric Theatre Company*. Singapore: Spier and Nando / Tien Wah, 2004.

Du Bois, W. E. B. *The Souls of Black Folk*. 1903. New York: Barnes and Noble, 2003.

———. "What is Civilization? Africa's Answer." 1925. In *A W. E. B. Du Bois Reader*, edited by Andrew G. Paschal, 208–9. New York: Collier's, 1971.

du Preez Bezdrob, Anné Mariè. *Winnie Mandela: A Life*. Cape Town, South Africa: Zebra / Struik, 2003.

Dyson, Michael Eric. *Come Hell or High Water: Hurricane Katrina and the Color of Disaster*. New York: Basic Civitas, 2007.

Effinger-Crichlow, Marta J. "Jones, Madame Sissieretta Joyner." In *African American Lives*, edited by Henry Louis Gates Jr. and Evelyn Brooks Higginbotham, 476–77. New York: Oxford University Press, 2004.

Eidsheim, Nina Sun. *Sensing Sound: Singing and Listening as Vibrational Practice*. Durham, N.C.: Duke University Press, 2015.

———. "Sensing Voice: Materiality and the Lived Body in Singing and Listening Philosophy." In *Voice Studies: Critical Approaches to Process, Performance and Experience*, edited by Konstantinos Thomaidis and Ben Macpherson, 104–19. New York: Routledge, 2015.

Elliott, Robin. "Blacks and Blackface at the Opera." In *Opera in a Multicultural World: Coloniality, Culture, Performance*, edited by Mary Ingraham, Joseph K. So, and Roy Moodley, 34–49. New York: Routledge, 2016.

Erlmann, Veit. "'A Feeling of Prejudice': Orpheus M. McAdoo and the Virginia Jubilee Singers in South Africa 1890–1898." *Journal of Southern African Studies* 14, no. 3 (1988): 331–50.

———. "Migration and Performance: Zulu Migrant Workers' Isicathamiya Performance in South Africa, 1890–1950." *Ethnomusicology* 34, no. 2 (1990): 199–220.

Fabi, M. Giulia, ed. *Clotel; or, The President's Daughter: A Narrative of Slave Life in the United States*. By William Wells Brown. New York: Penguin, 2004.

Fabian, Johannes. *Time and the Other*. New York: Columbia University Press, 1983.

Fauser, Annegret. "'Dixie *Carmen*': War, Race, and Identity in Oscar Hammerstein's *Carmen Jones* (1943)." *Journal of the Society for American Music* 4, no. 2 (May 2010): 127–74.

Fauser, Annegret, and Mark Everist, eds. *Music, Theater, and Cultural Transfer: Paris, 1830–1914*. Chicago: University of Chicago Press, 2009.

Feldman, Martha. *The Castrato: Reflections on Natures and Kinds*. Oakland: University of California Press, 2015.

Floyd, Samuel A., Jr., ed. *Black Music in the Harlem Renaissance: A Collection of Essays*. Knoxville: University of Tennessee Press, 1993.

———. *The Power of Black Music: Interpreting Its History from Africa to the United States*. New York: Oxford University Press, 1995.

Fonseca-Wollheim, Corinna da. "Little Time to Prepare: Now a Legacy to Keep." *New York Times*, February 1, 2013. http://www.nytimes.com/2013/02/02/arts/music/little -time-to-prepare-now-a-legacy-to-keep.html?_r=0.

Frankenberg, Ruth, ed. *Displacing Whiteness: Essays in Social and Cultural Criticism*. Durham, N.C.: Duke University Press, 1997.

Freire, Paulo. *Education for Critical Consciousness*. 1974. New York: Bloomsbury, 2013.

———. *Pedagogy of the Oppressed*. 30th anniversary ed. Translated by Myra Bergman Ramos. New York: Continuum, 2000; repr. New York: Bloomsbury, 2013.

Furman, Nelly. "Screen Politics: Otto Preminger's *Carmen Jones*." In *Carmen: From Silent Film to MTV*, edited by Chris Perriam and Ann Davies, 121–33. New York: Rodopi, 2005.

Gates, Henry Louis, Jr., and Gene Andrew Jarrett, eds. *The New Negro: Readings on Race, Representation, and African American Culture, 1892–1938*. Princeton, N.J.: Princeton University Press, 2007.

Gates, Henry Louis, Jr., and Cornel West. *The Future of the Race*. New York: Vintage, 1996.

Gaunt, Kyra D. *The Games Black Girls Play: Learning the Ropes from Double-Dutch to Hip-Hop*. New York: New York University Press, 2006.

Gauthier, Christopher R., and Jennifer McFarlane-Harris. "Nationalism, Racial Difference, and 'Egyptian' Meaning in Verdi's *Aida*." In André, Bryan, and Saylor, *Blackness in Opera*, 55–77.

Gerber, David, ed. *Anti-Semitism in American History*. Urbana: University of Illinois Press, 1986.

Gilbert, Tiffany. "American Iconoclast: 'Carmen Jones' and the Revolutionary Divadom of Dorothy Dandridge." *Women's Studies Quarterly* 33, no. 3–4 (Fall-Winter 2005): 234–49.

Gobbato, Angelo. Essay on the history of the opera scene in South Africa on the Cape Town Opera. Accessed June 2016 but no longer available at http://www.capetownopera.co.za/index.php/company/history Fall of 2015–June 2016.

Goldstein, Eric L. *The Price of Whiteness: Jews, Race, and American Identity*. Princeton, N.J.: Princeton University Press, (2006).

Gordon-Chipembere, Natasha. "Introduction: Claiming Sarah Baartman; A Legacy to Grasp." In Gordon-Chipembere, *Representation and Black Womanhood*, 1–14.

———, ed. *Representation and Black Womanhood: The Legacy of Sarah Baartman*. New York: Palgrave Macmillan, 2011.

Gordon-Reed, Annette. *The Hemingses of Monticello: An American Family*. New York: Norton, 2008.

———. *Thomas Jefferson and Sally Hemings: An American Controversy*. Charlottesville: University of Virginia Press, 1998.

Gossett, Philip. "Giuseppe Verdi and the Italian Risorgimento." The Jayne Lecture. *Proceedings of the American Philosophical Society* 156, no. 3 (2012): 271–82.

Graham, Sandra Jean. "Jubilee Singers." *Grove Music Online*. 11 Dec. 2017. http://www.oxfordmusiconline.com.proxy.lib.umich.edu/grovemusic/view/10.1093/gmo/9781561592630.001/omo-9781561592630-e-1002249936.

———. *Spirituals and the Birth of a Black Entertainment Industry*. Urbana: University of Illinois Press, 2018.

Graziano, John. "The Early Life and Career of the Black Patti: The Odyssey of an African American Singer in the Late Nineteenth Century." *Journal of the American Musicological Society* 53, no. 3 (2000): 543–96.

Guglielmo, Jennifer, and Salvatore Salerno, eds. *Are Italians White? How Race Is Made in America*. New York: Routledge, 2003.

Guilford, Gwynn. "It's Time to Stop Using 'Exoticism' as an Excuse for Opera's Racism." *Quartz*, July 23, 2014. http://qz.com/237569/its-time-to-stop-using-exoticism -as-an-excuse-for-operas-racism.

Guy-Sheftall, Beverly, ed. *Words of Fire: An Anthology of African-American Feminist Thought*. New York: New Press, 1995.

Hall, Stuart. "Encoding/Decoding." In *Culture, Media, Language: Working Papers in Cultural Studies, 1972–79*, edited by Stuart Hall, Dorothy Hobson, Andrew Lowe, and Paul Willis, 128–38. London: Hutchinson, 1980.

Hall, Stuart, Jessica Evans, and Sean Nixon, eds., *Representation*. 2nd ed. London: Sage, 2013.

Hartman, S. V., and Farah Jasmine Griffin. "Are You as Colored as That Negro? The Politics of Being Seen in Julie Dash's *Illusions*." *Black American Literature Forum* 25, no. 2 (Summer 1991): 361–73.

Heinze, Andrew R. *Is It 'Cos I's Black?" Jews and the Whiteness Problem*. David W. Belin Lecture in American Jewish Affairs. Ann Arbor: Frankel Center for Judaic Studies, University of Michigan, 2007.

Henderson, J. W. "Dr. Dvorak's Latest Work." *New York Times*, December 17, 1893.

Herwitz, Daniel. "The Coat of Many Colors: Truth and Reconciliation." In *Race and Reconciliation: Essays from South Africa*, 1–46. Minneapolis: University of Minnesota Press, 2003.

———. "Writing American Opera: William Bolcom on Music, Language, and Theater." *Opera Quarterly* 22, no. 3–4 (Summer–Autumn 2006): 521–33.

Heyward, Dorothy, and DuBose Heyward. *Porgy: A Play in Four Acts*. From the novel by DuBose Heyward; Theatre Guild acting version. New York: Doubleday, Doran, 1928.

Heyward, DuBose. *Porgy*. New York: Grosset and Dunlap, 1925.

Hickling, Alfred. "Bollywood Carmen: Bizet Goes Bhangra." *The Guardian*, June 5, 2013. https://www.theguardian.com/stage/2013/jun/05/bollywood-carmen-bizet -goes-bhangra.

Hisama, Ellie M., and Evan Rapport, eds. *Critical Minded: New Approaches to Hip Hop*. New York: Institute for Studies in American Music, 2005.

Hobbs, Allyson. *A Chosen Exile: A History of Racial Passing in American Life*. Cambridge, Mass.: Harvard University Press (2014).

Holiday, Anthony. "Forgiving and Forgetting: The Truth and Reconciliation Commission." In *Negotiating the Past: The Making of Memory in South Africa*, edited by Sarah Nuttall and Carli Coetzee, 43–56. Cape Town, South Africa: Oxford University Press, 1998.

Holloway, James. *Africanisms in American Culture*. 2nd ed. Bloomington: Indiana University Press, 2005.

hooks, bell. *Feminism Is for Everybody: Passionate Politics*. Cambridge, Mass.: South End, 2000.

———. *Feminist Theory: From Margin to Center*. 2nd ed. Cambridge, Mass.: South End, 2000.

Horne, Marilyn. "*Carmen Jones*." In *Marilyn Horne: My Life*, 68–76, 195–202. New York: Atheneum, 1983.

Horsley, Paul. "Song Cycle Exploits Presidential Tryst." *Kansas City (Missouri) Star*, February 7, 2002.

Howland, John Louis. *Ellington Uptown*. Ann Arbor: University of Michigan Press, 2009.

Huebner, Steven. "*La princesse paysanne du Midi*." In *Fauser and Everist, Music, Theater, and Cultural Transfer*, 361–78.

Hutcheon, Linda. *A Theory of Adaptation*. New York: Routledge, 2006.

Hutchisson, James M. *DuBose Heyward: A Charleston Gentleman and the World of Porgy and Bess*. Jackson: University Press of Mississippi, 2000.

Hyde, Christopher. "'The Summer King' Takes Risks, but Has Potential to Be a Classic." *Portland Press Herald*, May 9, 2014. http://www.pressherald.com/2014/05/09/_the_summer_king__takes_risks__but_has_potential_to_be_a_classic.

Ignatiev, Noel. *How the Irish Became White*. New York: Routledge, 1995.

Ingraham, Mary, Joseph K. So, and Roy Moodley, eds. *Opera in a Multicultural World: Coloniality, Culture, Performance*. New York: Routledge, 2016.

Isokariari, Mary. "Cape Town Soprano Singer's Got Talent." *The Voice*, July 7, 2013.

Joe, Jeongwon, and Sander L. Gilman. *Wagner and Cinema*. Bloomington: Indiana University Press, 2010.

Johnson, E. Patrick. *Appropriating Blackness: Performance and the Politics of Authenticity*. Durham, N.C.: Duke University Press (2003).

Johnson, Hall. "*Porgy and Bess*: A Folk Opera." *Opportunity* 14, no. 1 (1936): 24–28.

Johnson, James Weldon. *Black Manhattan*. 1930. New York: Arno / New York Times, 1968.

Jones, Eddie Wade. *Portrait of an Unsung Hero: Roland Hayes and His Music*. Memphis, Tenn.: Memphis State University (1989).

Jones, LeRoi [Amiri Baraka]. *Black Music: Essays by LeRoi Jones (Amiri Baraka)*. New York: Akashi Classics, 1968.

———. *Blues People: Negro Musicians White America*. 1963. New York: Harper Perennial, 2002.

Jorritsma, Marie. *Sonic Spaces of the Karoo: The Sacred Music of a South African Coloured Community*. Pittsburgh, Pa.: Temple University Press, 2011.

Kennedy, Randall. "Sally Hemmings and Thomas Jefferson." In *Interracial Intimacies: Sex, Marriage, Identity, and Adoption*, 50–59. New York: Pantheon 2003.

Kernodle, Tammy L. "'Sons of Africa, Come Forth': Compositional Approaches of William Grant Still in the Opera *Troubled Island*." *American Music Research Journal* 13 (2003): 37–59.

———. *Soul on Soul: The Life and Music of Mary Lou Williams*. Boston: Northeastern University Press, 2004.

Kertesz, Elizabeth, and Michael Christoforidis. "Confronting *Carmen* beyond the Pyrenees: Bizet's Opera in Madrid, 1887–1888." *Cambridge Opera Journal* 20, no. 1 (March 2008): 79–110.

Khumalo, Sibongile. "Graduation Addresses." University of Rhodes, April 18, 2009. https://www.ru.ac.za/media/rhodesuniversity/content/ruhome/documents/Ms%20Sibongile%20Khumalo-Rhodes%2009%20Grad%20Address.pdf.

Kimball, Robert, and William Bolcom. *Reminiscing with Noble Sissle and Eubie Blake.* 1st ed. New York: Viking, 1973. Reprint, New York: Cooper Square, 2000.

Kinney, Alison. "As the Met Abandons Blackface, a Look at the Legacy of African Americans in Opera." In *Hyperallergic*, August 3, 2015. http://hyperallergic.com/226687/as-the-met-abandons-blackface-a-look-at-the-legacy-of-african-americans-in-opera.

———. "Conversations with Black Otellos." *VAN*, June 14, 2016. https://van-us.atavist.com/black-otellos

Kirk, Elise K. *American Opera*. Urbana: University of Illinois Press, 2001.

Kozinn, Allan. "Living Colour and Robeson Opera among Highlights of New Jersey Arts Center Season." *ArtsBeat* (*New York Times* blog), May 14, 2014.

Kuykendall, Mae. "Seaton's *A Bed Made in Heaven*: Family, Race and Law in Nineteenth-Century America." In *Midwestern Miscellany XLI*, edited by Arvid F. Spoonberg, 73–87. East Lansing, Mich.: Midwestern, 2013.

Lanier, Shannon, and Jane Feldman. *Jefferson's Children: The Story of One American Family*. New York: Random House, 2000.

Laqueur, Thomas. *Making Sex: Body and Gender from the Greeks to Freud*. Cambridge, Mass.: Harvard University Press, 1990.

Larabee, Ann. "The Haunted Memory Machines of Sandra Seaton." *Midwestern Miscellany XLI*, edited by Arvid F. Spoonberg, 10–17. East Lansing, Mich.: Midwestern, 2013.

Levin, David J. *Richard Wagner, Fritz Lang, and the Nibelungen: The Dramaturgy of Disavowal*. Princeton, N.J.: Princeton University Press, 1999.

———. *Unsettling Opera: Staging Mozart, Verdi, Wagner, and Zemlinsky*. Chicago: University of Chicago Press, 2007.

Lewis, Jan Ellen, and Peter S. Onuf, eds. *Sally Hemings and Thomas Jefferson: History, Memory, and Civic Culture*. Charlottesville: University of Virginia Press, 1999.

Lindenberger, Herbert. *Situating Opera: Period, Genre, Reception*. Cambridge: Cambridge University Press, 2010.

Locke, Alain, ed. *The New Negro*. 1925. New York: Simon and Schuster, 1992.

———. *The Negro and his Music*. New York: Kennikat, 1936.

Locke, Ralph P. *Musical Exoticism: Images and Reflections*. Cambridge: Cambridge University Press, 2009.

———. "Spanish Local Color in Bizet's *Carmen*: Unexplored Borrowings and Transformations" in Fauser and Everist, *Music, Theater, and Cultural Transfer*, 316–60.

Lopez, A. J. "Introduction: The (Post)global South," *Global South* 1, nos. 1–2 (2007): 1–11.

Lorde, Audre. "The Master's Tools Will Never Dismantle the Master's House." 1984. In *Sister Outsider: Essays and Speeches*, 110–14. Berkeley, Calif.: Crossing, 2007.

Lott, Eric. *Love and Theft: Blackface Minstrelsy and the American Working Class*. New York: Oxford University Press, 1993.

Magee, Gayle Sherwood. *Charles Ives Reconsidered*. Urbana: University of Illinois Press, 2008.

Malan, Jaques. "Opera Houses in South Africa." In *The World of South African Music: A Reader*, edited by Lucia Christine, 126–29. Newcastle-upon-Tyne, Eng.: Cambridge Scholars, 2005.

Manning, Harriet J. *Michael Jackson and the Blackface Mask*. Surrey, Eng.: Ashgate, 2013.

Martin, Denis-Constant. *Sounding the Cape: Music, Identity and Politics in South Africa*. Oxford: African Books Collective, 2013.

Masters, Kim. "David Geffen, Samuel Goldwyn and the Search for the 'Holy Grail' of Missing Movies." *Hollywood Reporter*, February 23, 2017. http://www.hollywood reporter.com/features/david-geffen-samuel-goldwyn-search-holy-grail-missing -movies-977567.

Mbembe, Achille. *On the Postcolony*. Berkeley: University of California Press, 2001.

McClary, Susan. "*Carmen* as Perennial Fusion: From Habanera to Hip-Hop." In *Carmen: From Silent Film to MTV*, edited by Chris Perriam and Ann Davies, 205–16. Amsterdam: Rodopi, 2005.

———. "The Genesis of Bizet's *Carmen*." In *Georges Bizet: Carmen*, edited by Susan McClary, 15–28. New York: Cambridge University Press, 1992.

McKaiser, Eusebius. "Not White Enough, Not Black Enough." At "The Opinion Pages" on Latitude (*New York Times* blog), February 15, 2012. https://latitude.blogs.nytimes .com/2012/02/15/in-south-africa-after-apartheid-colored-community-is-the-big -loser/?_r=0.

McKoy, Sheila Smith. "Placing and Replacing 'The Venus Hottentot': An Archeology of Pornography, Race, and Power." In Gordon-Chipembere, *Representation and Black Womanhood*, 85–97.

McLucas, Anne Dhu. "Monodrama." *Oxford Music Online*. New York: Oxford University Press.

Meacham, Jon. *Thomas Jefferson: The Art of Power*. New York: Random House, 2012.

Meersmen, Brent. "Singing Winnie in Toronto." *Mail and Guardian*, June 8, 2007.

Meintjes, Louise. "Paul Simon's *Graceland*, South Africa, and the Mediation of Musical Meaning." *Ethnomusicology* 34, no. 1 (1990): 37–73.

Mhlambi, Innocentia Jabulisile. "Embodied Discordance: Vernacular Idioms in *Winnie: The Opera*." *African Studies* 75, no. 1 (2016): 48–73.

Midgette, Anne. "Alyson Cambridge Offers Ambitious but Flawed Recital." *Washington Post*, January 21, 2010.

Miles, Tiya. *Ties That Bind: The Story of an Afro-Cherokee Family in Slavery and Freedom*. Berkeley: University of California Press, 2005.

Monson, Ingrid, ed. *The African Diaspora: A Musical Perspective*. New York: Routledge, 2003.

———. *Freedom Sounds: Civil Rights Call Out to Jazz and Africa*. New York: Oxford University Press, 2007.

Moraga, Cherríe, and Gloria Anzaldúa, eds. *This Bridge Called My Back: Writings by Radical Women of Color*. 4th ed. Albany: State University of New York Press, 2015.

Morgan, Philip D. "Interracial Sex in the Chesapeake and the British Atlantic World, c. 1700–1820." In Lewis and Onuf, *Sally Hemings and Thomas Jefferson*, 52–84.

Morrison, Toni. *The Origin of Others*. Cambridge, Massachusetts: Harvard University Press, 2017.

Most, Andrea. *Making Americans: Jews and the Broadway Musical*. Cambridge, Mass.: Harvard University Press, 2004.

———. *Theatrical Liberalism: Jews and Popular Entertainment in America*. New York: New York University Press, 2013.

Muller, Carol A. *Focus: Music of South Africa*, second edition. New York: Routledge, 2008.

———. *Rituals of Fertility and the Sacrifice of Desire: Nazarite Women's Performance in South Africa*. Chicago: University of Chicago Press, 1999.

Muller, Wayne, and Hilde Roos. *Eoan: Our Story*. Johannesburg, South Africa: Fourthwall, 2013.

Murphy, Elaine. "Alumni Spotlight: Marvin Hayes." February 17, 2010. University of Southern California, Thornton School of Music. https://music.usc.edu/alumni-spotlight-marvin-hayes.

Murphy, Kerry "Carmen: *Couleur Locale* or the Real Thing?" In Fauser and Everist, *Music, Theater, and Cultural Transfer*, 293–315.

Nadell, Martha Jane. *Enter the New Negroes: Images of Race in American Culture*. Cambridge, Mass.: Harvard University Press, 2004.

Ndlovu, Siphiwe Gloria. "'Body' of Evidence: Saartjie Baartman and the Archive." In Gordon-Chipembere, *Representation and Black Womanhood*, 17–30.

Negus, W. E., et al. "Falsetto." *Oxford Music Online*. New York: Oxford University Press.

Neighbour, Oliver W. "Erwartung." *Oxford Music Online*. New York: Oxford University Press.

Nicholls, David G. *Conjuring the Folk: Forms of Modernity in African America*. Ann Arbor: University of Michigan Press, 2000.

Noonan, Ellen. *The Strange Career of Porgy and Bess: Race, Culture, and America's Most Famous Opera*. Chapel Hill: University of North Carolina, 2012.

Nuttall, Sarah. *Entanglement: Literary and Cultural Reflections on Post-Apartheid*. Johannesburg, South Africa: Wits University Press, 2009.

Nuttall, Sarah, and Carli Coetzee, eds. *Negotiating the Past: The Making of Memory in South Africa*. Cape Town, South Africa: Oxford University Press, 1998.

Oja, Carol J. *Bernstein Meets Broadway: Collaborative Art in a Time of War*. New York: Oxford University Press, 2014.

Olwage, Grant. "The Class and Colour of Tone: An Essay on the Social History of Vocal Timbre." *Ethnomusicology Forum* 13, no. 2 (2004): 203–26.

———, ed. *Composing Apartheid: Music for and against Apartheid*. Johannesburg, South Africa: Wits University Press, 2008.

———. "Discipline and Choralism: The Birth of Musical Colonialism." In *Music Power, and Politics*, edited by Annie J. Randall, 25–46. New York: Routledge, 2005.

———. "Scriptions of the Choral: The Historiography of Black South African Choralism." *South African Journal of Musicology* 22, no. 1 (2002): 29–45.

Parker, Roger. "Ballo in maschera, Un." *Oxford Music Online*. New York: Oxford University.

Patterson, Willis C. *The Saints Among Us*. Willis Patterson Publishing, 2011. https://www.facebook.com/people/Willis-C-Patterson/100002557401301.

Patterson, Willis C. *The Unlikely Saga of a Singer from Ann Arbor: The Autobiography of Willis C. Patterson, Basso*. Michigan Publishing, 2015. https://babel.hathitrust.org/cgi/pt?id=mdp.39015093623497;view=1up;seq=2.

Peterson, Bhekizizwe. *Monarchs, Missionaries and African Intellectuals: African Theatre and the Unmaking of Colonial Marginality*. Johannesburg, South Africa: Witwatersrand University Press, 2000.

Picard, Anna. "Pumeza Matshikiza: The Township Soprano Who Wooed the World." *The Guardian*, July 27, 2014.

Pirker, Michael. "Janissary Music." *Oxford Music Online*. New York: Oxford University Press.

Pogrebin, Robin. "ChevronTexaco to Stop Sponsoring Met's Broadcasts." *New York Times*, May 21, 2003.

Pollack, Howard. *George Gershwin: His Life and Work*. Berkeley: University of California Press, 2007.

Pooley, Thomas. "Extracurricular Arts: Poverty, Inequality, and Indigenous Musical Arts Education in Post-Apartheid South Africa." *Critical Arts* 30, no. 5 (2016): 639–54.

Powers, David M. *From Plantation to Paradise: Cultural Politics and Musical Theatre in French Slave Colonies, 1764–1789*. East Lansing: Michigan State University Press, 2014.

Powrie, Phil, Bruce Babington, Ann Davies, and Chris Perriam. Carmen *on Film: A Cultural History*. Bloomington: Indiana University Press, 2007.

Preston, Katherine K. *Opera on the Road: Traveling Opera Troupes in the United States, 1825–60*. Urbana: University of Illinois Press, 2001.

Quereshi, Sadiah. "Displaying Sara Baartman, the 'Hottentot Venus.'" *History of Science* 42 (2004): 233–57.

Radano, Ronald. *Lying Up a Nation*. Chicago: University of Chicago Press, 2003.

Radano, Ronald, and Philip V. Bohlman. "Introduction: Music and Race, Their Past, Their Presence." In *Music and the Racial Imagination*, edited by Radano and Bohlman, 1–56. Chicago: University of Chicago Press, 2000.

Roberts, Dorothy. *Fatal Invention: How Science, Politics, and Big Business Re-create Race in the Twenty-First Century*. New York: New Press, 2011.

Roberts, Kimberly C. "'We Shall Not Be Moved': A Candid Commentary on Our Society." *Philadelphia Tribune*, September 19, 2017.

Robinson, Paul. "Is *Aida* an Orientalist Opera?" *Cambridge Opera Journal* 5, no. 2 (July 1993): 133–40.

———. "Mérimée's Carmen." In *Georges Bizet: Carmen*, edited by Susan McClary, 1–14. New York: Cambridge University Press, 1992.

Rockwell, John. "Four Saints in Three Acts." *Oxford Music Online*. New York: Oxford University Press.

Roos, Hilde. "*Eoan—Our Story*: Treading New Methodological Paths in Music Historiography." *Historia* 60, no. 2 (November 2015): 185–200.

———. "Probing the Boundaries of Opera as Notated Practice in South Africa: The Case of Eoan." *Muziki* 11, no. 2 (2014): 79–88.

———. "Remembering to Forget the Eoan Group: The Legacy of an Opera Company from the Apartheid Era." *South African Theatre Journal.* 27, no. 1 (2014), 1–18.

Rosenblum, Joshua. "Bolcom: *From the Diary of Sally Hemings*." *Opera News* 75, no. 2 (August 2010): 56.

Ross, Alex. "Opera Startups: Small Companies in New York Take on the Met." *New Yorker*, April 4, 2016. http://www.newyorker.com/magazine/2016/04/04/operatic-startups-take-on-the-met.

Ross, Fiona C. *Bearing Witness: Women and the Truth and Reconciliation Commission in South Africa*. London: Pluto, 2003.

Rothman, Joshua D. "James Callender and Social Knowledge of Interracial Sex in Antebellum Virginia." In Lewis and Onuf, *Sally Hemings and Thomas Jefferson*, 87–113.

Rothstein, Edward. "Life, Liberty and the Fact of Slavery." *New York Times*, January 26, 2012.

Rushton, Julian. "Entführung aus dem Serail, Die." *Oxford Music Online*. New York: Oxford University Press.

Said, Edward. "The Empire at Work: Verdi's *Aida*." In *Culture and Imperialism*, 111–32, 344–45 (notes). New York: Vintage, 1993.

———. "The Imperial Spectacle." *Grand Street* 6, no. 2 (Winter 1987): 82–107.

———. *Orientalism*. New York: Pantheon, 1978.

Schenbeck, Lawrence. *Racial Uplift and American Music, 1878–1943*. Jackson: University Press of Mississippi, 2012.

Seaton, Sandra. "*From the Diary of Sally Hemings*." *Michigan Quarterly Review* 40, no. 4 (Fall 2001): 613–22.

———. "Program Notes." Recording of *From the Diary of Sally Hemings*, White Pine Music, (WPM221), 2010. Unnumbered pages.

———. "Program Notes." *Michigan Quarterly Review* 40, no. 4 (Fall 2001): 623–27.

Sharpe, Jenny. *Ghosts of Slavery: A Literary Archaeology of Black Women's Lives*. Minneapolis: University of Minnesota Press, 2003.

Sheppard, W. Anthony. "Exoticism." In *The Oxford Handbook of Opera*, edited by Helen M. Greenwald, 795–816. Oxford: Oxford University Press, 2014.

———. *Revealing Masks: Exotic Influences and Ritualized Performance in Modernist Musical Theater*. Berkeley: University of California Press, 2001.

Sinclair, James B. *A Descriptive Catalogue of the Music of Charles Ives*. New Haven, Conn.: Yale University Press, 1999.

Smith, Catherine Parsons. *William Grant Still*. Urbana: University of Illinois Press, 2008.

———, ed. *William Grant Still: A Study in Contradictions*. Berkeley: University of California Press, 2000.Smith, Jeff. "Black Faces, White Voices: The Politics of Dubbing in *Carmen Jones*." *Velvet Light Trap* 51 (Spring 2003): 29–42.

Smith, Valerie. *Not Just Race, Not Just Gender: Black Feminist Readings*. New York: Routledge 1998.

———. "Reading the Intersection of Race and Gender in Narratives of Passing." *Diacritics* 24, no. 2/3, Critical Crossings (Summer–Autumn 1994): 43–57.

Smittle, Stephanie. "A Glimpse of the 'Little Rock Nine' Opera at UCA." *Arkansas Times*, September 26, 2017.

Snyder, Jean E. *Harry T. Burleigh: From the Spiritual to the Harlem Renaissance*. Urbana: University of Illinois Press, 2016.

Somma, Donato. "'Just Say the Words': An Operatic Rendering of Winnie." *African Studies* 75, no. 1 (2016): 32–47.

———. "Madonnas and Prima Donnas: The Representation of Women in an Italian Prisoner of War Camp in South Africa." In *Cultural Heritage and Prisoners of War: Creativity Behind Barbed Wire*, edited by Gilly Carr and Harold Mytum, 261–74. New York: Routledge, 2012.

Somma, Donato, and Neo Muyanga. "'The Musical Thread': Neo Muyanga on Opera and South Africa; A Conversation between Neo Muyanga and Donato Somma." *African Studies* 75, no. 1 (2016): 74–97.

Southern, Eileen. *The Music of Black Americans: A History*. 3rd ed. New York: Norton, 1997.

———, ed. *Readings in Black American Music*. 2nd ed. New York: Norton, 1983.

Standifer, James A. *Porgy and Bess: An American Voice*. Directed by Nigel Noble. Narrated by Ruby Dee. Films for the Humanities and Sciences, FFH 10027. Documentary film, 1997.

Starr, Larry. *George Gershwin*. New Haven, Conn.: Yale University Press, 2011.

Stoever, Jennifer Lynn. *The Sonic Color Line: Race and the Cultural Politics of Listening*. New York: New York University Press, 2016.

Story, Rosalyn M. *And So I Sing: African-American Divas of Opera and Concert*. New York: Amistad / Penguin, 1990.

Sullivan, Jack. "Bolcom: *Diary of Sally Hemings*." *American Record Guide* 73, no. 5 (September 2010): 103–4.

Taylor, Timothy D. *Beyond Exoticism: Western Music and the World*. Durham, N.C.: Duke University Press, 2007.

———. *Global Pop: World Music, World Markets*. New York: Routledge, 1997.

Thackway, Melissa. *Africa Shoots Back: Alternative Perspectives in Sub-Saharan Francophone African Film*. Bloomington: Indiana University Press, 2003.

Thompson, Era Bell. "Why Negroes Don't Like *Porgy and Bess*." *Ebony* 14, no. 12 (October 1959): 50–52, 54.

Thompson, Krissah. "For Decades They Hid Jefferson's Relationship with Her: Now Monticello Is Making Room for Sally Hemings." *Washington Post*, February 19, 2017. http://wapo.st/2moRmRU.

Thurber, Jeanette. "Dvorak as I Knew Him." *Etude* 37 (1919).

Thurman, Kira. "The German Lied and the Songs of Black Volk." In "Colloquy Studying the Lied: Hermeneutic Traditions and the Challenge of Performance," by Convenor Jennifer Ronyak, *Journal of the American Musicological Society* 67, no. 2 (2014): 543–58.

Tillet, Salamishah. "A Police Bombing, Homes on Fire and an Opera the Grapples with It All." *New York Times*, September 15, 2017.

Tommasini, Anthony. "Reinventing Supertitles: How the Met Did It." *New York Times*, October 2, 1995. http://www.nytimes.com/1995/10/02/arts/reinventing-supertitles -how-the-met-did-it.html?pagewanted=all.

Tonkin, Boyd. "Pumeza Matshikiza on Soprano Megastardom, Her Township Education and Why the ANC Is a Stuck Record." *The Independent*, November 22, 2014.

Touré. *Who's Afraid of Post-Blackness? What It Means to Be Black Now*. New York: Free Press, 2011.

Trotter, James M. *Music and Some Highly Musical People*. 1880. London: Forgotten, 2012.

Turner, Kristen. "Class, Race, and Uplift in the Opera House: Theodore Drury and His Company Cross the Color Line." *Journal of Musicological Research* 34 (2015): 320–51.

Tutu, Desmond, et al. "Special Investigation into the Mandela United Football Club." *Report of the Truth and Reconciliation Commission* 2, chap. 6 (1998): 549–76. http:// www.justice.gov.za/trc/report/finalreport/Volume%202.pdf.

Tye, Larry. *Rising from the Rails: Pullman Porters and the Making of the Black Middle Class*. New York: Holt, 2004.

Viljoen, Santisa, and Marita Wenzel. "The Same, yet Different: Re-Encoding Identity in *U-Carmen eKhayelitsha*." *Journal of the Music Arts in Africa* 13, no. 1 (2016): 53–70.

Walker, Alice. "If the Present Looks Like the Past, What Does the Future Look Like?" In *In Search of our Mothers' Gardens: Womanist Prose*, 290–312. New York: Harcourt, 1983.

Watson, Steven. *Prepare for Saints: Gertrude Stein, Virgil Thomson and the Mainstreaming of American Modernism*. New York: Random House, 1998.

West, Cornel. *Race Matters*. New York: Vintage Random House, 1993.

Whooley, Owen. "Objectivity and Its Discontents: Knowledge Advocacy in the Sally Hemings Controversy." *Social Forces* 86, no. 4 (June 2008): 1367–89.

Wilkerson, Jane. *The Warmth of Other Suns: The Epic Story of America's Great Migration*. New York: Vintage, 2010.

Work, John W. "Negro Folk Song." 1923. In Gates and Jarrett, *New Negro*, 453. Originally appeared in *Opportunity* 1, no. 10 (October 1923): 292–94.

Wright, Josephine. "Jones, Sissieretta." *Oxford Music Online*. New York: Oxford University Press.

Wyatt, Robert, and John Andrew Johnson, eds. *The George Gershwin Reader*. New York: Oxford University Press, 2004.

Zanger, Anat. *Film Remakes as Ritual and Disguise: From Carmen to Ripley*. Amsterdam: Amsterdam University Press, 2006.

Index

NAOMI ANDRÉ is an associate professor in the departments of African and Afroamerican Studies and Women's Studies. She also is associate director in the Residential College at the University of Michigan. She is the author of *Voicing Gender: Castrati, Travesti, and the Second Woman in Early-Nineteenth-Century Italian Opera* and coeditor of *Blackness in Opera*.

The University of Illinois Press
is a founding member of the
Association of American University Presses.

———————————————————————

Composed in 10.5/13 Minion Pro
by Lisa Connery
at the University of Illinois Press
Cover designed by Jennifer S. Fisher
Cover illustration: Courtesy of Cape Town Opera,
photographer Bernard Bruwer

University of Illinois Press
1325 South Oak Street
Champaign, IL 61820-6903
www.press.uillinois.edu